The Politics of Cancer

The Politics
of Cancer

Samuel S. Epstein, M.D.

Sierra Club Books / San Francisco

*The Sierra Club, founded in 1892 by John Muir, has devoted
itself to the study and protection of the earth's scenic and
ecological resources—mountains, wetlands, woodlands, wild
shores and rivers, deserts and plains. The publishing program of
the Sierra Club offers books to the public as a nonprofit
educational service in the hope that they may enlarge the public's
understanding of the Club's basic concerns. The point of view
expressed in each book, however, does not necessarily represent
that of the Club. The Sierra Club has some fifty chapters coast to
coast, in Canada, Hawaii, and Alaska. For information about
how you may participate in its programs to preserve wilderness
and the quality of life, please address inquiries to Sierra Club,
530 Bush Street, San Francisco, California 94108.*

Library of Congress Cataloging in Publication Data

Epstein, Samuel S.
  The politics of cancer.

  Bibliography: p.
  Includes index.
  1. Cancer—Prevention. 2. Environmentally induced
diseases. 3. Cancer—Prevention—Political aspects.
4. Carcinogens. I. Title.
RC268.E67   362.1'9'699400973   78-985
ISBN 0-87156-193-X

Jacket design by Paul Bacon
Book design by Gary A. Head
Printed in the United States of America

10 9 8 7 6 5 4 3 2

To my parents

Contents

Preface

If one thousand people died every day of cholera, swine flu, or food poisoning, an epidemic of major proportions would be at hand and the entire country would mobilize against it. Yet cancer claims that many lives daily, often in prolonged and agonizing pain, and most people believe they can do nothing about it. Cancer, they think, strikes where it will, with no apparent cause. Some take out a cancer insurance policy, all hope not to be one of its victims.

But cancer has distinct, identifiable causes. It is not just another degenerative disease associated with aging. It can largely be prevented, but this requires more than just scientific effort or individual action. The control and prevention of cancer will require a concerted national effort. This book is offered as a contribution to that essentially political process.

There are four basic axioms of cancer causation which will be continually referred to:

1. *Cancer is caused mainly by exposure to chemical or physical agents in the environment.* To be sure, there are genetic aspects to cancer, and some cancers are sus-

1

pected to be caused by viruses, but these factors account
for only a small fraction of all cases.* Just as germs cause
infections, so do certain chemical and physical agents,
carcinogens, cause cancer.† While some carcinogens, such
as arsenic, asbestos, aflatoxins, and ionizing radiation,
occur naturally, there is increasing recognition of the dangers of synthetic petrochemical carcinogens, such as vinyl
chloride and bischloromethylether, which have been introduced into the workplace and environment in growing
numbers over the last few decases.

2. *The more of a carcinogen present in the human
environment, hence the greater the exposure to it, the
greater is the chance of developing cancer from it.*

3. *Although environmental carcinogens are the predominant causes of human cancer, the incidence of cancer
in any population of animals or humans exposed to a carcinogen may be influenced by a variety of factors.* The
development of cancer is of course profoundly influenced
by genetic, endocrine, immunological, viral, biochemical
and possibly even psychological factors. Additionally,
there are a wide range of other external factors which can
increase individual sensitivity to a given carcinogen or
carcinogens. Among these are excesses or deficiencies in
certain dietary components, exposure to other carcinogens
which enhance the effects of a particular carcinogen, and
exposure to *promoting* (or *co-carcinogenic*) agents which,

---

*There is little or no evidence that chemical carcinogens cause cancer by
activating latent viruses in human cells.

† The relation of carcinogens to cancer is pragmatic and has been established by observation of human and animal populations, and not by prior
understanding of the biological mechanisms involved. To be sure, a great deal
is known about the biochemical, immunological, and other effects of many
carcinogens at the cellular level. It now seems that the carcinogenic action of
certain chemicals is due to their direct interaction with cellular genes. Large
research programs and institutions have been built upon studies yielding such
information. However, the promise of improved treatment and prevention of
cancer based upon this knowledge of the mechanism of carcinogenesis has not
yet been fulfilled.

while not carcinogenic in themselves, may enhance the effect of an already present carcinogen.* These factors do not themselves cause cancer, but they can and do affect when a certain carcinogen will trigger cancer in an individual and how rapidly or slowly the course of the clinical symptoms and the disease will progress.

4. *There is no known method for measuring or predicting a "safe" level of exposure to any carcinogen below which cancer will not result in any individual or population group.* That is, there is no basis for the threshold hypothesis which claims that exposure to relatively low levels of carcinogens is safe and therefore justifiable.

This book has been shaped by the author's longstanding scientific involvement in toxicology and carcinogenesis, including several of the case studies discussed in this book. (It does not deal with nuclear radioactivity, a potent source of carcinogens, which would require a book in itself. Certainly, issues raised in this book apply directly to the dangers of radiation, but the solutions to the problems posed by nuclear materials are vastly different than those that apply to chemicals.) *The Politics of Cancer* is also based on the author's support of attempts to control human exposure to carcinogenic and other toxic chemicals, including many of those discussed in the following pages. In these efforts, he has worked with Congressional committees and regulatory agencies, and also with public interest groups and organized labor.

---

*For example, alcohol, which does not itself appear to cause cancer, other than possibly in the liver, increases the risk of cancer of the mouth, larynx, and esophagus, particularly in tobacco smokers. The "fertile ground" concept expresses the possible influence of such factors on the response of the host to any specific carcinogen.

Acknowledgments

The author most gratefully acknowledges the constructive comments and criticisms from friends who were kind enough to review the penultimate manuscript. These include: David Baltimore, Kenneth Bridbord, Shirley Briggs, Robert Harris, Michael Jacobson, David Kotelchuk, Claire Nader, Umberto Saffiotti, Irving Selikoff, and Carl Shy. Thanks are also due to Catherine Dollive, David Fine, Zafar Iqbal, Anson Keller, Sylvia Krekel, Marvin Legator, Richard Lemen, Congressman Andrew Maguire, Paul Meier, Anthony Mazzocchi, William Reukauf, Harry Snyder, Joel Swartz, Sidney Wolfe, and Arthur Upton for helpful comments on particular sections of the manuscript. The author also acknowledges help from Steven Stellman for background material in several sections of the book, particularly those dealing with epidemiology.

The author also thanks Jeff Cothran for stylistic assistance, and Pat Barcena, Pat Schaffner, and Willa Taylor for typing the manuscript.

It has been a pleasure to work with the staff of Sierra Club Books and Jon Beckmann, Director and Editor-in-Chief. All authors should have such an editor.

Chapter One

The Impact of Cancer

A Bittersweet Example

On March 9, 1977, an agency of the federal government, the U.S. Food and Drug Administration (FDA), proposed a ban on the use of saccharin, an artificial sweetener in foods. The public responded loudly. In outrage, citizens demanded that the government withdraw the proposal. Congress and the agency were barraged with thousands of letters, cables, and phone calls. The diet-soda generation had risen in arms.

Hearings were held. The news media were flooded with reports. The soft-drink industry paid for full-page advertisements in leading national newspapers to protest the FDA decision. Industry lobbies, responding to and organizing public opinion, gathered in strength.

Much of the controversy surrounding the saccharin ban arose from the public's sudden awareness and astonishment that this regulatory decision was based solely on the results of animal feeding tests. Further, the public was surprised that these tests were carried out using what seemed to be excessively high quantities of saccharin. In the case of the most recent study, rats had been fed concentrations of saccharin equivalent to a daily dose of 800 cans of diet soda. Predictably, comedians and editorial cartoonists had a field day. Johnny Carson joked that Canadian researchers who fed rats large quantities of saccharin in their coffee went broke paying for the coffee. The nation simultaneously laughed and stormed over the FDA decision.

Some people, though, weren't laughing. Public health activists were concerned that the standard scientific practices which had been used in the study of saccharin, in particular the use of rodents to test for cancer, were under attack. In turn, they were concerned that public misconception about the nature of this scientific research might cause legislative backlash and weaken the government's power to limit exposure to other chemicals suspected of causing cancer. This was not an idle concern. The scientific community lined up on opposite sides and issued conflicting statements about the saccharin question with the same vigor as the public. Statisticians, toxicologists, cancer researchers, environmental scientists, physicians, and chemists all joined in the fray.

Two quotations illustrate how far apart apparently informed scientific opinions could be. In March, 1977, Guy Newell, Jr., then acting director and now deputy director of the National Cancer Institute (NCI), testified: "Based on human data, we do not believe saccharin is a potent carcinogen for humans, if it is one at all."[1] David Rall, director of the National Institute of Environmental Health Sciences, a sister institute of the NCI, clearly disagreed with Newell:

> It may be that drinking just a couple of bottles [of a diet cola] a day may be risky for some people. FDA certainly should get saccharin out of diet pop. . . . When one looks at the data that have been accumulated from animal experiments over the years, there is plenty of reason to doubt that saccharin is safe. . . . In practically all of the studies that have been done including those in which animals

were fed saccharin at much lower doses than in the Canadian study, you find tumors in more of the saccharin-fed animals than in the controls.

Such diversity of opinion among scientists fed the public's concern and confusion. After all, how could the lay press and the nation be expected to make a decision on an issue about which the nation's leading scientists couldn't agree? What's more, why couldn't they agree? Isn't science by nature exact?

The fact is, much cancer research at its present stage of development must focus on statistical trends and tendencies in animal and human populations to link, in a causal chain, a particular agent or agents with a particular type of cancer. As was so clearly seen with saccharin, the ultimate judgment whether a substance causes cancer in humans is not always easy. The public has found, and scientists have had to admit, that there are many subjective and judgmental decisions being made about cancer — its causes, prevention, and control. Many of these judgments, particularly when regulation comes under discussion, have little to do with pure science. The economic impact of banning a substance or requiring its strict control, the technological feasibility of substituting new processes, the desirability of low-calorie foods in the nation's diet — all these topics are implicit in the saccharin issue. In short, the science of the saccharin decision is clearly mixed up with nonscientific considerations. Even the very basis of the research into saccharin's carcinogenicity is mixed up with economic and politics.

It is vital that the public learn where the science of cancer ends and social policy considerations begin. Further, it is important to realize that the basis of many so-called "scientific" decisions are in fact economic considerations, and not science. When regulatory judgments are made and laws are passed (or not passed) which touch on our lives and welfare, we must understand the real basis of the decision-making process.

Cancer is a problem which touches each of us in some way. We and our families are daily exposed to agents that cause cancer (called carcinogens), often unknowingly, while we breathe, eat, drink, work, and sleep. Moreover, we usually have no knowledge of what we are being exposed to. In order for us to respond to the cancer threat, we must all be equipped with the basic information needed to demand preventive policies and actions. If action is to be effective, it must be based on information and directed within the realistic limits of the political system.

The Impact of Cancer

The Human Costs

Cancer is now a killing and disabling disease of epidemic proportions. More than 53 million people in the United States (over a quarter of the population) will develop some form of cancer, from which approximately 20 percent of the U.S. population will die. [2] It is estimated that 665,000 new cancer cases were diagnosed in 1975, and there were 365,000 cancer deaths.* Cancer deaths that year alone were about five times higher than the total U.S. military deaths in all the Vietnam and Korean war years combined.

---

*The impact of cancer is often expressed in terms of mortality or of incidence rates. The mortality rate is the number of people in a particular population who die of cancer in a given time period, usually specified as a number per 100,000 population. The incidence rate is the number of new cases per year in the population, again usually per 100,000 population. Incidence rates are a more meaningful measure of the impact of cancer than are mortality, which also reflect curability. The longer the survival or the greater the cure rate for a given cancer, the more the incidence rate will exceed the mortality rate. Skin cancer, for example, has the highest incidence rate of all cancers, but because the chances of catching and curing the disease at an early stage are good, its mortality rate is small. Lung cancer, on the other hand, occurs less often than skin cancer, but once detected its prognosis is poor; hence its mortality rate approaches its incidence rate.

Cancer strikes not only the elderly, but also other age groups, including infants. Among males, cancer is the second leading cause of death for all age groups except 15–34 years, where it is exceeded by violent deaths, accidents, homicide, and suicide (Table 1.1). Among females, cancer is the leading cause of death for ages 35–54 years and the second leading cause for all other ages up to 75.

Black males, as a group, experience the highest incidence of cancer in the United States, while black females experience the lowest; whites are intermediate between these two, with males higher than females.[3] Strong racial variations exist for cancer at almost every body site. For instance, blacks have three to four times as much cancer of the esophagus as whites, twice as much cancer of the cervix, and prostate, and higher rates of cancer of the stomach, pancreas, and lung.[4]

The most common sites of fatal cancer are the lung and large bowel in men, and the breast and large bowel in women (See Tables 1.2 and 1.3 and Figure 1.1). Virtually every other organ in the body is also a potential site for cancer's attack. Leukaemia is the leading cause of fatal cancer in children.

A high and unmeasurable cost is the fear of contracting cancer oneself. Such fears are particularly well founded in individuals or groups at "high risk" of developing cancer from past exposures to carcinogens: hundreds of thousands of workers currently or previously exposed to occupational carcinogens; women treated with estrogens for "menopausal symptoms"; and women who have received repeated breast x-rays (mammography).

The Financial Costs

Obviously, cancer also places an enormous economic and social burden on the cancer victim, on the victim's family, and on society. It is a disease which can begin unobtrusively and linger on for years. Specialized treatment is often necessary. The total direct cost of treatment for an

Table 1.1 Top Three Causes of Death in 1971

Age in Years	Sex	First	Percent of All Deaths*	Second	Percent of All Deaths*	Third	Percent of All Deaths*
1–14	M	Accidents	49	Cancer	12	Congenital malformation	7
	F	Accidents	38	Cancer	12	Congenital malformation	8
15–34	M	Accidents	48	Homicide	13	Suicide	9
	F	Accidents	30	Cancer	13	Suicide	8
35–54	M	Heart disease	34	Cancer	18	Accidents	11
	F	Cancer	33	Heart disease	18	Stroke	7
55–74	M	Heart disease	43	Cancer	22	Stroke	8
	F	Heart disease	38	Cancer	26	Stroke	11
75+	M	Heart disease	46	Cancer	14	Stroke	14
	F	Heart disease	50	Stroke	18	Cancer	11

Most Frequent Causes of Death

Source: *Vital Statistics of the United States, 1971.* Vol. II, Mortality, Pt. A, U.S. DHEW, Public Health Service, 1975.
*Percent of all deaths for the given age group and sex.

Table 1.2 U.S. Mortality for the Three Leading Cancer Sites in Major Age Groups by Sex in 1975

Rank	Under 15 Male	Under 15 Female	15–34 Male	15–34 Female	35–54 Male	35–54 Female	55–74 Male	55–74 Female	75+ Male	75+ Female
1	Leukaemia	Leukaemia	Leukaemia	Breast	Lung	Breast	Lung	Breast	Lung	Colon and rectum
2	Brain and nervous system	Brain and nervous system	Brain and nervous system	Leukaemia	Colon and rectum	Lung	Colon and rectum	Colon and rectum	Prostate	Breast
3	Lympho- and recticulo-sarcoma	Bone	Testis	Brain and nervous system	Pancreas	Colon and rectum	Prostate	Lung	Colon and rectum	Lung

Source: American Cancer Society, "1978 Cancer Facts and Figures," New York, 1977.

Table 1.3   Estimates of New Cancer Cases and Cancer Deaths in 1978

Site	No. of Cases*	Deaths*
Lung	102,000	92,000
Colon-rectum	102,000	52,000
Breast	91,000	34,000
Uterus	48,000†	11,000
Mouth	24,000	8,000
Skin	10,000‡	6,000
Leukaemia	22,000	15,000

Source: American Cancer Society, "1978 Cancer Facts and Figures," New York, 1977.

*Figures rounded to the nearest 1,000.

†If carcinoma in situ included, cases total over 88,000.

‡Estimated new cases of non-melanoma about 300,000.

Incidence estimates are based on rates from NCI Third National Cancer Survey, 1969–71.

individual case continues to increase, with current estimates ranging between $5,000 and $30,000.[5] Indirect costs to the family are often much greater still, including loss of earnings from premature disability and death and the depletion of family financial resources. Dollar costs aside, the agony of watching a loved one die is an incalculable emotional burden.

Total national costs from cancer, both direct and indirect, were estimated by HEW in 1971 to be about $15 billion annually.[6] Projections for 1978 are in the region of $25 billion.*

---

*These figures underestimate the true costs, which are still largely unrecognized. For example, a recent National Occupational Hazards Survey by the National Institute for Occupational Safety and Health estimated that the costs of surveillance of workers exposed to just those few carcinogens currently regulated by the Department of Labor are as high as $8.5 billion. (The results of this survey are summarized in an NIOSH document, "The Right to Know," July, 1977).

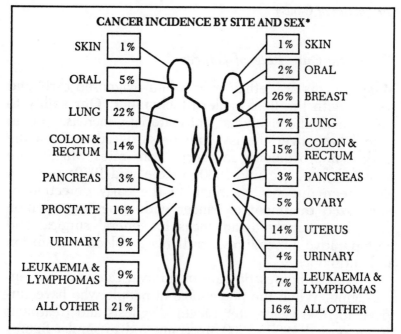

CANCER INCIDENCE BY SITE AND SEX*

	Male	Female	
SKIN	1%	1%	SKIN
ORAL	5%	2%	ORAL
		26%	BREAST
LUNG	22%	7%	LUNG
COLON & RECTUM	14%	15%	COLON & RECTUM
PANCREAS	3%	3%	PANCREAS
		5%	OVARY
PROSTATE	16%	14%	UTERUS
URINARY	9%	4%	URINARY
LEUKAEMIA & LYMPHOMAS	9%	7%	LEUKAEMIA & LYMPHOMAS
ALL OTHER	21%	16%	ALL OTHER

*Excluding non-melanoma skin cancer and carcinoma in situ of uterine cervix.

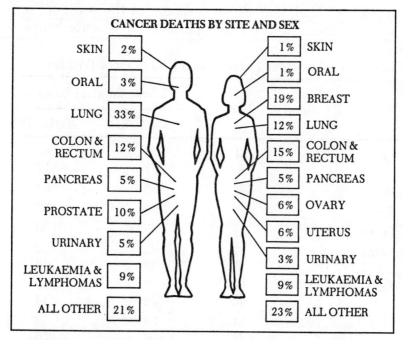

CANCER DEATHS BY SITE AND SEX

	Male	Female	
SKIN	2%	1%	SKIN
ORAL	3%	1%	ORAL
		19%	BREAST
LUNG	33%	12%	LUNG
COLON & RECTUM	12%	15%	COLON & RECTUM
PANCREAS	5%	5%	PANCREAS
		6%	OVARY
PROSTATE	10%	6%	UTERUS
URINARY	5%	3%	URINARY
LEUKAEMIA & LYMPHOMAS	9%	9%	LEUKAEMIA & LYMPHOMAS
ALL OTHER	21%	23%	ALL OTHER

Figure 1.1 Cancer Incidence and Deaths by Site and Sex

Source: American Cancer Society, "1978 Cancer Facts and Figures," New York, 1977.

The Static Cure Rate of Cancer

Many cancers are lethal, even when diagnosed early and treated with the best modern techniques. Our ability to treat cancer effectively has not materially increased on an overall basis over the last four or so decades. Even the modest improvements in cancer cure rates which were achieved from the mid-1930s to the mid-1950s seem to have been due not so much to the early detection or specialized treatment of cancer with drugs or radiation therapy as largely to advances in general surgical and postoperative procedures, particularly blood transfusion and antibiotics.

Modern figures on cancer survival rates are not encouraging. When the percentage of people who have survived for five years after cancer diagnosis and treatment in the period 1965– 1969 are compared to similar figures for 1950– 1959, it can be seen (Table 1.4) that with the exception of Hodgkin's disease, cancer of the prostate, and some relatively uncommon cancers such as acute lympho-

Table 1.4   Five-Year Survival Rates for Cancer (Whites)

Type of Cancer	Sex	5-Year Survival Rates %	
		1950– 1959	1965– 1969
Lung	M	7	8
	F	11	12
Breast	F	60	64
Cervix	F	59	56
Prostate	M	47	56
Colon	M	42	43
	F	46	46
Stomach	M	12	12
	F	13	14
Hodgkin's disease	M	31	52
	F	38	56

Source: CA—A Cancer Journal for Clinicians, 25:4 (1975).

cytic leukaemia, choriocarcinoma, and Wilm's tumor, no substantial overall progress has been made in treating cancer.[7]

Particularly for the major cancer killers, the odds of a cure have not improved much recently. The prognosis for lung cancer, the most common fatal type among men, remains poor; only about one of ten victims survives for five years after diagnosis. Victims of Hodgkin's disease now have about a 50 percent five-year survival rate, but Hodgkin's disease represents only about 1 percent of all cancers. Table 1.4 reflects the best available data as interpreted by the American Cancer Society. The NCI has recently completed a comprehensive survey of participating units in its Cancer Surveillance Epidemiology and End Results (SEER) program.[8] Results are even less encouraging than those of the American Cancer Society. This is the case despite the vast sums of money spent over the last 30 years, despite the high priorities for cancer research set by Congress, despite devotion of an entire federal agency (the National Cancer Institute) to the cancer problem, and in the face of continuing optimistic reassurances by the American Cancer Society.

The Increasing Incidence of Cancer

The Facts

Cancer is the plague of the twentieth century. In 1900, pneumonia and influenza headed the list of the ten leading causes of death in the United States, followed by tuberculosis, infectious gastrointestinal diseases, and heart disease. Cancer, number eight, caused less than 4 percent of all deaths (Table 1.5). By 1975, cancer was the second leading cause of death after heart disease, accounting for about 18 percent of all deaths.*

---

*The death rate from cardiovascular disease is now on the decline, having dropped 20 percent from 1968 to 1975, when the annual toll (994,513) fell below one million for the first time in more than a decade.

Table 1.5 The Ten Leading Causes of Death in the U.S. in 1900 and in 1975

	1900		
Rank	Cause of Death	Crude Death Rate per 100,000 Population	Percent of Total Deaths
	All causes	1,719.1	100.0
1	Influenza and pneumonia	202.2	11.8
2	Tuberculosis	194.4	11.3
3	Gastroenteritis	142.7	8.3
4	Diseases of heart	137.4	8.0
5	Cerebral hemorrhage	106.9	6.2
6	Chronic nephritis	81.0	4.7
7	Accidents	72.3	4.2
8	Cancer	64.0	3.7
9	Certain diseases of infancy	62.6	3.6
10	Diphtheria	40.3	2.3

Source: "Facts of Life and Death," National Center for Health Statistics, Public Health Service Publication no. 600, 1970, Table 12.

	1975		
Rank	Cause of Death	Crude Death Rate per 100,000 Population	Percent of Total Deaths
	All causes	888.9	100.0
1	Diseases of heart	336.2	37.8
2	Cancer	171.7	19.3
3	Stroke	91.1	10.3
4	Accidents	48.4	5.4
5	Influenza and pneumonia	26.1	2.9
6	Diabetes mellitus	16.5	1.9
7	Cirrhosis of liver	14.8	1.7
8	Arteriosclerosis	13.6	1.5
9	Suicide	12.7	1.4
10	Diseases of infancy	12.5	1.4

Source: American Cancer Society, "1978 Cancer Facts and Figures," New York, 1977.

To some extent, this increase in cancer mortality reflects the increased longevity which has occurred in the U.S. population during this century. Living longer increases the chances of developing cancer. However, there is also a greater cancer risk in each specific age group.[9] Thus a fifty-year-old man today is more likely to die of cancer than was a fifty-year-old man in 1950. It has been recently calculated, by Marvin Schneiderman, Assistant Director for Field Studies and Statistics of the NCI, that between 9.5 percent and 27 percent of the increase in the death rate from cancer over the past few decades is due to the increased cancer risk of specific age groups. The increased cancer death rate, therefore holds true despite the factor of age.* Standardized cancer death rate data, adjusted for age and based on the total U.S. population, also show an overall and progressive increase of about 11 percent over the last four decades.

Table 1.6 shows how the standardized cancer incidence rates (the number of newly detected cases per 100,000 population each year) have changed over the thirty-two-year period ending in 1969. These data were collected by the NCI during its periodic National Cancer Surveys and are adjusted to reflect changes in regions surveyed and, especially, changing age structures of the populations, i.e., to discount the effects of aging of the population. These are the most accurate nationwide data available on cancer incidence, and they reflect the general trend observed more recently in regional and local tumor registries, such as those of the states of Connecticut and California. As Table 1.6 indicates, there have been substantial increases between 1937 and 1969 in the incidence of cancer of a wide range of organs in males and females,

---

*This conclusion is based on the calculation of death rates for a standard population with a fixed percentage of people in each age category. Statisticians can then adjust the data to reflect a hypothetical constant age distribution and thus compensate for differences in aging.

Table 1.6 Changes in Age-Standardized Cancer Incidence
from 1937 to 1969

| Cancer Site | Group* | Percent Changes | | Net Change |
		1937–1947	1947–1969	1937–1969
Esophagus	WM	6	−28	Down
	WF	19	−18	Down
	BM	62	101	Up†
	BF	57	89	Up†
Stomach	WM	−23	−59	Down
	WF	−30	−67	Down
	BM	3	−48	Down
	BF	3	−56	Down
Colon	WM	17	26	Up
	WF	16	−1	Up
	BM	5	90	Up†
	BF	37	129	Up†
Rectum	WM	16	−22	Down
	WF	25	−29	Down
	BM	59	3	Up
	BF	62	−27	Up
Pancreas	WM	33	22	Up
	WF	12	21	Up
	BM	132	30	Up†
	BF	88	127	Up†
Lung	WM	115	133	Up†
	WF	63	108	Up†
	BM	202	234	Up†
	BF	71	213	Up†
Breast	WF	10	4	Up
	BF	9	25	Up
Uterus	WF	−6	−37	Down
	BF	−12	−49	Down
Ovary	WF	16	−10	Up
	BF	80	16	Up

(continued on following page)

Table 1.6   (*continued*)

Prostate	WM	17	23	Up
	BM	63	55	Up†
Bladder	WM	22	21	Up
	WF	8	−26	Down
	BM	25	118	Up†
	BF	44	−43	Down

Source: S. J. Cutler and S. S. Devesa, "Trends in Cancer Incidence and Mortality in the USA," in R. Doll and I. Voldopija, eds., *Host Environment Interactions in the Etiology of Cancer in Man*, International Agency for Research on Cancer, Lyon, France, 1973, pp. 15–34.

*WM = white male; WF = white female; BM = black male; BF = black female.

†Total increase exceeds 75 percent.

both black and white. Of the thirty-six categories of cancer type by sex and race listed in the extreme left-hand column of Table 1.6, the incidence of cancer has increased in two-thirds of them (twenty-four categories). In half of these (twelve categories) the incidence rate has increased by more than 75 percent. Similar substantial increases have occurred for malignant melanoma and thyroid cancer in white males and for lymphoma in black males and females.

These major increases in cancer incidence up to 1969 have been maintained progressively and more recently have become even more marked for certain sites.

As can be seen from Table 1.7, the increase in cancer incidence from 1970 to 1975 involves not only the lung but a wide range of organs in both sexes and racial groups and therefore cannot be largely due to smoking. In fact, the overall increase in total cancer incidence for all sites is comparable to that when cancer of the lung is excluded (see Table 1.8).

The differences between the increased incidence rates for cancer of all sites and all sites excluding the lung reflect the relative increase in the incidence of lung cancer

Table 1.7 Changes in Standardized Cancer Incidence (for Some Major Sites) from 1970 to 1975

Cancer Site	Annual Percent Changes in Incidence Rates, 1970– 1975*			
	WM†	BM	WF	BF
Lung	1.0	0.7	8.5	11.6
Bladder	2.4	8.2	3.2	10.0
Rectum	0.3	4.5	2.3	9.9
Colon	0.8	4.9	1.0	4.9
Melanoma (skin)	6.0	36.6‡		
Cervix			−6.5	−6.1
Uterus			9.0	12.0
Breast			2.3	8.9
All sites	0.9	2.3	2.2	6.1

Source: NCI, Third National Cancer Survey, 1969– 1971, and Cancer Surveillance Epidemiology and End Results (SEER) Program.

*The 1975 standardized overall cancer incidence rate (per 100,000) is 359.8 for white males; 413.2 for black males; 299.8 for white females; and 329.1 for black females.

†WM = white male; BM = black male; WF = white female; BF = black female

‡Estimate unreliable as based on small number of cases.

compared to all other cancers. For white males, lung cancer and all other cancers are increasing at about the same rate, whereas in black males, lung cancer is now increasing less rapidly. For white and black females, lung cancer is increasing more rapidly than all other cancers, reflecting the increase in smoking by females.

The rate of increase in the incidence and mortality of cancer seems to be sharper in blacks, particularly males, than in whites. Esophageal and bladder cancers are on the increase in blacks, although they are declining among whites. Cancer of the breast is also increasing among blacks at a time when it has leveled off among whites.

Table 1.8 Changes in Cancer Incidence Rates from 1970 to 1975

Group	Average Percent Increase in Incidence Rates, 1970–1975			
	Cancers of All Sites		Cancers of All Sites except Lung	
	Annual	5-Year	Annual	5-Year
White male	0.9	4.7	0.9	4.6
Black male	2.3	11.9	2.7	14.3
White female	2.2	11.6	1.8	10.2
Black female	6.1	34.6	5.7	32.2

Source: As for Table 1.7. NCI, Third National Cancer Survey, 1969–1971; SEER Program; and statement of M.A. Schneiderman before the U.S. Department of Labor, Occupational Safety and Health Administration, OSHA Docket 090, April 4, 1978.

Cancers of other sites including prostate, pancreas, lung, and ovary are also on the increase in blacks.

The actual probability, at today's death rates, of a person born today getting cancer by the age of eighty-five is 27 percent for both men and women. This is up from 19 percent for men and 22 percent for women in 1950.[10]

It is clear that there has been a real and absolute increase in cancer incidence and mortality during this century which cannot be explained away by increased life span or by smoking. A significant acceleration in the long-term upward trend of cancer mortality is now underway. The increase offers additional support for the conclusion by most experts that cancer is environmental in origin and that the recent increase in the incidence of cancer is due to industrial pollutants.

Attempts to Deny the Facts

Many industry groups have tried to argue away this increase in cancer. Their arguments were summarized in a January, 1978, report by the American Industrial Health

Council, an organization recently created by the chemical industry to fight effective regulation of carcinogens in the workplace:

> If we use the turn of the century as a time against which to compare today's cancer problem, there has indeed been an increase in the incidence of cancer . . . but the increase is predominantly attributable to (1) greater longevity (the incidence of cancer increases with age), and (2) pandemic cigarette smoking. [11]

The American Industrial Health Council attempts to support its arguments with graphs that show a decrease in cancer death rates when lung cancer (which in the general population is largely due to smoking) is excluded. The council argues that cancer is on the decline, that its present incidence can largely be attributed to smoking and diet, and that industrial chemicals are responsible for no more than 5 percent of all cancers in the United States. However, it is easy to see from industry data that two sites have accounted for most of the decrease, stomach and cervix, and that this decrease has been more than matched by increases at other sites. The lower rate of cervix cancer is due in part to widespread Pap screening programs which detect and treat precancerous conditions, not to the disappearance of its possible environmental causes. *
The decline in stomach cancer is still unexplained. As is obvious from Tables 1.7 and 1.8, smoking is not a significant cause of the increased incidence of cancer in the past decade.

The industry position is based on oversimplification of a complex statistical problem. Cancer is probably not one disease but a spectrum of diseases with common features but different—though proximate—causes. Cancer strikes different parts of the population with different

---

*The decrease in cervix cancer rates is probably less real than apparent, as a large portion of older women (perhaps as many as 30–50 percent in some areas of the country) have had hysterectomies.

force. Any attempt to represent the effect of cancer with a single summary statistic for many cancer sites lumped together necessarily masks the real situation. As Table 1.6 shows, the incidence of many different types of cancer has risen dramatically in recent decades. There is also growing evidence incriminating the role of industrial chemicals as major causes of cancer.

Environmental Causes of Cancer

An informed consensus has gradually developed that most cancer is environmental in origin and is therefore preventable. The striking increase in cancer death rates in this century cannot be accounted for by aging alone and cannot be due to genetic changes in the population, which would take generations to propagate throughout the population. Furthermore, a series of epidemiological studies have concluded that environmental factors cause from 70 percent to 90 percent of all cancers. Such estimates are derived from a comparison of cancer incidence and mortality in different countries all over the world.[12] Countries at low risk for a given type of cancer are assumed to establish the background rate for that cancer type. A higher cancer rate in other countries is then attributed to environmental factors peculiar to them. Genetic differences between countries or regions are largely discounted in view of evidence that groups which migrate from one country to another tend to develop cancers at the sites and rates prevalent in their adopted countries.[13]

Striking geographical variations in the incidence and mortality of a wide range of specific organ cancers (sometimes as much as 2,000 percent) are now well recognized, and in some instances the environmental causes for its excess rates in certain regions have been discovered.[14] The high incidence of cancer of the mouth in Asia, representing some 35 percent of all Asiatic cancers (in contrast to less than 1 percent of European and North American cancers), is clearly due to the common habit of chewing betel nuts and tobacco leaves. The high incidence of liver cancers in the Bantu and in Guam is well recognized and is likely to be due to dietary contamination with aflatoxin, a potent fungal carcinogenic toxin, and to eating cycad plants containing naturally occurring (azoxyglucoside) carcinogens, respectively. The high incidence of cancer of the esophagus in Zambians drinking a homemade alcoholic brew (kachasu) and in residents of the Calvados area of France incriminates strong alcoholic spirits, possibly contaminated with carcinogens such as nitrosamines.

Environmental factors incriminated as causes of human cancer encompass a wide range of influences including background and man-made radiation, smoking, naturally occurring plant, fungal, bacterial, and chemical carcinogens, and industrial chemical carcinogens contaminating air, water, food, consumer products, and the workplace. While it is known that smoking accounts for up to 80,000 cancer deaths each year, there is no reliable method for calculating the numbers of deaths caused by other classes of carcinogens. For instance, it has been claimed, particularly by the chemical industry, that industrial chemicals are a relatively trivial cause of cancer, accounting for only about 5 percent of all cancers in adult males.[15] This figure is based on estimates of the effects of those workplace chemicals *known* to cause cancer. But in view of the limited number of epidemiological studies that have been carried out in the workplace there is every reason to suspect that many other industrial chemicals are carcinogenic, but not yet so identified. Also, there is no way of currently determining how many workers are unknowingly exposed to industrial carcinogens, so figures based on known workplace carcinogens will seriously underestimate the carcinogenic hazards of industrial chemicals.* Two or more carcinogens, furthermore, can interact

---

*The majority of industries has not been evaluated for cancer and other chronic effects. This alone makes it impossible to estimate the number of cancers that are industrially related.

synergistically and thus greatly increase the carcinogenic effects over those induced by either carcinogen alone. For example, the incidence of lung cancer among asbestos workers who smoke cigarettes is many times greater than either that of nonsmoking asbestos workers or of smokers among the general population.[16] The additional lung cancers due to synergistic effects would not have occurred in the absence of the occupational exposure to asbestos.

Cancers caused by industrial chemicals are not restricted to the workers immediately exposed to them. These chemicals are discharged or escape from plants handling them into the air, water, and soil of the surrounding communities. (Workers can also carry them home on contaminated clothes to their families.) Examination of overall cancer death rates on a state and county basis, using the recently published maps of the National Cancer Institute showing the geographical distribution of overall cancer mortality rates and rates for most major sites in men and women, clearly shows excess rates for people living in industrialized areas, particularly in the vicinity of petrochemical plants.[17]* While some of the excess cancers in males are due to exposures within the plant, the excess female cancers are most likely due to contamination of the community air or water by carcinogens originating from the plant. In a growing number of instances, chemical monitoring has demonstrated the presence of occupational carcinogens such as asbestos, vinyl chloride, benzene, and nitrosamines in the air outside plants.

The extent and importance of proximity of residence to industry, and possibility of exposure to industrial chemical carcinogens, as a substantial factor in causes of cancer in the general public is becoming increasingly recognized. Table 1.9 lists the five states with the highest overall cancer death rates for both men and women during the period 1950–1969 and contrasts these with the five states

---

*The pattern of distribution for each cancer site and sex and ethnic group tends to be distinctive.

with the lowest rates. As can be seen, the five highest rates, both for men and women, are all found in the northeast in some of the country's most heavily industrialized states. (The cancer maps further show that within any given state much higher rates are found in highly industrialized than rural counties.) In contrast, the states with the lowest cancer death rates are in predominantly rural western and southern states, where there is relatively little industry. The combined cancer death rate for the five highest states is 45 percent greater than that for the five lowest among males, and 38 percent greater among females. These large differences between urban industrial and rural environments, taken in the aggregate, point strongly to an important role of industrial pollution, possibly together with pollution from non-industrial sources, such as automobiles. One would be hard pressed to explain away differences of this large magnitude on the basis of possible differences in smoking, medical care, lifestyle patterns, or other such factors. New Jersey and Wyoming, for instance, have almost identical per capita tobacco sales (New Jersey's sales are 2 percent higher), but New Jersey's female cancer death rate is 36 percent higher than that of Wyoming.

Differences in cancer mortality rates among states and counties are even more striking when specific types of cancer rates are compared. As Table 1.10 shows, the excess rates for lung, bladder, and colon-rectal cancers are much greater for females living in New Jersey than in Wyoming or North Carolina. Similar but less marked excesses are also seen for breast cancer, a cancer not generally considered to result from exposure to industrial chemicals. When comparisons are extended to the United States as a whole, the strongest association in any county between cancer death rates and the location of petrochemical plants are found for bladder cancer.

While it is not possible to use cancer maps to determine the precise factors responsible for the striking differences in overall cancer rates and in rates for cancer of specific organs among counties all over the United States, the location of large petrochemical plants in counties with excess rates—with the strong likelihood of pollution of nearby communities—is the most plausible explanation. Calculations based on figures such as those in Tables 1.9 and 1.10 seem to suggest that such pollution may be a cause of 30 to 40 percent of cancers in the general population, but it would be unwise to interpret these figures except in a general way, as they may also reflect an incremental role of non-industrial sources of air pollution. It is clear, however, that industrial chemicals are major causes of cancer in the general population as well as the workforce.*

The New Era of Petrochemical Carcinogens

The recognition that environmental agents are the major cause of cancer, and the identification of the specific causal roles that many of them play, has led to an increased concern about the carcinogenic and other toxic effects of the many new chemicals which are being produced and dispersed into the environment. A measure of this concern and evidence that the petrochemical industry itself can no longer cope with the risks of its own operations is the industry's skyrocketing insurance premiums, with renewals sometimes fifty times higher than old rates. We are living in a new era of organic chemicals, not just familiar ones, but exotic ones which have never previously existed on earth, and to which no living thing has previously had to adapt. Organic chemicals containing carbon, hydrogen, and chlorine (or other halogens) are rarely, if ever, found in nature. Organochlorines are nondegradable or poorly

---

*In testimony supporting the recent proposals by the Department of Labor for the regulation of occupational carcinogens, Marvin Schneiderman of the NCI estimated that up to 30 percent of all cancers in white males were related to occupational exposures (OSHA Docket 090, April 4, 1978).

Table 1.9   States with the Five Highest and the Five Lowest Cancer Mortality Rates

	Five Highest States		Five Lowest States		Difference between Highest & Lowest
	State	Mortality Rate*	State	Mortality Rate	
Males					
	New Jersey	205.01	Utah	133.13	
	Washington, D.C.	203.75	New Mexico	136.30	
	Rhode Island	203.17	Wyoming	138.93	
	New York	199.24	Idaho	139.02	
	Connecticut	195.68	North Carolina	140.11	
	All five	200.36	All five	138.51	45%
Females					
	New York	138.01	Utah	102.06	
	New Jersey	147.92	North Carolina	106.97	
	Rhode Island	143.37	Arkansas	108.03	
	Washington, D.C.	141.73	Wyoming	109.09	
	Maine	140.46	Idaho	110.15	
	All five	147.37	All five	107.09	38%

Source: Based on T. J. Mason and F. W. McKay, "U.S. Cancer Mortality by County, 1950–1969," DHEW Publication (NIH) 74-615, Washington, D.C., 1973.

*Age-adjusted annual mortality rate for all cancers per 100,000 population.

Table 1.10 Comparison of Cancer Death Rates: New Jersey, Wyoming, and North Carolina, White Females*

Cancer Death Rates	State			Excess Rate for New Jersey (%)	
	New Jersey	Wyoming	North Carolina	Wyoming	North Carolina
Overall	147.9	109.1	107.0	36	38
Lung	7.2	4.4	4.5	64	60
Bladder	2.9	1.6	2.1	81	38
Leukaemia	5.7	4.8	5.6	19	20
Colon and rectum	21.7	12.4	10.9	71	99
Pancreas	6.3	5.1	5.2	24	21
Breast	30.6	21.1	19.3	45	59

Source: Based on T. J. Mason and F. W. McKay, "U.S. Cancer Mortality by County, 1950–1969," DHEW Publication (NIH) 74-615, Washington, D.C., 1973.

*Age-adjusted annual mortality rate per 100,000 population.

degradable, persist in the environment and in the body, and are fat soluble and have accumulated and concentrated in the food chain. As a class, it also contains a disproportionately high number of carcinogens (several of which will be discussed in the case studies that follow). Literally thousands of them are being released into the environment, and not in lots of a few pounds or gallons but by the millions and billions of pounds and gallons. The intricate biochemical defenses that living beings throughout evolution have developed to cope with their environment are now being constantly violated by foreign materials introduced into the environment in petroleum products, synthetic organic chemicals, and organic pesticides (Table 1.11).

Petroleum Products   Petroleum first achieved commercial importance in 1859, but significant quantities were not produced until the development of the internal combustion engine in the late nineteenth century. The growing use of gasoline led to the development in 1913 of large-scale hydrocarbon cracking processes, which for the first time made available large quantities of low-molecular-weight hydrocarbons, the starting material for the production of many organic compounds.[18] After World War II, catalytic cracking made possible yet another dramatic increase in hydrocarbon production from petroleum sources. The age of chemical solvents had begun. The growth of refining capacity is traced in Table 1.12.

Synthetic Organic Chemicals   Prior to 1900, the great bulk of all organic raw materials was derived from coal tar, and, to a lesser extent, from the distillation of wood. In 1931, the U.S. National Bureau of Standards and the American Petroleum Institute began a systematic study of petroleum hydrocarbon synthesis and uses. This culminated after World War II in a fundamental shift of organic chemical production to the petroleum industry, which, along with increased hydrocarbon production from catalytic cracking of petroleum, gave birth to a new petrochemical industry. Benzene provides a good example of the exponential growth of a petrochemical product. Its production in the United States rose from 125 million gallons in 1940 to 410 million in 1955 to 1.5 billion in 1976.

Insecticides Large-scale use of insecticides began in the 1870s, when the potato beetle was spreading rapidly eastward across the United States. Inorganic pesticides, calcium arsenate and copper sulfate, for example, were used to control pests and fungi, and they dominated these agricultural markets until World War II. Organic pes-

Table 1.11 Rate of Increase in Production from 1945 to 1970 of Selected Groups of "New" Chemicals

Chemical	Percent Increase
Synthetic fibers	5,980
Plastics	1,960
Nitrogen fertilizers	1,050
Synthetic organic chemicals	950
Organic solvents	746

Source: Barry Commoner, *The Closing Circle*, N.Y., Knopf, 1971.

Table 1.12 Growth in U.S. Crude Refining Capacity from 1900 to 1960

Year	Capacity (millions of barrels, daily)
1900	0.50
1931	3.91
1952	7.70
1960	10.36

Source: Kirk and Othmer, eds., *Encyclopedia of Chemistry and Technology*, 15:3 (1968); and W. L. Nelson, *Petroleum Refinery Engineering*, N.Y., McGraw-Hill, 1936.

ticides, which were expensive and variable in supply, were limited to a few natural products, such as rotenone, nicotine, and pyrethrum. The inorganics, however, tended to leave toxic residues which accumulated in the soil until levels were reached which made further growing of crops unprofitable. In 1939, when DDT was developed for widespread use, synthetic organic insecticides began to gain importance. After the war, many other chlorinated organic pesticides were developed, such as chlordane, toxaphene, dieldrin, and aldrin. As will be seen in chapter 7, many of these compounds, which have been released into the environment in mammoth quantities (DDT at 2.75 million pounds per month in 1945), are highly persistent and carcinogenic.

As is apparent, the end of World War II marked a turning point in the growth of the chemical industry. American enterprise, with its enormous productive capacity, had to create new products at an unparalleled pace in order to keep its large plants and refineries operating. It set to work aggressively developing "needs" for new types of goods and services. As a by-product of this prodigious effort, more new chemicals to be used in making these goods were created, which in turn required the creation of new markets to produce them on a large, and hence economically profitable, scale. Table 1.11 shows the rate of production of a variety of chemical substances which had not existed on the face of the earth until a few decades ago.

This productive spiral continues to accelerate, dipping occasionally only to wait for markets to stabilize, for new products to catch on, or for capital to become available. Figure 1.2 shows the trend in production for chemicals, plastics, and synthetics over the past ten years. Annual growth rates of 15 percent or more are not uncommon for the organic chemical industries, at a time when the rest of the economy is advancing by only 4 or 5 percent per year.

This pattern of growth applies not just to a handful of chemicals but to tens of thousands of them. As of November, 1977, the Chemical Abstracts Service computer registry of chemical compounds contained over four million

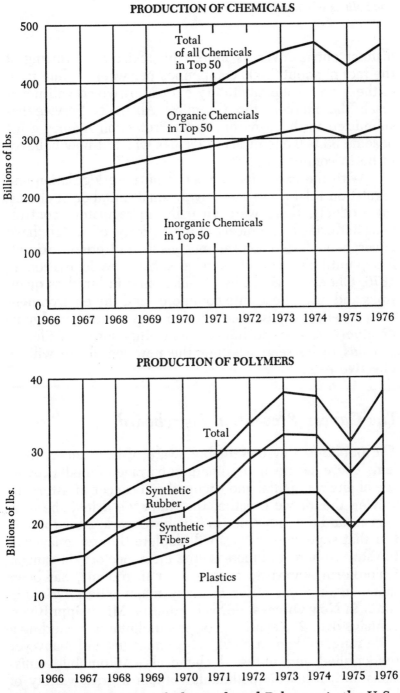

Figure 1.2 Production of Chemicals and Polymers in the U.S. from 1966 to 1976.

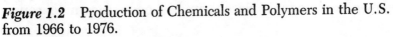

Source: Chemical and Engineering News, May 2, 1977.

distinct entries. What's more, the registry is growing at the rate of about 6,000 compounds per week. While most of these are exotic laboratory curiosities which will never reach the market, the Chemical Abstracts Service has submitted to the Environmental Protection Agency a list of some 33,000 chemicals in its files which it now believes to be in common use. [19]

With the exception of special-purpose legislation and regulation relating to a relatively small number of chemical products, there were virtually no regulatory controls over industrial chemicals, the majority of which have never been tested for carcinogenesis and other toxic effects, until the advent of toxic substances legislation in 1976. Chemicals could be manufactured in limitless quantities and introduced into commerce and the environment with no effort to discover whether they were carcinogenic or otherwise toxic to humans and other forms of life. (It remains to be seen whether the new legislation will be effective.)

The Cancer Prevention Scoreboard

The public is now undeniably aware of the cancer problem. There has been an unending barrage of media coverage of environmental and occupational cancer disasters involving the air we breathe, the water we drink, the food we eat, and the industries in which we work. Now there is fear that supersonic planes will deplete the ozone layer of the stratosphere and increase the incidence of skin cancer. Chloroform, known to cause cancer in rodents, has been found in drinking water in many major cities. Drinking water in New Orleans, derived from the Mississippi River, contains over 200 synthetic organic pollutants, including a wide range of known chemical carcinogens and many yet unidentified and untested chemicals. Automobile emissions and urban air pollutants contain a great variety of known carcinogens. Saccharin has been shown to cause cancer in animals. Many food additives and animal feed additives are proven carcinogens. In addition to these, a still wider range of chemicals used in the workplace are known to be carcinogenic, potentially exposing millions of workers to cancer hazards.

- Asbestos workers have a high lung cancer rate relative to the general population.
- Some plastics workers develop a rare form of liver cancer, besides other more common cancers, from exposure to vinyl chloride.
- Workers with nickel and chromium have high lung cancer rates.
- Dye workers have high rates of bladder cancer.
- Workers exposed to benzene have increased rates of leukaemia.

The public has responded to this assault of information on cancer risks with generally fatalistic reactions: "Everything causes cancer, so why bother?" or "You've got to go somehow, so it might just as well be cancer." Industry on the other hand, has been quick to minimize the scope and extent of cancer risks, to attribute them to personal habits such as smoking and diet, and to exaggerate the difficulties and costs of their control. In this denial of responsibility, industry has been supported by academic consultants who usually speak under the guise of independent scientific authority. And industry has not failed to exploit the awakening anticancer consciousness of consumers with appropriate responsive campaigns, such as for low-tar cigarettes.

The cancer prevention scoreboard has low entries in all categories, except confusion. While there is clearly need for improved understanding of the scientifically complex problems behind cancer, there is an even greater need for corrective political action. The decisions that are made today will have long-lasting effects on our own and on future generations.

Part I
The Science of Cancer

The human animals that provide the raw material are available in immense numbers; the wild ones are an independent lot and some of them behave in peculiar enough ways to satisfy the demands of the most imaginative investigator.

Richard Doll, British epidemiologist.

Chapter Two

Cancer: The Human Experiment

Historical Background

From earliest times, it has seemed logical to search for the cause of a disease by examining the characteristics common to those contracting it. The logic of this approach includes studying groups of people who have differing chances or risks developing the disease, not just those already afflicted with it. The science that encompasses such studies is called epidemiology. Epidemiological studies, by exploiting the "natural experiments" that people perform on themselves or that society or the environment inflict on them, are as close as we can reasonably get to performing actual experiments on humans.

Epidemiology has been much more successful in the study of acute infectious diseases, such as typhoid and cholera, than in the study of chronic diseases like cancer. Most infectious diseases spread rapidly and can be reproduced in the laboratory. Various hypotheses as to cause, effect, and prevention can thus be tested quickly, and once an infectious agent is isolated, it can be comparatively easily shown to cause the disease.

The epidemiology of cancer is more complex. In its broadest sense, cancer epidemiology is the study of the environment of the types of people who do and who do not get a particular type of cancer. Unfortunately, cancer epidemiology is a search for clues to the causes of cancer in a world where clues are both scarce and difficult to interpret.[1] It is a search for factors that differentiate cancer patients from other individuals, pursued in the hope that discovering such factors will lead to the development of preventive methods for those who have not contracted the disease. Epidemiological evidence is often the first clue that a problem exists. Occasionally, it is the only clue as to cause and prevention. The peculiar nature of cancer, especially the long natural history of the disease, in which clinical evidence of illness often occurs several decades after initial exposure to a carcinogen, makes cancer epidemiology frustrating, often controversial, and sometimes a useless exercise.

Some Perspectives and Pitfalls of Cancer Epidemiology

The fundamental problem of epidemiological research is that it is quite difficult to assemble a large enough number of cancer cases of a particular type upon which to draw conclusions about its causes. In numbers of people affected cancer is a major killer, but from a statistical point of view a particular type of cancer is a relatively rare event. For example, the overall incidence of lung cancer in the general population in 1970 was about forty cases for each 100,000 people, although its incidence is much higher in the middle-aged and elderly.[2] As the probability of an individual contracting lung cancer in that year was thus about one in 2,500, an extremely large number of people would have to be observed to ensure that there would be enough cases of the disease to study. The very task of assembling a sufficient number of persons to satisfy the statistical requirements of such an investigation is often the principal obstacle to the study, demanding as it does access to large population groups and substantial financing for salaries of interviewers, statisticians, and other investigators.

Identifying a sufficient number of cancer cases, together with their medical and exposure histories, is central in the use of epidemiology as a tool for investigating the cause of the cancer. To assist in this undertaking, a number of localities and states have set up cancer registries for the purpose of identifying all new cases of cancer. The nation's oldest such registry is that of the state of Connecticut, which maintains computerized files for use by epidemiologists and statisticians.[3]

Even in the best of circumstances, however, registries cannot predict what types of exposure to ask patients about, so that the "right" type of questions may simply not be asked. Cancer cells are not, after all, labeled for "carcinogen of origin." The clinician discovering cancer at a specific site may not have any useful idea what its cause could have been and what past exposures of the patient should be investigated.

Even when a particular chemical product or process has been shown to be carcinogenic in animals, hence suspect in humans, recognized human cancer cases due to the chemical may, for a long time, be too few to show up above background levels in the general population induced by other carcinogens.* Additional difficulties may be posed by latency, which for some carcinogens is decades (twenty to forty years for smoking and up to fifty years for asbestos).

Quite apart from these intrinsic difficulties in per-

---

*For this and other reasons, epidemiology is weak at identifying relatively low levels of cancer risk. The lowest clearly identified excess cancer risk, after some twenty years of intensive study, is the 30 percent excess risk for childhood leukaemia following irradiation in later pregnancy.

forming adequate epidemiological studies, there are also methodological problems which plague even the best designed ones. The most serious is the inability to obtain adequate data on exposure to carcinogens at times which preceded the finding of cancer by many years. It is nearly impossible to reconstruct industrial exposures to chemicals twenty years or more in the past if specific measurements were not recorded, because in that period the original processes often have changed radically or disappeared altogether. Even for chemicals voluntarily taken by people, such as saccharin, reliable information on how much was ingested or even whether it was taken at all, is difficult to obtain from interviews. This is the case because persons who have a disease which they suspect to be related to a particular chemical may selectively "recall" its use even sometimes when it never took place, and ignore other relevant chemical exposures.

Another major difficulty in most epidemiological studies is sorting out the relevant from the irrelevant. Claims of relationships between certain influences or exposures and disease may be due, not to those particular influences, but to other factors such as diet, location of residence, or lifestyle which the investigator may have overlooked or discounted.

Basic Epidemiological Techniques

The basic epidemiological techniques used in investigating environmental and occupational causes of cancer can be illustrated by describing their use in the tobacco-cancer problem.

The Informed "Hunch"

The informed hunch is often an important first step in developing a hypothesis about which type of exposure might be linked with a given cancer. It was responsible for early suspicions linking tobacco and lung cancer.

Lung cancer has not always been a major killer. In 1912 a British doctor published a book on the then obscure disease, wondering: "Is it worthwhile to write a monograph on primary malignant tumors of the lung?"[4]

In 1939, however, a German researcher observed that many lung cancer patients he was treating were heavy cigarette smokers.[5] About the same time, a similar observation was made in the United States by the now renowned heart surgeon, Michael DeBakey. These observations stimulated speculation, but without some way of comparing the lung cancer patients to healthy people, there was no way to exclude a host of other factors besides smoking as causes for the cancer. The main problem was that the number of lung cancer cases then seen by any one doctor was relatively small. The epidemic of what is now the most common cause of cancer deaths had only just begun. Only when the number of cases began climbing in the decades after World War II, could scientists begin to check out this hunch further.

Many, if not most, leads for epidemiological studies were developed in just this way, through astute observations by clinicians. The association, for example, between maternal medication with diethylstilbestrol and vaginal cancer in their daughters was developed after a doctor noted a number of similar cases of cancer and began a thorough investigation of use of the drug by obstetricians. This testifies to the importance of close links and communications between clinicians and epidemiologists in the cancer research effort.

Follow-up Studies

By the late 1950s a number of classical epidemiological studies on lung cancer and other disease complexes thought to be due to cigarette smoking were in progress in different countries. Some of these were follow-up or prospective cohort studies, which is to say a large number of healthy people are followed for several years in order to determine which of them contract and die from a specific disease.[6] A follow-up study begun in 1959 by E. Cuyler Hammond of the American Cancer Society is a good example.[7] In a massive and expensive effort by volunteers in twenty-five states, about one million men and women were questioned about their age and disease and smoking histories. The American Cancer Society managed to keep track of over 90 percent of the initial subjects for a dozen years. Updated questionnaires were supplied every four years or so, or, if a subject died, a death certificate showing the cause of death. The number of deaths observed among people in a specific category was divided by the number expected for people in the category, yielding a value known as the Standard Mortality Ratio (SMR).

The American Cancer Society found that the SMR from lung cancer increased dramatically with the number of cigarettes smoked and with the inhalation of smoke. It also found that the SMR for ex-smokers decreased as the time since quitting lengthened. More recent analysis also shows some lessening of the lung cancer death rate among smokers who switched from high to low-tar cigarettes.[8]

A single epidemiological study cannot alone validate or invalidate an assumed link between exposure and disease. However, over the past twenty-five years a parade of other follow-up studies conducted in the United States, England, Japan, and elsewhere, has extended and confirmed the causal association between smoking and lung cancer.*

---

*However, these studies have generally failed to inquire into occupational histories and have thus neglected a possible role of exposure to occupational carcinogens. Of further interest in this connection is the fact that deaths from pleural mesotheliomas due to asbestos are listed as lung cancers in the International List of Causes of Disease (which is used as the basis for reporting cancer mortality data). Thus, malignant lung disease due to occupational exposure or by such exposure interacting with the effects of tobacco smoke are misrepresented as being exclusively lung cancer deaths exclusively due to tobacco. It is thus likely that the role of occupational exposure to industrial chemicals as a cause of lung cancer has not been adequately recognized.

Case-Control Studies

The logistic problems of follow-up studies, which require enrollment of great numbers of healthy subjects in order to observe a statistically meaningful number of cases of disease, prompted epidemiologists to develop the case-control approach. A case-control (or retrospective) study depends on locating patients with a particular disease (the cases) and another group of people, either healthy or with some unrelated disease (the controls) and asking them the same set of questions. This approach is particularly appropriate for use in hospitals, where most people with serious disease eventually come. (In studies of lung cancer, the questions asked obviously include detailed smoking histories.) A figure called the relative risk is estimated from the replies. Relative risk is to a case-control study what an SMR is to a follow-up study, namely, a measure of the strength of association between exposure and disease. Both of these are measures of risk relative to the control group. But follow-up studies have an advantage over case-control studies in that they can be used to calculate absolute disease rates as well as relative ones. Thus, one can determine whether the incidence of the disease being studied is unusually large or small in the population being studied. However, this advantage is far outweighed by the enormous logistical difficulties and scale follow-up studies.

The case-control studies of lung cancer and smoking performed during the last twenty-five years have confirmed the conclusions of the follow-up studies. However, case-control studies have also shown that not all types of lung cancer are affected by smoking to the same extent. A type of lung cancer called adenocarcinoma is much less closely related to smoking than the more usual types, squamous, or oat cell, cancers.[9] Some of the studies also showed that the risk of lung cancer is greater among urban than rural dwellers, thereby supporting the case for an additional role of air pollution in lung cancer. A final important finding was that the risk of lung cancer is lower in smokers of filtered than non-filtered cigarettes.[10]

By 1964, based on the remarkable agreement of seven follow-up and twenty-nine case-control studies, U.S. Surgeon General Luther Terry, in his famous report on smoking and health, could bluntly state: "Cigarette smoking is causally related to lung cancer in men."[11]

Historical Follow-up Studies*

Many of the currently accepted occupational causes of cancer have been verified in human populations through a technique which exploits the follow-up approach, but in which the initial population of exposed workers, known as the cohort, is identified many years after the initial exposure. This is called a historical-follow-up or a retrospective-cohort study. This method has been successfully used by NIOSH and other investigators to identify such carcinogens as asbestos, vinyl chloride and benzene.[12]

In brief, the cohort of workers is defined to be all those engaged in a particular process at some time in the past. In the follow-up, a variety of documents are searched, such as employment, social security, or motor vehicle records, to ascertain the vital status of each cohort member at some later time. Causes of all deaths are obtained from death certificates. Then, based upon actuarial tables the SMR is calculated. The greater the SMR, the stronger is the inference of carcinogenicity.

Epidemiology: Conduct and Misconduct

Epidemiological investigation of a chronic disease, such as cancer, is difficult under the best of circumstances. But because of the major economic impact of a finding that an industrial product or process can cause cancer, industries have often compounded these difficulties by failing to undertake necessary studies or encouraging interpretation or even manipulation of the data to bias the studies in their favor.

---

*Also known as "cohort studies."

Until recently, most industries have been opposed to any epidemiological study of their workforce. They have either refused to cooperate in proposed studies, and in many cases have failed to accumulate meaningful records, or even destroyed these records. One reason for this has been their realization that such records could possibly damage the company in prospective Workman's Compensation claims or negligence suits.

Since passage of the 1970 Occupational Safety and Health Act, some companies have agreed to cooperate with government studies or else have hired their own staff or outside consultants to do the job. This apparent willingness to investigate the cancer risk to workers often masks a biased operation in which the preordained outcome is a clean bill of health. Indeed, a collection of statistical devices with built-in biases for handling data have become standard strategy to avoid regulation of carcinogens and other toxic chemicals. The tobacco industry alone has remained stalwart in its assertion that epidemiology, inasmuch as it is entirely statistical, is inappropriate for the study of cancer. This self-serving argument has been abandoned by virtually every other industry in favor of more sophisticated methods of manipulating numbers.

Many studies begin and end with the observation that workers in a given plant have a lower cancer or disease rate than the general population. This may in fact be correct, but it does not prove that workers in that industry are free from cancer or other illness due to occupational exposure, for it is well known that workers in any industry will have a death rate significantly lower than that of people of similar age drawn from the general population.[13] The general population includes disabled and chronically ill individuals, while the industrial population is at least healthy enough to perform work.* Thus, even when a working population develops cancer from an industrial carcinogen, the overall increase in worker death rate may

*This is sometimes known as the "healthy worker effect."

not be great enough to exceed the death rate of a similar age group in the community. The only meaningful comparison group for any given work force under investigation is a control group of workers from other industries where there is no exposure to the suspected carcinogens.

The most common error in conducting prospective studies is failure to obtain an adequate follow-up. If a large number of persons have been lost to follow-up, serious errors in computing cancer death rates can arise. For example, industry studies on retirees often find living retirees in a far greater percentage than they find the death certificates of retirees who have died. Whether by mischance or by inadequate effort to identify deaths, this means seriously underestimating the death rate for employees of the industry. A related problem is simply attempting to do a study on too few people, known as the "too few" technique. If the cohort size is too small, then even a greatly increased risk of cancer or any other disease cannot be detected statistically.[14]

Another common error of cohort studies is to follow workers for too short a period of time. Since most cancers have a latent period of at least ten years (and many have twenty-year or greater latencies), it is essential to follow workers for at least this much time before a meaningful cancer death rate can be expected. An example of the "short follow-up" technique is the current industry claim of the rarity of leukaemia following occupational exposure to benzene. This claim is, in part, based on an average follow-up of only three years.[15] Another example is the claim for the rarity of cancer in workers exposed to vinyl chloride. In this case the effects of vinyl chloride on workers with long-term exposures have been masked by including in the study many workers only recently exposed and by having a follow-up of only a few years, thereby resulting in a deceptively reduced cancer mortality rate.

Any particular epidemiological study can demonstrate various permutations and combinations of these different statistical devices, as will be illustrated in the various case studies in chapters 5, 6, and 7. For instance, using the "too few" and the "short follow-up" techniques, Shell Chemical Company has claimed that the pesticides aldrin and dieldrin are not carcinogenic, since workers engaged in their manufacture apparently did not have an increased cancer risk. Shell also used this argument as the basis for its claim that the overwhelming data on the carcinogenicity of these pesticides in rodents should be discounted in favor of the allegedly conclusive human evidence of safety.*

Cancer, Geography and the Environment

What do we know of other factors, besides smoking, that are causes of cancer? Are these factors environmental or genetic? Differences all over the world in the incidence of cancers of particular organs help answer these questions.

We now know that the incidence of various types of cancer exhibits great geographical variation. For example, in Scotland, the rate of lung cancer among men is the highest in the world, 78 cases per 100,000. In the United States, for white males, the rate is half that of Scotland and in Portugal only one-seventh. The death rate for stomach cancer in Japan is eight times that of U.S. whites, which is now the lowest in the world and still decreasing. The death rate from prostate cancer for U.S. blacks is the world's highest, ten times that of the Japanese. [16]

An almost unbelievable geographical variation exists in a broad belt of central Asia. The Ghurjev district of Khazak in the USSR has an extremely high incidence of esophageal cancer, over 500 cases per 100,000 males. In a

---

*In an attempt to improve the quality and reduce the bias of epidemiologic studies on the basis of which regulatory decisions are made, the Interagency Regulatory Liaison Group has developed guidelines for cohort studies, released in draft form on May 31, 1978, which recommend minimal criteria for the acceptability of such studies, including availability of supporting documentation, definition of follow-up procedures, discussion of potential bias, and disclosure of source of sponsorship and funding.

small section of Iran near the Caspian Sea, the rate of this disease among women varies by a factor of as much as thirty over a distance of only 100 miles. This high-cancer region has been mapped and inexplicably has a very sharp edge.[17] Similarly inexplicable is the fact that breast cancer also varies geographically by a factor of six, from its lowest national incidence in Japan to its highest in the Netherlands.[18]

Cancer of the mouth is relatively rare in the United States, accounting for less than one-half of one percent of all cancers. In parts of Asia, however, it accounts for up to thirty-three percent of all cancers. In this instance, the reason for such a striking difference is known. It results from the habit among many Asians of chewing betel nuts and leaves, wads of which are wrapped around shredded tobacco and lime and held in the mouth for long periods.[19]

The fact that there are such geographical differences in cancer rates does not tell us whether environmental or genetic factors are involved. However, epidemiological studies have shown that when people migrate from one area to another, their disease patterns tend to adjust to that of the country to which they migrate. A 1968 study on the offspring of Japanese migrants to the United States showed that their stomach cancer rate was reduced by two-thirds, their colon cancer rates tripled, and their rates of cancer of the pancreas and lung, and of leukaemia increased (Table 2.1). These changes in cancer patterns were all in the direction of matching the comparable cancer rates for the U.S. white population. Since this second-generation group tended only to intermarry among themselves or with new migrants from Japan their genetic characteristics as a group remained basically the same. Such studies give strong evidence for the environmental rather than genetic causation of cancer.

The National Cancer Institute has recently published an "Atlas of Cancer Mortality for U.S. Counties: 1950–1969."[20] This is a set of colored maps ranking U.S. coun-

Table 2.1 Mortality Rates of Offspring of Japanese Migrants to the U.S.

Cancer Site	Relative Cancer Mortality Rates		
	Japanese	Offspring of Migrants	U.S. Whites
Stomach	100	38	17
Colon	100	288	489
Pancreas	100	167	274
Lung	100	166	316
Leukaemia	100	146	265

Source: W. Haenszel and M. Kurihara, "Studies of Japanese Migrants. I. Mortality from Cancer and Other Diseases Among Japanese in the United States," *J. Natl. Cancer Inst.* 40(1968): 43–68.

ties by cancer mortality rates of white males and females, adjusted for age. A similar study for non-whites was subsequently published. [21]

The "Cancer Atlas" has proved a valuable resource for epidemiologists. Its value lies in its use of 3,056 U.S. counties in forty-eight states as the basic units for the study. These units are sufficiently small to be homogeneous in factors which might influence cancer risk, yet large enough to provide statistically useful estimates of cancer rates at specific body sites. Since the U.S. Census provides basic social and economic information also broken down by counties, it is possible to correlate these with the cancer death rates, and thus to test hypotheses about the association between cancer mortality and suspected socioeconomic variables.

For example, males show a striking variation in distribution of cancer mortality rates, with highest rates of certain cancers in counties with heavy concentrations of petrochemical industries. Salem County, New Jersey, where 25 percent of the men are employed by the chemical industry, has the highest mortality from bladder cancer for white males in the United States.* High bladder cancer rates are also found in industrial cities like Buffalo, Toledo, and Chicago. Liver and lung cancer rates are high in the refinery and shipbuilding areas of the Texas Gulf Coast and Louisiana. Lung cancer is also high in counties where copper, lead, and zinc smelters are located. The fact that the corresponding cancer rates among women in some cases show less striking variations strongly suggests the cancers in the men are substantially occupational in origin.†

However, excess cancer rates are also seen in women living in industrial areas, for example close to petrochemical plants and shipyards. This makes it clear that environmental factors are critically involved. Further confirmation of the risks of living near chemical plants has come from a recent NCI study showing higher rates of cancer of the lung in men and women, as well as cancer of the nasal cavity, skin, testis, and other sites in men living in counties with major petroleum refineries.[22]

The nature of these environmental factors involved in geographical clustering of excess cancers in heavily industrialized locations is gradually becoming clearer. Evidence is accumulating of the discharge or escape of a wide range of occupational carcinogens from inside petrochemical and smelting plants into the air and water of the surrounding community. Although only relatively few investigations of this kind have so far been made, carcinogens such as ni-

---

*Interest in the high cancer rates in New Jersey has been recently highlighted by the discovery of a cluster of six cases of acute childhood leukaemia in the 21,000 population of Rutherford over the last five years. On the basis of chance alone, not more than one case should have occurred in this time. While Rutherford is now being monitored for chemical carcinogens, the possibility that the ITT radar station in Rutherford may be implicated does not appear to have been considered yet.

†The present-day cancer incidence reflects exposure perhaps ten or twenty years ago, when the percentage of women in the industrial work force was much lower than at present. Thus, male–female differences in cancer incidence, except of course for sex organs, can give evidence of occupation-related cancer.

trosamines, vinyl chloride, kepone, benzidine, arsenic and asbestos, have all been found and measured in nearby communities outside particular industries. Another source of family exposure is the carcinogenic chemicals and dust brought home on workers' skin and clothes.

In tracking down specific industrial and environmental correlations with cancer, the cancer maps are valuable only up to a certain point. At best, the data can be used to obtain clues or leads as to identification of possible high risk groups, which must be further investigated by additional epidemiological methods and chemical monitoring of the industries. For example, the bladder cancer map reveals a clustering of high risk counties for both white males and females in easily delineated industrial locales. Since many different types of industry tend to be located near each other, however, identifying the specific industries responsible can be difficult. Also, other variables known or suspected to cause cancer are more prevalent in urban industrial areas. Explanations for higher cancer rates in these areas should also take other possible urban-rural differences into account.

Epidemiology versus Animal Testing

In conclusion, epidemiology is used to study the incidence of cancer in populations who have already been exposed to carcinogens. While of obvious value in helping to establish causal relationships, these studies must invariably rely for their data on people who have already contracted cancer, or who do so during the course of the study. In preventive terms, it is a case of "locking the barn door after the horse has run out," at least for the population being studied.

In contrast, animal testing of new chemicals not yet introduced into commerce allows relatively simple and rapid determination of carcinogenicity, allowing the possibility of subsequent control prior to human exposure.

The major categories of known human carcinogens, the majority of which are occupational carcinogens or industrial processes (the remainder being drugs), are listed in Appendix I. In the case of the five industrial processes, the precise chemical identity of the causative agents is unknown. As can be seen, there is very good general correspondence between the human and the experimental animal data.

The bottom line on carcinogenesis testing is this. You can drown an animal in a pool of some substance, suffocate an animal under a heap of it, or beat an animal to death with a sock full of it, but if it isn't carcinogenic, you can't give an animal cancer with it.

William Hines and Judith Randal,
Washington, D.C. Journalists.

Chapter Three

Cancer: The Animal Experiment

Whenever it is announced that a chemical has been shown to be carcinogenic in animals, there is usually an accompanying disclaimer that "the chemical has not been found harmful to humans." Every time you read this kind of statement in the press, or hear it announced on the radio or television, you should mentally insert the word "yet." You should ask yourself the question, "If the chemical *is* carcinogenic to humans, how would we know?" As we have seen, we can only know if the appropriate epidemiological study has been done and its results are conclusive beyond doubt—which is rare—or if the chemical induced an extremely rare tumor.

This chapter explains the rationale for animal experiments, the standard test methods used on animals, and how animal test results should be interpreted. It also deals with some current controversies in interpretation, particularly when major economic interests are threatened.

54

Some Historical Perspectives

Experiments studying causes of cancer in laboratory animals are not new, but the systematic use of animals to test whole classes of chemicals (e.g., food additives) for the purpose of deciding whether they can be safely used or not is a relatively recent development. This lies at the heart of much of the modern cancer controversy. However, there is now overwhelming agreement by most qualified scientists that if a chemical causes cancer in well-designed animal tests, then there is a strong likelihood that it will also cause cancer in exposed humans.[1] Experience continues to prove that this is, indeed, the case.

Distasteful as it may seem to some to use animals in experimental research, even in accord with standard humane guidelines for the prevention of unnecessary pain and suffering, there is no practical and reasonable alternative to their use. Modern medicine, including vaccines, antibiotics, drugs, and transplants, would not have been possible had it not been for animal studies. The same is also true for cancer research.

During the early 1900s scientists, familiar with the classic writings more than 100 years earlier of Percival Pott on the role of soot in scrotal cancer among chimney sweeps, tried unsuccessfully to reproduce this in animals using coal tars prepared from soot.[2] Then, in 1916, two Japanese scientists succeeded in inducing skin tumors on rabbit ears by daily application of coal tar for a period of more than six months.[3] This single experiment suddenly opened up the use of animals in cancer research.

It is important to appreciate the difficulty that early investigators experienced in inducing cancers in laboratory animals. First, the time required to produce cancer in an animal was found to be much longer than the time to produce an infection such as rabies or typhus. Such unforeseen delays alone caused many researchers to abandon their experiments. Second, the Japanese scientists were fortunate in their choice of the rabbit as a test animal, for rabbits appear to be particularly sensitive to the effects on skin of this kind of carcinogen. It took three more years before the results of the coal tar experiments were confirmed. [4]

Another reason why work proceeded so slowly was that, in addition to the experimental difficulties in inducing cancer, scientists in the early 1920s didn't believe that cancer could even be caused by a particular chemical. The conventional wisdom of the day was rather that the tumors resulted from a generalized irritation of cells and tissues, irrespective of the identity of the agents causing the irritation.

During the 1930s, the experimental foundation of chemical carcinogenesis was firmly established by a research team led by Sir Ernest Kennaway at the Royal Cancer Hospital in London. [5] In a short period, his team demonstrated the carcinogenicity in mice of tars extracted from pitch and oils. They showed that the cancer-causing activity was greatest in the chemical fractions with the higher boiling points. [6] These chemicals, called polycyclic aromatic hydrocarbons, are found in cigarette smoke and air pollutants, and are the products of incomplete combustion of organic matter.

In their most dramatic experiment, the London researchers produced tumors by applying a pure synthetic chemical, dibenz[a,h]anthracene, which was also known to be one of the many components of tar. [7] This was the first time it had ever been shown that an individual pure chemical, rather than a mixture such as coal tars, could cause cancer. Finally, one of the group, J. H. Cook, proceeded to test various chemical fractions extracted from a pitch sample originally weighing two tons, and thereby identified benzo[a]pyrene, another powerful skin carcinogen and also a major component of tobacco smoke. [8]

About the same time, epidemiological studies in the United States and elsewhere were finding a clear relationship between the high incidence of bladder cancer among workers in the dye industry and their exposure to particular chemicals, such as benzidine and 2-naphthylamine.[9] In order to study the basic mechanisms involved here, it was logical to try to reproduce this disease in animals by exposing them to these dye chemicals. Not until 1938 was this successfully performed by Wilhelm C. Hueper, one of the great early pioneers of environmental and occupational carcinogenesis.[10] His good fortune was to have chosen the dog as the test subject, rather than the usual experimental animals, rodents. Dogs and humans have similar sensitivity to 2-naphthylamine, which induces bladder cancer in both, whereas rodents are relatively resistant to this carcinogen, and when cancers are induced they are found in organs other than the bladder.

From Mouse to Humans

Unless we can relate the occurrence of cancer among other species of animals, however induced, to human cancers, the most elegant animal experiment will have been at best academic.

The legitimate inference that what is found to cause cancer in one species must also be assumed to cause cancer in others (known as the species-to-species extrapolation) is fundamental to cancer research. This inference rests on over half a century of intensive scientific investigation into the biology and chemistry of carcinogenesis and carcinogens in many organisms, including humans. Acceptance of the extrapolation principle is grounded in the fact that fundamental life processes in mammalian and other animals are basically the same as those in humans. Thus information on the origin of cancer drawn from observations of animal experiments can be applied, with appropriate reservations, to man. While the substance of these reservations has often been the source of intense controversy in specific instances, the basic fact that extrapolation is a reasonable undertaking is nearly universally accepted by biomedical researchers and is indeed fundamental to all experimental biology and modern medicine.

By the time a cancer has developed in a test animal, a great many events have taken place at the molecular, cellular, and organ levels. Also, a relatively long period of time, the latency period, has passed since the initiation of the cancer process. Cancer probably begins with a single identifiable event within a cell, such as the breakage of some critical genetic component of the cell by the carcinogen. While such events are probably frequent, and normally handled by cellular repair and detoxification mechanisms, in certain cases they may go unrepaired, and the cancer process begins. The cancer cells grow in an uncontrolled fashion, invade local tissues, and often spread (*metastasize*) to distant parts of the body.[11]

There are very striking similarities between cancer in humans and other living organisms with regard to the widest possible range of biological characteristics. Cancer is found in multicellular organisms, including insects, fish, and even plants. The probable reason for this is the essential similarity of their cellular ultrastructures, in particular their genetic structure and coding. Carcinogenic chemicals thus tend to be similarly active in many different test animals. However, there are often differences in the susceptibility of various animal species, in differing strains of any species, and in different individuals in any particular strain or sub-strain. Additionally, the target organ affected by the carcinogen may vary from species to species. Nevertheless, if a carcinogen is active in any one species, it is likely to also be active in others, including man.

The use of small mammalian animals, particularly mice and rats, has been and continues to be standard practice in routine carcinogenicity testing. Considerations of convenience apart, the key role of these rodents in carcinogenicity testing has been repeatedly endorsed by numerous expert committees and authorities, as illustrated by the following statement from the National Academy of Sciences in 1960:

The rat and mouse have been shown to be susceptible to the carcinogenic action of a large variety of compounds and, indeed, most of our knowledge of chemical carcinogenesis is based on the use of these species. The hamster and guinea pig are relatively resistant to the carcinogenic action of several compounds which produce tumors readily in the rat and mouse. On the other hand, no known carcinogens for the hamster and guinea pig are inactive in the rat and mouse.[12]

It must be realized that the activity of many known human carcinogens was first recognized in rodent tests. These include 4-aminobiphenyl, bischloromethylether, aflatoxins, vinyl chloride, mustard gas, melphalan, and diethylstilbestrol. Conversely, all chemicals known to induce cancer in man, with the possibile exception of arsenic, also do so in experimental animals, generally rodents.[13] In any one instance where a chemical is found to be carcinogenic in a proper animal test, there is no possible way in which absolute assurances can be given that the chemical will also be carcinogenic in humans. However, the general similarity in response to carcinogens of a very wide range of species, including humans, and also the good track record of animals as predictors of human response, afford strong reasons for accepting the results of well-conducted animal experiments as surrogates for human experience.

The predictive value to humans of carcinogenicity tests in mice has been repeatedly challenged by industry.*

---

*Few epidemiological studies have been undertaken for carcinogens found active in rodent tests, and industry sometimes equates this absence of epidemiological data with evidence of noncarcinogenicity in humans. Accordingly, industry argues that regulation should primarily, if not exclusively, be directed at those few carcinogens identified by human epidemiologic studies. A reductio ad absurdum of this position has been put forward by Vaun Newill, Medical Director of Exxon Corporation, in *Cancer Bulletin* 29 (1977): 177–78: "A regulatory program based on experimental screening models to evaluate new chemicals prior to their introduction into the environment, however, will hinder the better documentation of this correlation [between human and animal carcinogenicity data] than we have presently. When a carcinogen is prevented from entering the environment on the basis of screening results, there can be no data regarding that exposure in man."

It has been claimed by Shell Chemical Company and other segments of the chemical industry that the mouse is an unsuitable animal for carcinogenicity testing of products such as pesticides because it is unusually sensitive and because it has a high incidence of spontaneous tumors. These criticisms have been particularly focused on the supposed unreliability of mouse liver tumors as an indication of response to carcinogenic chemicals.* There are just no scientific grounds for these allegations. On the basis of an extensive review of the literature on chemical carcinogenesis, Lorenzo Tomatis of the International Agency for Research on Cancer in Lyon, France, published recent studies which demonstrate that the results of carcinogenicity tests in mice are closely similar to and predictive of those in rats or other rodents.[14] Tomatis found that of fifty chemicals producing liver tumors in mice, all induced tumors of the liver or other organs when adequately tested in rats and hamsters.

A major deficiency in current carcinogenicity tests is their simplistic nature, dictated in part by practical considerations, such as testing the effects of one chemical at a time. Carcinogenicity tests thus do not adequately reflect the realities of multiple concurrent and sequential exposures to a wide range of carcinogens in the general environment and the workplace. Because of the relatively small numbers of animals that can be tested and the impossibility of predicting human sensitivity from animal tests, there is also substantive evidence of interactions between individual carcinogens making the carcinogens together much more potent than either separately. Also interactions between carcinogens and a wide range of noncarcinogenic chemicals may increase the potency of the carcinogens. For example, the incidence of liver cancers induced in trout by feeding as little as 0.4 parts per billion

---

*Those industries such as Shell which challenge the significance of the induction of cancers in test mice by their products continue to use the failure of other products to induce cancers in mice as proof of their safety.

(ppb) of aflatoxin is sharply increased by addition of various noncarcinogenic oils to the diet.[15] Similarly, the carcinogenic effects of low concentrations of benzo[a]pyrene on mouse skin are increased 1000-fold by the use of the noncarcinogenic n-dodecane as a solvent.[16] Benzo[a]pyrene and ferric oxide injected in the trachea of adult rodents induce a high incidence of lung tumors, only if the animals are pretreated at birth with a single low dose of another carcinogen, diethylnitrosamine. The quantitative response to a particular carcinogen can be substantially influenced by a wide range of factors, including interaction with other carcinogenic and noncarcinogenic chemicals. Thus, these so-called *synergistic* effects further confound attempts to find safe levels of carcinogens. Such interaction studies clearly confirm that threshold levels of carcinogens cannot possibly be predicted by calculations based on setting a dose arbitrarily lower than the lowest apparently carcinogenic animal dose in a particular experimental situation. Epidemiology has given important clues on interactive effects between carcinogens, such as smoking and asbestos or uranium, and between carcinogens and noncarcinogenic chemicals, such as arsenic and sulfur dioxide. There are now critical needs for large-scale interactive tests designed to elucidate such additive and synergistic interactions as they occur in daily life.

Principles of Animal Testing

Test Guidelines

The National Cancer Institute has recently published a set of specific recommended procedures for carcinogenicity testing in rodents.[17] Useful guidelines have existed since the early 1960s, but they are too general for current regulatory needs. As the results of more and more animal tests are now subject to public scrutiny, the proposed NCI guidelines will probably have an increasing influence on carcinogenicity testing.

There is now general acceptance of the need to conduct tests in accordance with accepted humanitarian principles.

Test Animals

Just as the chemist pulls a bottle of chemicals off the shelf and is assured of reasonably standard quality, so does the cancer biologist like to use particular species and strains of animals in which a reasonably standard response can be expected.[18] As noted above, the two species used more than any others are rats and mice. There are various strains of each species available, each with its own characteristic biological properties and sensitivities. There are some important advantages to using highly inbred rodent strains. Their incidence of spontaneous cancers and of cancers following treatment with various chemical carcinogens is more predictable than is the case with random-bred animals. Additionally, strains can be selected that are either highly sensitive or highly resistant to certain classes of carcinogens.

On the other hand, as human populations represent a genetic smorgasbord, it is more likely that random-bred animals will give results more in line with expected human responses. A compromise, which is now currently favored, is to use a hybrid of two inbred strains which combines the advantages of predictable responses with genetic heterogeneity.

Routes of Tests

Among the many possible methods and routes by which a carcinogen can be administered to an animal are feeding, inhalation, and skin painting. The same carcinogen administered through different routes can produce cancer in either different or in the same organs; there is no way of predicting the type and site of response. The most common test route for tests of food additives and other dietary compounds is by incorporating the test substance in animal feed or administering it directly into the stomach by a tube (this process is called *gavage*). Feeding is also a standard test method for administering many other types of possible carcinogen. Feeding of test animals can be and is also used when the route of human exposure is by the skin or lungs, especially when there is a likelihood that cancers will result in internal organs, such as the liver or kidney.

When exposure on the human skin results in skin cancer (or is suspected to cause skin cancer), as in workers exposed to petroleum and shale oils, then skin painting in animals is the proper method to use. Skin painting, however, is not sufficiently sensitive for investigating carcinogenic effects of chemicals such as amine hair dyes and textile fire retardants, which are absorbed through the skin and induce cancers at distant sites.* A technical background statement in the NCI "Guidelines for Carcinogen Bioassay in Small Rodents" makes this clear:

> Although this type of test (skin painting) might provide useful information on some chemicals, it might be unreliable for measuring the effects of such chemicals on internal organs. [19]

If a chemical is suspected of causing lung cancer when inhaled by humans, the logical way of testing is by inhalation. However, inhalation studies are technically difficult and relatively expensive. They are also complicated by the fact that a rodent, unlike humans, can breathe only through its nose, filtering the chemical being tested through a highly developed defense system and possibly reducing its effects. Despite the obvious importance of inhalation as a major route of human exposure,

---

*The insensitivity of skin painting is due to the fact that it is difficult to apply sufficiently high concentrations of test material by this route. For this reason, a positive result is all the more significant.

particularly for air pollutants, industrial chemicals, pesticides, and cosmetics, relatively few chemicals have so far been adequately tested for carcinogenicity by long-term inhalation.[20]

Dosage

In well-designed tests, a range of doses is used. If the dose of a carcinogen is too low, few or no animals in the typically small test groups may get cancer. If it is too high, animals will die quickly from toxic effects of the chemical, well before cancer has had a chance to develop. To estimate the proper dosage range for carcinogenesis research, it is usual to perform preliminary toxicity tests to determine the maximum tolerated dose (MTD), i.e., the highest quantity of chemical which can be administered over the course of a prolonged carcinogenicity test without the animals losing substantial weight or becoming sick or dying. In well-designed studies, additional doses, based on one or more fractions of the maximum tolerated dose, are also tested. The various dosages used in an experiment are usually expressed as so many milligrams (mg) of chemical per kilogram (kg) of animal body weight, mg/kg. This allows a comparison of the effects of equivalent doses in different animal species with different typical body weights.

The duration and periodicity of the dose are also important. Some carcinogens will induce only a relatively low incidence of cancers when given in one large dose, but will produce a higher incidence when broken up into a series of intermittent and lower doses over the course of months.

Use of Relatively Large Dosages Perhaps the aspect of cancer research most misunderstood by the public is the necessity to use much larger doses of a substance being tested than humans could possibly be exposed to. The superficial absurdity of a rat consuming the human equiva-

lent of about a thousand cans of diet soda per day from
fetus to adulthood has been exploited by industry, misinterpreted by the press, and misunderstood by the lay public, which has come to believe that anything given in large
enough doses will cause cancer in animals.* This simply is
not true. The need for large dosages of chemicals (as the
highest of a range of doses) in some experiments is a reflection of the facts (1) that some carcinogens are much
less potent than others and (2) that animal experiments,
no matter how well planned, must make use of finite animal resources. To illustrate this point, let us suppose that
humans and rats are equally sensitive to some chemical
carcinogen which causes one case of cancer in every
10,000 persons (or rats) to which it is given. If 220,000,000
Americans were exposed to this chemical, 22,000 cases of
cancer would occur. On the other hand, if fed to the typical fifty rats used in an experiment, the chances that even
one rat would get cancer is one-half of one percent; 10,000
rats would have to be fed the chemical (at human dosages)
to observe even one cancer.[21]

Given that a human-level dosage might not produce a
detectable result in a small rat population, even for a carcinogen which may be the cause of many thousands of
cases in humans, the only alternative is to increase the
dose, and thereby increase the probability of inducing a
cancer in a particular animal. Once the dosage is increased above real-life levels, scientists must begin to
make assumptions about their findings in the following
vein. If the equivalent of, let us say, 1,000 cans of
saccharin-containing soda per day produces one tumor in
50 rats, then it is plausible to assume that 100 cans will
produce one-tenth as many tumors, or one tumor in 500
rats. Continuing the argument, the equivalent of 10 cans

*In addition to being carcinogenic at relatively high dose levels, saccha-
rin is also carcinogenic in rats at doses in the diet extending down to 0.01
percent, equivalent to the amount of saccharin in one and one-half cans of
diet soda.

per day would produce one-tenth as many as before, that is, one tumor in 5,000 rats. Finally, one can per day would produce one tumor in 50,000 rats. If, as we assume, humans and rats are equally sensitive to this carcinogen, one can of soda per day would produce one tumor in 50,000 people, or about 4,000 cases of cancer in the nation's population.*

Two basic assumptions are involved in the above argument. First, as stated, we assumed humans to be as sensitive as rats. Of course, in any particular situation, humans may either be less sensitive or more sensitive than rodents to the toxic or carcinogenic effects of the chemicals in question. For example, the lowest dose of thalidomide inducing birth defects in pregnant women is 0.5 mg/kg/day; the corresponding values for the mouse, rat, and dog are 30, 50 and 100 mg/kg/day, respectively. Thus, humans are 60 times more sensitive than are mice to thalidomide, 100 times more sensitive than rats and 200 times more sensitive than dogs.[22] Moreover, certain aromatic amines, such as 2-naphthylamine, are potent bladder carcinogens for man, monkeys and dogs, but not for rats, mice and other rodents, in which tumors at other sites are produced.[23] Hence there is no known method for predicting a safe human level for carcinogens on the basis of experimental animal data, if indeed such safe levels for humans exist at all.[24] Second, we assumed that equal proportions of tumors would occur at all dosages, known technically as a linear dose–response extrapolation. This assumption is the least strong, because it is simply not practically verifiable by direct experimentation. As a conservative method for extrapolating animal data from high to low doses, however, it has become standard practice. By conservatism, we mean use of a mathematical method which errs, if at all, on the side of safety to humans. As former NCI Director Frank Rauscher, Jr., admitted to an American Enterprise Institute roundtable on saccharin on

---

*This argument has been simply explained in R. W. Rhein and L. Marion, *The Saccharin Controversy* (New York: Monarch Press 1977), p. 58.

April 21, 1977, "In protecting the public's health, there is no choice but to assume that the extrapolation is linear."

The justification for the conservative approach to the absence of a threshold for carcinogens or the inability to determine its existence rests largely on our ignorance of the nature of the lower ends of dose—response curves. There is, in fact, no evidence at all of the existence of thresholds for the irreversible processes involved in carcinogenesis. There is also no evidence of complete repair of DNA damaged by any carcinogen; any residual unrepaired DNA would perpetuate the carcinogenic hazard.*

Finding the Evidence

One of the most poorly conducted areas of animal cancer research is the identification of the cancer in the animals' bodies. The process of finding a cancer in the fresh carcass of a mouse or rat is different from the discovery of cancer in a human by a doctor. The rodent cannot complain of painful symptoms before death. Also, since carcinogens may cause cancer in any of a wide range of organs, the entire body of the animal must be meticulously searched. This is not possible if, through neglect or poor husbandry, the animal has been allowed to die and decompose before an adequate autopsy, as is often the case.

The Statistical Significance of the Evidence

The ideal experiment is one in which either the chemical being tested induces no tumors in the test group with none in controls, in which case the chemical is determined to be noncarcinogenic, or the chemical induces a

---

*Jerome Cornfield, in "Carcinogenic Risk Assessment," *Science* 198 (1977): 693–99, proposed a hypothetical model for carcinogenesis which in effect gives a threshold. Cornfield, however, stressed that his model is based on the assumption that all of a carcinogen below a given dose level, administered on a single occasion, could be inactivated instantaneously, by some unknown defense mechanism. According to Schneiderman of the NCI, the unverifiable and unrealistic nature of Cornfield's assumption invalidates his model.

high incidence of tumors in the test group with none in controls, in which case the chemical is determined to be carcinogenic. Unfortunately, the results are rarely this clear. Typically, the test animals have a certain percentage of tumors, which are considered to be induced, and the controls have a smaller percentage, which are considered to be spontaneous. It is then the job of the statistician to sort out the data and decide whether the difference in tumor yield between the test and control groups is statistically significant or simply due to chance. The statistician is also concerned with the time from the initial dose which elapses before the tumors appear, as not only do carcinogens increase the number of cancers in test animals in contrast with those occurring spontaneously in controls, but they also induce these cancers earlier in the life of the test animals. The statistician thus deals with four factors in a standard carcinogenicity test: the number of animals tested; the number of given types of cancers induced in each animal and in each test and control group; the time required to induce these cancers; and the number of tumors in both the test and control groups. Apart from the individual importance of each of these factors, their effects interact with each other statistically.

A critical factor in these tests is the number of animals tested. The greater the number of animals tested in each of the various dosage groups and in the control group, the more meaningful is any observed difference. A 20 percent tumor rate among the test group, compared to a 5 percent spontaneous rate among controls, unambiguously indicates a carcinogenic response in a group of 200 animals. But in a group of only 20 animals with the same exposure the difference between 20 percent and 5 percent is not statistically significant and the carcinogenic effects of the exposure cannot be established.

Short-Term Tests

Over the last two decades, some dozen or so short-term tests have been developed for predicting the carcinogenicity of chemicals by methods which, in contrast to conventional animal tests, are inexpensive and rapid, taking a few days or sometimes a few hours.[25] Short-term tests are based on underlying chemical, physical, or biological properties which are shared, or rather are believed to be shared, by carcinogens but not by noncarcinogens. The successive appearance of each short-term test has characteristically been initially greeted with uncritical enthusiasm. This becomes progressively dampened when subsequent studies on a more extensive series of chemicals reveal poor correlations with carcinogenicity, at which stage the test gradually falls into more limited use or disuse.

The most recent short-term test was developed in 1975 by Bruce Ames of the University of California, Berkeley.[26] This test was based on his original finding that 93 percent of a selected group of 174 carcinogens induced mutations in bacteria, while none were induced by another group of 46 noncarcinogens. Besides the rapidity and economy of the Ames test, an additional attraction is that it was considered to have been based on the detection of specific types of damage to the genetic material, DNA, which have been thought to be critically involved in the cancer process. The test system has been subsequently refined by the incorporation of several types of rodent liver extracts to allow activation of the chemicals tested, and thus to crudely approximate some types of metabolic transformations in the body.

Since its introduction, the test appeared promising and is now being widely used. It allows large numbers of chemicals to be screened rapidly. The pharmaceutical, pesticide, and other chemical industries are using it on a routine basis early in developmental phases to screen chemicals presumed to be carcinogenic. Additional applications of the test include looking for carcinogens in complex, ill-defined organic mixtures such as extracts of air and water pollutants or hair dyes, and for carcinogenic metabolites in the urine or blood of workers with suspected exposure to carcinogens.

Apart from responsible uses of the test, it has also been used by some industry to argue that animal tests are too expensive, impractical, and unreliable and, in the absence of conclusive human epidemiological evidence of carcinogenicity, should be replaced by the Ames test. This would create a "no-lose" situation. A negative Ames test would be taken to exculpate any chemical from questions of carcinogenicity and to allow its marketing. Depending on economic considerations, a positive test could either be accepted or rejected in the full knowledge that regulatory agencies would be reluctant—and rightly so—to base regulatory actions on the results of tests in bacterial systems.

An example of misuse of the Ames test is afforded by the recent controversy surrounding the fire retardant, Fyrol FR-2, which is now used in some polyester children's sleepwear. During attempts to ban the carcinogenic flame retardant Tris,* Stauffer Chemical Company of Westport, Conn., advertised and sold a substitute, Fyrol FR-2, claiming that it was found to be inactive in the Ames test and therefore safe. Suspecting that this claim was in error, since Fyrol FR-2 is similar to Tris in chemical structure, Fyrol was then independently tested and found to be positive. Meanwhile, Stauffer was already marketing Fyrol FR-2 which had found its way into approximately two to three million pairs of children's sleepwear (mainly those sold by J. C. Penney Co.).

A wide range of problems in the Ames test itself have begun to surface. First, it gives positive results (called false positives) for various noncarcinogens, such as iron salts and vitamin C. Second, it misses several important classes of carcinogens (false negatives).† These include

---

*Manufactured by Velsicol Chemical Company.

†In classic quality-control terminology, a false negative result represents a "consumer risk" (in that it underestimates risk to the consumer), and a false positive a "producer risk" (in that it overstates risk to the producer). Units of producer and consumer risk are not fixed and can be expressed in terms of duration of disease-free life or dollars, and the proper balance between these can be expected to vary according to particular circumstances.

heavy metals; a wide range of carcinogens activated by intestinal rather than liver enzymes, such as cycasin and cyclamates; carcinogens of the chloroform class; and major classes of carcinogenic organochlorine pesticides, such as dieldrin and heptachlor. Third, the correlations between mutagenic effects in the tests and carcinogenicity are much less good than the 90 percent originally claimed and range down to 63 percent for selected groups of compounds.[27] More recently Stephen Rinkus and Marvin Legator of the University of Texas, Galveston, have concluded an exhaustive analysis of the correlation between the results of the Ames test and carcinogenicity.[28] This was based on 477 chemical carcinogens which they classified in forty different structural categories. For some classes of carcinogens, the correlation was shown to be excellent, whereas it was poor or nonexistent in others.* In fact, correlation was shown to be just a function of the structural type of carcinogen selected for test. This means that for randomly selected test compounds the results of the Ames test cannot be meaningfully correlated with carcinogenicity. Fourth, the test has become more and more complicated as more types of liver activation systems have had to be introduced in attempts to decrease false negatives. These activation systems are so difficult to standardize and reproduce that the test can no longer be regarded as a simple routine screen. Fifth, the test only picks up genetic damage at the gene level, and cannot detect chromosomal mutations, which are considered to be involved in cancer and other diseases in humans. Sixth and finally, based on recent studies with the carcinogen dimethylbenzanthracene, fundamentally different types of molecular biological interactions with DNA appear involved in its effects in the Ames test and in its carcinogenic effects on the skin of mice.[29]

While it is clear that the Ames test, especially when combined with a battery of other such short-term tests

---

*In fact, about half of the carcinogens discussed in the case studies presented in this book are inactive in the Ames test.

based on mutagenicity, has useful applications, it is equally clear that its practical role has been exaggerated and now needs critical, independent reevaluation. In the meanwhile, reliance by regulatory agencies on the Ames test, as envisioned in recent proposals by the Occupational Safety and Health Administration on regulation of occupational carcinogens and by the EPA Office of Toxic Substances, seems unwise. At present, there just is no reliable substitute for animal carcinogenicity tests.

The Practicality of Animal Testing

The practicality of animal testing is often challenged by industry on the grounds that too many new chemicals are being introduced into commerce each year to be handled by conventional animal testing and that the cost of such testing would be prohibitive. In fact, this has been used as one of the main arguments for the need for short-term tests. However, based on various recent estimates including those by the Council on Environmental Quality, it seems that the number of these new chemicals which actually reach commerce is under 700 annually. There is every reason to believe that current facilities could be expanded to cope without excessive strain with this number of chemicals. In addition, there are large potential facilities at the National Laboratories, such as Oak Ridge, Tennessee, and Argonne, Illinois, besides an underutilized facility at the National Center for Toxicological Research, in Arkansas. There seems every reason to believe that the NCI bioassay program, given high priority, could increase its present efforts to handle 700 or so chemicals.

With regard to expense, the annual costs of testing one chemical for carcinogenicity in groups of fifty mice and rats of each sex at two dose levels is $200,000 at the most. Properly conducted carcinogenicity tests also provide information on a wide range of chronic toxic effects, including testicular damage leading to sterility, central nervous system damage leading to paralysis or behavioral changes, and damage to the liver leading to cirrhosis. The $140 million costs for testing 700 chemicals would be unlikely to result in substantial increases in production and retail product costs. These testing costs should be contrasted with chemical industry 1975 gross sales of $72 billion (of which they represent about 0.2 percent) and after tax profits in excess of $5.5 billion.

The costs of testing should be further contrasted with the far greater costs of failure to test and regulate, including the majority of the $25 billion recognized annual costs of cancer due to preventable causes and the even greater costs of surveillance of workers exposed to occupational carcinogens. It is clear that the costs of failure to test and regulate are inflationary.

Part II

The Science and Politics of Cancer

Chapter Four

Introduction to the Case Studies

In the next three chapters case studies on some twelve individual carcinogens or classes of carcinogen are examined.* These are grouped according to their site of greatest social impact: in the workplace (chapter 5), in consumer products (chapter 6), and in the general environment (chapter 7). While convenient, this grouping is somewhat artificial. Carcinogens such as asbestos, vinyl chloride, and benzene pose major hazards to the exposed work force. However, these same carcinogens also escape or are discharged into the air outside the plants where they are being processed or manufactured and can produce cancer and other disease in people living in the local community. While carcinogenic pesticides are widely recognized as environmental contaminants, they represent still greater hazards to workers engaged in their manufacture, formulation, and application. Concerns about carcinogens in con-

---

*The case studies are generally based on information available up to April, 1978.

sumer products, such as sex hormones used as drugs and animal feed additives, have stimulated subsequent concerns about their role as occupational carcinogens.

While discussions of each substance are particular, all the case studies deal essentially with two basic sets of questions:

(1) *What do we know?* What are the patterns of manufacture and use of the product or process? What are the patterns of human exposure? What is the evidence of carcinogenicity from animal tests or epidemiological studies? What will be the economic and social impacts of regulation and of failure to regulate?

(2) *To what use has this information been put?* How has the affected industry reacted? What was the response of the regulating agency? What roles have public interest groups and organized labor taken? Also of concern are the roles of the Congress, courts, press, professional and scientific communities, and the nature of public perceptions.

A few common themes will emerge throughout the case studies. Most of the information we have on the products and processes involved has come from industry itself, either through in-house technical staff or indirectly through commercial consultants and laboratories. Apart from their general poor quality, built into most industry-sponsored studies is a tendency to minimize risks and maximize benefits, and to emphasize the difficulties and costs of regulation. They may fail to ask the relevant questions to assess risks and benefits, and in doing so fail to undertake the necessary studies to answer them. Worse yet, the results are occasionally manipulated or even destroyed.

The most serious effect of this information bias is the inappropriate shift in the burden of proof from the private to the public sector. The consumer or worker who bears the risk from exposure to an untested or poorly tested product then must also bear the burden of raising questions about its safety or proving its dangers or of ensuring that the federal government proves its dangers.

The regulatory role of federal agencies is often complicated by inherent ambiguities and inconsistencies in the statutes under which they operate. Be that as it may, the major problem here is not one of inadequate laws but of unwillingness to enforce the law. The track record of federal agencies in regulating industry and in protecting workers and consumers from carcinogenic hazards reflects extreme laxness often compounded by undue responsiveness to special interests.

Over the last decade, virtually all regulatory actions against carcinogens in the workplace, in consumer products, and in the environment have been developed only at the initiative of public interest groups or organized labor. The scientific community has been largely indifferent. The exceptions are the few independent professionals who have worked with public interest groups and labor, and a small but influential segment of the scientific community working closely with industry in efforts to impede or block attempts to regulate environmental and occupational carcinogens. Over two decades ago, President Eisenhower warned against the growing national threat of the military–industrial complex. The medical–industrial complex now appears to be as serious a threat.

'Tis a sordid profit that's accompanied by the destruction of health. . . . Many an artisan has looked at his craft as a means to support life and raise a family, but all he has got from it is some deadly disease, with the result that he has departed this life cursing the craft to which he has applied himself.

Bernadino Ramazzini, an Italian physician,
considered the founder of occupational medicine,
1705.

Chapter Five

The Workplace: Case Studies

The total U.S. work force numbers approximately 100 million.* Various categories of workers are at high risk of exposure to carcinogens. These include approximately 670,000 workers in the petrochemical industry, 365,000 in metallic and nonmetallic mining, and 1.1 million in the metal processing and smelting industries.[1] These figures do not reflect the extent of exposure to occupational carcinogens. Estimates by HEW in 1978 indicate that from 8–11 million workers have been exposed to asbestos since World War II. On the basis of a recent National Occupational Hazard Survey, the National Institute for Occupational Safety and Health (NIOSH) estimates that 880,000

---

*Of these, 41 million are women. The numbers of women in the work force are growing. In 1977, 48 percent of all U.S. women were in the work force, as opposed to 38 percent in 1960.

workers are currently exposed to just those carcinogens or other toxic substances that are currently regulated by the Department of Labor's Occupational Safety and Health Administration (OSHA).[2] The range of industries involving exposure to occupational carcinogens is shown in Table 5.1

In general, workers are denied knowledge of what chemicals they are exposed to, and in what concentrations.[3] They are also not informed whether these have been adequately tested, whether they are toxic under conditions of exposure in the plant, or whether they are carcinogenic. This is in striking contrast to chemicals in consumer products, which must be tested in animals before they can be used, and for which there are labeling requirements, however imperfect.

The toxic and carcinogenic chemicals to which workers may be exposed at relatively high concentrations in the workplace also are discharged or escape into the air and water of the surrounding community. The worker may be exposed to the same chemical carcinogens through consumer products and the general environment as in his or her workplace.

What are the conditions of exposure to toxic and carcinogenic chemicals in the workplace and what precautions are taken to protect workers from such exposures? What is the role of government, industry, and the medical community in preventing and regulating such exposures? The British medical journal *Lancet* gives some answers to these questions in a recent editorial, "The Medical Industrial Complex":

> Involved in this sinister complex are numerous big industrial manufacturing firms who are reluctant to believe that any product they use or manufacture, from asbestos insulation to benzidine or beta-naphthylamine, can be harmful. The medical men and scientists directly employed by these firms are chiefly concerned with their employers' and their own profits, and are indifferent to the health of the exposed employees. Some of the firm's employers

Table 5.1 Occupations Associated with an Excess Risk of Cancer

Site of Cancer	Carcinogen	Occupations
Liver	Arsenic, vinyl chloride	Tanners, smelters; vineyard workers; plastic workers
Nasal cavity and sinuses	Chromium, isopropyl oil, nickel, wood and leather dusts	Glass, pottery and linoleum workers; nickel smelters, mixers and roasters; electrolysis workers; wood, leather, and shoe workers
Lung	Arsenic, asbestos, chromium, coal products, dusts, iron oxide, mustard gas, nickel, petroleum, ionizing radiation, bischloromethyl-ether	Vintners; miners; asbestos users; textile users; insulation workers; tanners; smelters; glass and pottery workers; coal tar and pitch workers; iron foundry workers; electrolysis workers, retort workers; radiologists; radium dial painters; chemical workers
Bladder	Coal products, aromatic amines	Asphalt, coal tar, and pitch workers; gas stokers; still cleaners; dyestuffs users; rubber workers; textile dyers; paint manufacturers; leather and shoe workers
Bone marrow	Benzene, ionizing radiation	Benzene, explosives, and rubber cement workers; distillers; dye users; painters; radiologists

Source: P. Cole and M. B. Goldman, "Occupation," chapter 11 in J. F. Fraumeni, Jr., ed., *Persons at High Risk of Cancer* (New York: Academic Press, 1975), pp. 167–84.

have, it is alleged, ignored even legal regulations and got away with it. Another alleged tack is for the firm, singly or in combination with like firms, to set up supposedly independent research institutes whose scientists seem always to find evidence to support the stance taken by the firm, despite massive contrary evidence. Thus, when some high-sounding institute states that a compound is harmless or a process free of risk, it is wise to know whence the institute or the scientists who work there obtain their financial support. But there are Government agents, Federal and State, to enforce safety measures and draw up others, to see that regulations are in force, and to monitor dangerous processes. Alas, it seems that these people, too, are often involved in the medical/industrial complex, and are reluctant to enforce regulations, to emphasize risks to employees, or to see that measures are taken to warn or protect them against industrial hazards. They also seem, as individual contractors or as members of research organizations, to attract an undue proportion of Federal research grants.

The indictment is a strong one, and it is coupled with accounts of factories where employees work in fogs of asbestos dust and beryllium dust, or with beta-naphthylamine and benzidine slopped about. Ever greater numbers of employees are being recognized as suffering from pulmonary asbestosis, berylliosis, bladder and lung cancer, and mesotheliomas. The greatest danger, as far as the numbers exposed go, seems to be asbestos, and the carcinogenic properties of this material are creating general alarm. Large numbers of the general public are exposed to it through the drinking water in one city. The number of industrial hazards and of workers killed or injured by them seems to be increasing, and the public has reason to be worried. The industrial/medical complex is now required to answer the case, and as its credibility has been seriously impugned it had better be a clear answer.[4]

This chapter presents case studies on four substances: asbestos, vinyl chloride, bischloromethylether, and benzene. These are chosen to illustrate some fundamental problems of exposure to carcinogens in the workplace.[5]

Asbestos

Asbestos, known as the "magic mineral,"[1] has been used in one form or another for centuries.* Virtually indestructible, it is highly resistant to fire, has high tensile strength, and its fibers can be spun into yarn and woven into cloth. The asbestos industry has grown phenomenally since the first North American asbestos mine opened in 1879 in Thetford, Quebec, with a first-year output of 300 tons. Johns-Manville was founded in the United States in 1901 and Turner Brothers, still the largest British company, in 1916. World production of asbestos in 1920 was only 20,000 tons, about 0.5 percent of present levels (about 4.3 million tons). Of the present world output, 1.7 million tons are mined in Canada (and fabricated largely in the United States) and 2.5 million tons in the Soviet Union. At the heart of this booming industry is a research effort which has led to use of asbestos in cement, asphalt, wallboard, pipes, textiles, insulation, food and beverage processing, brake linings, and countless other everyday products.[2] It has also led to approximately 50,000 deaths per year in the United States from cancer and other diseases.[3]

Occupational Exposure

Occupational exposure to asbestos dust occurs in a wide range of operations from the mining and processing of the ore to its fabrication and use in many industries, particularly construction, shipbuilding, insulation, and textiles.

By 1918 enough was known about the dangers of asbestos to lead to the decision of U.S. and Canadian insurance companies to stop selling life policies to asbestos

---

*Asbestos is a generic name for a group of naturally occurring fibrous mineral silicates, which consist of two major classes: serpentines, largely represented by chrysotile, a relatively pure magnesium silicate that comprises 90–95 percent of the world's asbestos production; and amphiboles, including five main types (actinolite, amosite, crocidolite, anthophyllite, and tremolite) in which the magnesium component is partially or wholly replaced by other cations.

workers.[4] It was not until the early 1920s that descriptions of a new respiratory disease resulting from exposure to asbestos (*asbestosis*) first appeared in the medical literature. An often fatal disease, involving progressive scarring of the lungs and leading to respiratory disability and heart failure, asbestosis is akin to black lung and other chronic chest diseases (*pneumoconioses*) which afflict miners and processors of various kinds of minerals and fibers. In England, where it was first studied and reported in the medical literature, asbestosis was covered under Compensation laws in 1931, after which some efforts were made to improve working conditions and reduce exposure to asbestos dust.[5]

By the 1930s, based on numerous case reports of asbestosis and lung cancer occurring together in asbestos workers, scientists began to suspect that asbestos is carcinogenic. But no full-scale studies were made on asbestos plant workers until the 1950s, when the British epidemiologist Richard Doll investigated employees with at least twenty years exposure in an asbestos textile plant. Doll found that this group experiences ten times the lung cancer deaths of non-asbestos workers of the same age.[6]

Also during the 1950s, Irving Selikoff, now a leading occupational epidemiologist at Mt. Sinai Hospital in New York City, noted that fifteen of seventeen of his patients employed at Union Asbestos and Rubber Company in Paterson, New Jersey, had developed asbestos-related lung disease. By the early 1960s, the disease incidence was climbing at an alarming rate, prompting Selikoff to inquire into the employment records of workers in this and other asbestos plants. After being refused this information by industry, he contacted the New York and New Jersey locals of the International Association of Heat and Frost Insulators and Asbestos Workers, the union representing many of the men. Selikoff then conducted a cohort study based on all men belonging to those locals who had been employed in the asbestos industry over a particular length of time. Starting with 632 workers listed on the union rolls in 1943, he inquired into their fates, checking how many had died and the cause on each death certificate. This type of study is ordinarily difficult because it involves tracing the whereabouts of a worker twenty years after employment in a particular job. In this case the union had kept fairly detailed records of work histories. The union also administered the death benefits for its members, who as retirees had good reason to keep in touch right up to the time of their deaths.

By 1973, 444 of the original 632 workers were dead.[7] Table 5.2 is an epidemiological analysis which shows the number who had died of various causes, compared with the number who would have been expected to die of each cause.*

Table 5.2 shows that by 1973 this cohort of workers had experienced a death rate 50 percent greater than the average white male. Among these "excess" deaths, lung cancer by far exceeded the expected experience of such a group of men by a factor of seven. The rate of all cancers combined was four times as great for these men, and there were thirty-five cases of mesothelioma, which for non-asbestos workers should not have occurred at all.† Finally, even the rates of cancer of stomach, colon, and rectum were more than three times that expected.

Conditions at the Johns-Manville plant in Scarborough, Ontario, give further insight on conditions of occupational exposure to asbestos. This plant opened in 1946 for the manufacture of asbestos and silica cement pipes and fiberglass insulation. Within a few months, men were working without respirators in dust that was so thick that

---

*The ratio of observed to expected numbers of deaths is the *standard mortality ratio*. The larger this ratio is than 1, the more likely it is that a particular occupational exposure was the cause of death.

†Mesothelioma is a form of cancer of the lungs (pleural mesothelioma) or abdomen (peritoneal mesothelioma). It should be noted that deaths from pleural mesothelioma are reported as lung cancer deaths in cancer mortality records (based on the International List of Causes of Disease) and can thus be falsely attributed to smoking rather than asbestos.

Table 5.2 Causes of Death in 444 Asbestos Workers

Cause of All Deaths	Number of Deaths, 1943–1973		
	Expected	Observed	Ratio (observed/expected)
Total deaths, all causes	300.65	444	1.48
Cancer—all sites	51.26	198	3.86
Lung cancer	11.68	89	7.62
Pleural mesothelioma	0	10	. . . .
Peritoneal mesothelioma	0	25	. . . .
Cancer of stomach	5.10	18	3.53
Cancer of colon-rectum	7.50	22	2.93
Asbestosis	0	37	. . . .
All other causes	249.39	209	0.84

Source: I. J. Selikoff and E. C. Hammond, "Multiple Risk Factors in Environmental Cancer," chapter 28 in J. F. Fraumeni, Jr., ed., *Persons at High Risk of Cancer* (New York: Academic Press, 1975), pp. 467–83.

they could not see more than a few yards ahead of them.* Even after a new ventilation system was installed in 1952, counts of 50 million fibers per cubic meter (m^3) of air persisted in some areas. Selikoff visited Scarborough in the mid-1960s and predicted a high incidence of cancer deaths in the coming decade. Management dismissed these concerns as alarmist, and made little attempt to improve working conditions. Since then, over fifty workers of a total work force of approximately 500 have been disabled by chronic respiratory diseases and there have been twenty-seven deaths from lung cancer.

Regulation of Occupational Exposure

The ultimate acceptance of the carcinogenicity of asbestos has not been easily achieved. Even today, the controversy

---

*Dust counts were probably about 80 million fibers per cubic meter (m^3) of air.

persists, but now the questions are not "whether" but "how much" and "what type." The importance of this issue is directly related to the vast economic stake which industry has in winning its battle with the government over the standard regulating levels of exposure to asbestos in the workplace.

When OSHA began hearings in 1972, the industry fought strenuously against any reduction in permissible exposure levels on the alleged grounds that the dangers of asbestos were minimal.[8] The basis for the industry case was strongly argued by academic consultants, some from medical schools or schools of public health, some of whose research and publications were supported directly or indirectly by grants or funds from the industry or industry-financed foundations.[9]

Regulatory standards for asbestos are based on the number of fibers in a unit volume of air.[10] The current OSHA standard is 2 fibers per cubic centimeter or 2 million fibers per cubic meter, over an eight-hour working day.[11] In the course of an average day, a worker inhales about 8 cubic meters of air, equivalent to an allowed inhalation of 16 million asbestos fibers. Even where the standard is met total exposure levels are much higher. Current optical microscopic techniques for counting fibers in the workplace only detect those which are relatively long, more than 5 microns in length. Smaller fibers, or fibrils, which can only be counted by electron microscopy and not by optical microscopy, may outnumber the longer ones by as much as 100 to 1.* Thus, occupational exposure to asbestos at currently regulated levels of 2 million fibers, may result in the daily inhalation of as many as 1.6 billion short fibers. It should be recognized that these are be-

---

*Asbestos counts in the workplace are invariably counted by optical microscopy and hence reported as fibers per cubic meter of air. In contrast, electron microscopy is the only practical technique for measuring public exposure in the general environment, and these counts of fibrils and fibers are translated into mass and reported in nanograms rather than counts per cubic meter.

lieved to be more carcinogenic than the long fibers. It should finally be recognized that there are critical needs for the development of practical and sensitive methods for monitoring of total asbestos fibers, both long and short, in the air breathed by exposed workers.

The key issue in the 1972 OSHA hearings was the proposal by NIOSH to lower the then temporary exposure standard of 5 million asbestos fibers per cubic meter of air to 2 million fibers, the 1969 British standard. This lower standard, however, was primarily designed to protect just against asbestosis, without any consideration of the cancer problem.* The asbestos industry argued at the hearings that the 5 million standard exposure level did not cause much disease, and that to lower it further would create severe economic dislocation and unemployment. In spite of the threat of job losses, organized labor fought strongly for the improved standard, pointing out that asbestos is a major health hazard not only for asbestos workers, but also for workers in many other chemical and manufacturing industries which use asbestos in many forms.

The involvement of the asbestos industry in health research, and its propagandizing of the public is long-standing. While the asbestos industry takes some pro forma precautions in the open scientific forum, these are not apparent in its public relations literature. Some good examples of this can be found in a recent publication by the Quebec Asbestos Mining Association (QAMA) of a bilingual pamphlet, "Asbestos and Your Health."

> Can a little bit of asbestos kill you? No—long-term medical studies of workers who are exposed to asbestos show that low to moderate levels of exposure do not lead to an increased rate of disease. In these studies, a higher-than-normal incidence of disease was found only among employees exposed to extremely high asbestos concentrations for long periods of time.

---

*Later, the British standard was subsequently shown by U.S. investigators to be inadequate for protection against asbestosis, let alone against lung cancer.

Note the deliberate omission of the word "cancer."
Also, the statement is simply false. Short term and low-
level exposures are known to cause disease.

> The lung's normal cleaning mechanisms quickly remove
> the majority of inhaled particles, including respirable-
> sized asbestos fibers.

On the contrary, the majority of fibers either remain
in the lung or move to the gut, where it is suspected they
contribute to the development of cancer of the gastrointestinal tract.

> Some cases still occur among long-service employees
> whose exposure began at a time when little was known of
> the amount of asbestos a human could tolerate . . . With
> expanding medical knowledge and today's improved dust
> control measures, however, there is every reason to be-
> lieve that these cases will decrease in the future and
> asbestos-related disease will cease to be an occupational
> problem.

The controls which industry fought for at the OSHA
hearings were sufficient to cause levels of disease among
New York insulation workers at which 20 percent died of
lung cancer, 10 percent of gastrointestinal cancer, 10 percent of mesotheliomas, 10 percent of other cancer, and 10
percent of asbestosis.

Over the past decade, industry has also supported
major scientific studies at McGill University in Montreal,
by the Industrial Health Foundation in Pittsburgh and by
Tabershaw-Cooper Associates on the West Coast, all of
which have minimized the danger of working with asbestos. One of the most controversial of these studies, involving more than 11,000 employees and ex-employees of
Quebec asbestos mines, was carried out by J. Corbett
McDonald, then in the Department of Epidemiology and
Public Health at McGill. In presenting his results to the
OSHA hearing officers, McDonald introduced himself as

a full-time employee at McGill University, and an independent research worker.

> "I do not work, nor am I associated with any asbestos producer or manufacturer. The research I shall be describing is supported by grants, not to me but to McGill University, from a number of sources — the Institute of Occupational and Environmental Health, the Canadian government, the British Medical Research Council, and the USPHS [U.S. Public Health Service]."[12]

However, anyone glancing at his paper, published in 1971 in the Archives of Environmental Health, would have noticed, in the customary small typeface at the end of the text, the acknowledgment:

> This work was undertaken with the assistance of a grant from the Institute of Occupational and Environmental Health of the Quebec Asbestos Mining Association.[13]

McDonald made several claims on the basis of his study. First, he maintained that "the findings suggest that our cohort of workers in the chrysotile [a kind of asbestos] mining industry had a lower mortality than the population of Quebec of the same age." Second, he claimed that while indeed some workers did seem to get more lung cancer than others the "excess" cancer deaths were confined to those workers who had been much more heavily exposed than the rest. Lastly, he concluded that "these findings strongly suggest . . . that chrysotile is less likely to cause malignant disease of the lung and pleura than other forms of asbestos, such as crocidolite."

Criticism came swiftly from independent scientists in the United States. Major objections were directed not only at the overall design of the study, but at the statistical analysis of the data as well. McDonald had selected a method for computing death rates which seemed to ignore the long latency period of lung cancer. This resulted in an underestimate of the excess deaths which occurred among men with a long duration of employment.[14] Faced with mounting criticism and complaining that his "life had been made hell," McDonald resigned his position at McGill.[15] Taking his asbestos–cancer research funds, including continuing support from the National Cancer Institute (NCI),[16] he returned to England, where the London School of Hygiene and Tropical Medicine appointed him to the Trade Union Congress Chair of Occupational Medicine.

Another illustration of the industry position was afforded when a recent NIOSH study demonstrated an increased risk for lung cancer and other lung diseases among South Dakota gold miners exposed to asbestos dust levels even lower than the 2 million fiber standard proposed by NIOSH in 1972.[17] A sharp response from Paul Kotin, the medical director and senior vice president of Johns-Manville, the world's largest asbestos manufacturer, was subsequently circulated in attempts to minimize the impact of these findings and to persuade the safety of exposure to levels of 2 million fibers.[18]* The NIOSH group prepared a rebuttal which defended their original analysis and demanded:

> Why should it surprise Drs. Kotin and Chase that asbestos at concentrations less than 2 million fibers per cubic meter is associated with excessive risk of respiratory cancer? Indeed, it is known that asbestos fibers have been previously demonstrated to be carcinogenic to man at all fiber concentrations studied under adequate epidemiologic method.[19]

On December 15, 1976, John F. Finklea, as Director of NIOSH, communicated with Morton Corn, then Assistant Secretary of Labor for OSHA, pointing out that the 1969 British 2 million fiber standard, which had been the basis of the 1972 proposed NIOSH standard, had since been shown to be excessively high and should be re-

---

*These and other current positions on chemical carcinogenesis are in striking contrast to views expressed by Kotin when in government employ in 1970 (see Appendix II), and in even more striking contrast to his testimony at the Myrex cancellation proceedings (FIFRA Docket 293, EPA, November, 1973).

duced. Finklea referred to studies on exposures as low as 250,000 fibers per cubic meter, at which workers had twice the likelihood of the general population of dying from lung cancer or asbestosis. Finklea further proposed that the standard should be lowered to a maximum of 100,000 fibers. NIOSH clearly recognized that even this proposed lower standard did not represent a safe exposure level. Finklea finally stated:

> Because it is not possible to specify a safe exposure level for a carcinogen, only a ban on the use of asbestos can ensure complete protection against this mineral's carcinogenic effect. Therefore, emphasis should be placed on prohibiting the occupational use of asbestos in other than completely closed operations and on substituting other products whenever possible. Asbestos should be replaced where technically feasible, by substitutes with the lowest possible chronic toxicities. [20]

NIOSH also pointed out that all forms of asbestos, including chrysotile, amosite, crocidolite, and tremolite, can induce asbestosis and also cancer.

The OSHA standard still rests at 2 million fibers, twenty times in excess of the level that NIOSH now recommends. The stance of industry in fighting even the unsatisfactory OSHA standard is further illustrated by the record of R. T. Vanderbilt Company, Norwalk, Connecticut, which owns a number of talc mines in upstate New York and Vermont. [21] Shortly after OSHA promulgated its 1972 standard, R. T. Vanderbilt belatedly realized that the high asbestos content of its talc threatened its market, as several purchasers of its products had been advised by NIOSH to switch to other, safer materials. Vanderbilt, realizing it had missed its legal chance to comment on the regulations before they became law, put pressure on Congressmen Robert McEwen (R-N.Y.) and Jerry Pettis (R-Cal.) to help out. On June 20, 1973, McEwen wrote OSHA Secretary John Stender, "Should these mines be forced to close, you can readily understand that it would have a serious and adverse economic effect in that area." [22]

Over the objection of his own Health Standards Chief, Standards Director Gerald Scannell encouraged Vanderbilt in December, 1973, to do its own sampling to determine whether or not their talc contained asbestos, and to advise their customers of the results of the tests. Vanderbilt took the hint and immediately redefined tremolite so as to exclude its classification as asbestos, even though it is clearly defined as such in the legal standard. Vanderbilt then notified its customers "that our talc products used in their manufacturing processes are not subject to the asbestos standard."

The illegality of this procedure came to a head after an OSHA inspector cited a Vanderbilt customer, Borg Warner, for a violation of the asbestos standard on July 9, 1974. This involved a material purchased from Vanderbilt, Nytal, which was accompanied by "self-certification" that it contained no asbestos. The case went to the Occupational Safety and Health Review Commission, the highest arbiter of OSHA cases. On June 28, 1976, Judge Jerry W. Mitchell, ruled against the company.[23] In the lengthy interim, OSHA issued a field directive supporting Vanderbilt's claim that its talc was asbestos-free, but failed to order its field operatives to enforce the directive.

The seriousness of this evasion is emphasized by the results of a NIOSH epidemiological investigation on workers at Vanderbilt's mines. This identified "both respiratory diseases and lung cancers which appear to be significantly above those expected."

Smoking and Occupational Exposure

Many epidemiological studies have indicated that asbestos workers who smoke have a much greater lung cancer risk than asbestos workers who don't smoke. Industry has argued that these studies prove that smoking and not asbestos is the real problem for asbestos workers, and that the development of lung cancer in these workers was their own fault for smoking. However, recent studies, including one by NIOSH in 1977, indicate that the smoking effect is less clear-cut than earlier reports suggested, and that nonsmoking asbestos workers also have excess risks of lung cancer.[24] Additionally, smoking is unrelated to the risks of developing mesotheliomas which occur with equal and increased frequency among smoking and nonsmoking asbestos workers.

Public Exposure

In 1960 an alarming report came from J. C. Wagner in South Africa of sixteen new cases of the rare mesothelioma.[25] While six of these were in asbestos mine workers, none of the other ten had ever worked in the mines. All had lived in the vicinity of the mines, though, many as children. Public or non-occupational mesotheliomas have since been reported from nine other countries, including the United States. These cases are generally thought to be due to exposure of family members to asbestos brought home on the clothes of asbestos workers. Additional sources of exposure include contamination of the air with asbestos from nearby plants or factories. High concentrations of asbestos fibers have recently been demonstrated in communities adjacent to asbestos industries.

The indestructibility of asbestos, its indiscriminate use, and the careless disposal of its waste products make it difficult to predict the extent and level of exposure of the general public. For instance, Certain-Teed Products Corporation, an asbestos-cement pipe manufacturer, has in the past dumped about 2,700 tons each year of crushed asbestos pipe in an open-air landfill site in Ambler, Pennsylvania.

> The dump not only snakes diagonally through the very center of the town, which has a population of 8,000, but it is fifty feet high, anywhere from one to two city blocks wide, and about ten city blocks long. In fact, it is estimated to contain some million and a half cubic yards of waste material . . . Kids play on an asphalt basketball

court that has been built smack on top of material from the dump, and is literally covered with loose asbestos fiber and wads of waste material containing (chrysotile) asbestos.[26]

Drinking water is an additional possible source of non-occupational exposure to asbestos. Reserve Mining Company, a subsidiary of Armco and Republic Steel, for years has been dumping taconite mine wastes, rich in asbestos fibers, into Lake Superior at levels of about 67,000 tons a day. Not unreasonably, this gave rise to fears that polluting the drinking water of Great Lakes communities with asbestos would lead to excess cancer rates, especially of the stomach and colon.[27]

In April, 1974, Federal District Judge Miles Lord issued an injunction in Duluth, Minnesota, restraining the Reserve Mining Company from further dumping its taconite mine wastes into Lake Superior. Reserve Mining witnesses attempted to prevent this ruling by testifying that there were no alternatives to this lake dumping, although it appears that the company had developed plans for land disposal sites as early as 1970.

It is not yet known whether the resulting asbestos contamination of drinking water of Lake Superior towns, including Duluth, will lead to cancer. Preliminary studies with laboratory animals have so far yielded ambiguous results. Certainly, it has been established that persons occupationally exposed to asbestos have an increased risk of alimentary tract cancer* as well as lung cancer. Without waiting for answers to these questions, a Federal Appeals Court reversed Judge Lord's decision, on grounds that it was not based on adequate proof of risks to health, and permitted Reserve Mining to resume dumping its tailings into the lake, pending the development of alternate land disposal sites.

---

*These include pharynx, esophagus, stomach, and colon and rectum cancers.

In May, 1975, Congress approved $4 million to build a water treatment plant in Duluth to filter out the asbestos fibers from drinking water. The State of Minnesota appropriated $2.5 million in local funds for the project, which became operative in November, 1976. Reserve Mining is now phasing out lake dumping, and is building a land disposal site, in accordance with a court order that dumping is to be terminated by 1980.[28]

In addition to environmental exposure to asbestos in air and water, the general public receives a wide range of further exposures.[29] Particularly important sources are construction operations involving the spraying of asbestos, the use of crushed stone containing unbound asbestos in roads and driveways, and demolition. Exposure to asbestos also results from its use in fireproofing and insulation, air ducts, automobile brake linings, cement water pipes, filter pads for beers, wine, and drugs, and cosmetic talcs. Resulting levels of public exposure can be high. For example, counts of 10 million fibers per cubic meter of air have been found in the vicinity of construction sites during asbestos spraying, and counts of 3 million fibers have been found in public buildings treated with asbestos as a fire retardant.[30]

Regulation of Public Exposures

In an ineffective attempt to protect the general public from asbestos air pollution, EPA developed an emission standard for asbestos as a hazardous air pollutant in April, 1973. The standard, however, is only based on visible emissions and on poorly enforced work practices, and not on asbestos fibril counts.*

Acting on a petition from a public interest group, the Health Research Group, the Consumer Product Safety

---

*The only effective method of measuring community exposure to asbestos is by counting fibrils using electron microscopy, which in fact is rarely done. Results are expressed as a mass in nanograms per cubic meter.

Commission announced in December, 1977, that patching and spackling compounds containing asbestos would be banned from the $400 million market by June, 1978. Under the commission's order, fifty manufacturers ceased production in January, 1978, leaving retailers the next six months to clear their shelves. While these patching compounds are used primarily by professional builders, about 10 percent of the market is for home hobbyists and craftsmen.

The Future

Realization is gradually dawning that except under the most restrictive conditions all forms of asbestos have become too expensive in terms of human disease for commercial use. Further illustration of this are the individual and class action suits for asbestos cancer and disease, in the multimillion-dollar range now being filed by some of the four and one-half million workers employed in Naval shipbuilding yards during World War II.

The Navy has since abandoned the use of asbestos in shipbuilding in favor of alternative materials, including fiberglass. However, there are also reasons for concern on the use of fiberglass as an asbestos replacement. Experimental studies indicate that fiberglass, particularly the more modern short-fiber products which were introduced into large-scale use in the early 1960s, may produce a type of disease and cancer similar to that produced by asbestos.[31] Epidemiological studies are now only suggestive of an increased cancer risk, probably because exposed workers have not been followed up for the three or so decades it generally takes for asbestos fibers to induce cancer. Industry is attempting to quiet these concerns in moves which reflect the growing shift from asbestos to fiberglass for insulation and a wide range of consumer products, including draperies. An interesting insight into such tactics was afforded by a recent letter to *New Times* by Johns-Manville's Kotin, bearing no reference at all to his industry employment, protesting that "epidemiological studies show that there is no chronic health effect in humans as a result of exposure to fibrous glass."[32]

Apart from fiberglass, other possible replacements for certain asbestos applications include long inorganic fibers made from aluminum or zirconium, such as those manufactured by Imperial Chemical Industries of England.

Another area of growing concern relates to the emerging trend in the asbestos industry to relocate in lesser developed countries, such as Mexico and Taiwan, where their capital investment is welcomed and not restricted by governmental health and safety regulations.[33]

On April 26, 1978, HEW Secretary Joseph Califano issued the most explicit warning ever made by government on the dangers of asbestos. Califano estimated that as many as half of all workers exposed to asbestos could develop serious diseases such as cancer of the lung and gastrointestinal tract, mesotheliomas, and asbestosis. Califano also estimated that from 8 to 11 million workers may have been exposed to asbestos since the start of World War II. Besides urging exposed workers to have a chest X-ray, HEW is sending a "physician advisory" letter regarding the dangers of asbestos to the nation's 400,000 doctors. While Califano properly stressed the added danger of smoking to asbestos workers, an impression of "blaming the victim" appears to have been created by the absence of any balancing reference to the more urgent needs for control of exposures in the workplace.

Califano's statement appears to have been prompted by the growing number of lawsuits filed against federal agencies for having failed to notify workers in the past of the known hazards of asbestos exposure.* As such, Califano's statement is also important for what it failed to say. Workers were not informed of their rights to sue the government. Nor were any plans announced for organiza-

---

*Some 500 asbestos workers have already collected $20 million in damages, including $5 million from the federal government.

tion of a surveillance program, including contacting and examining former government workers. Nor was any mention made of the long overdue need to implement the recommendation of NIOSH for a 100,000 fiber standard as the only meaningful way to protect against asbestos-induced cancers and disease. Finally, no mention was made of the growing evidence of the hazards to the public-at-large, particularly those living in the vicinity of asbestos plants, from low-level exposures to asbestos.

In spite of all the problems of omission and emphasis in the Califano statement, its significance is epochal. It opens the door of national health care policies to preventive medicine. Specifically, the statement recognizes in principle that prospective surveillance is needed for groups at high risk of cancer. It is likely that the high costs of surveillance may well act as future incentives to reduce risks of occupational exposure to carcinogenic and other highly toxic agents, forcing the ultimate realization that prevention is cheaper than "cure."

Summary

While the dangers of asbestos have been well recognized for over five decades, the industry was able to largely ignore these until studies in the 1950s by Doll in England and by Selikoff in the U.S. (sponsored by the asbestos insulators union) established the relationship between asbestos and asbestosis and cancers at various sites. Since then the industry has employed scientific expertise to advocate its position in professional journals and to successfully resist and prevent effective government regulations. With an estimated 8 to 11 million workers having been exposed since World War II, the toll of asbestos occupational disease and cancer is now reaching epidemic proportions. Workers have begun to exercise legal initiatives, including third-party and medical malpractice suits, resulting in multimillion dollar awards.

Concerns are also mounting on the dangers to the public from "low-level" asbestos contamination of air and water and from asbestos-containing consumer products.

As the realization is dawning that asbestos is too expensive in terms of disease and death to continue using, the industry is beginning to develop the strategies of relocating in lesser developed countries and promoting the use of fiberglass as an asbestos substitute in the United States. There are serious unresolved questions as to the dangers of fiberglass and there are possibilities that it may be no less hazardous than asbestos.

The massive human toll taken by asbestos is probably the single most important incentive to the development of coherent national policies recognizing preventive medicine as a major future component in the delivery of health care.

Vinyl Chloride

One of the most common pejoratives applied to modern times is "the plastic age." And just as age-old natural materials like wood, glass, and metal have been replaced by cheaper synthetic plastics, this seems to imply, so has the value of our lifestyle been degraded. Many things we now touch or use daily are made of plastic. Yet the plastic transformation of our society has only taken place over the last forty years. The consequences to society of its plasticization, in terms both of high energy and health costs, have only recently been appreciated. One of the major costs is from cancer.[1]

Manufacture

Plastics are the leading product of the modern petrochemical industry. This era of plastics dawned in the 1930s with the realization that petroleum was the cheapest and simplest starting material for the synthesis of the vast array of organic chemicals now used by modern industry. Petroleum then gradually replaced coal, which had been previously used for this purpose, and is now almost the exclusive basis of the organic chemical industry.

Vinyl chloride (VC) lies at the heart of the plastics industry. VC was first discovered in 1837. Large-scale production, however, did not start until the 1930s, when it was synthesized from chlorine and ethylene, largely for the manufacture of synthetic rubber.[2] Production levels increased rapidly after World War II at a rate of 15 percent per year, reaching a total of about 7 billion pounds this year.

VC is a simple chemical consisting of a small single molecular unit (a *monomer*) which is normally a gas but can be shipped and stored as a liquid under pressure. VC reacts under conditions of heat and pressure and in the presence of plasticizing chemicals to form large molecular chains (*polymers*) of polyvinyl chloride (PVC) resins. The polymerization of the VC monomer never proceeds to completion, but always leaves some unreacted VC entrapped in the PVC resin. Depending on the production process, this unreacted VC has concentrations ranging as high as 8,000 parts per million (ppm).[3] This residual VC can be dissolved out of the polymer or released by heating it.[4]

PVC resins are molded, injected, and extruded in the fabrication of a wide array of plastic products. These include phonograph records, wire and cable insulation, floor coverings, garden hose, furniture, upholstery fabrics, car bodies, coating of fabrics and wallpaper, containers, bottles, and food wrappings. It is difficult to get an accurate count of the number of U.S. workers involved in all the various stages of PVC production. There are about seventeen VC manufacturing plants, employing about a thousand workers, and forty PVC plants, employing about six thousand workers.[5] There are no figures available, however, on the number of fabricating plants or on the number of their employees. These must run into the hundreds of thousands.

Suppression by the Industry of Data on the Carcinogenicity of Vinyl Chloride

In May, 1970, an Italian toxicologist, Pierluigi Viola, reported at an international cancer congress in Houston, Texas, that long-term intermittent exposure of a small group of rats to 3 percent of VC in air (30,000 ppm) resulted in the production of cancers in a wide range of organs.[6] Prior to this, there had apparently been no studies in the plastics industry on the possible carcinogenicity of VC, although tens of thousands of workers the world over had been exposed to it for over three decades and at least seven fatal cases of liver cancer had occurred in VC/PVC workers prior to 1970.[7] Disturbed by Viola's public report, a consortium of giant European chemical industries, led by Italy's semi-governmental Montedison, and with contributions from British, Belgian, and French firms, financed a major study initiated in July, 1971, by Cesare Maltoni of the Bologna Cancer Institute.[8] An extensive series of tests were conducted in which adult, infant, and pregnant mice, rats, and hamsters were exposed to VC in inhalation chambers at concentrations ranging from the relatively low 50 ppm level to the toxic 100,000 ppm (10 percent) level. By late 1972, Maltoni had confirmed and extended Viola's results. VC was shown to be a potent carcinogen, inducing a rare type of liver cancer (called angiosarcoma) as well as more common liver cancers (hepatomas) and cancers of other organs, including kidney, brain, and lung. The cancers were subsequently found even at the lowest level tested, 50 ppm.* The overall

---

*At that time the permissible exposure level for U.S. workers was 500 ppm.

tumor incidence was concentration-dependent, with higher doses increasing the incidence and rate of development of the cancers.[9]

In October, 1972, the Manufacturing Chemists Association, the major trade association of the U.S. chemical industry, entered into an agreement with the European consortium to share their information, but not to disclose it without prior consent.[10] In January, 1973, the U.S. industry representatives visited Maltoni and were given full details of his studies. The Manufacturing Chemists Association (and Maltoni) subsequently failed to disclose this information, in spite of the fact that NIOSH, in the same month, had publicly requested all available data on the toxic effects of VC. In March, 1973, the Manufacturing Chemists Association recommended to NIOSH a precautionary label for VC that made no reference to toxic or carcinogenic effects on animals or humans.

Also in March, 1973, following complaints of an unpleasant taste, Schenley Distillers found 10-20 ppm levels of VC in their liquors sold in PVC bottles. On the basis of these findings, and still knowing nothing about the carcinogenicity data, FDA then banned the use of these liquor bottles. In December, 1973, the Society of Plastics Industry, the plastics industry trade association, provided the FDA with data on migration of VC from PVC containers to food, but made no reference to problems of carcinogenicity.

On January 22, 1974, B. F. Goodrich announced that since 1971 three PVC workers in their Louisville, Kentucky, plant had died of angiosarcoma of the liver. On that same day, the Manufacturing Chemists Association revealed the by now fifteen-month-old Italian data to NIOSH.

According to a recent special committee report of the American Association for Advancement of Science, the Manufacturing Chemists Association "appears to have deliberately deceived NIOSH regarding the true facts. . . . Because of the suppression of these data, tens of thousands of workers were exposed without warning, for perhaps some two years, to toxic concentrations of vinyl chloride." [11]

Distortion by the Industry of Data on the Carcinogenicity of Vinyl Chloride

The first published case reports of angiosarcoma of the liver in VC/PVC workers generated an intensive epidemiological investigation of cancer mortality in the industry in several countries. A British Petroleum Corporation study, published in *Lancet* in 1975, concluded that the longer one worked in a VC plant, the less was the risk of getting cancer. [12] Closer examination by NIOSH, however, questioned the interpretation of the English data. Expected death rates in workers exposed to VC for fifteen or more years were artificially reduced, and rates in workers with lesser exposures were artificially inflated. Re-analysis of the data by NIOSH, using standard methods, showed a clear excess of mortality from all causes and all cancers, besides angiosarcoma of the liver (Table 5.3).

Exaggeration by the Industry of the Costs of Regulating Occupational Exposure to VC

As information on the carcinogenicity of VC began to surface, OSHA was prodded into action. On April 5, 1974, OSHA reduced permissible exposure levels from 500 ppm to a new emergency standard of 50 ppm. Under pressure from labor and independent scientists, who insisted that the new standard was still too high for safety, OSHA then proposed reducing this further to 1 ppm. [13] Even at that time, it had been shown that exposure of small numbers of rats to 5 ppm VC induced an increased incidence of cancer, and there was no evidence then (or now) of any safe exposure level for VC, or indeed to any other carcinogen.

Table 5.3 Comparison of Causes of Death in VC Workers Reported by British Petroleum (BP) and Recalculated by NIOSH

Cause of Death, Reported by BP and Recalculated by NIOSH	Standard Mortality Ratios* for Workers Exposed to VC for Varying Times		
	Years of Exposure		
	9 or less	10–14	15 or more
All causes			
BP	112	107	61
NIOSH	79	137	353
All cancers			
BP	123	58	73
NIOSH	86	76	428
Digestive system cancer			
BP	106	47	121
NIOSH	75	62	702
Lung cancer			
BP	129	101	62
NIOSH	90	133	366

Source: J. K. Wagoner, P. F. Infante, and R. Saracci, "Vinyl Chloride and Mortality." *Lancet* 2(1975): 194–195.

*Values greater than 100 indicate excessive deaths relative to expected population values.

Nevertheless, industry objected strongly to the 1 ppm proposal on the grounds that it was both unnecessary and beyond their compliance capability. To bolster these claims, contracts were given out by the Society of Plastics Industries to Arthur D. Little, Inc., of Cambridge, Massachusetts. Also, OSHA gave out a contract to Foster D. Snell, a division of Booz, Allen and Hamilton, for the purpose of estimating the economic impact of the new standard. The consulting firms predicted costs as high as $90 billion and losses up to 2.2 million jobs, persuasive arguments in the depressed economic climate of 1974.

However, these estimates were shown by the subsequent experience of the plastics industry to be gross exaggerations.[14] In spite of massive industry lobbying and pressures, OSHA stood firm on the new 1 ppm standard, which was passed on April 1, 1975.

Within one year, the VC/PVC manufacturing industry had successfully met the new standard, and without any major economic dislocation. B. F. Goodrich, one of the industry giants, redesigned its manufacturing technology to enclose VC manufacturing and handling processes and plug possible sources of leaks. Additionally, a "stripping" process was developed to reduce levels of the unreacted VC monomer in the PVC resin and to decrease VC loss in the process. The initial capital costs of the compliance technology were only $34 million. Contrary to the estimates of the industry consulting firms, B. F. Goodrich found that the new clean-up technology actually cut labor costs and could be profitably leased. (In spite of this, B. F. Goodrich increased the price of its PVC products in 1976, claiming higher production costs and blaming these on regulatory standards.) The experience of Union Carbide is similar. In late 1975, an official expressed surprise as to how unexpectedly easy it had been for his company to comply with the 1 ppm standard. However, earlier intercompany reports had documented the economic advantages of compliance through recovering and recycling VC which would have otherwise been discharged into the environment. Estimates of the economic impact of compliance had ignored the major costs to industry from losses of VC gas, with resulting air pollution of the plant and adjacent community. They had also ignored or discounted the major costs to society, both direct and indirect, from failure to regulate, with resulting VC-induced disease. Finally, these estimates did not reflect the emergence of a small and booming industry manufacturing the monitoring equipment now required to meet OSHA regulations.

Cancer and Other Diseases Due to VC

Long before the 1974 reports of angiosarcoma in VC/PVC workers, VC was known to be toxic to experimental animals and to humans at relatively high concentrations. Studies on experimental animals in the early 1960s, by Dow Chemical Company and others, established that VC induced toxic effects in the liver and kidney at concentrations as low as 500 ppm, then the U.S. occupational standard.[15] At higher levels skin and bone abnormalities were also noted.

Acute toxic effects, such as headaches, disorientation, dizziness, drowsiness, and loss of consciousness had been noted in VC/PVC workers as long ago as 1949.[16] In the same year, the Russian scientific literature reported the occurrence of chronic gastritis, hepatitis, and skin lesions from VC exposure. In 1957 there appeared the first report of a new occupational disease among vinyl plastic workers called acroosteolysis, characterized by a thickening or clubbing of the fingers and toes, spasmodic contraction of the blood vessels, painful bone changes, and arthritis of the knuckles. Additional cases of acroosteolysis have since been noted from plastic plants all over the world. By 1966, it was recognized that liver damage, hepatitis and cirrhosis, was common among PVC workers and in some cases occurred after only one or two years of employment. Scattered cases of chronic lung disease have been noted since 1970 in workers inhaling PVC dust; any possible role of unreacted VC contained in or absorbed on the dust is not yet known. Also, a characteristic "meat-wrapper asthma" has been noted among supermarket and wholesale meat workers who, in packaging cuts of meat, use a "hot wire" or "cool rod" to cut and seal the sheet of PVC plastic film used.[17] In the cutting process, fumes are often given off, particularly by the hot wire. While the industry has ascribed the asthma to common irritants, such as hydrochloric acid, it is not known yet whether there are long-term health hazards caused by unreacted VC liberated from the film.

Since 1974, more than forty deaths from angiosarcoma of the liver have been recorded in VC/PVC plants in the United States and elsewhere.* More ominously, four cases have been reported in PVC fabricating plants where VC exposure levels were under 10 ppm. Cancers at various other sites, including the brain, lung, and kidney, have also been found in VC/PVC workers; it should be noted that cancers were also induced at these sites in the animal tests. While the occupational exposure preceding the cancers has usually ranged from thirteen to twenty years, there have been four reports of liver angiosarcoma following less than six years of human exposure. The true incidence of VC cancers in exposed workers is still unknown, because of the long latency periods. However, the ever-increasing number of reported VC cancer cases in organs other than the liver indicates that they can no longer be considered a rarity.[18]

Despite the growing evidence of chronic human disease and the many thousands of workers at risk worldwide, the industry failed for more than twenty years to undertake any carcinogenicity tests in animals. Such tests could as easily have detected the carcinogenic effects of VC in the 1950s as they eventually did in the 1970s.

There are still elements of the academic community who minimize the risks of VC exposure. A recent brochure from the University of Louisville's Vinyl Chloride Project, a multimillion dollar NCI-funded program for the prevention and detection of VC-induced occupational cancer and other diseases, states:

> The low incidence of cancer development among people with prolonged exposure to vinyl chloride is a reflection of

---

*At least seven fatal cases of primary carcinoma of the liver, subsequently diagnosed as angiosarcoma, had been recognized in VC/PVC workers before 1970. Six of these cases occurred in the United States between 1961 and 1968, and the other in Sweden.

the body's ability to remove the chemical agent safely without developing cancer. Some individuals do not have this capability and develop cancer after years of exposure.[19]

The brochure makes no reference to the fact that the present apparent "low incidence of [VC] cancer" may simply reflect its long latency period. Additionally, the independence of this University project has been questioned following recent disclosure of its receipt of undisclosed support from the Manufacturing Chemists Association.*

Public Exposure to VC

The public and the regulatory agencies are now beginning to realize that what goes on in a plant often affects the health of those living nearby in the community. The closer you live to a plant manufacturing VC or PVC or fabricating PVC products, the more VC you are likely to breathe. EPA has estimated that 4.6 million people live within five miles of VC/PVC plants.[20] No estimates are available for the presumably greater number of people living near the uncounted PVC fabricating plants scattered over the country. Measurements by EPA in 1974 and 1975 indicated that in 90 percent of cases, VC levels in the vicinity of VC/PVC plants were below 1 ppm; EPA estimated that average exposure within a five-mile radius would be about 17 parts per billion (ppb). Higher levels, however, were found in 10 percent of communities sampled—33 ppm at a distance of one-third of a mile from the center of one plant.

EPA also estimated that VC/PVC plants were losing 220 million pounds of VC into the air annually, mainly from PVC plants. These considerations, together with reports of excess birth defects in Ohio women living near

---

*This was admitted at an NCI site visit meeting at the University of Louisville on September 26 and 27, 1977.

VC/PVC plants, prompted EPA in October, 1976, to propose regulating VC as a "hazardous air pollutant" and to limit plant emissions to 10 ppm. These regulations would be expected to reduce VC emissions by about 95 percent of previous levels and to reduce community exposure by a similar amount. However, no regulations have yet been developed for plants fabricating PVC products nor for municipal incinerators, which discharge VC into the air from thermal processing and combustion of plastic products, respectively.

The results of a June, 1977, EPA investigation of an elementary school in Saugus, California, located across the road from Keysor-Century Corporation, which manufactures PVC and phonograph records, are disturbing.[21] Levels as high as 2.8 ppm VC have been measured in the air in classrooms. It appears that this heavy contamination largely results from VC losses during tank car unloading at the plant in the night.

Recently, the occurrence of VC disease in the general population has been suggested by preliminary findings of an incidence of 18 congenital malformations per 1,000 live births in women living in three Ohio communities near PVC plants, in comparison with an incidence of 10.5 per 1,000 in those living at a distance.[22] Most of these malformations were of the brain. In addition, an excessive number of brain tumors in adult males were found in those communities near the PVC plants. A similar excess of birth defects over a period from 1966 to 1974, has been recently noted in Shawinigan, Quebec, where a large VC/PVC plant is located.[23] These various effects have been associated with the detection of VC in the air of communities adjacent to VC/PVC plants.

Another way in which the public has been exposed to VC is from aerosol propellants in consumer products such as insecticides, hair sprays, disinfectants, and furniture polishes.[24] EPA studies show that during use of hair or insect sprays, users breathed VC in the 100 to 400 ppm range. After much prodding, the FDA banned the use of

VC as a propellant in cosmetic products, including hair sprays. However, the FDA did not consider the matter serious enough to order a recall of VC-containing products so that the public could avoid further exposure. The Health Research Group eventually pried out from the FDA the brand names of hair sprays that used VC as a propellant, identifying Clairol as a top selling product. According to a recent survey by Consumer Product Safety Commission staff, no new consumer products containing VC have been manufactured since 1974, and no VC-containing products remain on the market in 1978.

The FDA also showed reluctance in moving against the use of PVC containers for food products, although it was aware that unreacted VC was leached out of the container walls by the foods or fluids inside. By 1974 the FDA knew that VC levels as high as 9 ppm had been found in vegetable oils sold in rigid PVC containers.[25] High levels were also found in other PVC-packaged products, including beverages and cosmetics. While the FDA banned the use of rigid PVC containers for food products and beverages, it did not recall them from the market. The FDA still allows the use of PVC film for wrapping foods.

Extensive research is now being done by industry with the object of reducing VC levels in PVC products, especially those intended for food packaging and medical applications.[26] However, as indicated in a recent trade journal article, the prospects of success seem slim:

> At present conventional devolatilizing techniques cannot be successfully offered to PVC. . . . It cannot be expected, however, that a completely monomer-free PVC resin will be a commercial reality in the near future.[27]

Summary

Vinyl chloride (VC) is a simple gaseous chemical which can be polymerized to form a wealth of plastic materials. Despite recognition for several decades of a wide range of chronic toxic effects in animals and exposed workers, it was not until 1970 that the carcinogenicity of VC was first established experimentally. A consortium of European plastics manufacturers then funded further carcinogenicity testing of VC which confirmed and extended the earlier findings. These results, which were shared with the Manufacturing Chemists Association, remained unpublished for over eighteen months until the announcement by B. F. Goodrich in January, 1974, of the occurrence of three fatal cases of an extremely rare cancer, angiosarcoma of the liver, among its VC/PVC workers. On the same day, the Manufacturing Chemists Association revealed the results of the animal tests showing VC to be a potent carcinogen in rodents, inducing angiosarcoma of the liver and a wide range of cancers at other sites at exposures of 50 ppm and below.

In the absence of available information on the carcinogenicity of VC in animals, its effects in exposed workers were only first recognized because of the occurrence of the three rare angiosarcomas of the liver. Had VC only induced lung cancer, its carcinogenicity would in all probability have remained unrecognized or ascribed to smoking.

The present occupational standard of 1 ppm was promulgated by OSHA in spite of estimates by industry of grossly exaggerated costs and unemployment. While the standard affords some degree of protection to workers in VC/PVC plants, it does not protect the greater number of workers in PVC fabricating plants, nor does it prevent exposures to VC of the public-at-large, particularly those living in the vicinity of VC/PVC plants, with attendant risks of cancer and also possibly birth defects.

My own company is very conscientious and careful about the chemicals we use in the manufacturing process.

Ellington M. Beavers, Medical Director and Vice President, Rohm & Haas Company, 1974.

Bischloromethylether

It is surprising how quickly the scandals of yesterday become today's respectable textbook classics. A standard 1975 medical text, *Occupational Medicine,* contains the following matter-of-fact account of the discovery of bischloromethylether (BCME) as a potent human carcinogen:

> [Dr. William Figueroa] reported on lung cancer found in chloromethylmethylether workers and suggested another occupational hazard that increases the risk of lung cancer. They surveyed and studied a chemical manufacturing plant with approximately 2,000 employees where periodic chest X-ray surveys had been carried out for many years. In 1962, management became aware that an excessive number of workers suspected of having lung cancer were reported in one area of the plant, and promptly engaged consulting services to identify and resolve what appeared to be a serious problem.[1]

Claims of "prompt" action by this company, Rohm and Haas (R&H), one of the world's dozen largest chemical manufacturing companies, have often been reiterated in the medical literature. The facts prove the contrary. As shown, among others, by Philadelphia Inquirer reporters William Randall and Stephen Solomon in the award-winning investigative book, *Building Six,* the response by R&H was not prompt.[2] As documented in the book, the company did its best not only to obstruct studies of the lung-cancer outbreak, but also to discredit those studies.[3] Finally, R&H tried to block protection of other workers by fighting against adequate exposure standards for BCME and other occupational carcinogens.[4]

Discovery of BCME

BCME was developed in 1948 by R&H chemist Robert Kunin at the company's Bridesburg laboratories in Pennsylvania. Attempts to scale up the laboratory process to a

100-gallon batch, however, revealed that BCME was intensely caustic, so much so that it virtually destroyed the plant machinery. By 1950, BCME was replaced by the closely related chloromethylmethylether (CMME), which in its industrial form contains from 1 to 7 percent BCME as a contaminant. Based on BCME and CMME, R&H chemists developed manufacturing processes for ion-exchange resins and promoted their application in various technologies, including water purification, and fabrication of nuclear weapons and fuel for power plants.

The scale-up of the BCME manufacturing process is typical of the way in which industries move newly developed technology from the laboratory to the production line. BCME is not an end-product chemical, but an intermediate which is produced and used at the production site during synthesis of ion-exchange resins. In 1948, after R&H chemists were convinced they had developed a valuable material, the first stage of large-scale production commenced in the "semi-works," so-called because it was a sort of half-way house for testing chemical processes on a larger scale than the laboratory.

As long as BCME synthesis had been confined to the laboratory, work proceeded under ventilated hoods, which drew toxic fumes up and away from the chemist. At the semi-works, however, there was no such ventilation. And the chemical was prepared not in test-tube quantities but in 100-gallon batches in open kettles that continued to be used after BCME was replaced by CMME in 1950.

In 1954, the process was moved from the semi-works to Building 6, a windowless five-story building also used for the manufacture of insecticides such as Rothane, a mainstay of R&H's operations. Randall and Solomon quote an R&H spokesman's description of the CMME process in building 6:

> The operation started at the top floor, where the CMME was actually manufactured by shovelling paraformaldehyde flakes and aluminum chloride into kettles of hy-

drochloric acid. There were a good bit of fumes from the aluminum chloride, a fine powder, as soon as the air hit it. The kettle had to be charged quickly or it would become gummy. The men would cough, then turn away. . . . Then the CMME would go down a chute to the level below, where agitators would mix it in kettles that men would have to open from time to time so they could check on its progress. When they did lift the lids, vapors came rolling up at them. Then the mixture was dropped to the level below, where water was poured in on top to quench the reaction. This time, when the men hit the switch on the agitator, the fumes billowed out and they would have to run from the building gasping for air, then wait to go back in again. [5]

One of the insecticide workers who shared the building with the CMME process, was quoted:

When the CMME fumes hit the floor, it was like a London fog. Everybody had to run outside to breathe. It was so goddamn hot in there you couldn't wear a mask. They were old rubber masks and you couldn't get your breath through them and so whenever there was a spill, and it happened a couple of times a day when the foreman pushed the men a little and they added the flakes a little too fast, everyone in the whole building got a shot. And if you tried to smoke after getting a shot of that stuff, it made you puke." [6]

Medical Problems

By 1962 it had become obvious that there was something wrong at R&H. Fourteen BCME workers had died of lung cancer in the preceding seven years. Their average age at death was 50, ten years younger than the average age of death of lung cancer victims. Among these was a woman of 28 and men aged 33, 38, 41, 43, and 49. The national death rate for lung cancer in white males in that age group was then about 15 per 100,000. To have seen even one or two lung cancers in workers under 50 in a

2,000-person plant should have immediately alarmed the company.

R&H claims that it "warned" its employees about the possibility of the cancer risk as soon as it knew. None of the employees has ever recalled any such warning. A memorandum, which the company maintains was read to small groups of its employees in 1962, contains a cryptic reference to "our concern over the cases of cancer that have appeared among building 6 personnel." It is clear, however, that the main thrust of the memorandum was different:

> The personnel department is currently in the process of making arrangements for the next chest X-ray survey of the Bridesburg employees . . . During several of these surveys, cases of TB (tuberculosis) have been uncovered, and as a result, people who worked around these individuals have been and are now being checked to be sure they have not contracted the disease. [7]

"Making arrangements" refers to the company's consultation with Katherine Boucot Sturgis, a well-known Philadelphia chest specialist, who for several years had been X-raying some Bridesburg employees as part of the Philadelphia Pulmonary Neoplasm Research Project. Sturgis' advice came in two parts. First, she agreed to add the entire building 6 and semi-works personnel to her yearly project X-rays, although this was never in fact done. Second, she recommended R&H to contract with Norton Nelson of New York University, to do carcinogenicity tests on BCME. Sturgis agreed to turn over all her findings directly to the company, but none of her patients, the workers, seems to have received any warning from her or the company.*

---

*Recently juries have awarded damages in lawsuits against company-retained doctors who concealed medical findings from employees. They rejected company arguments that, since the company bought the medical service, only they were entitled to know the results of the examinations.

Animal Experiments

The negotiations between R&H and Nelson over company sponsored carcinogenicity tests on BCME collapsed after two years, apparently over Nelson's insistence on permission to publish any findings. After another year's delay R&H instead contracted with Hazelton Laboratories, a commercial testing company, to do carcinogenicity tests on BCME, CMME, and other chemicals in use at the Bridesburg Plant. By 1966, Hazelton reported that BCME and CMME, as well as some of the other chemicals, were carcinogenic.

Meanwhile, the New York University team had also begun a study of the carcinogenicity of BCME and CMME using government funds. By 1971 they found that BCME was one of the most potent carcinogens ever tested.[8] At 0.1 ppm in the air they breathed, rats developed a high incidence of lung cancers.

Human Experimentation

Between 1962 and 1968, when the screening phase of the Philadelphia project ended and the X-rays stopped, workers continued to die. Although their impending deaths were often picked up on X-rays, too late to save them, no meaningful effort was made to prevent further exposure. The X-ray reports were sent to the R&H medical office and were simply filed away. Even in 1968, one of the Philadelphia project physicians noted an excess of R&H lung cancer deaths, but failed to draw any conclusions, not having been told of worker's exposure to the carcinogenic BCME in the semi-works and building 6.

Then, in 1971, one of the workers with lung cancer was referred to William Figueroa, an internist at the Germantown Dispensary and Hospital near Philadelphia for treatment. Figueroa was surprised to find that this worker had never smoked, since the type of lung cancer

he had (oat cell) is rare in nonsmokers. The worker recalled several other men who had previously died of
cancer after working at similar jobs in the plant. Figueroa
consulted one of his former professors at Hahneman Medical College, Philadelphia, William Weiss, who had
conducted much of the Philadelphia Pulmonary Neoplasm
Research Project, to see what information was available
for the other men. He also attempted to obtain occupational exposure histories for the group of 125 R&H workers for whom he had X-rays and medical and smoking histories. As he later found out, of the fifty-four lung cancer
deaths at R&H, four occurred in the project group during
the screening period from 1963 to 1968.[9] R&H, however,
insisted that they had no work histories and exposure records on any of these 125 workers, and that they did not
know why these workers had been selected for screening.
Subsequently, R&H did manage to produce some of these
records at a workman's compensation hearing to show that
a particular worker had not been exposed to BCME and
was therefore ineligible for benefits.

The importance of knowing which of the 125 workers
had been exposed to BCME and which had not was critical to a prospective-type epidemiological investigation of
the lung cancer epidemic at R&H. Figueroa had to calculate a death rate among exposed workers and compare it
with that of the general population. He knew that 4 of the
125 workers had lung cancer, but without the exposure
data, he could not calculate a cancer rate and thus, assess
the significance of these findings. In the absence of company cooperation, Figueroa turned to his only available
source of information, the lung cancer patient who, in his
years of working at R&H, had come to know many of the
plant employees. From memory, the man reconstructed
the work histories of many of the plant employees on the
Pulmonary Neoplasm Project list. The results were as-
tonishing. Of the 125 men screened, only 44 had definite
exposure to BCME. (Thus, the death rate was 4 out of 44,

or 9 percent.)* This excessive rate, coupled with the young age of many of the victims, was remarkable. Figueroa immediately published his findings in the *New England Journal of Medicine*.[10] His paper stands as an indictment of BCME as a potent carcinogen and, more telling, an indictment of R&H.

Simultaneous with the appearance of Figueroa's publication, NIOSH released the results of an investigation at a Diamond Shamrock CMME plant, Redwood City, California, initiated in 1971.[11] This study also showed a high incidence of lung cancers in relatively young workers. A number of other epidemiological studies in the United States and Germany have since confirmed the extreme carcinogenicity of BCME.[12]

Industry Fights Back

In 1972 R&H launched a campaign to discredit the experimental and epidemiological findings on the carcinogenicity of BCME. They informed NIOSH of their position that none of the cases of lung cancer in their plant could possibly have been due to BCME exposure; that instead they were caused by smoking and air pollution.

In the spring of 1973, R&H Senior Vice-President for Health Ellington M. Beavers, who in 1971 had refused to provide Figueroa with exposure data on BCME, was appointed to OSHA's Standards Advisory Committee on Occupational Carcinogens. Beavers urged the committee to reject proposals for minimal regulation of occupational exposure to carcinogens, and argued against the identification of occupational carcinogens by animal tests, recommending instead the need for more convincing human studies.

R&H and the Manufacturing Chemists Association

---

*More recent follow-up of the Pulmonary Neoplasm Project screenees resulted in the identification of seven more lung cancer deaths at R&H.

also lobbied strongly against enactment of a workplace exposure standard for BCME, which was finally promulgated in an emasculated form in a package of standards for fourteen occupational carcinogens in January, 1974.

It has recently been discovered that BCME can be formed spontaneously in reaction mixtures containing the common chemicals hydrochloric acid and formaldehyde.[13] This places many thousands of workers in danger of potential exposure to BCME. For example, many textile workers use formaldehyde in making permanent press fabrics, which are then treated with an acid wash.

A Needless Tragedy

Fifty-four workers at R&H have so far died of lung cancer. Yet the deaths due to BCME were unnecessary, as shown by the experience of Dow Chemical Company, R&H's closest competitor in the manufacture of CMME and BCME.

On the basis of findings in the late 1940s that BCME was an intense lung irritant to animals, Dow enclosed the manufacturing process at its Midland, Michigan, facility since its inception in 1949. Dow's Research Laboratory director commented on the cost of providing this type of protection:

> At first thought, it seemed to me that such methods would be so expensive that they could not be used in normal chemical manufacture. Actually, this may not be true. The enclosure for the manufacture of chloromethylether need not be a six-foot wall of concrete, but only a normal airtight building . . . If such operation proves impractical, I believe we should abandon large-scale work with chloromethylether.[14]

A 1972 NIOSH field inspection of the Dow facility reported that

> the industrial hygiene philosophy employed is to completely contain the product inside the process equipment

and to have local exhaust ventilation at points of potential leakage, such as around seals with rotating shafts. This allows the worker to be in the production area without having to rely upon respiratory protection.[15]

In fact, the health record of Dow BCME employees is difficult to evaluate. In its twenty-five years of operation, only about 120 workers were known to have been potentially exposed. Dow claims that only one of the workers, a heavy cigarette smoker, developed lung cancer. R&H had allowed eighteen years to elapse before, in 1967, it finally followed Dow's example of enclosing the CMME manufacturing process.

Summary

Bischloromethylether (BCME) is used to manufacture ion-exchange resins and appears virtually indispensable as an intermediate product in nuclear fuel processing. BCME has been manufactured on a large scale at only two industrial sites during the past 25 years, and by only two chemical companies, Dow Chemical and Rohm & Haas. While Dow engineered its process from the start to reduce human exposure to BCME, Rohm & Haas scaled up production with little regard for its obvious toxicity or emerging information on its carcinogenicity.

Workers in Rohm & Haas started dying of lung cancer in the early 1960s. The company attempted to conceal this information, and subsequently to ascribe the cancer to smoking. When the need for animal testing became inescapable, Rohm & Haas aborted negotiations with New York University over the issue of open publication of results, contracting instead with a commercial testing laboratory. Even after BCME was shown to be one of the most powerful carcinogens ever tested in animals, and in the face of the increasing lung cancer death toll in its employees, Rohm & Haas resisted paying compensation to its employees' families and vigorously fought attempts by OSHA in 1973 to regulate BCME and other occupational carcinogens.

Benzene

Benzene is one of twelve chemicals used in largest volume by U.S. industries. Both production and manufacturing capacity have increased steadily by about 5 percent per year over the last decade. U.S. benzene production in 1977 was approximately 11 billion pounds, some 90 percent of which was produced in petroleum refining and petrochemical industries, and the remainder in the coke ovens of the steel industry.[1] The manufacture of tires accounts for approximately half of all benzene used. Commercially, benzene is also used as an intermediate in the production of a wide range of chemicals, such as nitrobenzene, phenol, cyclohexane, cumene, maleic anhydride, and detergent alkylate. Another major usage is as an octane booster in gasoline. Further end-products of the use of benzene include nylons, pesticides, adhesives, laminates, coatings, inks, paints, varnishes, and moldings.

Occupational Exposure

The occupational hazards of benzene have long been recognized, although their seriousness has, until recently, been underestimated. While in the past exposures in the range from 100 to 500 ppm were commonplace, current levels in some workplaces are generally lower, reflecting the 1971 occupational standard of 10 ppm. Workers in petroleum and petrochemical refineries, in chemical plants (especially those manufacturing rubber products and solvents), and in the steel industry are at particularly high risk from benzene exposure. Additional categories of workers exposed include printing pressmen and lithographers, shoemakers, gasoline pump attendants, and professional artists and craftsmen.

A National Occupational Hazard Survey published by NIOSH in 1977, found that nearly 50,000 full-time workers are exposed to benzene, of whom 55 percent work at facilities that have no engineering controls or protective equipment.[2] More than 75 percent of the workers do not receive periodic blood tests to check for benzene toxicity. NIOSH estimates that about 2 million workers are now exposed to benzene.

Public Exposure

While benzene has been well known as an occupational problem for more than eighty years, recognition of the hazards posed to the general public is only recent. Public exposure to benzene falls into three major categories: communities near industries producing, processing, or using the chemical; the general public (from gasoline); and the homeowner (from benzene-containing consumer products).

Based on recent estimates by Stanford Research Institute, it is clear that while these exposures are at much lower levels than occupational exposures, they are virtually unregulated at present and affect much of the U.S. population (Table 5.4).[3] These rough estimates of general population exposure in the vicinity of petroleum refineries and gasoline service stations have, in general, been subsequently confirmed by limited industry monitoring, including that by the American Petroleum Institute.

Over half the benzene supply in the United States comes from a small number of petroleum refineries in Texas, California, Louisiana, and Illinois.[4] These four states, together with Pennsylvania and New Jersey, account for about 70 percent of the total national refining capacity. It is estimated that more than 6 million people who live in the vicinity of these refineries are being constantly exposed to benzene emissions in the 0.1 to 1 ppb range. An additional 64,000 people living still closer to the plants received exposures up to 2 ppb.[5]

Table 5.4 Industries Causing Exposure of the General Public to Benzene

Source	Number of People Exposed to Various Concentrations of Benzene, ppb*					Total Number of Exposed People
	0.1–1	1–2	2–4	4–10	Over 10	
Petroleum refineries	6,529,000	64,000	4,000	. . . .	. . . .	6,597,000
Chemical manufacturing	7,497,000	970,000	453,000	644,000	319,000	9,883,000
Solvent operations	208,000	5,000	2,000	. . . .	. . . .	215,000
Coke ovens	15,726,000	521,000	50,000	2,000	. . . .	16,299,000
Gasoline stations						
People using self-service	. . . .	. . . .	. . . .	. . . .	37,000,000	37,000,000
People living nearby	87,000,000	31,000,000	. . . .	. . . .	. . . .	118,000,000
Urban exposures from autos	68,337,000	45,353,000	. . . .	. . . .	. . . .	113,690,000

Source: S. J. Mara and S. S. Lee, "Human Exposures to Atmospheric Benzene," Center for Resources and Environmental Systems Studies, Report No. 30, Stanford Research Institute, 1977.

*Based on estimates of annual averages.

A wide range of chemical manufacturing plants throughout the United States, but particularly concentrated along the Gulf Coast, leak substantial quantities of benzene into the atmosphere.[6] A 1971 study by Mitre Corporation indicated that annual losses are in the region of 260 million pounds, about 2.5 percent of total production. The worst offenders seem to be facilities manufacturing aniline and maleic anhydride. The actual concentrations to which local populations are exposed are highly variable, depending on factors such as height of gas stack, temperature of exhaust gas and wind patterns, but more critically on proximity to the plant. Average benzene levels are estimated to be in the 100 to 3,000 ppb range directly outside some plants, with progressive reduction at increasing distances.

Relatively little is known about the amounts of benzene used in solvent industries, for purposes such as manufacture of tires, natural and synthetic rubber products, adhesives, printing inks, paints, paint removers, leather and leather products, and floor coverings.[7] Limited monitoring data have found benzene levels as high as 700 ppb within a quarter of a mile of a B. F. Goodrich Company solvent operation.[8] There is a gradual trend, particularly in the rubber industry, to substitute toluene as a much safer and effective alternative for benzene.

Sixty million tons of blast furnace coke are produced from coal each year in sixty-five U.S. steel plants, most of which are concentrated in four states: Pennsylvania, Indiana, Ohio, and Alabama.* For each ton of coke, about four gallons of "light oil," most of which is benzene, are produced as a by-product. Most coke ovens are old and "leaky," allowing the escape of benzene and other volatile toxic materials such as carbon monoxide, hydrogen sulfide, and sulfur oxides. Benzene levels are estimated to range as high as 50 ppm inside the plants and 300 ppb

---

*These plants consist of an estimated 13,000 ovens contained in about 230 coke oven batteries.

immediately adjacent to them, decreasing to a few ppb at twelve miles distance. It is further estimated that about 16 million people are exposed to annual average concentrations in the 0.1 to 1 ppb range and 50,000 in the 2 to 4 ppb range.[9]

By far the most extensive operations resulting in benzene exposure to the general population are gasoline stations, of which there are about 200,000 in the United States. With the gradual phasing out of gasoline lead additives, the use of benzene as an octane booster has doubled over the last four years to current levels from 1 percent to 2.5 percent in most gasoline brands. Most of the vapor liberated during a typical fill-up operation results from the displacement of benzene trapped within the gas tank, and not from the gasoline being pumped. Recent measurements in U.S. self-service stations found benzene levels averaging 250 ppb immediately adjacent to the gas pumps. It is estimated that about 37 million people are intermittently exposed to such benzene levels through the use of self-service facilities. Gasoline attendants, of course, are continuously exposed to them. So are also the 118 million people, more than half the U.S. population, who are exposed to levels between 0.1 to 2.0 ppb by virtue of living near a gas station.[10] And automobiles themselves are mini-dispensers of benzene, both from tailpipe emissions and evaporation from the gas tank. Estimates of average benzene levels from these sources range from 1 to 4 ppb in downtown Dallas, Los Angeles, St. Louis, and Chicago, where the highest levels were found. Concentrations in the suburbs of these cities were from two to ten times lower.[11]

Many commonly used consumer products contain benzene. These include solvents, adhesives (including the cement in bicycle tire patch kits), carburetor cleaners, and paint and wood strippers. A popular paint stripper, Red Devil Paint and Varnish Remover, contains over 50 percent benzene. Recent NIOSH measurements in a closed garage after a half-hour of furniture stripping found benzene levels ranging from 75 to 225 ppm.[12] Professional artists, craftsmen, and hobbyists are often exposed under poorly ventilated conditions to benzene in their homes, studios, and workshops from the uses of common materials, such as resin and fluorescent dye solvents, paint and varnish removers, and silk-screen washes. Another NIOSH survey at the Cooper Union School of Art and Architecture in New York, measured benzene levels of 37 ppm in a breathing zone sample on a photoetcher. A 1977 investigation by a New York public interest group, the Center for Occupational Hazards, found the following benzene consumer products readily available.[13] Seventeen of twenty randomly selected hardware stores sold products listing benzene on their label, but with little or no indication of the dangers involved. Paint removers are

Brand Name	*Products*
Red Devil's Paint Products	Red Devil's Paint and Varnish Remover Liquid #99 Liquid #66 No-Wash #88 Paste #77
Wilson Imperial Products Products	Imperial Wonder-paste Paint Remover Imperial Rapid Brush Cleaner Imperial Cleanwood Wil-Bond Sanding Liquid
KWIK Products	KWIK Liquid No-Wash Paint and Varnish Remover KWIK Semi-Paste Paint and Varnish Remover
Classic	Classic Rubber Repair Cement
Kleen Kutter	Klean Kutter Paint Remover

Source: Art Hazards Project, Center for Occupational Hazards, Inc., 1976.

particularly hazardous since they may be from 15 to 100 percent benzene.

A most dramatic example of community exposure to benzene and other carcinogenic solvents is afforded by the case of the Galaxy Chemical Company, Elkton, Maryland.[14] This company started operations in 1961 for the purpose of recovering solvents from the wastes of major chemical industries, such as Du Pont. The company first stored these wastes in tanks vented directly to the atmosphere. Following processing at Galaxy, the "bottoms" or residues were discharged into open drying beds. After evaporation, the final wastes were dumped in nearby landfills. Additionally the company periodically had large spills of carcinogenic and other chemicals.* Complaints of foul odors commenced as soon as the plant opened and became almost constant by 1964. Monitors outside the plant in 1970 found levels of benzene as high as 23 ppm and other solvents such as carbon tetrachloride, at levels of 140 ppm.

By 1974, a local pathologist, Pietro Capurro, who had himself been involved in the monitoring, noted an excess of lymphoma cases in Elkton. Capurro, after trying in vain to get help from the Maryland State Department of Health, prepared in March, 1974, a preliminary manuscript reporting his findings, but not specifying Galaxy as the source of the pollution. Medical World News subsequently interviewed Capurro and printed an article naming Galaxy as the pollution source. The director and owner of Galaxy, Paul Mraz, claimed that Capurro's article was defamatory and resulted in the loss of business, and sued Capurro for over $2 million. The case came to jury trial in December, 1977. Edward Radford, Professor of Epidemiology at the School of Public Health,

---

*According to a deposition of the director and owner of Galaxy, Paul Mraz, the company "spilled" about 1,000 gallons of trichlorethylene in 1965, and several hundred gallons of acrylonitrile in 1971 or 1972. Mraz estimated that the company "spilled" on the average of 1,250 gallons of chemicals each year.

University of Pittsburgh and consultant to Galaxy, claimed that Capurro was "reckless and irresponsible" in writing the draft of his article, and that Galaxy could not possibly have been responsible for the admitted excess of lymphoma cases in Elkton. On the basis of the scientific and other evidence,* the jury found for Capurro. Mraz has appealed this verdict to the Maryland Special Court of Appeal, which is expected to hear the case during its September, 1978, term.

Galaxy Chemical Company was dissolved in 1975, and has since reopened as Solvent Distillers, again under the ownership of Mraz.† In spite of some improvements in the operations of the new company, complaints of odor persisted, as indicated at the trial. Continuous monitoring in 1976 revealed periodic benzene levels in the 200 to 900 ppb range.

Occupational Diseases[16]

Virtually all knowledge of the effects of benzene on humans comes from studies on exposed workers. Benzene is highly toxic, inducing a wide range of acute and chronic adverse effects. Unless contaminated with other more readily absorbed solvents, benzene is poorly absorbed through the intact skin. The primary route of entry into the body is inhalation, with rapid absorption from the lungs into the blood. Benzene accumulates in various organs and sites of the body in proportion to their fat content. Most is rapidly metabolized, primarily by liver enzymes, to water soluble derivatives which are excreted in the urine. One of the early metabolic products of benzene is benzene epoxide, which is highly reactive and may ul-

---

*The author was a witness for the defense.[15]

†Solvent Distillers has been renamed Spectron, Inc. On May 8, 1978, an explosion at the plant involving release of white fumes from barrels containing polyurethane and ink resins resulted in the evacuation of more than fifty residents from Elkton. Mraz characterized the vapors as "nonlethal."

timately be responsible for the toxic bone marrow effects
noted below.

Aplastic Anaemia   Benzene is a potent marrow poison,
inducing a wide range of toxic effects, the best recognized
of which is aplastic anaemia, which is characterized by pal-
lor and fatigue and can exist alone or together with a condition known as *pancytopenia*. In this condition, bleeding
can occur in the skin and elsewhere in the body, and there
also is increased susceptibility to infection.

It is difficult to assess the long-term outcome of aplastic anaemia. While the immediate prognosis of early and
mild cases may be good if benzene exposure is discontinued, apparently complete recovery is sometimes followed by the development of acute leukaemia up to
twenty or so years later.

Case histories of aplastic anaemia/pancytopenia in
benzene-exposed workers have gradually been accumulating in the U.S. and European literature over the last five
decades. Cases have been reported in a wide range of occupations, including printers in rotogravure plants, rubber
workers, aircraft construction workers, and leather and
shoe workers. One of the most important series of studies
has been based on Turkish shoe workers, who between
1955 and 1960 started using adhesives containing high
levels of benzene, and were exposed to levels in the 150
to 650 ppm range.[17] Individual cases of aplastic anaemia
were noted in 1961. By 1977, 46 workers had developed
aplastic anaemia, of whom 14 died from the disease. Five
of these workers later developed leukaemia, from which
they subsequently died.

Chromosomal Effects   Since the early 1960s, several
European studies have shown that there is a relatively
high incidence of chromosome abnormalities in the lymphocytes (white blood cells) of workers, with varying degrees of marrow damage following benzene exposure.[18]
These abnormalities were generally found in workers intermittently exposed to benzene levels from 25 to 150

ppm. The literature has been conflicting with regard to chromosome damage at lesser exposure levels.

By the summer of 1977, Dow Chemical Company had completed extensive chromosome tests on some forty workers in its Freeport, Texas, plant exposed to "low" benzene levels, believed to be under 10 ppm. The Dow scientists reportedly found clear-cut evidence of chromosome damage, particularly in men over forty. The Michigan corporate offices of Dow initially decided not to disclose these results.* The news, however, leaked out. NIOSH sent two letters to Dow in late 1977 and another in January, 1978, requesting details of this study, which Dow finally released in March, 1978. This study confirmed the occurrence of chromosome damage in workers with average exposure levels of 2 to 3 ppm.

Unpublished studies from Sweden also seem consistent with the results of the Dow studies, with the findings of chromosome damage in industrial workers and crews of petrol tanker ships, following exposure to benzene in the 5 to 10 ppm range.[19]

The occurrence of chromosome damage in the absence of any other evidence of benzene toxicity is important for several reasons, particularly when found at relatively low exposure levels. First, there are theoretical grounds for associating induced chromosome damage with the subsequent development of leukaemia. Second, similar abnormalities are induced by X-rays, which can also produce leukaemia. Third, these changes can persist long after there has been apparent recovery from benzene poisoning, and well before leukaemia develops. Finally, these changes are commonly found in leukaemic blood cells.

Leukaemia in Humans   Four major types of this fatal form of cancer of white blood cells are recognized: acute myelogenous, chronic myelogenous, acute lymphocytic, and chronic lymphocytic. The association between acute

---

*This would have jeopardized the industry position of fighting against the 1977 proposed OSHA reduction of the benzene standard to 1 ppm.

myelogenous leukaemia in humans and benzene exposure is unequivocal. There are three major lines of supporting evidence for this: First, benzene is known to be toxic to bone marrow, producing aplastic anaemia/pancytopenia and also chromosomal abnormalities, both of which are probable precursors of leukaemia. Second, there have been over 100 case reports of acute myelogenous leukaemia following occupational exposure to benzene, many of which first developed as aplastic anaemia. Finally, and most important, various epidemiologic studies have concluded that benzene induces leukaemia and is thus a carcinogen.

For example, an impressive series of studies has been done by Muzaffer Aksoy based on 28,500 shoe workers in Istanbul, Turkey, exposed to benzene levels from 210 to 650 ppm over a period ranging from one to fifteen years. [20] Of these cases, 26 developed acute myelogenous leukaemia from 1967 to 1973; this is an annual incidence of 13/100,000 and about four times that seen in the general population. Additionally, the average age of these leukaemia cases was 34 years, which is much lower than the 60-year average age of leukaemia deaths in adults.

Similar results have been reported in Italian shoe and rotogravure workers in Milan and Pavia, where the risk of acute myelogenous leukaemia was calculated in 1964 to be approximately twenty times greater than that of the general population. It is of particular interest that no new cases of aplastic anaemia or leukaemia were observed in the rotogravure industry during the ten-year period following the substitution of toluene for benzene in 1964. [21]

In 1974, J. Thorpe, Associate Medical Director, Exxon Corporation, published a large-scale epidemiological study of leukaemia mortality, based on 36,000 employees and retirees of eight European affiliates exposed to "low levels" of benzene from 1962 to 1972. [22] Thorpe found no excess risks of leukaemia. However, there was a wide range of problems in this study, some of which were admitted by the author. These included inadequate follow-up of older employees (who were most likely to develop leukaemia), incomplete exposure histories, inadequate measurement of exposure levels, and suspect diagnosis reporting. As one critic expressed it, "With case finding techniques as apparently relaxed as those in the Exxon study by Dr. Thorpe, one cannot help but doubt the accuracy of the data presented."[23]

A recent epidemiological study by Peter Infante of NIOSH* involved a cohort of 748 men who had been exposed to benzene from 1940 through 1949 at the Akron and St. Mary's, Ohio, plants of the Goodyear Tire and Rubber Company, while engaged in the manufacture of "pliofilm," a natural rubber cast film.[24] A virtue of this study was the "purity" of the exposure; that is, the workers were exposed only to benzene, rather than to the mixture of other organic solvents usually encountered in the rubber industry. Although a 1946 report by the Ohio Industrial Commission indicates that benzene levels in the pliofilm operation were relatively low, ranging from zero to 10 ppm, the value of this study is probably more qualitative than quantitative. Of 140 deaths observed by 1975, 7 were leukaemias, mainly acute myelogenous, while only 1 or 2 would have been expected from U.S. death rates. The risk of workers in this plant dying from leukaemia was calculated to be about ten times that of the general population. Unpublished reports from Lund, Sweden, in 1977 also indicated a high incidence of acute myelogenous leukaemia in gasoline pump attendants.

There is a clear relationship between benzene and acute myelogenous leukaemia, and there is growing information incriminating benzene in other forms of leukaemia and other malignancies. Much of this evidence, however, comes from studies in which there are mixed exposures to other solvents besides benzene, such as in the rubber industry. For instance, a 1963 HEW study reported a 54 percent increase in death rates for "cancer of

---

*Now in OSHA.

the lymphatic and haematopoietic system," besides excess cancers of other sites in the rubber industry compared with other manufacturing industries.[25] A comprehensive study of rubber workers by scientists of the University of North Carolina showed an excess death rate from all forms of leukaemia, including lymphatic leukaemia, and also lymphosarcoma and Hodgkin's disease. Other studies of the rubber industry have also confirmed the findings of excess lymphatic leukaemia. There have also been scattered case reports on the association between benzene exposure and lymphosarcoma, Hodgkin's disease, multiple myeloma, and reticulum cell sarcoma.[26] For instance, six cases of Hodgkin's disease have been recently reported in Turkish shoe workers following one to twenty years of occupational exposure to benzene.

Leukaemia in Animals

In 1897, a German physician, G. Santesson, investigating an outbreak of skin haemorrhages in a group of women working with benzene, was able to reproduce these effects in rabbits by injection and skin application of the chemical. Since then, there have been numerous investigations on the effects of benzene in animals. In general, these have shown that benzene is a marrow toxin, depressing marrow function, and producting an aplastic anaemia/pancytopenia-like condition. In more recent studies, chromosome damage, of a type similar to that found in occupationally-exposed workers, has been found in circulating lymphocytes.[27]

Attempts to induce leukaemia and other cancers in experimental animals by chronic administration of benzene have on the whole been unsuccessful until very recently. It has been customary to regard benzene as one of two major exceptions to the rule that all chemicals found to be carcinogenic in humans will also induce cancer in animals (arsenic is the other). However, there are grounds for questioning whether benzene is really an exception.

First, many claimed negative animal experiments are inadequate in that they used too few animals or observed them for too short a period. Second, there are several animal studies which, while individually flawed, together are highly suggestive of the induction of leukaemias or lymphomas. Examples are a 1932 German study, in which eight out of forty-four surviving mice developed leukaemia or lymphosarcoma, and a 1963 Japanese study, in which fibrosarcomas were induced in five of eight mice surviving chronic benzene administration.[28] Finally, two recent unpublished studies seem to confirm the carcinogenicity of benzene. The preliminary results of one study were presented by Cesare Maltoni at a meeting sponsored by Chemical Week in New Orleans, October 21, 1977. Groups of sixty to seventy rats of both sexes were fed benzene at doses of 50 and 250 mg/kg. Five rare ear gland tumors, five skin tumors and three other tumors were found in the high dose group. No such tumors occurred in 300 controls. The second, still incomplete, study from New York University has established that benzene induces leukaemia in rodents. This study is based on exposure of groups of forty to sixty rats and mice to benzene by inhalation at 100 or 300 ppm for up to two years. So far, one rat and one mouse have died from chronic myeloid leukaemia, another mouse from acute leukaemia, and a third mouse from a leukaemic-like disease. Additionally, most mice at the higher dose level developed severe anaemia.

Regulatory Developments

The year 1977 was a year of regulatory confrontation for benzene, as moves were finally made by federal agencies to limit and control exposures in the workplace, in the general environment, and in the home.

Regulation in the Workplace The 1977 occupational standard of 10 ppm was originally based on a standard developed by the American Conference of Governmental Industrial Hygienists in 1969.[29] This is one of several industry-oriented organizations in whose hands occupational standards were set prior to passage of the 1970 Occupational Safety and Health Act. The American National Standards Institute is another such organization. Standards set by these organizations are often referred to as "consensus standards," although the consensus did not generally reflect the views of consumers or organized labor. While Section 6(a) of the Occupational Safety and Health Act allows conferring of federal authority on such standards, these have recently come under increasing scrutiny and revision. The consensus standard, adopted as an OSHA standard in 1971, allowed average benzene exposures of 10 ppm, with an acceptable ceiling of 25 ppm, and periodic excursions up to 50 ppm. Both the consensus and resulting OSHA standard were based on the general toxic effects of benzene, without any consideration of risks of leukaemia, in spite of the substantial evidence of this effect which then existed.

The risks of leukaemia could no longer be ignored when the results of the Turkish shoe worker study by Aksoy were published in 1974.[30] Accordingly, NIOSH submitted a criteria document to OSHA on benzene admitting that "the possibility that benzene can induce leukaemia cannot be dismissed."[31] Nevertheless NIOSH recommended retention of the 10 ppm standard. Resentment against this standard surfaced on April 23, 1976, when the United Rubber, Cork, Linoleum and Plastic Workers of America wrote to Secretary of Labor William J. Usery urging that an Emergency Temporary Standard regulating occupational exposure to benzene be issued in order to protect workers from leukaemia. According to the Act, an Emergency Temporary Standard may only be issued if there is a condition of grave danger, and if action by OSHA can mitigate this. Under the Nixon and Ford administrations, OSHA showed extreme reluctance to engage in such emergency rule-making. Usery denied labor's request on May 18, 1976.

In June, 1976, the National Academy of Sciences released an EPA-contracted review on the "Health Effects of Benzene," prepared by its industry-dominated Committee on Toxicology.[32] This emphasized the need for further research and study but admitted that "benzene must be considered as a suspect leukemogen," a conclusion which was, however, sharply qualified:

> It is probable that all cases reported as "leukaemia associated with benzene exposure" have resulted from exposure to rather high concentrations of benzene and other chemicals.

This statement has been exploited by the American Petroleum Institute and other industry as the basis for their view that further study rather than further regulation of benzene is needed, and in support of their objections to the 1977 proposed OSHA standard of 1 ppm.

These views of the National Academy of Sciences Committee are also in sharp contrast to the unequivocal statement that benzene was a leukemogen, contained in an updated criteria document submitted to OSHA in August, 1976, by then director of NIOSH, John Finklea, clearly reversing the agency's 1974 assessment.[33] The updated document stated, "It is apparent from the literature that benzene leukaemia continues to be reported, . . . [thus] no worker [should] be exposed to benzene in excess of 1 ppm in air." The document also recognized that the risks of leukaemia were such that no safe level of exposure to benzene can be established. NIOSH followed this move by a letter to OSHA on October 27, 1976, recommending that the standard be revised downwards from 10 to 1 ppm.

The next development was the completion, in January, 1977, of the NIOSH pliofilm industry study by Infante, which clearly confirmed excess leukaemia risks from benzene at apparently relatively low exposure levels.[34] OSHA, already sensitized by the 1976 update of the NIOSH criteria document, reacted promptly to these new studies. In February, 1977, OSHA alerted industry to the imminent and urgent need for reducing exposure levels, by issuing a "guideline" recommending a new standard of 1 ppm and outlining probable requirements for engineering controls, monitoring, and employee medical surveillance. Reaction from the industry was prompt. Without waiting for the formalization of the guidelines into proposed standards, the National Petroleum Refiners Association, in a March press release, attacked the proposal as unnecessary and unjustified, claiming that it would entail a $267 million capital outlay and subsequent annual costs of $75 million.[35]

On April 29, 1977, Secretary of Labor F. Ray Marshall and Assistant Secretary for OSHA Eula Bingham announced an Emergency Temporary Standard of 1 ppm, reducing the 25 ppm ceiling level to 5 ppm and eliminating permissible peaks of 50 ppm.[36] This was scheduled to go into effect on May 21, 1977, and to become a permanent standard six months from then. In announcing the measure, Marshall recognized the historic and critical importance of the proposal by declaring that

> [this] signals a new day for an agency which in the past has been criticized for acting too slowly when lives were at stake. . . . We are going to focus our primary attention in OSHA on major, rather than minor problems. . . . We are going to catch whales rather than minnows.[37]

OSHA made it clear that it did not regard the 1 ppm standard as safe, but rather as the lowest feasible level for the current detection and control of benzene exposure. In fact, practical instrumentation is available which is sensitive down to 0.05 or 0.1 ppm. OSHA pointed out that if this new level was not found to be adequately protective, it would then urge for the large-scale substitution of less harmful solvents for benzene. Of the 2 million workers whom NIOSH estimates are exposed to benzene, only approximately 153,000 workers and 1,200 work sites will be covered by the emergency standard. For the time being, however, gasoline pump attendants and industries using less than 1 percent benzene in any liquids or formulations are exempted. OSHA indicated that the costs of meeting the emergency standard would be of the order of $40 million, and that for the permanent standard a maximum of $500 million. These are fractions of the costs claimed by the American Petroleum Institute and the National Petroleum Refineries Association.

The practicality of the emergency standard and also of a zero exposure standard were further emphasized in May, 1977, by an Economic Impact Statement submitted to OSHA. This stressed that benzene has already been or soon will be replaced by other chemicals in a wide range of processes; that most benzene is already used by large industry in closed systems; and that the price of benzene has quadrupled from 1973 to 1976, providing economic incentives for the further use and perfection of closed systems. The impact statement also quoted the American Petroleum Institute to the effect that since 1970, 90 percent of benzene exposures in the petrochemical industry are under 1 ppm.

The proposed emergency standard came under immediate attack from several quarters, from industry as being too stringent, and from labor and the Health Research Group as being too weak. Sheldon Samuels, of the Industrial Union Department of AFL-CIO, filed a petition on the same day in the U.S. Court of Appeals for the District of Columbia Circuit, on the basis that there is no known safe exposure level for a carcinogen. Labor and the Health Research Group made no secret of their strong support for the OSHA action as a first step in the right direction.

The Manufacturing Chemists Association on behalf of the chemical industry, and the American Petroleum Institute, on behalf of ten major oil companies, strongly protested the proposed standard. On May 29, 1977, the American Petroleum Institute petitioned the Federal Court of the New Orleans Circuit for a stay of execution of the emergency standard, which was granted. The petition was transferred in June to the District of Columbia Circuit, which denied an appeal by OSHA and continued the stay. The industry's position in the appeals brief was inconsistent and questionable. Shell Oil claimed that the emergency standard would make it necessary for them to monitor about 150 workplaces. A survey by the Oil, Chemical and Atomic Workers Union however, showed that Shell owns only seventeen chemical plants and eight refineries. Standard Oil of Ohio claimed that it had only about ten respirators that it could use for the new regulations, whereas the workers in its Toledo refinery found over 100 cartridge and 32 self-contained respirators in that one plant alone. Union Oil Company of California made similar statements.[38]

Some industry groups, however, were more cooperative. Goodyear Tire and Rubber Company said that it expected to be able to meet the new emergency standard and reported that it was well along in replacing benzene in its operations. Other chemical industries, and also some universities, announced that they were switching from benzene to safer solvents, such as toluene and petroleum ether. A memorandum from Atlantic Richfield to its employees said, "We believe some aspects of OSHA's new standard may be overly restrictive, but intend to comply as quickly as possible with all of its provisions."

Public hearings on the proposed OSHA standard began on July 19, 1977. OSHA's main exhibit, apart from the 1976 NIOSH criteria document, was the Infante study. Also testifying was Louis Beliczky, of the Rubber Workers Union, who called for a stricter standard and for economic protection through "rate retention" of workers found to have toxic effects from benzene exposure. Sidney Wolfe, of the Health Research Group also testified in favor of stricter standards, pointing out that the only safe exposure level for benzene, as for other carcinogens, is zero and that this could be achieved by product substitution and engineering controls. It should be noted that support for the zero exposure standard has been clearly stated by

Donald Hunter in 1969 in his internationally recognized standard text on occupational diseases:[39] "The safe concentration of benzene vapour in a factory or workshop is zero parts per million." The Health Research Group also demanded that all employers proposing to use benzene should first be required to obtain a "use permit," which would allow OSHA to regulate more effectively, to physically inspect the workplace before issuing a permit, and to institute uniform work practices and labeling.

The industry attacks against the standard focused on three major points: They claimed that the Infante study was invalid, that the current 10 ppm standard was a safe threshold against leukaemia risks, and that any possible remaining risks were far outweighed by the benefits to society of the continued use of benzene under currently regulated conditions.

The major criticisms against the Infante study, by then published in *Lancet* (July 9, 1977), were presented by the chief industry witness, Irving Tabershaw, long-time industrial consultant and editor of the industry-oriented *Journal of Occupational Medicine.*[40] Tabershaw attempted to recalculate the Infante data so as to minimize the excess leukaemia incidence in the exposed work force. He did this by the device of computing mortality rates on groups of workers as a whole, in a way similar to that used by McDonald to minimize the cancer risk of asbestos miners, rather than by computing rates on workers at risk for specified periods of exposure time. The latter approach is essential to the analysis of mortality rates for diseases with a long latency period, such as cancer. The Tabershaw argument was published in a letter to *Lancet* on October 22, 1977, together with a counter-rebuttal by Infante.[41]

One of the industry witnesses was Robert E. Olson, Chairman of the Department of Medicine, St. Louis University, whose seventeen-page testimony, a quarter of which was devoted to listing his own academic achievements, attacked the Infante study on the grounds, among others, that none of its authors had an M.D. Olson made

it clear that he was under the impression that the literature had established thresholds for carcinogenic effects:

> The carcinogen, vinyl chloride, shows clear-cut threshold
> behavior in both animals and man. The threshold for
> tumor induction by vinyl chloride in animals is 10 ppm, a
> concentration at which hepatic glutathione levels were not
> depressed and no tumors occurred. After 25 years of ob-
> servation, doses of vinyl chloride in the air of approxi-
> mately 2000 ppm in industrial plants have been shown to
> cause tumors in man, whereas levels below 200 ppm have
> not.[42]

Stranger still was Olson's belief that benzene could
not be regarded as a human carcinogen, because human
experience had not been validated in animal experiments.
"In my opinion benzene cannot be called a primary carcinogen, because no cancer has been demonstrated in
animals after benzene exposure and no mutagenic activity
has been demonstrated in mutant microorganisms (Ames
test)." Robert Synder, Professor of Pharmacology, Thomas
Jefferson University, another industry witness, agreed
with Olson on this point: "The major stumbling block to
general acceptance of the theory that benzene induces
leukaemia has been the inability to produce any form of
this disease in mice or rats exposed to benzene." (These
statements are reversals of the usual industry position of
demanding human validation of carcinogens established in
animal tests.)

A leading industry witness was James J. Jandl,
Professor of Medicine at Harvard University Medical
School and a prominent hematologist, testifying on behalf of Organization Resources Counselors, Inc., a New
York-based consulting firm that represents about fifty top
national corporations, including Du Pont and Union Carbide. Jandl maintained that leukaemia had been caused
only by long-discontinued exposures in the 50 to 100 ppm
range. He further reported that of 4,448 case reports of

workers exposed to 100 to 1,000 ppm of benzene since 1939, which he had reviewed, "only" 169 (4 percent) had developed aplastic anaemia, and of these 148 (88 percent) had recovered completely. Jandl provided no documentation for these case reports. Apart from the fact that he found eleven deaths from aplastic anaemia or leukaemia, his follow-up period for the aplastic anaemia cases averaged only three years. The literature, however, makes it clear that the latency period for leukaemia can extend for fifteen years or more.

Jandl also supported the industry position of "blaming the victim," claiming that only hypersusceptible workers developed leukaemia following benzene exposure, and that these could be detected by periodic surveillance and screening programs. One of the flaws in this argument, apart from the fact that there was no evidence presented for it, became apparent in a report subsequently submitted by Dow Chemical Company, which found a four-fold excess of leukaemias in employees exposed to benzene in its Michigan plant, in spite of the fact that the company has elaborate pre-employment and blood screening programs for exposed workers.

The Jandl testimony included a critical but poorly substantiated analysis of the Infante study, unfavorable references to the "explosive interest" of Aksoy on "an alleged but undocumented 28,500 Turkish workers in the shoe making industry," and sarcasm directed against OSHA, which he charged with engaging in "self-serving . . . dramatization."

The final argument presented by the Manufacturing Chemists Association at the OSHA hearings summarized the views of its consultants and alleged that "the best available evidence" indicates that there are two thresholds for toxic effects of benzene, 100 ppm for leukaemia and 40 ppm for aplastic anaemia. Anyway, argued the Manufacturing Chemists Association, why worry about aplastic anaemia, especially in view of Jandl's reassurances that the mortality rate for this disease is so low? For these reasons, they protested, why revise the standard downwards, especially as this would involve considerable expense?

A permanent benzene standard of 1 ppm was signed into law by OSHA on February 2, 1978, effective March 13. The American Petroleum Institute and the National Petroleum Refiners Association have joined in filing a petition in the U.S. Court of Appeals in New Orleans challenging the new standard on the grounds that there is no evidence of health hazards at exposure levels below 10 ppm and that the health benefits of the standard do not justify the costs that would be imposed. A temporary stay of the standard was granted March 13 by the U.S. Court of Appeals for the Fifth Circuit. (As of June, 1978, the case is before a New Orleans federal apellate court.)

Regulation of Public Exposure   By early 1977, evidence of OSHA's growing concerns on occupational hazards of benzene encouraged the extension of these concerns to similar hazards in the general environment and home.

On April 14, 1977, the Environmental Defense Fund petitioned EPA to list benzene as a "hazardous air pollutant" under section 112 of the Clean Air Act. EPA did so on June 7, 1977, and recommended that industrial emissions of benzene be reduced to the "lowest possible level." This action required the agency to develop appropriate standards and abatement programs within a subsequent ninety-day period.

EPA, meanwhile, was preparing the scientific basis for its proposed action. This consisted of three key documents: "Benzene Health Effects Assessment, an External Review Draft," dated October, 1977, the chief author of which is Bernard D. Goldstein, a hematologist at New York University Medical Center;[43] "Human Exposure to Atmospheric Benzene," a preliminary draft by Stanford Research Institute, dated October, 1977;[44] and "Preliminary Report on Population Risks to Ambient Benzene Exposures," prepared by the Carcinogen Assessment Group of EPA.[45] The first document is a comprehensive literature review up to the summer of 1977, confirming the leukemogenicity of benzene at levels under 100 ppm, confirming the occurrence of chromosome damage in levels down to 25 ppm, and dismissing any suggestion that only the "susceptible" worker develops aplastic anaemia or leukaemia from exposure to benzene. The Stanford Research Institute document identified all major industrial sources of benzene emissions into the air, estimated the average and worst-case levels of exposure for various population groups, and concluded that exposure levels of the general population were in the 1 ppb range, although much higher levels could be found in the vicinity of various industries. On the basis of these two documents, the third EPA document estimated that thirty to eighty cases of leukaemia could be anticipated each year in the general population from exposure to estimated average 1 ppb levels. These are minimal estimates, as they ignore the likelihood of synergistic interactions between benzene and other environmental carcinogens, which could result in much greater numbers of leukaemias and cancers.

Flanked by its lawyers and consultants, the American Petroleum Institute, Organization Resources Counselors, the Manufacturing Chemists Association, the American Iron and Steel Institute, and other concerned industries launched into an attack on the EPA position at a meeting of the Environmental Health Advisory Committee, December 12, 1977. The Stanford Research Institute document was attacked as speculative and based merely on estimates, rather than hard monitoring data, which the industry claimed could have easily been obtained from them by the government.

Direct questioning of the industry by members of the advisory committee, however, made it clear that in the summer of 1977, EPA had requested industry to supply it with monitoring data in the general environment, but received virtually no response. Just before the advisory committee meeting the American Petroleum Institute released some limited monitoring data which agreed well with the Stanford estimates. Additionally, EPA had submitted a draft of the Stanford Report to the industry and had included all their limited comments in the final draft, which the industry subsequently attacked at the advisory committee meeting.

The industry was questioned as to the availability of the Dow study on chromosome abnormalities in workers exposed to levels of benzene believed to be under 10 ppm which NIOSH had repeatedly requested since late 1977. Dow finally made these data available on March 1, 1978. The results of the Dow studies clearly demonstrated the occurrence of a statistically significant incidence of chromosome abnormalities in a group of fifty-two workers exposed to benzene for an average period of fifty-six months, ranging from one month to twenty-six years, at estimated time-weighted average levels of 2–3 ppm.[46]

Shell Oil submitted a written statement which chided EPA for failing to differentiate between a carcinogen and a leukemogen. The statement reflected puzzlement that thresholds for benzene could not be found for the general public, since "they can be determined for workers." Finally, Shell dismissed the Stanford document as based largely on estimates rather than on hard monitoring data when, like the rest of the industry, Shell had failed to supply such information requested by EPA.

Jandl attacked the EPA position which he claimed was unscientific. However, he was unable to explain why he based his claims for the high recovery rate from benzene-induced aplastic anaemia and the rarity of leukaemia on an average of only three years follow-up.

In February, 1978, the Advisory Committee concluded that available scientific evidence strongly supported the proposed EPA action to regulate benzene as a "hazardous air pollutant."

Consideration of the health risks both to the general population and the work force from exposure to benzene is clearly going to be influenced by the costs of achieving reduction in emissions. It is likely that there will be increasing emphasis on the important fact that steps taken to reduce benzene emissions will also result in concomitant reduction of emissions of a wide range of other toxic and carcinogenic chemicals. This is certainly the case for coke oven emissions, as well as for emissions from petrochemical plants.

The NCI maps on cancer mortality have already focused attention on excess cancer rates in counties with heavy concentrations of petrochemical industries. In October, 1977, William J. Blot of the NCI published a further study based on thirty-nine counties where at least 100 persons and at least 1 percent of the population work in petroleum refining plants.[47] Blot found a 6 percent higher overall cancer death rate in petroleum counties than in matched non-petroleum counties. Much higher excesses were found for cancers of various sites: nasal cavity, 48 percent higher; lung, 15 percent higher; skin, 10 percent higher; testes, 10 percent higher; stomach, 9 percent higher; and rectum, 7 percent higher. Excess lung cancer rates were also found in female residents of the petroleum counties, clearly suggesting the role of carcinogenic emissions from industry into the surrounding community. The NCI study suggested that some of the excess cancers could also be due to other classes of carcinogens emitted by refineries or other chemical industries located nearby.

While OSHA, NIOSH, and labor were moving to reduce occupational exposure to benzene, and EPA, prodded by the Environmental Defense Fund was moving to control industrial emissions to the general environment, concerns were growing that the home and arts and crafts schools are major sources of exposure, particularly for artists, craftsmen, and hobbyists. The only current regulatory restriction for such products is a requirement under the Federal Hazardous Substances Act for special labeling if they contain 5 percent or more benzene. In May, 1977, two public interest groups, the Health Research Group and the New York Center for Occupational Hazards, petitioned the Consumer Product Safety Commission to ban benzene-containing household products, including paint strippers and adhesives.[48] The petition noted the poor or nonexistent labeling practices of the manufacturers of these products and concluded that "there is no safe way for artists, craftspeople, hobbyists or children to work with benzene in their home or studio." The Commission has not yet taken action on this petition.

Summary

Literally millions of Americans are exposed to benzene, in many instances almost continuously, from sources including coke ovens, petroleum refineries, petrochemical plants, gasoline stations, auto exhaust, and a variety of consumer products including rubber cement and paint remover. While exposure to benzene has been known for nearly 100 years to cause blood diseases, growing epidemiological evidence over the last two decades has shown that it also causes aplastic anaemia and leukaemia, as well as chromosomal damage.

Following initiatives by organized labor and public interest groups, steps were taken in 1977 by OSHA, EPA, and the Consumer Product Safety Commission to regulate benzene exposure in the workplace, general environment, and the home. Industry, led by the Manufacturing Chemists Association and the American Petroleum Institute and with the support of their academic consultants, attacked EPA estimates on environmental levels of benzene, while having failed to previously supply such information on request and in spite of the fact that the government estimates agreed well with industry findings. Industry also attempted to discredit the epidemiological evidence on the leukemogenicity of benzene and to assert that there was a "threshold" below which it was safe to expose workers to benzene, in spite of the overwhelming rejection of the threshold concept by the informed and independent scientific community. Industry also argued against accepting human evidence on the carcinogenicity of benzene because earlier studies had failed to produce these effects in animals, while at the same time rejecting more recent animal studies which appear to confirm the carcinogenicity of benzene.

Out of the industry experience in mobilizing support to attack proposed federal regulations of benzene, a new organization, the American Industrial Health Council, was spawned from the Manufacturing Chemists Association to fight current attempts by OSHA to develop "generic" standards for carcinogens in the workplace.

Chapter Six

Consumer Products: Case Studies

Consumer products represent the most direct way in which the consumer is exposed to industrial chemicals. Regulatory responsibility for different classes of consumer products is shared by various agencies, including the Food and Drug Administration (FDA), for food and animal feed additives, cosmetics, and drugs; the Consumer Product Safety Commission, for household products, including cleaning agents, flame retardants, refrigerants, and paints; the Environmental Protection Agency (EPA), for pesticides; the United States Department of Agriculture (USDA), for grading and labeling of meat, poultry, fruits, and vegetables; and the Federal Trade Commission, for advertising of all classes of consumer products, including tobacco which is otherwise virtually unregulated. Requirements for testing and labeling of the various classes of consumer products, and for evidence of their efficacy, are inconsistent. The ways the consumer is exposed to chemicals in these products are highly varied.

Smoking is generally regarded as a voluntary action, although it is usually initiated in adolescence and in response to massive advertising campaigns. However, smoking also exposes nonsmoking bystanders involuntarily. Similarly, the use of certain food additives, such as saccharin, is also generally considered voluntary, especially in the case of adults deliberately taking it in various beverages such as diet sodas and foods or as drugs. However, exposure of the embryo to the carcinogenic effects of saccharin, and other carcinogenic food additives, is clearly involuntary. Many classes of additives, such as the food dye Red #40, are so ubiquitous and poorly labeled in the food supply that the consumer, wishing to avoid them, has only limited options to do so. Consumer options are similarly limited for a wide array of chemicals, including: flame retardants in fabrics and textiles; chemical additives to cattle or poultry feed, residues of which are found in meat products; pesticide residues in food; and residues of chemicals that migrate from plastic food packaging. Drug taking, especially prescription drugs, is essentially involuntary and often without informed consent of the consumer-patient. The pharmaceutical industry and prescribing physicians usually do not make available to the patient full information on risks, not to speak of benefits.

This chapter presents a series of five case studies: tobacco, Red dyes #2 and #40, saccharin, acrylonitrile, and female sex hormones.

A custom lothsome to the eye, hateful to the nose, harmful to the braine, dangerous to the lungs, and in the blacke stinking fume thereof, neerest resembling the horrible Stigian smoke of the pit that is bottomelesse.

James I, 1604

Tobacco

Within 24 hours of setting foot on the soil of the New World, Christopher Columbus picked up the tobacco smoking habit from American Indians and later introduced it to Europe. The habit spread like wildfire, being particularly popularized in England by Sir Walter Raleigh, whose smoking, like his politics, was offensive enough to James I to eventually have him beheaded.

A century later, the Italian physician, Bernardino Ramazzini, one of the great pioneers of industrial medicine, noted that Italian tobacco workers, who prized their jobs, did so in spite of headaches and stomach disorders from tobacco dust.[1] "The sweet smell of gain," Ramazzini commented, "makes the smell of tobacco less perceptible and less offensive to those workers. . . . This vice will always be condemned and always clung to." Emotional and other considerations apart, this clinging is now seen to be the result of physiological habituation or addiction to nicotine.

Many people feel that the book on tobacco has been closed, that we know as much as we need to about its cancer-causing properties, and that whatever lessons need to be learned about the prevention of tobacco-related diseases have already been learned. But the continued study of the relation between tobacco smoking and disease is still necessary for several reasons: first, to provide further understanding on how tobacco smoke causes cancer, cardiovascular and other diseases; second, to provide information on the interaction of tobacco smoke with other environmental and occupational carcinogens and toxic chemicals; third, to further educate the public on the hazards of smoking in order to better pressure the government and voluntary health agencies, such as the American Cancer Society, to develop more aggressive approaches to regulating tobacco sales and advertising; and finally, to provide surveillance of the tobacco industry, including monitoring the effects of constantly changing tobacco products and markets.*

---

*Further research would be largely unnecessary if the government were to ban tobacco advertisement and mount a massive campaign to persuade people to give up smoking. An even more effective curtailment of the industry would result if it were forced to accept financial responsibility for each tobacco-related death.

The pattern of cigarette smoking in the United States is changing.[2] The total number of adult smokers, particularly in the upper socioeconomic groups, has been declining since 1970. However, the number of smokers among teenagers and pre-adolescents, particularly young girls, is on an alarming rise. In 1977, 27 percent of all teenage girls smoked cigarettes, compared to 22 percent in 1964. This is happening despite a growing awareness among all age groups that smoking is a serious health hazard.[3] Because of the long time from the first cigarette puff to the appearance of cancer, current trends will not affect disease rates for many years to come. Even so, the male lung cancer rate is increasing at a lesser rate than previously. The rate for women, however, continues to climb as sharply as before and may eventually reach that of men.[4]

The Chemistry of Tobacco Smoke[5]

The chemical composition of tobacco smoke is quite complex, which probably comes as a surprise to most smokers, who tend to think of smoke only in terms of nicotine and "tar." Tobacco is a cured, dried plant leaf. When burned in a paper wrapper, it produces a variety of products from incomplete combustion of the leaf, the wrapper, and the many curing agents, additives, and fillers also present in cigarettes. These combustion products are either completely vaporized or are released as a suspension of microscopic particles in the smoke. The gas phase of the smoke contains a great variety of toxic and carcinogenic gases, some of which are listed in Table 6.1. These include several nitrosamines, such as dimethylnitrosamine (DMN), nitrosopyrrolidine, nitrosopiperidine, and N-nitrosonornicotine (found exclusively in tobacco smoke), which are all potent carcinogens.

The gas phase of cigarette smoke also contains a number of other chemicals which are either tumor promoters, such as formaldehyde, or impair the lung's natural defenses by disabling the cilia, as nitrogen oxides do, thereby permitting carcinogens from tobacco smoke and polluted air to penetrate and remain in the lungs.

When the gas phase is separated from tobacco smoke by filtration, a moist substance called total particulate matter is left behind. When the moisture and nicotine are

Table 6.1   Quantities and Concentrations of Some Gaseous Components of Cigarette Smoke

Substance	Quantity (μg/ cigarette)	Concentration (ppm)	TLV* (ppm)	Activity†
Acetaldehyde	770	3,200	100	CI
Acetone	578	1,100	1000	....
Acrolein	84	150	0.1	CI
Ammonia	80	300	25	....
Benzene	67	....	....	CA
Carbon dioxide	50,600	92,000	5000	....
Carbon monoxide	13,400	42,000	50	....
Dimethylnitrosamine	0.08	....	....	CA
Formaldehyde	90	30	2	P
Hydrazine	0.03	....	....	CA
Hydrogen cyanide	240	1,600	10	CI
Hydrogen sulfide	....	40	10	....
Nitric oxide	....	250	5	....
Nitrosopiperidine	0.01	....	....	CA
Nitrosopyrrolidine	0.1	....	....	CA
Toluene	108	....	....	....
Vinyl chloride	0.01	....	1	CA

Source: E. L. Wynder and D. Hoffmann, *Seminars in Oncology,* 3(1976): 5–15; and I. Schmeltz, D. Hoffmann, and E. L. Wynder, in *Trace Substances in Environmental Health,* D. D. Hemphill, ed., 7(1974): 281–95.

*Threshold limit value, maximum concentration permitted for workers exposed to the same substance in the air of their workplace.

†CA = carcinogen, CI = ciliotoxic agent, P = promoter.

then removed, a dry condensate known as tar remains. The tar contains literally innumerable chemicals, at least 1,200 of which have been identified. Many of them are known carcinogens and tumor promoters.

The Epidemiology of Lung Cancer[6]

Many factors are involved in the association between tobacco smoking and lung cancer.

Type of Tobacco Product Smoked Cigarette smokers have a higher lung cancer rate than cigar or pipe smokers.[7] This is probably due to the fact that the smoke of cigars and pipes is more alkaline than that of cigarettes and is not likely to be inhaled so deeply. Alkaline nicotine is more toxic than its neutral form and is more readily absorbed through the mouth and nose. Because of the rapid absorption of nicotine, cigar and pipe smokers need to smoke less to maintain a given nicotine level. Additionally, cigar and pipe smokers usually inhale less than cigarette smokers.[8] Among those few cigar and pipe smokers who inhale, lung cancer and coronary heart disease rates are as high as for cigarette smokers. Additionally, cancers of the lips, tongue, mouth, and esophagus are as high if not higher among pipe and cigar smokers, irrespective of the degree of inhalation.

Quantity Smoked Nearly every epidemiological study has found a dose–response relation. The more cigarettes, cigars, or pipes smoked per day, the greater is the cancer risk.[9]

Duration of the Habit The longer a smoker continues to smoke, the greater is the risk of cancer.[10]

Inhalation Most recent studies confirm the obvious notion that inhalation increases the risk of cancer.[11] An interesting sidelight comes from studies of smoking in

France, where the lung cancer rate is the lowest in the Western world, yet cigarette consumption is among the highest. This is probably due to the fact that French smokers inhale less than Americans. One reason for this is that French smokers favor the government-distributed brand, Gauloises, made with a black variety of tobacco rather than the blond Burley blends of American and English cigarettes; black tobacco smoke is highly alkaline, while blond smoke is acidic.*

Smoking Cessation   There is ample evidence that stopping smoking decreases the cancer risk, even for long-term smokers.[12] However, the extent of relief is still unclear (see Table 6.2).

Tar Yield   It has long been assumed that the major carcinogens in tobacco smoke are found in the particulate rather than the gas phase. Tar condensates have been measured annually by the Federal Trade Commission for over a decade and the results must now be displayed in advertisements.

When filter cigarettes first became popular in the mid-1950s, their major role was the reduction of tar. This single step has led to lower death rates among smokers of filtered cigarettes, compared with smokers of high-tar cigarettes.[13] However, death rates among filter cigarette smokers are in excess of those in nonsmokers.

Only half the cigarettes smoked in the United States in 1960 were filtered. Today over 90 percent are filtered and have tar levels less than 20 mg per cigarette. Federal Trade Commission ratings have also shown a very marked increase of cigarettes with tar levels under 10 mg, as many as 28 brands being available by June, 1977.

One problem with low-tar cigarettes is that they have a lower nicotine/tar ratio than unfiltered cigarettes. To

---

*The nicotine from alkaline smoke is more easily absorbed through the mouth and tongue, allowing the smoker of French cigarettes to satisfy the craving for nicotine without inhaling the carcinogenic smoke.

Table 6.2 Comparison of Relative Lung Cancer Death Rates for Men Aged 50–69 for Cigarette Smokers, Ex-Smokers, and Nonsmokers

Smoking Habits	Death Rates Relative to Nonsmokers
Nonsmokers	1.0
Current smokers (cigarettes/day)	
1–9	3.5
10–19	8.8
20–39	13.8
40 or more	17.5
Current smokers with different inhalation practices	
None or slight	10.6
Moderate	11.7
Deep	13.9
Ex-smokers of 1–19 cigarettes/day who had quit for specified number of years	
1 or less	7.2
1–4	4.6
5–9	1.0
10 or more	0.4
Ex-smokers of 20 or more cigarettes/ day who had quit for specified number of years	
1 or less	29.1
1–4	12.0
5–9	7.2
10 or more	1.1

Source: E. C. Hammond, "Smoking in relation to death rates of one million men and women," National Cancer Inst. Monogr. *19*:129–204, 1966.

compensate for this lower nicotine content, smokers of filtered cigarettes may inhale more and use more cigarettes than would be the case if they smoked unfiltered cigarettes. Thus filter cigarette smokers may end up inhaling more tar than they would from high-tar cigarettes. Low-tar cigarettes also produce higher levels of carbon monoxide, due to relatively incomplete combustion, and increased carbon monoxide inhalation appears to promote heart disease. Additionally, there may well be unrecognized risks from the extensive use of untested flavor additives in low-tar cigarettes. From all points of view, there is absolutely no better way to deal with these problems than to stop smoking.

Histology of Lung Cancer   There are several different types of lung cancer. The most common type, *squamous carcinoma*, comprises cancers of the epithelial cells lining the trachea and bronchi and is caused by smoking. A second type, called *oat cell carcinoma*, is also strikingly related to cigarette smoking. Smoking probably causes a third type, *adenocarcinoma*, but much less frequently than the other types.

Worldwide Data   Many countries now either support limited epidemiological surveys on smoking or participate in programs developed by international health agencies. The British Tobacco Research Council, an industry trade association, publishes reports on the use of tobacco products by Britons, as does the Verband der Cigarettenindustrie in Germany.

Recently, a high degree of correlation has been demonstrated between the present lung cancer mortality rate in nineteen different countries and their per capita cigarette consumption thirty years ago.[14]* Three countries that did not fit this correlation well were France, Ireland, and Japan. The French data can be explained by the fact that smokers in that country tend to inhale less than Americans. The Japanese anomaly was thought due to the Japanese custom of *kazami*, in which the cigarette is

---

*The thirty-year lag reflects the long latency period for lung cancer.

puffed, but not inhaled. The Irish data are largely un-explained.

Differing Cancer Rates in Various Groups   Until about 1950, few American women smoked. The rapidly rising cancer rate among women today reflects the smoking habit established about thirty years ago and continued since then. The cigarette-smoking habit is now increasingly common among working people, while the white-collar classes, particularly professional men, are giving it up in increasing numbers. Also, a greater proportion of black men smoke than whites and they are more likely to use nonfilters than whites. The lung cancer incidence rate among black males in this country is about one-third greater than that for white males.[15]

Smoking and Air Pollution   Various surveys in England and the United States have indicated that smokers of a given age, sex and level of tobacco consumption have a higher lung cancer rate if living in urban areas with high air pollution levels, than if living in the relatively unpolluted suburbs. It seems likely that there is a synergistic interaction between smoking and air pollution.*

Lung Cancer among Nonsmokers and in Workers   About 20 percent of lung cancer deaths occur in nonsmokers, and the incidence of lung cancer in nonsmokers is on the increase. While there is a marked increase in the incidence of lung cancer in asbestos workers and uranium miners who smoke, there is also an increase, though a lesser one, in nonsmokers who work in these industries. An important role of exposure to occupational carcinogens in lung cancer deaths exclusively attributed to smoking is

---

*According to Schneiderman of the NCI, there has been an increase in lung cancer from 1947 to 1970 on the order of 10 to 20 percent, which cannot be accounted for by smoking.

likely. It must be recognized that the role of work history and occupational exposures to carcinogens was ignored in the classical epidemiological studies relating smoking to lung cancer. This has led to a possible overestimate of the risks of smoking compared to the risks of exposure to occupational carcinogens or interaction between the two. (This has been compounded by the fact that lung cancer mortality rates based on the International List of Causes of Disease fails to distinguish between lung cancer of different histological types, some of which, such as adenocarcinoma, are unlikely to be due to cigarette smoking and other forms of malignant disease of the lung, such as pleural mesothelioma, which is due to asbestos and not smoking.) As Schneiderman of the NCI has recently pointed out (see statement to OSHA, Docket 090, April 4, 1978), "We are unable to say how much of the risks attributed to cigarettes is a 'pure' cigarette risk and how much is cigarette times another, possibly on-the-job hazard."

It should be noted that these various epidemiological studies proving the tobacco–cancer relationships were all based on analysis of groups of individuals with varying smoking habits as compared to nonsmokers. In the absence of population groups with such differences in exposure, epidemiology cannot readily establish causal links between disease and exposure. (This is why epidemiology is of limited value for the detection of such environmental carcinogens as food additives and pesticides to which the population-at-large is extensively exposed.) One possibility that has not been adequately recognized is that some cancer cases identified in these epidemiological studies derive from exposure to occupational carcinogens, such as asbestos, as well as or instead of tobacco smoke.

This epidemiological summary would be incomplete if it left the impression that lung cancer is the only type of cancer caused by smoking. Tobacco smoking is also incriminated in cancers at other sites, including the lip, tongue, mouth, larynx, pharynx, esophagus, urinary blad-

der, pancreas, and possibly kidney and liver.* In addition
to cancer, smoking is the major cause of chronic bronchitis and emphysema in the United States. Smoking also
has a striking relationship to coronary heart disease,
stroke, aortic aneurism, and other diseases, including
peptic ulcers.

Astoundingly enough, industry claimed for some time
that the association between tobacco and all of these diseases showed that their product could not possibly be at
fault. In this they were supported by academic consultants, including the well-known statistician, Joseph Berkson,[16] of the Mayo Clinic, who protested in 1958, "I find it
quite incredible that smoking should cause all of these diseases. It appears to me that some other explanations must
be formulated." In view of the fact that tobacco smoke
contains hundreds of identifiable chemical components, it
is now surprising that smoking causes so few diseases.

Involuntary Smoking

Passive or involuntary smoking is the inhalation by nonsmokers of the secondhand products of cigarette smoking,
usually in situations not of their own choosing. This type
of exposure is potentially serious, because the toxic and
carcinogenic chemicals released from the burning tip of a
cigarette enter the atmosphere totally unfiltered. This so-
called sidestream smoke contains high concentrations of
tar, carbon monoxide, nicotine, and nitrosamines. (The
smoker thus breathes the double load of mainstream and
sidestream smoke.) Many nonsmokers are highly sensitive
to cigarette smoke, the most noticeable effects of which
are eye and throat irritation. In poorly ventilated enclosed
areas, such as bars, automobiles and conference rooms,

---

*The attributable risk" (the proportion of a disease to a given cause) of
lung cancer due to smoking has been estimated as 0.8 to 0.85 (80–85 percent); for bladder cancer, 0.4–0.5; for pancreas cancer, 0.3–0.4.

allowing one pack of cigarettes to burn has produced levels of nitrosamine carcinogens ten times higher than in inhaled smoke itself, a tar concentration of 17 mg/m^3 and carbon monoxide levels of 70 ppm.[17] In such an environment, the carboxyhemoglobin level of a nonsmoker, a measure of carbon monoxide inhalation, has been found to double. Such studies have shown that this environment for the passive smoker, especially the elevated carbon monoxide, is particularly dangerous for people with cardiovascular disease, and can aggravate or bring on anginal symptoms.[18] It is not yet known what effect such exposure has on lung cancer risks, although on theoretical grounds it is likely that they are increased.

A second category of involuntary smoker is the fetus. Many studies have found a marked decrease in birth weight of infants born to mothers who smoked during the second half of pregnancy, even as little as one cigarette per day.[19] The immediate effect of maternal smoking on the health of the child can be seen in the poorer survival rate for these infants with a lower birth weight. The 1974 surgeon general's report estimated that of 87,000 perinatal deaths in the United States, 4,600 were a direct result of the mother's smoking. The smoking mother is also 80 percent more likely than the nonsmoker to have a spontaneous abortion. Other effects also occur, such as the increased carbon monoxide in the mother's blood causing a more rapid heartbeat in the fetus. In addition, both nicotine and the carcinogen benzo[a]pyrene cross the placental barrier and reach the fetus, which at that stage in development is particularly sensitive to carcinogens. Children of smoking parents also have a higher incidence of bronchitis and pneumonia than the children of nonsmokers. Finally, the role parents play as models for their children should not be overlooked; children of smokers are probably more likely to smoke than children of nonsmokers. In spite of such evidence, the Tobacco Institute, supported by the NCI's Gori, says that there is no hazard in involuntary smoking and that there is no need for regulatory controls to protect the nonsmoker.

Financial Costs of Smoking

While it is difficult to properly calculate the financial costs of smoking, it seems clear that these are much greater than the $6 billion annual tax revenues generated.[20] Annual costs in the United States include treatment and deprivation of earnings of the 80,000 or so tobacco-cancer victims and the approximately 200,000 victims of respiratory and cardiovascular diseases caused by smoking. The costs of passive smoking have not yet been adequately recognized, let alone estimated. Other direct costs include the millions of public research dollars spent on tobacco-induced diseases, income loss from tobacco-induced diseases, and excess fire protection costs. In the latter category for example, fire protection and fire damage costs from smoking in Massachusetts alone are estimated to be $18 million and $26 million, respectively. Recent estimates of total annual costs from smoking are in the $20 billion range.

The Role of Government in Prevention of Tobacco-Related Cancer

What is the government doing to reduce the number of cases of tobacco-related cancers? The only major effort now federally funded is a coordinated set of projects administered by the NCI, known as the Smoking and Health Program. The program's fundamental premise is that since an outright ban on cigarettes is not possible now, the best compromise is to develop a "less harmful cigarette."[21] However, it is inappropriate for the taxpayer to fund this research through the NCI, especially when it is clear that the industry will profit from apparent successes in the research program. The most serious criticism of the Smoking and Health Program, apart from its token budget, is its lack of antismoking education activities. Instead of opposing smoking as its main goal, the government program merely seeks to reduce the risks entailed in smoking, thereby supporting the industry efforts to persuade smokers to persist in their habit but switch to "less harmful" cigarettes.

The avowed goal of the Smoking and Health Program is to attempt to reduce the risk for the smoker who refuses to or allegedly cannot quit. The project consists of a range of activities with this common theme. The major current tobacco blends are analyzed to identify their chemical constituents. These are then tested in animal models to determine their individual roles in tobacco cancer. On the basis of these results, an experimental cigarette is "built," which contains a minimum of toxic products. Flavor agents or additives are then added to this "less harmful cigarette" to make it more palatable to the average smoker. The possibility of toxic or carcinogenic effects from these tobacco additives does not seem to have been adequately investigated.

To oversee the smoking program, the NCI set up the Tobacco Working Group, consisting of health and industry experts, including vice presidents and research directors of Liggett & Myers, the Brown & Williamson Tobacco Company, R. J. Reynolds Industries, Lorillard Research Center and Philip Morris, not to mention representatives of major consulting firms, such as Hazelton Laboratories and Arthur D. Little, Inc. Apart from the industrial domination built into the Tobacco Working Group, research and educational activities were trivial in relation to the importance of smoking as the number one cancer killer. The Tobacco Working Group, which was disbanded in 1977, funded only a single large-scale epidemiological study on smoking and cancer and failed to fund studies on interactions between smoking and industrial chemicals in the workplace and in the general community. Additionally, the pattern of research support awarded by the Tobacco Working Group has demonstrated clear conflicts of interest in that much of the support was awarded to the members of the Group or to the institutions to which members of the Group belonged.

An example of how similar were the perspectives of

the Tobacco Working Group to those of industry is the statement by its recent director, Gio Gori, who is deputy director of the NCI's Division of Cancer Cause and Prevention, that a so-called "practical threshold" exists for each brand of cigarette, constituted by the number that can be smoked daily without increasing lung cancer risks. This suggestion was rebutted by Marvin Schneiderman, Associate Director of Field Studies and Statistics, who has demonstrated that any level of smoking increases risk.[22] Although the Tobacco Working Group was disbanded, NCI policies and programs on smoking appear unchanged.

The NCI, with a current annual budget of some $900 million, last year spent less than $7 million on all its tobacco research projects, most of which went to the Smoking and Health Program discussed above. Much of this research support is channelled through a prime commercial contractor, Enviro Control, of Rockville, Maryland. Less than $2 million a year is spent by the NCI on educational programs, in contrast with the $400 million the industry now spends annually on cigarette advertising in magazines and newspapers.

The Role of the Government in the Increase of Tobacco-Related Cancer

The extent of federal support of the industry is not generally appreciated. This support is more than amply compensated by massive revenues from tobacco sales. Federal, state, and local governments collect about $6 billion in tobacco taxes annually. In 1977, $97 million was spent by the government in direct assistance programs and in indirect support of the industry. This includes a $50 million USDA research program studying better ways to grow and process the crop, and contract-supported research at the universities of Kentucky and North Carolina. Other federal subsidies include inspection and grading of domestic crops, administration of tobacco price support programs, and loans for sales abroad under the 1954 Food for Peace program! In December, 1977, President Carter pledged continued federal support for tobacco growers, expressing the view that the assistance programs and health dangers of tobacco should be considered as separate issues.

In a speech on January 12, 1978, HEW Secretary Joseph Califano announced, on the occasion of the 14th anniversary of the surgeon general's classic report on smoking and health, an antismoking campaign particularly aimed at the nation's youth.[23] Calling smoking "slow-motion suicide," he asked the major broadcasting networks to increase antismoking commercials; called for a ban on smoking in most public areas of HEW buildings; endorsed the Civil Aeronautics Board proposal to ban cigarettes on commercial airliners; urged an increased tax on cigarettes; asked insurance companies to give premium discounts to nonsmokers; and asked the FDA to amend labeling on oral contraceptives to indicate the even greater risk of strokes and heart attacks for smokers.*

A significant omission was the lack of any reference to federal tobacco subsidies. Asked to comment on the apparently contradictory thrusts of the Carter and Califano statements, White House Press Secretary Jody Powell commented:

> The Administration does not feel that there is any logic in asking thousands of families and communities to bear the burden of economic ruin which would result if we abolished the part of the farm program because of the habits of an entire nation.[24]

The subsidies, it should be noted, go largely to tobacco conglomerates, and not to small tobacco farmers.

The reaction of the tobacco industry to Califano's speech was summarized by Raymond J. Mulligan, Presi-

---

*While these proposals are of course to be welcomed, they are proposals largely to other regulatory agencies and not yet backed up with any regulatory force.

dent of the Liggett Group, Inc., who called the Secretary "a silly ass."[25] The Kentucky state legislature went further and demanded Califano's resignation. It is clear that an administration attack on tobacco price supports would be damaging to the base of Carter's political support in the South. It is not clear how the administration weighs political expediency against 300,000 American deaths each year.

The Role of Industry

The tobacco industry did not welcome the early reports of the adverse health effects of smoking. During the 1950s, when many of these studies were just getting under way, the industry did its best to discredit them by sponsoring their own studies in search of contrary results and by supporting highly publicized and unproductive forays into improbable areas of research. These strategies were relatively successful for many years, as the few independent scientists who devoted their careers to tobacco and health research were repeatedly forced to enter public forums to respond to industry challenges.

It is important to understand the claims of the tobacco industry, because many of them are being echoed in the present-day debates over other environmental carcinogens. The standard gambit then, as now, was that the health research implicating smoking was based only on statistics and not on medical observations. If a real cause and effect sequence from cigarette smoking inhalation to cancer could be shown, the industry cried, rather than all these statistics, that indeed would constitute proof.

Another favorite industry fallback was, and still is, the genetic, or constitutional issue. This claims that some people, predestined by their genes to get cancer, are also by nature predisposed to smoke cigarettes. In simpler terms, cancer causes smoking![26] The logical conclusion of this argument is that "susceptible" people somehow should be identified and discouraged from smoking so that the rest of the population can continue to be exposed "safely." This line of reasoning is sometimes applied to the debate on exposure standards in the workplace, where other industries talk of finding and screening out "hyper-susceptible" workers.

In terms of funding research, the tobacco industry remains at consultant's length from the NCI smoking program, as it would not do to have government money paid directly to tobacco companies for health research. On April 12, 1977, the industry launched its own Tobacco and Health Research Institute on the University of Kentucky campus. In a three-day conference held in Lexington to mark the dedication of this institute, the thrust of research to be undertaken there was revealed. Of nineteen talks given by well-known speakers invited from academia, ten were devoted to the genetic factors and immune response involved in "hypersusceptibility" to tobacco smoke. Indeed, the title of the program, "Pulmonary Disease: Defense Mechanisms and Populations at Risk," only hinted at the reality. The institute appears to have adopted the tobacco industry's tactic of shifting the burden of proof away from themselves and onto the victims.

Early efforts at regulating the sale of tobacco, based on health reports in the 1950s, inspired massive counter-lobbying by the industry and tied up the Federal Trade Commission for years in administrative logjams.[27] Even when the writing at last appeared on the wall with the famous 1964 warning of Surgeon General Luther Terry that smoking presents "a health hazard of sufficient importance . . . to warrant remedial action," industry decided to dig its heels in still more firmly.[28]

The biggest blow against cigarette smoking was initiated in 1970 by John Banzhaf II, Director of a public interest group known as Action on Smoking and Health. Banzhaf petitioned the Federal Communications Commission to use the Fairness Doctrine to require TV and radio stations that broadcast cigarette ads also to give equal time to antismoking ads. The commission and the courts agreed with Banzhaf. Tough antismoking spots began giving the

public the other side of the smoking story. So strong were
the spots that the cigarette industry decided to remove
their ads from the airwaves, which had the effect of removing the anti-smoking spots also.

The tobacco industry's voluntary withdrawal from TV
and radio advertising was one of the most successful gam-
bles in the history of mass marketing. The industry thus
saved hundreds of millions of advertising dollars, which
were then used to strengthen its printed advertising,
which would continue unthreatened by antismoking
commercials. Advertising revenues to newspaper and
magazine publishers have increased nearly seven-fold
since 1970, reaching a current annual total of approximately $400 million. Also, to get further media exposure,
the industry sponsors athletic contests, such as the Virginia Slims Tennis competition.* A new organization of
health professionals called "Doctors Ought to Care" has
filed a request that the U.S. attorney general forbid tele-
vising the Virginia Slims Tournament under that name on
the grounds that such advertising is against Federal
Communication Commission regulations.

The latest marketing gimmickry is the introduction
by R. J. Reynolds of a new brand of cigarettes called
Reals. Reals were launched in 1977 with a $50 million
promotional campaign described in the press as "the most
heavily advertised cigarette introduction of all time," and
as "the biggest marketing campaign in the history of consumer packaged goods." The industry itself promises that
"before long you won't be able to turn around out there
without having Real hit you over the head."[29] The thrust
of this advertising campaign was that Reals are "natural"
cigarettes containing no synthetic flavoring or other additives. The clear and misleading inference is that Reals are

*In 1975, the Florida Chapter of the American Cancer Society offered to
cosponsor the tournament. The offer was abruptly withdrawn when the national office in New York found out what was happening.

safer than other cigarettes and should be favored by health-conscious consumers.

Senator Edward Kennedy (D-Mass.) is currently exploring new initiatives designed to deter adolescents from smoking. These are based on the use of HEW funds to support private and public educational programs on TV and through other media. Additional approaches also being considered by Senator Kennedy include mandating the use of more effective and explicit labels on cigarette packs.

The Role of the American Cancer Society

Much of the early work on the causal association between smoking and cancer was supported by the American Cancer Society. In fact, the society was one of the few major health groups to request President Kennedy in 1961 to take action against tobacco. Having made this important contribution, the society took the position that the matter was out of its hands. In its own words, the Society "had used [its] resources to uncover the health risks of smoking. Now it was up to the government to take a stand and to respond accordingly."[30]

This attitude has typified subsequent policies of the American Cancer Society. Following publication of the 1964 surgeon-general's report, the society expressed disappointment at the failure of government to act. However, when Banzhaf petitioned the Federal Communications Commission in 1971 for equal time against tobacco ads, the society refused to support him, let alone defend the subsequent FCC ruling in his favor.

Since the Banzhaf episode, the record of the society has remained mixed. It has supported ordinances to prohibit or restrict smoking in public places, to request more stringent warnings on cigarette packs, including use of the word "death," and to establish a graduated federal excise tax on cigarettes based on their tar and nicotine content. The society has also recently mounted a "Target 5" Campaign designed to reduce the number of young people and adults who smoke, and to reduce the carcinogenicity and toxicity of tobacco smoke.

The Target 5 Campaign stands little chance of success without a well-organized lobbying activity. The society, however, does not appear to have made plans to lobby Congress or to file petitions with the Federal Trade Commission and other concerned agencies. In addition to one part-time lobbyist in Washington, D.C., Tanny Pollster, whose major role seems to be to insure adequate funding for the NCI, in early 1978 the society hired Marvella Bayh, wife of Senator Birch Bayh, as a full time lobbyist. While this recent move is to be welcomed, it would not seem unreasonable to expect that the Society should develop strong lobbying activities in order to secure legislative and regulatory support for its anti-smoking programs and objectives.*

The Role of the Press

The press is now the almost exclusive medium of major advertising for the tobacco industry. The massive coverage given the Vietnam War, with some 40,000 U.S. deaths in all the war years combined, and the violent crime deaths of some 20,000 per year contrasts with the virtual silence of the press on a single agent responsible for about 300,000 preventable deaths a year. The enormous revenues generated probably account for the apparent lack of interest of the press in devoting proportionate space to tobacco health hazards.

There are, however, some notable exceptions. The *Reader's Digest*, which does not accept cigarette advertisements, has published a series of authoritative articles on the dangers of smoking over the last two decades, and the *New Yorker* has published several outstanding articles by Thomas Whiteside on the political and advertising strategies of the tobacco industry.

---

*Under the Tax Reform Act of 1976 (Sec. 4911, Tax Code Amended, 1976), tax exempt organizations such as the American Cancer Society are allowed to spend up to $1 million annually on lobbying.

The Role of the Courts

The courts have not been helpful in the past in gaining legal redress for victims of tobacco cancer. At least fifty such suits have been filed, but none has ever resulted in an award. During the 1950s and 1960s, the main argument of the plaintiffs was that the producers had failed to supply a product of marketable quality and that they had not fulfilled their responsibility to make sure that cigarettes were harmless, while implying such in their advertising. The successful defense of industry was that there had been no way to foresee the harm their product might do a consumer.

The farthest such a case has ever gone was *Green* v. *American Tobacco Co.* Edwin Green of Miami contracted lung cancer in 1956, after smoking Lucky Strikes for thirty years. A jury found in favor of the company at first, but the Court of Appeals, acting on an appeal by the heirs of the by then deceased Green, directed a new jury trial. The second jury found that Luckies were indeed "reasonably fit for general public consumption," since as one juror later told reporters, if it took twenty to thirty years to affect the plaintiff, they must be reasonably safe. This juror, however, gave up smoking after the trial.[31]

A new appeal by the heirs against this adverse decision resulted in a temporary reversal, in which the Court stated:

> We are now left in no substantial doubt that under Florida law the decedent was entitled to rely on the implied assurance that the Lucky Strike cigarettes were wholesome and fit for the purpose intended and that under the facts found by the jury [his widow is] entitled to hold the manufacturers absolutely liable for the injuries already found by a prior jury to have been sustained by him.[32]

But this consumer triumph was short-lived. In April, 1969, thirteen years after the case had been started and with Edwin Green long in his grave, the U.S. Fifth Circuit Court reversed the decision and found in favor of American Tobacco.[33] Shortly afterwards, the universal labeling of cigarette packages with health warnings seemed to virtually close the door on this type of law suit. The smoker now stands warned with every pack he buys and with every advertisement he reads, that cigarette manufacturers do not claim their product to be entirely harmless. The main impact of this warning, advocated by many to help discourage smoking, may in the end be to release tobacco companies from liability and further shift the burden of smoking-induced disease to the victim.

On December 20, 1976, Donna Shimp, an employee of New Jersey Bell Telephone Company, obtained a court injunction ordering Bell to provide a workplace free of cigarette smoke for its nonsmoking employees.[34] The court took into account expert testimony that carbon monoxide, nitrogen oxides, tar, and nicotine given off by cigarette sidestream smoke can aggravate lung and heart disorders, and that up to 10 percent of the population may be allergic to the smoke. The court ruled that smoking was not necessary to the operation of Bell's business, and that no employee should have to assume the risks of inhaling smoke as a condition of employment. The court also noted that, considering that smoking is prohibited near certain telephone equipment because "delicate parts" may be damaged, a human being should be entitled to at least as much protection.

Probably one of the most effective ways of decreasing the tobacco death toll would be to make the industry pay for tobacco-caused cancer and other diseases, as well as other national costs. Cigarette companies have in the past successfully defended themselves against lawsuits by claiming an "assumption of risk" by the victim or his or her family. This claim could be countered by the fact that the industry advertises widely to entice people, including minors, to start smoking. Such advertisements create "an attractive nuisance," often with fatal consequences. Perhaps what is needed now is a series of large successful lawsuits against the industry, still a distant hope.

The Role of Consumer Groups

The rights of the nonsmoker to breathe air unpolluted by tobacco smoke have been vigorously asserted recently by a number of public interest groups created especially for this purpose. Recent information on the dangers of passive smoking have lent further emphasis to these rights. Prominent among these is the Washington-based Action on Smoking and Health. This public interest group has appeared before the Federal Trade Commission in hearings to beef-up warnings on cigarette packages, and to impose stricter advertising rules; before the Federal Communications Commission to get "little cigar" commercials off the air and more antismoking ads on; and before the FDA to provide labels on birth control pills warning women about higher disease risks among pill takers who smoke. At the instigation of Action on Smoking and Health, the Civil Aeronautics Board voted on November 23, 1977, to ban all cigar and pipe smoking on commercial airlines and took steps that could eventually prohibit cigarette smoking as well.

Environmental Improvement Associates, the New Jersey-based group set up by Donna Shimp after her court victory against Bell, is demanding smoke-free working conditions for the nonsmoker. The first "Nonsmoker's Guide to Washington," produced by Washingtonians for Nonsmokers Rights, a project of the Washington, D.C., Lung Association, lists restaurants and hotels which offer non-smoking areas, besides tips on handling smokers tactfully and effectively. The guide also gives a good rundown on the legal rights of nonsmokers.

Future Trends

The facts speak for themselves. There is a steady and progressive overall increase in tobacco consumption in the United States.[35] The smoking habit is extending to younger and younger ages. The administration has made it clear that it opposes effective regulation of the industry and that it intends to continue subsidies. NCI expenditures on tobacco research are not only trivial but indirectly support the industry by focusing on "less harmful" cigarettes, rather than on an aggressive antismoking campaign. The American Cancer Society's efforts are weak where it really counts, at the legislative and regulatory levels.

It is true that cigarettes in the United States and other developed countries, have 50 percent less tar and nicotine and that the carcinogenic activity of the remaining tar has been decreased. It is also true that filters are becoming more effective at removing selected gases, such as volatile phenols. However, the possible benefits, in terms of reduced cancer risks, are probably counterbalanced by increased tobacco consumption and inhalation in some smokers due to the lowered nicotine content of low-tar cigarettes and due to consumers being misled by the illusion of safety of the low-tar cigarettes. Additionally, smokers of low-tar cigarettes are likely to have increased risk of heart disease from the higher carbon monoxide content of these cigarettes.

More hopeful trends, however, are that the middle class are giving up smoking, and that vigorous public interest groups are carrying the battle into the legal and political arenas.

An important recent development has been the adoption of tough public smoking regulations, effective July 1978, by the New Jersey Public Health Council under the state sanitary code. The council acted following refusal of the New Jersey legislature to address this problem. According to the new regulation, smoking is restricted in restaurants seating more than 50, and prohibited except in areas designated as "smoking permitted," which may not exceed 75 percent of the total area. The nonsmoking area must be equally attractive and convenient and have ventilation adequate to prevent build-up of levels of carbon monoxide above those outside the restaurant. The New Jersey legislature, under pressure from the hotel and restaurant lobby, is threatening to override these new regulations.

A similar move to restrict smoking in restaurants and other public areas in New York was recently proposed by Assemblyman Alexander B. Grannis (D-Manhattan). In May, 1978, Grannis charged that the Retail Tobacco Dealers of America, Inc., which had failed to register under the state's lobbying law, had illegally generated over 30,000 postcards—the largest outpouring of public opinion in this year's legislative session—protesting the proposed bill. Regardless of the success or failure of the New Jersey and New York initiatives, they clearly presage the likelihood of increasing controls and restrictions on smoking by local government.

As the antismoking campaign is beginning to gain ground among professionals and upper socioeconomic classes in developed countries, the tobacco industry is intensifying its promotional campaign in the Third World. British American Tobacco, Inc., is moving aggressively to exploit these newer markets unrestricted by government regulation or social pressures.* Efforts by international organizations, such as the World Health Organization and the International Union Against Cancer to counter this dangerous trend in the Third World are effectively neutralized by actions of the U.N. Development Program and the Food and Agriculture Organization to encourage investment in tobacco as a cash crop.

Summary

Tobacco plays a central role in the modern subculture, fulfilling emotional and physical "needs" which are assiduously and skillfully promoted and nurtured by the industry, with increasing emphasis on the enticing of adolescents. Smoking is the single most important cause of lung

---

*Philippine Kent cigarettes have about three times as much tar as British Kents.

cancer, as well as cancers at other sites, chronic bronchitis and emphysema, and cardiovascular diseases. There is growing evidence that switching to filter cigarettes may not reduce cancer risks and may actually increase the risks of cardiovascular disease. There is also growing evidence on potential hazards to nonsmokers from "secondhand smoke." Conservative estimates indicate that the costs of smoking approximate 300,000 deaths and $20 billion annually.

The response of government to this national disaster is fragmented and contradictory, reflecting the $6 billion annual tax revenues and the political influence of the Southern congressional network. The USDA openly subsidizes the tobacco industry and, with the blessing of President Carter, sponsors research to improve crop yields. Educational and research activities of the NCI are weak. They include programs to develop "less harmful cigarettes" which are made palatable by chemical additives. The FTC has banned cigarette advertising from broadcasting, but not from print. Sensitive to $400 million advertising revenues, the press has engaged in a "conspiracy of silence" to ignore or minimize the human death toll from tobacco. While the American Cancer Society played an important role in the early 1960s in proving and drawing attention to the dangers of smoking, its more recent activities, particularly at the legislative and regulatory levels, have been weak and diffuse. Although the courts are beginning to uphold the rights of nonsmokers to unpolluted air, they have failed to take the only single effective step of controlling smoking, that is finding the industry liable for the costs of disease due to tobacco.

Recent trends that may have powerful impact on the tobacco market include regulatory initiatives being developed at the state and local levels, and industry attempts to counter the possible slowing of tobacco consumption in the United States by opening up massive new markets in lesser developed countries, where the population is poorly informed on the dangers of smoking.

Artificial colors are highly objectionable on ethical grounds because they deceive, and on hygienic grounds because they injure.

Harvey Wiley,
Chief, Bureau of Chemistry,
USDA, 1907

Red Dyes #2 and #40

Food is the single most important route of exposure for humans to synthetic chemicals. In a year the average American eats about 1,500 pounds of food containing about 9 pounds of chemical additives (other than sugar and salt). Several thousand chemicals are added to food for a wide range of purposes.[1] These include preservatives, flavoring agents, stabilizers, and colors and are known as *intentional food additives*. An additional class of chemicals, which become incorporated in food during some phase of processing, packaging or storing (such as pesticide residues or chemicals migrating from packaging materials) are known as *indirect food additives*.

Chemicals added to foods and beverages solely for the sake of improving their appearance are popularly known as *cosmetic food additives*. Since antiquity, foods and beverages have, to some extent, been artificially tinted to make them look more appealing and appetizing. Until the relatively recent development of synthetic colors, "natural" pigments such as lead, chromium, and arsenic compounds, were popular additives, although somewhat unpredictable in their coloring—as well as their toxicity. More sensibly, natural plant dyes have also been used for the same purpose.

The use of cosmetic additives often entails consumer deception, in that they make a food look better and more appealing than it really is, or than its condition really warrants.[2] Current labeling laws do not require that the consumer be given explicit information on the presence or concentration of these artificial colors in foods, which are instead labeled "artificial colors," FD&C (Food, Drug and Cosmetic) or U.S. certified colors. Additionally, many colored foods, such as cheese, butter, and ice cream, are exempt from even these minimal labeling requirements. This taken with absence of alternative, uncolored foods and beverages hardly allows the consumer to exercise free choice in the marketplace. To make matters worse, there is mounting evidence of the toxicity and carcinogenicity of synthetic colors, and this is in no way indicated on the labels of beverages or foods containing them.

Natural plant dyes were the cornerstone of the industry until the latter part of the last century, when they were ousted by synthetic dyes based on coal tars.[3] The coal-tar dye industry had its origin in 1856, when an English college student, William Henry Perkin, attempting to synthesize quinine, succeeded only in obtaining a dirty reddish-brown precipitate. Intrigued, he repeated the reaction using a simpler starting material, aniline sulfate, and from the resulting black residue extracted a purple compound which was light-fast and stuck to textile fibers. Within the year, this new compound, which he dubbed mauve, appeared so useful that the Perkin family began manufacturing it on a large scale. Similarly, in 1897, a German company, BASF, discovered a highly profitable technique for the synthesis of indigo from a derivative of coal tar, naphthalene. Indigo, long one of the most important dyes, had for centuries been manufactured from plant extracts.

The burgeoning synthetic dye industry was initially a closed German enterprise, stimulated by their expertise in organic chemistry and favorable tariff and financing laws. This lucrative industry got a sudden boost in the United States during World War I, when, deprived of German products, the American chemical industry developed its own synthetic methods and new dye products.

The largest single class of dyes are chemical derivatives of coal tars. These compounds are used for coloring beverages, food, cosmetics, and textiles, as well as paints and inks. The largest single user of FD&C colors is the beverage industry. At least two of the colors, tartrazine and amaranth, you probably ate or drank recently. Their common names are Yellow #5 and Red #2, respectively. According to FDA estimates, some children eat as much as one quarter of a pound of coal-tar dyes each year.

Many coal-tar derivatives and dyes are also known carcinogens, among them 2-naphthylamine and benzidine, which induce bladder cancer in occupationally exposed workers.[4] As knowledge of the carcinogenicity of so many coal-tar dyes is well established, why should it come as any surprise that some dyes used by the food industry have also been shown to be carcinogenic? According to a recent analysis of FDA data by the Health Research Group, most of the nine coal-tar dyes (currently used as food additives) have not been adequately tested for carcinogenicity.[5]*

However, there are pressures from industry to continue using coal-tar food dyes. In this, they have been abetted by the past regulatory laxness of the FDA. The Food Protection Committee of the National Academy of Sciences, with close ties with the food industry, from which it received about 40 percent of its funding, has taken the position that use of these dyes is "legitimate."[6]

A ban on the use of all cosmetic food additives would not cause undue marketing problems. As established in a Gallup poll commissioned by *Redbook* in March, 1976, 59 percent of all women surveyed favored banning all additives used only to improve the appearance of food. Ban-

---

*As an example, the Center for Science in the Public Interest petitioned the FDA on February 15, 1976, to ban Orange B, an azo dye similar to Red #2 and used mainly in hot dogs sold in the southeastern United States, on the grounds that its safety had not been demonstrated. In May, 1970, in the absence of any FDA action, the manufacturer of Orange B, the Stange Company of Chicago, announced it would voluntarily withdraw the product from the market, as it had been shown to be contaminated with the potent bladder carcinogen 2-naphthylamine.

ning cosmetic additives might also discourage the fad for non-nutritious "junk foods" such as soda pop, candies, and cookies, in which food colors are extensively used. Instead this might encourage use of more expensive natural dyes, such as beet juice. It should be noted that support for such a ban has not come from the FDA or from scientific and nutrition communities, but largely from public interest groups, such as the Health Research Group, the Center for Science in the Public Interest, and the Consumer Federation of America.

Red #2

The Congress probably did not consider cancer when it passed the Pure Food and Drug Act of 1906, which approved an initial seven coal-tar food colors, including Red #2, or amaranth. This was done over the strenuous objections of Harvey Wiley, chief of the Bureau of Chemistry, USDA, the agency then responsible for enforcing the Act. In the wake of Upton Sinclair's 1906 exposé of the meat industry in his classic book, *The Jungle*, food law reformers were more concerned with preventing people from dropping dead from bacterial contamination and poisonous adulterants than from long-term risks such as cancer. Not surprisingly, therefore, the government permitted color manufacturers to have their products "certified" as safe, a procedure made mandatory by the 1938 Federal Food, Drug, and Cosmetic Act. This certification was supposed to be the public's guarantee that food additives were harmless. The burden of proof, however, was then on the government to demonstrate that a given additive was harmful. Nevertheless, sixteen previously "approved" coal-tar colors were tested and banned by the government before 1960, when a new set of Color Additive Amendments to the 1938 Act shifted the burden of proof, now requiring industry to prove new products to be safe. Far from being onerous, however, the new laws were actually beneficial to industry, as they allowed continued use of unsafe and inadequately tested additives by registering them provisionally.

The recent history of Red #2 is a saga of past regulatory incompetence coupled with preoccupation with industry interests.[7] Between 1960 and 1975, the FDA extended the provisional registration of the dye fifteen times. Meanwhile, Red #2 was becoming one of the most widely used cosmetic food additives, accounting for over $14 million in direct annual sales, and being incorporated in $10 billion worth of food.

In 1970 the FDA learned of some new Russian studies in which the dye was shown to induce birth defects and cancer in laboratory animals. One of these studies concluded that "chemically pure amaranth possesses carcinogenic activity of medium strength and should not be used in the food industry."[8] FDA scientists meanwhile had become convinced, on the basis of their own and the Russian studies, that Red #2 should be banned. On November 18, 1971, an internal FDA memorandum from scientists of the Bureau of Foods recommended:

> It would be prudent to limit FD&C Red #2 only to indirect or incidental applications involving food; that is, limit use of the color to such applications as food packaging where migration to food is nil, color marking of animal food additives, and to external uses in drugs and cosmetics.

The FDA, however, still refused to take any regulatory action, claiming that it could not examine the Russian data or check the purity of the dye used in their tests. In the wake of pressure by the Health Research Group and publicity about its procrastination, the FDA decided to pass the problem to the National Academy of Sciences, which initially rejected the request as too routine. However, under pressure from its Industry Liaison Panel, the academy subsequently conceded and set up an ad hoc subcommittee of its Food Protection committee. The subcommittee produced a report in June, 1972, favorable to the industry, finding "insufficient reason" to ban Red #2 or reduce its use.[9]

About the same time, the FDA decided to undertake on its own an extensive series of tests designed to finally resolve all the safety problems of Red #2. The first set of FDA tests showed that the dye is metabolized in all major organs in the body. A second group of studies explored the question of whether Red #2 causes adverse inheritable genetic mutations. Initial results were inconclusive, but the results of another set of experiments, begun in 1972, remained unanalyzed for over three years through "administrative oversight." A third set of studies showed that the dye would kill rat embryos at daily doses in excess of 15 mg/kg. Applying the standard 100-fold margin of safety used by the FDA for such toxic effects, this would result in setting a "safe level" of 0.15 mg/kg in humans, equivalent to less than one can of cherry soda daily. The FDA attempted to "resolve" this problem by proposing an unprecedented 10-fold reduction in the safety factor for Red #2, thus setting "safe levels" of 1.5 mg/kg.[10]

The big news, however, was the fourth set of FDA tests, those on carcinogenicity. These were initiated in March, 1972, using five groups of fifty male and fifty female rats each, four of them to be given different dosage levels and one to act as a control group. In January, 1973, only nine months into the two-year study, a technician noticed that one rat's identification tag did not match its cage number. Subsequent investigation revealed a fiasco.[11] There was widespread mixing of animals among assigned dosage groups, and a general neglect of husbandry that had left many rats dead and decomposed in their cages. Of the original 500 animals, 231 were unusable and 71 more had only a few of the necessary organs available for examination, leaving only 198 intact animals. Enough data were salvaged, however, to demonstrate that at the highest dose, at least, the dye induced a large number of malignant tumors in female rats surviving to two years. That was enough to finally force FDA Commissioner Schmidt to ban the food color in January, 1976, though not enough to motivate recall of colored foods from grocers' shelves.

In spite of the fact that industry could conceivably have continued its fight for years to come, particularly in view of the obvious inadequacies of the FDA carcinogenicity tests, Red #2 seems to have been allowed to die a natural death, largely because of forceful protests by consumer and public interest groups, especially the Health Research Group. Allied Chemical, one of the six major U.S. manufacturers of Red #2, also holds the patent on what is claimed to be the best—in fact, the only—available substitute, Allura red, or Red #40.

Red #40

In 1965, Allied began to introduce Red #40 into the profitable food coloring market, and contracted with Hazelton Laboratories to do the required testing. The mainstay of the Hazelton studies was a planned two-year carcinogenicity test, using a total of 300 rats fed various concentrations of the dye. However, after only six weeks of testing, an epidemic of respiratory disease killed many young animals. To halt the infection, survivors were treated with antibiotics. The total mortality was so high that the test had to be terminated prematurely at twenty-one months, leaving only 59 of the original 300 rats available for examination. Clearly, this study has very limited value as a chronic toxicity or carcinogenicity test.[12] The only finding of note admitted by a Hazelton pathologist was kidney damage in some of the higher-dosed animals that died at six months. This diagnosis was subsequently discounted by senior Hazelton staff in a "retrospective histo-pathological analysis," and all references to toxic

kidney effects were omitted from the final FDA report.[13]*
On the basis of their Red #40 study, Hazelton scientists
nevertheless concluded that Red #40 was noncarcinogenic. Other Hazelton tests, including studies on
birth defects in rats and rabbits, gave suspicious or margi-
nal results. These findings were transmitted by Allied to
the FDA in 1970, which accepted the Hazelton data and
approved the dye for use in foods and drugs in 1971 and
for cosmetics in 1974.

The FDA approval allowed Allied to go ahead with
aggressive marketing and claims of safety. In early 1971,
Allied claimed:

> Allura red has undergone one of the most extensive bat-
> teries of testing ever used for a food colorant. The screen-
> ing included two series of feeding tests — one lasting two
> years, another lasting five years.[14]

In fact, no five-year study was ever reported to the FDA.

The permanent approval given Red #40 by the FDA
in 1971 contradicted its own guidelines, endorsed by several worldwide health organizations, that food additives
should be tested for carcinogenicity in at least two animal
species. In 1974, an expert committee of the World
Health Organization refused to grant even temporary approval for the dye, "as only very limited information is
available."[15] Not surprisingly, the dye has not been approved for use in Canada, Sweden, Norway, Japan, Italy,
Israel, France, Austria, United Kingdom, or Australia.
The FDA has since claimed that they gave approval for
the dye in 1971 because they were under the impression
that it would be used only for maraschino cherries.[16]

---

*On April 8, 1976, then Commissioner Schmidt testified before congres-
sional hearings that the FDA had found major deficiencies in Hazelton testing, which it intended to investigate, stating that the firm did not examine
many animals with gross lesions histologically, reported on nonexistent slides,
and rewrote their own pathologists' reports.

Meanwhile, use of Red #40 was growing in the United States. It has become the standard coloring agent in a great many common beverages and foods, especially "junk" foods such as imitation fruit drinks, soda pop, hot dogs, jellies, candy, ice cream, and even cosmetics and pet food. With more than a million pounds certified by the FDA in 1976, Red #40 has grown in six years from zero sales to the second most prevalent food coloring agent in the U.S., behind only Yellow #5. It is now virtually impossible to eat most normal meals uncontaminated by the dye. At the current rate of consumption, a child of today will consume one-third of a pound of this coal-tar dye in his or her lifetime.[17]

Faced with an urgent need for new test data to unblock foreign markets, Allied again contracted with Hazelton in late 1974 for further studies on rats and mice. About a year into this study, the results to date were presented to FDA. Nothing of particular interest had been observed in the rat experiment. However, early in the mouse test animals started developing cancers of the lymphatic system (*lymphomas*). Furthermore, the incidence of these cancers seemed related to dosage. An FDA advisor recommended that a large number of apparently healthy mice be sacrificed ahead of schedule — at 42 weeks — in order to see whether there were any undetected lymphomas in either controls or test animals.[18] This action nearly wrecked the study, because it markedly reduced the number of mice in each group remaining at risk, that is, who could survive to develop cancer later in their lives.

On February 25, 1976, the Center for Science in the Public Interest petitioned FDA to prohibit the use of Red #40 on the grounds that it had been originally allowed into the food supply on the basis of very crude studies that did not establish the dye's safety. On the same day, Allied Chemical was meeting with FDA to inform them of "ambiguous findings" in the 1974 mouse feeding study: six of a small group of dye-fed mice had died of cancer, whereas all controls had survived. However, as the experiment proceeded the controls eventually began developing tumors.[19] The FDA responded by asking Allied to undertake a further study, but did not ban the dye. Allied agreed and contracted again with Hazelton in spring of 1976. The refusal of FDA to take any regulatory action at this stage seems contrary to its own guidelines, as spelled out by its own 1969 panel of experts. The guidelines define carcinogens not only in terms of an increased production of tumors in test animals, but also in terms of "an earlier occurrence of tumors in the treated animals than in the controls, the incidence being the same in both."

Apparently sympathetic to the position that Red #40 was industry's last good, cheap synthetic food color, the FDA convened in December, 1976, a special working group of senior researchers and statisticians, together with the NCI and the National Center for Toxicological Research. This group receives monthly reports on the mouse studies, and undertakes independent analysis of the results. In the group's own words:

> Consideration of the results of these studies by the working group will ensure that any decision subsequently reached by FDA regarding the safety and use of FD&C Red No. 40 are legally sound and scientifically supportable . . . The completion dates for the two mouse studies cannot be precisely ascertained.[20]

In April, 1978, on the basis of one completed mouse test and another then in its seventy-sixth week, an interim report by the working group concluded that "experiments provide no evidence at this time" that Red #40 is carcinogenic. This conclusion was made in spite of the fact that mice on the lowest dose of color in the incomplete study have a higher incidence of tumors than in controls. Pending "final assessment," the FDA has initiated no regulatory action.

The comment of Sidney Wolfe, of the Health Research Group, that the working group is "playing a very deadly statistical game," seems apt.[21] It is now about three years since questions of carcinogenicity of Red #40 were first raised. The FDA's refusal to have taken and to now take regulatory action, with continuing involuntary exposure of almost the entire U.S. population to the probably carcinogenic food color, constitutes an inappropriate shift in the burden of proof from industry to the public.

Summary

Red #2 and #40 are coal-tar dyes without any nutritional benefits which are added to foods, particularly junk foods, for cosmetic purposes, and in the general absence of explicit labeling which would allow the consumer the exercise of free choice. A recent Gallup poll established that about 60 percent of women surveyed favored the banning of all such cosmetic food additives.

Many coal-tar derivatives, including some previously used as food additives and since banned, are human carcinogens. There are serious questions as to the carcinogenicity, besides other chronic toxic effects, including birth defects, of those dyes in current food use. It is estimated that some children eat as much as one quarter of a pound of coal-tar dye additives each year.

The history of Red #2 and Red #40 reflects regulatory sluggishness of the FDA and the continued sacrifice of the interests of the consumer to the special interests of the food and chemical industries. Between 1960 and 1975, the FDA extended the provisional registration of Red #2 annually for a total of fifteen times, pending the submission by industry of the required toxicological data, meanwhile, allowing the dye to insinuate itself into an $11 billion food market.

In face of mounting evidence of carcinogenicity, including that derived from one of its own bungled tests, the FDA refused to take regulatory action against the dye until it finally acceded to pressure from consumer and public interest groups and in 1976 reluctantly banned the dye.

Red #40 was approved for food use by the FDA in 1971 on the basis of tests by Hazelton Laboratories, under contract to Allied Chemical Company, the manufacturer, which were so inadequate that they were rejected by the World Health Organization and most countries. With the banning of Red #2, the use of Red #40 has expanded and it is now the second most commonly used food dye in the United States. Subsequent tests have raised further and still unresolved questions on the carcinogenicity of Red #40. The FDA, in permitting the burden of proof to be shifted from industry to the public, is allowing continued use of the dye pending final resolution of these questions.

Anyone who says saccharin is injurious to health is an idiot.

Theodore Roosevelt, 1907

Saccharin

Saccharin was discovered in 1879 by Ira Remsen, then professor of chemistry and later president of Johns Hopkins University, and also a good friend of President Theodore Roosevelt.[1] Remsen, though a good chemist, was a poor businessman. Constantin Fahlberg, the student who had helped him develop saccharin, took out a patent on its synthesis in his own name and made a fortune. Remsen did not make a nickel.

Manufacture and Current Usage

The method by which Remsen originally synthesized saccharin, known as the Remsen–Fahlberg method, was its major source for many years.[2] A superior method, known as the Maumee synthesis, was later introduced to get rid of the bitter after-taste caused by an impurity in the process, *o*-toluenesulfonamide.

Saccharin is a non-nutritive and non-caloric artificial sweetener, about 350 times sweeter than sugar. The current saccharin market is large and profitable. The foods and beverages in which it is used have a net annual value of about $2 billion.[3] Sherwin-Williams is the only domestic producer of saccharin, although some is imported from Japan and Korea. In 1976, about 7 million pounds of saccharin were used in foods, 75 percent in diet sodas (a can of pop contains about 150 mg of saccharin), 15 percent in dietetic foods, and 10 percent in "table top" sweeteners. The relatively minor nonfood uses of saccharin include flavoring of mouthwashes, toothpaste, cosmetics, cigarette paper, and animal feeds. Saccharin is also used as a nonprescription drug and as a flavoring agent in prescription drugs, especially antibiotics for pediatric use.

Saccharin is consumed by about 14 percent of the general population, largely by teenagers. In comparison, and contrary to popular belief, saccharin is used regularly by only about one-third of all diabetics.

Efficacy or Benefits

Saccharin is currently approved by the FDA as an intentional food additive. The current food additive law requires proof of safety and "function," but not of "efficacy" or benefit. This means that an additive must perform its registered function. For instance, a sweetener must sweeten food or a color must color food, but this function does not necessarily have to serve any useful purpose.

Claims have been made by the Calorie Control Council,[4] an industry trade lobby, and a variety of other groups such as the American Diabetic Association, the American Weight Watchers Association, and the Grocery Manufacturers Association of the value of saccharin in the treatment of diabetes, obesity, dental caries, and other disorders. None of these claims, however, has been backed up by any published studies. In fact, the relatively scant available literature seems to indicate the contrary. The first clue to this came in 1947, when it was shown that as little as 50 mg of saccharin, equivalent to about one-third of a can of diet soda, decreases blood sugar in humans by about 16 percent.[5] Since appetite and hunger can be triggered by a drop in blood sugar, ingestion of saccharin may induce a person to eat more, hardly a good prescription for a low-calorie sweetener. These effects were subsequently confirmed in animal studies, in which it was also shown that rats fed low doses of saccharin actually ate more and gained more weight than saccharin-free controls.[6]

In 1956, a cooperative study by the nutrition department of the Harvard School of Public Health and the dietary department at the Peter Bent Brigham Hospital, Boston, on the use of saccharin and cyclamates in the management of diabetics and the obese concluded:

> No significant difference was apparent when the weight loss of users and non-users of these products was compared. No correlation was found between the length of time these products were used and weight loss, nor was the degree of overweight associated with the use of these products.[7]

In 1974 a report by an expert subcommittee of the National Institute of Medicine of the National Academy of Sciences chaired by Kenneth Melmon, concluded:

> The data on the efficacy of saccharin or its salts for the treatment of patients with obesity, dental caries, coronary artery disease, or even diabetes has not so far produced a clear picture to us of the usefulness of the drug.[8]

More recently, eminent diabetes and dietetic experts, including Jesse Roth, Director of Endocrinology and Diabetes at the National Institutes of Health, the late Max

Miller, Chief of the Diabetic Clinic at Case Western Reserve Medical School, and Ann Galbraith, Chief Dietician at the Massachusetts General Hospital and past-president of the American Dietetic Association, have all endorsed this particular conclusion of the Melmon subcommittee. Further confirmation on the lack of any substantive evidence on the medical efficacy of saccharin was presented at hearings before Congressman Paul Rogers (D-Fla.) on March 22, 1977, by Sidney Wolfe, of the Health Research Group,[9] and before Senator Gaylord Nelson (D-Wisc.) on June 7, 1977, by Donald Fredrickson, Director of the National Institutes of Health and Donald Kennedy, FDA Commissioner.[10]

Carcinogenicity Tests

Saccharin has been extensively tested for carcinogenicity in rodents over the last three decades. The majority of these studies are still unpublished, having been sponsored by industry or government, and until recently never subject to independent scrutiny. The quality of these studies is variable in regard to design, execution, and interpretation.

Approximately a dozen conventional feeding tests, one dating back to 1948, have shown that saccharin is carcinogenic in both rats and mice.[11] While each of these individual studies may be criticized on some grounds or other, taken together the weight of evidence proving the carcinogenicity of saccharin is overwhelming. The dietary concentrations of saccharin tested and found to be carcinogenic have ranged from as low as 0.01 percent, equivalent to a daily consumption of about one and a half bottles of diet pop, to 7.5 percent, equivalent to daily consumption of about 800 bottles.

In addition to cancer of the urinary bladder, the predominant tumor induced in these tests (Table 6.3), saccharin also induced cancers in female reproductive organs, and lymphomas or leukaemias (Table 6.4).

Table 6.3 Tumors of the Bladder in Rats Fed Saccharin

Study	% Saccharin in Diet	Sex of Rat	Number Animals at Risk (%)	
			Control	Treated
Lessel, 1959	5	F	0/20	2/20 (10%)
Litton, 1972	5	F	0/20	1/26 (4%)
FDA, 1973	5	F	0/24	0/28
	5	M	1/25 (4%)	1/21 (5%)
	7.5	F	0/24	4/31 (13%)
	7.5	M	1/25 (4%)	7/23 (30%)
WARF, 1973	0.05	F	0/17	1/17 (6%)
	5	M	0/16	7/16 (44%)
Munroe et al. (Canada), 1973	0.2	F	0/56	1/56 (2%)
	0.2	M	0/57	1/51 (2%)
	2	M	0/57	2/52 (4%)
Arnold et al. (Canada), 1977	5	M	1/78 (1%)	19/83 (23%)
	5	F	0/85	2/89 (2%)

Source: Based on a table prepared by Melvin Reuber, included in testimony of Public Citizen's Health Research Group, before the Subcommittee on Health, House Commerce Committee Hearings on Saccharin, March 21, 1977.

Table 6.4 Tumors Other Than the Bladder in Rodents Fed Saccharin

Study	% Saccharin in Diet	Equivalent Pop "Bottles/Day"	Animal (Sex)	Number Animals With Tumors (%)		Type of Tumor
				Controls	Treated	
FDA, 1948	0.01	1.6	Rats (M)	0/20	8/14 (57%)	Lymphosarcoma
	5	800	Rats (F)	0/20	9/17 (53%)	Lymphosarcoma
Schmähl (Germany), undated	0.2	32	Rats (M)	4/104 (4%)	6/104 (6%)	Lymphoma
	0.5	80	Rats (F)	4/104 (4%)	8/104 (8%)	Lymphoma
WARF, 1973	0.05	8	Rats (F)	0/17	1/17 (6%)	Malignant
	0.5	80	Rats (F)	0/17	2/15 (13%)	tumors of the
	5	800	Rats (F)	0/17	4/20 (20%)	uterus & ovary
FDA, 1973	0.01	1.6	Rats (F)	6/20 (23%)	14/30 (47%)	Breast
	0.01	1.6	Rats (M)	6/29 (21%)	14/25 (56%)	Breast
NIHS (Japan), undated	0.2	32	Mice (F)	0/14	3/18 (17%)	Ovary
	1	160	Mice (F)	0/14	7/11 (64%)	Ovary
Bio-Research, 1973	1	160	Mice (M)	9/19 (11%)	14/29 (48%)	Lung

Source: Based on a table prepared by Melvin Reuber, included in testimony of Public Citizen's Health Research Group, before the Subcommittee on Health, House Commerce Committee Hearings on Saccharin, March 21, 1977.

Three of the most important studies were those by WARF (the Wisconsin Alumni Research Foundation) in 1973, the FDA in 1973, and Arnold, *et al.*, in Canada's equivalent of the FDA, the Health Protection Branch, in 1977. These studies examined two generations of animals, saccharin exposure for the second generation commencing in embryo. The WARF study confirmed that saccharin over a dose range from 0.05 to 5 percent, induced cancer of the bladder, the uterus, and the ovary. The 1973 FDA study involved groups of thirty male and female rats fed saccharin over a dose range from 0.01 percent to 7.5 percent. This study confirmed the induction of bladder cancer and also found breast cancer. The 1977 Canadian study was a crucial one because it was based on feeding pure saccharin, produced by the newer Maumee synthesis, to large numbers of rats over the course of two generations. A higher incidence of bladder cancer was produced in the second generation, warning of the increased sensitivity of the embryo to the carcinogenic effects of saccharin. Ortho-toluenesulfonamide (OTS), a common contaminant in most commercial saccharin,[12] was also tested and shown to be noncarcinogenic. The details of this study have been reviewed and confirmed by a panel of ten independent pathologists.

An extensive FDA analysis of the Canadian study concluded:

> The upshot of the Canadian study is that the feeding of a "pure" sodium saccharin to rats for their lifetime, when either exposed from weaning or from time of conception, resulted in a significant incidence of urinary bladder tumors. The results confirm the findings of the earlier FDA and WARF studies. Further, the Canadian study showed that OTS was not the responsible agent, that urinary pH was not a factor, and that urinary calculi are likely not a factor. Therefore, the conclusion must be drawn that there are now at least three studies that show saccharin to be a urinary bladder carcinogen in the rat.[13]

David Rall, Director of the National Institute of Environmental Health Sciences, commented, "It's absolutely a superb scientific study—it was very well done. I think the data are pretty convincing that saccharin is carcinogenic."[14]

The Calorie Control Council has repeatedly attacked the Canadian carcinogenicity test, which precipitated the FDA ban, as being unscientific.[15] However, prior to initiating the saccharin test in 1973, the Canadian government sent the council a full plan of its intended study with a request for suggestions and comments. The council returned the plan without criticism. In October, 1976, the council invited Harold Grice, of the Canadian Health Protection Branch, to report on the progress of the study at its annual meeting in Ottawa. At that stage, Grice was able to report that o-toluenesulfonamide was not carcinogenic, although the results of the saccharin test were not yet complete. The council seemed delighted by this news, and expressed no critical comment on the design of the study. Only after the subsequent findings of the carcinogenicity of saccharin did the council attack its scientific credibility.[16]

In addition to the findings of carcinogenicity in the Canadian and other conventional feeding tests, saccharin has also been shown to induce bladder cancer in various other types of studies, including one in which pellets were implanted in rodent bladders, and another in which rats were fed saccharin after their bladders had first been primed by local instillation of very low doses of a nitrosamine-type carcinogen.[17]

Quite apart from problems of carcinogenicity, a metabolite of saccharin isolated from the urine of saccharin-fed rats, has recently been shown to induce bacterial mutations.[18]

Human Studies

A series of studies have been made on human populations consuming saccharin, with a view to determining whether this is associated with an excess risk of bladder cancer. The majority of these studies have either compared national bladder cancer rates with the patterns of saccharin usage[19] or studied patients with bladder cancer to determine if they had been heavy saccharin users.[20] Other studies have examined the incidence of bladder cancer in diabetics,[21] on the reasonable assumption that diabetics are more likely to be saccharin users than the general population. In general, these studies have not identified an excess bladder cancer risk in saccharin users, or presumed saccharin users. These apparently negative findings have been widely hailed by the industry as conclusive evidence that saccharin is noncarcinogenic, and that the extensive findings of carcinogenicity in animal tests should hence be disregarded.

Closer examination, however, reveals that the quality of these data does not support the claims of safety. The inherent limitations of epidemiology are particularly applicable in the case of saccharin. First, there may be a latency period of decades between exposure and disease, as with bladder cancer induced by occupational exposure to aromatic amine carcinogens. Second, the success of epidemiology depends on the availability, for comparative studies, of large populations of exposed and unexposed individuals. None of the studies done so far have identified and contrasted a large number of patients with bladder cancer who used and who did not use saccharin. Third, epidemiology, even under ideal conditions, is unlikely to be able to detect relatively small increases in cancer incidence. Yet, increases of this order could still result in a large number of excess cancer cases in the U.S. population.

Viewed against these general limitations, it is clear that none of the apparently negative human saccharin studies can be used to give it a clean bill of health. Large-scale usage of saccharin commenced in the 1960s, so that judging from what is known of other known bladder carcinogens, not enough time has elapsed for any significant excess of saccharin-induced cancers to have appeared in the general population. With regard to the diabetic studies, the number of cases involved are inadequate to detect any but the grossest increase in cancer incidence. Additionally, diabetics are more likely to die at a relatively young age from complications of their disease, rather than from cancer. Finally, there is no reason at all for the epidemiological studies on saccharin to have focused exclusively on bladder cancer, to the exclusion of cancer at other sites. Not only is there no necessary correspondence between the sites of action of carcinogens in different species, such as rodents and humans, but also the rodent studies clearly show that saccharin induces cancer in many sites other than the bladder.

In the fall of 1977, *Lancet* published a paper entitled "Artificial Sweeteners and Human Bladder Cancer," by a team of government and university scientists written under the auspices of the Canadian National Cancer Institute, a voluntary fund-raising agency.[22] This study was based on recent interviews of all patients with newly diagnosed bladder cancer in three Canadian provinces. Each case was then matched to other individuals of similar characteristics living nearby, so-called neighborhood controls, who were also asked the same questions. It was found that men who used saccharin had a 65 percent greater risk of developing bladder cancer than those who didn't. It was also found that this risk increased with both duration and amount of use.

Regulation and Politics

Questions on the safety of saccharin are longstanding. In 1911 saccharin was declared "a poisonous and deleterious substance" and banned from general food use on the basis of digestive disturbances and other evidence of toxicity in human studies. Until 1959 the use of saccharin was restricted to those with special medical needs who took it as a prescription drug or used it as a "table top" sweetener or in diet foods in preparations labeled:

> Warning: to be used only by those who must restrict intake of ordinary sweets.

Saccharin was first suspected of being carcinogenic in 1948 on the basis of an FDA chronic toxicity test. The questions of carcinogenicity were raised again in 1959 when, with the explosion of the soda pop market, saccharin first came into widespread general use, initially as a one-tenth mixture with cyclamates, another artificial sweetener. These questions became more pressing in 1969, when cyclamates were banned on grounds of carcinogenicity, leaving saccharin the entire diet pop market.

In 1972 saccharin was removed from the GRAS (Generally Recognized as Safe) food additive list on the grounds of the WARF study. This action had the legal force of allowing a future ban on saccharin if there was any question of safety, irrespective of the provisions of the Delaney Amendment to the 1938 Federal Food, Drug, and Cosmetic Act which requires an automatic ban on food additives causing cancer in animals or man.

A recent report to Congress by the General Accounting Office, identified twenty-three studies since 1970 which indicate potential carcinogenic hazards of saccharin.[23]

On March 9, 1977, Acting FDA Commissioner Sherwin Gardner announced a proposal to ban the use of saccharin in foods and beverages. The FDA press release stated that this action was based on the results of a recently completed Canadian carcinogenicity test in which rats developed bladder cancer after being fed daily the equivalent of 800 cans of diet soda. The press release, however, hastened to reassure that "saccharin has been in use for more than eighty years and has never been found to harm people." The press release also stated that this action was unequivocally required by the terms of the Delaney Amendment.

This FDA press release was misleading. It implied that the Canadian carcinogenicity test was an isolated experiment. It questioned the value of the Canadian study by emphasizing the high doses of saccharin inducing carcinogenic effects, while ignoring the fact that this is standard practice in carcinogenicity tests. It cast doubt on the value of the study by ignoring the dozen or so other carcinogenicity studies known to the FDA, including its own 1948 and 1973 studies. In contrasting the Canadian study with the alleged human experience of safe use, the FDA press release in no way indicated the limitations of the human studies, which are so serious as to invalidate any inferences of safety. Finally, in invoking the Delaney Amendment as the legal basis for the proposed ban, the FDA showed an apparent ignorance of its own laws, which anyway require a ban on the basis of safety requirements of general food law.

The way the FDA handled this matter has been regarded by some as inept, and by others as a deliberate attempt to provoke a consumer and congressional backlash against the Delaney Amendment, which was implied to be both inflexible and unscientific. It was well known that many upper-level agency officials, including previous commissioners, notably Charles Edwards,* were openly sympathetic to the industry position that the Delaney Amendment was an unnecessary and unfair restriction to their freedom to add known carcinogens, at supposedly safe levels, to the American food supply.

Not unexpectedly, the FDA press release provoked a sharp reaction from the industry. The Calorie Control Council barraged Congress with cables and letters in protest, and took out full-page advertisements in leading national newspapers complaining about the unreasonable and unscientific proposal of the FDA.[24] These advertisements went so far as to equate the proposed ban with an attack on democracy and freedom of choice of the consumer. The American Diabetic Association claimed that saccharin was necessary for the treatment of diabetes. The

---

*Edwards' career is a classic case of the "revolving door" between industry and Government. Prior to becoming FDA Commissioner he was a Senior Executive at Booz, Allen & Hamilton, a major management consulting firm. After a stint in the FDA, he returned to industry as Senior Vice-President for Research at Becton-Dickinson Medical Supply House. Edwards is now president of the Scripps Clinic and Research Foundation, San Diego, California.

American Cancer Society attacked the ban on the grounds that the animal carcinogenicity data should be disregarded because saccharin was of great medical benefit and safe on the basis of human experience. The past president of the society, R. Lee Clark, protested that "banning saccharin may cause great harm to many citizens while protecting a theoretical few."[25] While the American Cancer Society cannot be necessarily faulted for this ill-considered statement, it has yet to retract or modify this position.

Even the apparently informed scientific community joined in the attack. At hearings before Congressman Rogers on March 2, 1977, Guy Newell, Deputy Director of NCI, Kurt Isselbacher, Professor of Medicine at Harvard and chairman of the Harvard University Cancer Committee, and Arnold Brown, Professor of Pathology at the Mayo Clinic and then candidate for the NCI directorship, vigorously attacked the proposed FDA ban. Isselbacher, a well-known physician (although not a recognized authority on carcinogenesis or epidemiology), asserted:

> I would submit to you that in the case of saccharin, the available data indicates, in my view, that the risk to humans for developing cancer from saccharin in the amounts ingested by the average individual is remote, while the harm, I believe, which may occur to millions in the absence of a non-nutrient sugar substitute, is great.[26]

Brown recommended that the admittedly unequivocal animal carcinogenicity data be ignored, because of the alleged evidence of safe human use, and also that the Delaney Amendment be relaxed.* A lone voice on the

---

*Brown's highly qualified position on the predictive value of animal carcinogenicity tests also raised serious questions as to his fitness for the NCI directorship, as subsequently expressed in a letter of May 17, 1977, from Congressmen Andrew Maguire (D-N.J.) and Henry Waxman (D-Cal.) to HEW Secretary Califano. These questions are thought to have been instrumental in Brown's failure to gain the NCI post. Brown is still chairman of the Clearinghouse on Environmental Carcinogens, an advisory committee to the NCI bioassay program dealing with carcinogenicity testing in animals.

side of the FDA at the Rogers hearings was that of Sidney Wolfe, of the Health Research Group, who ably marshalled the scientific evidence supporting the ban.[27]

This was then the background of events confronting the incoming FDA commissioner, Donald Kennedy, who within a few days of assuming his new post in April, 1977, issued a press release in which he made a determined effort to set the record straight. Commissioner Kennedy confirmed the proposed ban of saccharin in foods, beverages, and cosmetics, but also proposed in the Federal Register of April 15, 1977, that saccharin should be made available as an over-the-counter, nonprescription drug to diabetics and others requiring it for medical reasons. The hooker in this was the legal requirement that the industry would have to show evidence of efficacy, in accordance with the Kefauver–Harris amendments to the Federal Food, Drug, and Cosmetic Act. Kennedy also explained that the basis for the proposed saccharin ban was the general safety requirements of food law, quite apart from the Delaney Amendment. He endorsed the scientific merits of the Canadian cancer tests as confirming earlier carcinogenicity studies and explained that the relatively high test doses used were in accordance with standard test practices. He also explained that there was no valid basis for concluding that human experience had demonstrated the safety of saccharin, and quoted FDA estimates that lifetime ingestion of saccharin by the general population could lead to 1,200 excess cases of bladder cancers annually.

Finally, Kennedy dismissed claims for the medical benefits of saccharin:

> I know of no other drug whose only use is to change the taste of food. I know of no other drug which is to be taken not for what it can accomplish in itself, but because the only alternative—in this case sugar—must be avoided.

Kennedy's actions could not, however, diminish the growing anti-ban and anti-Delaney sentiment, which was supported by the Calorie Control Council, the food chemical industry, and its extensive cadre of consultants. The council launched a massive lobbying campaign in the general press and in Congress protesting that the FDA ban was undemocratic and an outrage depriving millions of Americans of an important and useful additive, besides being unscientific: "We find it incredible that the new Commissioner would move to propose an action of this significance on less than scientifically supportable data." However, in spite of all the strident rhetoric on the importance of saccharin to the American consumer and on its alleged medical efficacy, the industry has not, so far, produced any scientific evidence to support these claims.

More than 100 senators and representatives have backed over a dozen bills to amend the Delaney Amendment or exempt saccharin from the ban. Congressman James Martin (R-N.C.) gathered vocal support for a bill allowing industry to continue using a carcinogen in food for economic reasons. Congressman Andrew Jacobs (D-Ind.) in the words of a recent article in *Consumer Reports,* "hit a comedic high and a know-nothing low" with a bill* calling for saccharin to be labeled "Warning: the Canadians have determined that saccharin is dangerous to your rat's health."[28]

The voices of sanity and restraint in Congress were few and far between, notably Senator Gaylord Nelson and Congressman Paul Rogers, Richard Ottinger (D-N.Y.), and Andrew Maguire (D-N.J.). Senator Kennedy attempted to dampen the hysteria by referring the saccharin problem to the Office of Technology Assessment (OTA), which issued a well-balanced report on June 7, 1977, concluding:

1. The doses of saccharin used in the rat cancer tests were admittedly high, but were valid.

---

*Uncrazying of Federal Regulations Act of 1977, March 28, 1977.

2. The most convincing animal cancer tests indicate that saccharin is a weak carcinogen in rats.

3. Saccharin is also likely to be a relatively weak carcinogen in people.

4. Though weak, for several important reasons saccharin should be regarded as having the potential of posing a significant health hazard to humans.[29]

Accepting the position of the OTA that neither the risks nor the alleged benefits could be adequately expressed in terms of the expected number of human cancer cases, Senator Kennedy stated in a June 10 press conference:

> I believe that, because of the division in the scientific community, because of the division in the OTA Panel, because of the genuine uncertainty on each side of the risk/benefit equation, the individual ought to be fully informed and then allowed to make a personal decision.

While this statement seems reasonable, it does not reflect the fact that the informational process is largely proceeding via full-page ads taken out by the Calorie Control Council and other partisan groups, and that the majority of saccharin users, adolescents, are hardly likely to be able to make reasoned decisions on the risks and benefits of saccharin. These considerations are still more cogent for the unborn generation exposed prenatally to saccharin.

Senator Kennedy also announced his intent to support legislation to suspend the FDA ban on saccharin for eighteen months to allow a detailed study of food additive law by the National Academy of Science. Kennedy proposed that saccharin-containing foods be labeled with a warning during this interim period. In his press release, Senator Kennedy appeared to rely on unsupported advice that the carcinogenic hazards from saccharin were remote and that its benefits were real.

The subsequent decision by Congress on October 17, 1977, to postpone the FDA ban for eighteen months was understandable in the circumstances. While heading off the concentrated industry attacks on the Delaney Amendment, quite apart from the proposed saccharin ban, the decision offered an opportunity for more deliberate examination by Congress of the underlying facts on risks and benefits. In an attempt to limit further public exposure to saccharin during this interim period, Senator Nelson introduced legislation on September 14, 1977, to restrict usage of saccharin to those with a specific medical requirement and to require that saccharin products be labeled with a cancer warning. Senator Nelson, moreover, warned Congress of the unwise precedent it was setting by interfering with the specifics of the regulatory process and by legislating special treatment on a product-by-product basis:

> By delaying a regulatory restriction on the use of saccharin in the food supply, Congress is risking the public health for the benefit of large economic interests. Saccharin is one of 2,100 food additives approved for use directly in food. Approximately 10,000 are approved for indirect uses, such as in packaging. Does Congress expect to react to every request for special consideration of food additives?[30]

Nevertheless, Congress subsequently passed the eighteen-month moratorium, which was signed into law on November 21, 1977, by President Carter. Subsequent to this, the Canadian government, however, banned the use of saccharin in beverages and foods on the grounds of its carcinogenicity. Saccharin is still available in drugstores in Canada as a nonprescription drug.

The voices of reason are now beginning to be raised in the scientific community. At a September 16–17, 1977, Washington conference on saccharin organized by the Society for Occupational and Environmental Health, leading protagonists discussed available data on carcinogenicity testing, epidemiology, and the efficacy of saccharin. There was a clear scientific consensus that the animal carcinogenicity data were sound and created a strong presumption of human cancer risk; that the earlier human studies provided no indication of safety; and that indeed the 1977 Canadian epidemiological study raised further serious questions as to the carcinogenicity of saccharin. In short, participants other than industry concluded that the use of saccharin entails significant risks and provides no matching benefits for the general population nor for those alleged to have special medical needs.

Summary

Saccharin is a 100-year-old non-nutritive, non-caloric sweetening agent. Formerly popular mainly among diabetics, its use has exploded over the last twenty years as a staple of the diet food and drink craze. Its major current consumption is in diet pop by teenagers, and not by diabetics and the obese. The public now firmly believes that foods containing saccharin are effective in weight control, and has been persuaded by the soft drink industry (through the Calorie Control Council) that these benefits outweigh any possible health risks.

The Calorie Control Council has also carefully cultivated the popular but mistaken belief that animal tests using large doses of a weak carcinogen are absurd, and has in this way undermined the public's trust in the use of standard animal tests for carcinogenesis, and their predictive value to humans. As a result, a powerful industry lobby backed up by popular sentiment has prompted Congress to take the extraordinary action of suspending the FDA's power to regulate saccharin until April, 1979, pending further scientific study.

In fact, there is no available evidence that saccharin is in any way effective in the treatment of diabetes and obesity. Some published studies indicate just the contrary. More than a dozen animal tests over the last thirty years have demonstrated the carcinogenic effects of saccharin in the bladder and other sites, particularly female reproductive organs, and in some instances at doses as low as the equivalent of one to two bottles of diet pop daily. Additionally, recent epidemiological studies have shown that saccharin usage is associated with a 65 percent increased risk of bladder cancer.

As a result of congressional interference with the regulatory authority of FDA, 14 percent of the U.S. population, including growing embryos, are being exposed to a carcinogen added to their diet more for its market value than for its nutritive or medical value.

Acrylonitrile

The old talmudic saying, "Don't be concerned by the bottle itself, but rather by what's inside it," doesn't seem to apply to modern experience with acrylonitrile. Monsanto, Inc., found this out at great expense, when the contents of its newly marketed plastic bottles were shown to contain the potent carcinogen, acrylonitrile.

Plastic Bottles

It all started about 1972, when Pepsi Cola and Coca Cola carried their rivalry into the search for a plastic bottle that would be lighter than glass, but tough enough to stand the pressure of carbonation. Each of the soft drink giants went to a chemical giant for help — Pepsi to Amoco Chemical Corporation, and Coke to Monsanto. Engineers at both Amoco and Monsanto then set about finding suitable plastic bottles for their respective clients. Amoco came up with a bottle for Pepsi made from a polyester, polyethylene terephthalate.* Monsanto developed its bottle made from another widely used acrylonitrile (AN) plastic, a co-polymer of styrene and acrylonitrile.

---

*Coincidentally, this polyester was selected by Hoechst Chemical Co. as a replacement for the fire retardant Tris, which the Consumer Product Safety Commission banned because of its carcinogenicity and mutagenicity.

Then came the test-marketing period. While both companies initially had a tough time interesting the public in their new products, the Pepsi bottle seems to have caught on well, and has since generated orders for about 50 million pounds, most being supplied by Goodyear Tire and Rubber Company.[1] Goodyear claims that its bottles have exceptional clarity, that they can be safely inciner-ated without giving off toxic fumes, and can be compacted for landfill and recycled. During this time, the rival AN, marketed by Monsanto under the name Cycle Safe, started running into problems of carcinogenicity, which the company had failed to anticipate in the earlier devel-opmental stages.

Carcinogenicity and Other Problems

In a series of carcinogenicity tests sponsored by the Man-ufacturing Chemists Association in the laboratories of Dow Chemical Company, AN was administered to rats by feeding and inhalation. A high incidence of cancers of the breast, brain, and stomach were found in test animals.[2] Other studies showed that AN induced a wide range of birth defects in pregnant rats[3] and mutations in bacterial (Ames) systems.[4]

Evidence on human effects was quick to follow. On May 23, 1977, the medical director of Du Pont reported, on the basis of preliminary epidemiological studies, that he had identified sixteen cases of cancer, with eight deaths occurring between 1969 and 1975 among 470 workers ex-posed to AN from 1950 to 1956 in the company's textile fibers plant in Camden, South Carolina.[5] This was nearly three times the incidence of cancers that would have been expected in a similar group of unexposed workers. Six of these were lung cancers, three were colon cancers, and seven were in various other organs.

These findings should not have come as a complete surprise to anyone. There is an obvious similarity of chemical structure between VC, known by the industry since 1970 to be carcinogenic, and AN, which should at least have triggered earlier questions.

acrylonitrile
or
vinyl chloride   vinyl cyanide

$$CH_2 = CH-Cl \qquad\qquad CH_2 = CH-CN$$

Relevance of Carcinogenicity Data to Safety of Coca Cola Bottles

AN, like VC, is a small gaseous monomer, which under the influence of heat, pressure, and plasticizers can be reacted to form long-chain polymers, and then fabricated into solids or films. As with VC, the polymerization reaction never proceeds to completion, and there is always some unreacted AN monomer in the final polymeric product. The unreacted monomer will dissolve or leach out of bottles made from the polymer into the fluid it contains. The amounts leached out will vary widely, depending on the conditions in which the bottle was fabricated, its thickness and size, and the duration and temperature of storage of the product. This problem of leaching and migration of toxic or carcinogenic monomers or other chemicals from plastic bottles or food wrappings into their contents is a problem of major importance in the food, cooking oil, beverage, and cosmetic industries. It is not just unique to AN and VC.

Monsanto at first contended that there was no detectable migration of AN into the contents of the bottles, and that the bottles met the migration limits of 50 ppb (0.05 ppm) set by the FDA for food-contact or wrapping materials. Monsanto has since admitted, however, that it did not have test methods sufficiently sensitive to back these claims. In fact, FDA extraction tests indicated that significant migration does occur.

Regulatory Developments on the Plastic Bottle

In January, 1977, on the basis of interim results of the still incomplete Dow carcinogenicity tests, the Natural Resources Defense Council petitioned the FDA to set a zero tolerance for AN migration, and to ban the plastic beverage bottles. In face of sharp protests from Coca Cola, the FDA acted on this request on March 11, 1977, and announced a ban on the sale of the bottles after they had been marketed for little over a year. The ban was made final in September, 1977. Monsanto was left with 20 million bottles worth $2 million, and with lost 1977 sales exceeding $30 million. The FDA ban also extended to the use of AN bottles manufactured by Borg-Warner for apple juice.*

Following the final September ban, J. Virgil Waggoner, Monsanto's executive vice president complained, "We do not agree with these findings. We believe that our Cycle Safe bottles are safe and that this action is unwarranted."[6]

In November, 1977, Monsanto appealed the FDA ban in the U.S. Court of Appeals, where a three-judge panel will eventually review the case. Meanwhile, in October, 1977, Coca Cola announced that they were switching to the rival Amoco bottles.

Regulatory Developments in the Workplace

Current production of AN is approximately 1.6 billion pounds, and involves about 125,000 workers, 10,000 of whom are exposed to AN on a regular basis.[7] Besides the planned use of AN in Coca Cola bottles, it is widely used in the manufacture of acrylic and other synthetic fibers,

---

*This prompt FDA action, on the basis of incomplete test results, contrasts sharply with its foot-dragging on Red #2 and stll more recently on Red #40.

such as Orlon, Acrilan, Creslan, synthetic rubber, and other plastics.

In the wake of unfavorable publicity, following disclosure of excess cancers among AN workers at Du Pont, the company voluntarily reduced its exposure limits from the then OSHA 20 ppm standard to 2 ppm in June, 1977.

In January, 1978, on the basis of the experimental and epidemiological carcinogenicity data, OSHA concluded that AN constitutes "a potential carcinogenic risk to humans." Accordingly, OSHA issued an emergency temporary standard of 2 ppm for all workplace exposure to AN. Countering industry's argument that the lengthy induction period of cancer makes such an emergency standard unnecessary, OSHA director Eula Bingham stated:

> As a carcinogen, AN can pose its life-threatening danger in a very brief period of exposure. Without this emergency temporary standard, employees would continue to be exposed to this threat during the period of time necessary to complete normal rule-making procedures.[8]

Bingham also explained her reluctance to issue an absolute-zero exposure level. Noting that even though OSHA clearly recognizes that no safe level exists for carcinogens, she explained, "In this case a level was chosen to immediately minimize the hazard to the greatest extent possible within the confines of feasibility." The emergency standard was promptly challenged in the Cincinnati Circuit Court by the manufacturers of AN, including Monsanto, American Cyanamid, Borg-Warner, and Vistran Company, a subsidiary of Sohio. At this writing, in May, 1978, the matter is before the courts.

Summary

The case of acrylonitrile (AN) is a clear-cut example of inadequate premarket testing of a major ingredient of a food and soft drink container. It is also a paradigm of the larger problem society faces as industries rush to market new products or, without regard for the deliberate process of testing needed to exclude possible public health hazards.

Following the original and unwise decision by Monsanto and Coca Cola to market AN bottles, evidence of the substance's carcinogenicity was found in test animals by Dow Chemical and in exposed workers by Du Pont. The subsequent banning of AN bottles by the FDA and regulation of AN in the workplace by OSHA have been challenged in the courts by Monsanto, the same company that has recently launched a massive national advertising campaign to prove to the public that synthetic chemicals are essentially safe unless misused, and to assert that regulatory controls such as the Delaney Amendment are "unscientific."

Nobody has shown a cause-and-effect relationship between Premarin and cancer. It does not cause cancer. It just accelerates it.

A vice president,
Ayerst Laboratories, November 23, 1977

Female Sex Hormones

Hormones are low-molecular weight chemicals secreted into the bloodstream by the endocrine glands which influence most biochemical and metabolic processes in the body.[1] The group that regulates all aspects of reproductive development and function are the steroidal sex hormones, of which three major classes are recognized: estrogens and progestins, both female hormones, and androgens, male hormones. Natural estrogens are a mixture of three related hormones, estradiol, estrone, and estriol.* The balance between the levels and functions of the different sex

---

*While estradiol is the main secretory product of the ovary, the liver readily interconverts these hormones.

hormones is exquisitely sensitive and imbalance, occurring spontaneously or following their administration for therapeutic or other purposes, seems to be associated with excess risks of cancer.

In addition to natural estrogens, diethylstilbestrol (DES) is a synthetic chemical which has high estrogenic potency, although it is chemically unrelated to steroids.

Uses

Second to tranquilizers, female sex hormones are the most commonly prescribed drugs in America today.[2] They are also extensively used as feed additives that stimulate growth in poultry, cattle, and hogs.

Oral Contraceptives   During research on progestin fertility drugs in the mid-1950s, it was found that contamination with small amounts of estrogens reversed their effects, and instead effectively prevented pregnancy. Starting in 1956, large-scale trials of oral contraceptives in Puerto Rican and Haitian women, based on combinations of estrogens and progestins, demonstrated the nearly complete effectiveness of the "combination pill," which is now used commonly throughout the world.[3] A second type of oral contraceptive is the "sequential pill," so-called because its three phase cycle consists of two weeks on estrogen, one week on estrogen and progesterone, and one week off.

In June, 1960, the FDA approved the first oral contraceptive pill, Enovid, marketed by G. D. Searle Company. This was rapidly followed by competitive products from other pharmaceutical companies, including Syntex, Ortho Pharmaceutical, and Eli Lilly. This enormous experiment, in which a nonmedicinal drug was mass-marketed without adequate prior safety testing, took place with the approval of the FDA and an uncritical medical establishment. In this they were aided by a "diplomatic immunity" extended by the press to the pill for nearly a decade after its introduction.[4]

About eight million U.S. women now regularly use oral contraceptives, representing a pharmaceutical market in excess of $100 million annually. The industry is highly protective of this market and, while enthusiastically promoting the unchallenged effectiveness of the pill, has shown extreme reluctance to admit or investigate any possible hazards involved. Searle, for example, set up a "Bad Press Committee" designed to counter any bad publicity in the medical and popular literature on Enovid.[5] In fact, until quite recently, national preoccupation with the effectiveness of the pill has been so great as to virtually repress the alarming information which has gradually accumulated on its dangers.

Estrogen Replacement   Tantalized by promotional campaigns of "Feminine Forever," five million menopausal U.S. women regularly use estrogens for "estrogen replacement therapy," with an annual market over $80 million, a market which has approximately quadrupled over the last decade.[6] The object of estrogen replacement therapy is to "replace" the dwindling supply of estrogens secreted by the ovaries as the menopause approaches and menstruation ceases.

Since Victorian times, the medical profession has tended to view the menopause and some of its discomforting symptoms as an illness to be treated, rather than as a natural process.[7] The symptoms for which estrogen replacement therapy is recommended in a standard medical text include

> hot flashes alternating with chilly sensations, inappropriate sweating, paresthesias [tingling], formication [sensation of crawling ants], muscle cramps, and myalgias and arthralgias [muscle and joint soreness]. There is an unbearable uneasiness that gives rise to manifestations of anxiety, overbreathing, palpitation, dizziness, faintness, and syncope. Untreated, a few women become chronic invalids, some experience years of ill health, and most feel gen-

uinely miserable and understandably lack vigor and initiative."[8]

In spite of this impressive plethora of symptoms, there is a growing body of informed opinion, particularly among younger, pro-feminist physicians, that what gynecologists label as estrogen-deficient illness in large measure reflects societal attitudes toward loss of fertility, as well as other social and family pressures to which middle-aged women are often subject.[9] While it is true that a small proportion of women do experience severe postmenopausal problems, these are usually only temporary. Many women, however, are untroubled by their menopause, and continue to secrete reduced but significant quantities of estrogens from their ovaries and adrenals.

Why, then, do doctors prescribe estrogens to such an extent? For one thing, treatment is immediately satisfactory in those few women with disabling problems, such as persistent hot flashes, drenching sweats, and vaginal atrophy:

> Replacement-therapy is probably the most gratifying use of hormones both to patient and physician . . . The physician can achieve brilliant clinical results with small doses of hormones.[10]

A more important reason, however, is the reliance of the medical profession for guidance on the sales-representatives and promotional literature of the pharmaceutical industry. The most popular formulation for estrogen replacement therapy is Premarin,* a brand of natural estrogens which is currently prescribed for about 13 percent of all women in the 45 to 64-year age bracket.[11]

The synthesis of DES in Britain in 1938 made available a cheap estrogenic drug which was widely used from

---

*So named because it is manufactured from the urine of *pregnant mares*.

1940 to 1960 for replacement therapy in over three million women. Unlike natural estrogens, DES can be taken by mouth without loss of effectiveness. Based on the belief that habitual miscarriage and other complications of late pregnancy are due to estrogen deficiency, DES was widely used from 1945 to 1970 for the treatment of threatened miscarriages and for preventive purposes in women with a history of habitual miscarriage. The DES dosage varied widely from 2.5 to 150 mg per day, and the duration of treatment from 3 to 212 days, most women being treated with 50 mg daily for 150 days. Apart from being ineffective, this treatment has resulted in vaginal cancer in the daughters of the treated women and sterility and congenital genito-urinary defects in their sons, apart from excess breast and other cancers in the treated women themselves.

Other Medical Uses[12]   Estrogens are prescribed for various gynecological problems, such as menstrual cramps and irregularity and genital itching, for some of which they appear effective. They are also extensively used for many other purposes for which the evidence of their usefulness seems slender. These include: acne and hirsutism, probably reflecting an assumption that feminine hormones can "soften" or neutralize these "masculine" conditions; "feminizing" ingredients in cosmetics; and, osteoporosis or thinning of bones, which normally occurs with aging and sometimes results in fractures and collapse of vertebrae, particularly in the upper back, producing the familiar "dowager's hump." An unquestionably effective but relatively minor use of estrogen is as a component in the treatment of advanced prostate cancer.

Another common use of estrogens is in the postcoital contraceptive, or "morning-after pill"[13] for preventing the risk of pregnancy resulting from unprotected intercourse. DES is still prescribed for this purpose at many university health clinics, although not authorized for this purpose by the FDA. It is also made available to rape or incest victims by some agencies, at an approximately 250 mg dosage over a five-day period, equivalent to the estrogen content in about a two-year supply of oral contraceptives.* There are, however, questions as to how effective DES really is as a postcoital pill. Quite apart from possible risks of cancer to any young woman from this massive dose of estrogen, there are also carcinogenic and other hazards to her infant if she is pregnant and the DES fails to terminate the pregnancy.

Feed Additives In late 1954, DES was approved by the USDA for use as a growth stimulant in poultry, hogs, and cattle. Its estrogenic effects make animals grow to marketable weight faster and on less feed. Poultry farmers found the increased growth and fat content of young roosters gave them the appearance of capons without the trouble and expense of castration, and, in advancing the feminine characteristics of young hens, yielded a product that according to one feed manufacturer was "juicier, more tender, and with better flavor." This effect, however, was largely achieved by increasing the conversion of feed to fat, rather than protein. Similar effects were achieved with DES fed to or implanted as pellets under the skin of cattle, two million head of which were put on DES-treated feed within three months of its availability. It has been estimated that a beef animal given DES reaches market weight of about 1,000 pounds approximately thirty-five days sooner than an untreated animal, saving about 500 pounds of feed per animal. The direct savings to the cattle and feedlot industry were estimated in 1974 as over $90 million a year. These advantages are, however, achieved at the expense of meat quality, which is reduced.

---

*The FDA will approve use of DES for such emergency situations if a manufacturer provides patient labeling and special packaging. The FDA has not given approval for any manufacturer to market DES as a postcoital contraceptive, and has withdrawn from the market the 25 mg DES tablets formerly used for this purpose.

A Department of Agriculture meat inspector, John S. White, made attempts in 1963 to draw attention to the inferior quality of DES-beef. Following threats of disciplinary action and dismissal if he attempted to pursue his concerns and findings, White resigned and subsequently published his conclusions in a farming journal in 1966.[14]

Interestingly enough, the original research on the basis of which DES was first introduced as a feed additive was conducted at Iowa State University, in Ames, which had a licensing agreement with the manufacturer, Eli Lilly, and received a royalty from its sales.[15] This research was of questionable quality, being characterized in a 1972 report of the Agribusiness Accountability Project as "an example of land grant [college] research at its worst — it is at once a service to industry and a disservice to consumers—DES has produced a royalty of $2.9 million for ISU, which means that the taxpayer has helped Eli Lilly . . to sales of $58 million."[16]

Carcinogenic Effects of "Estrogens"

There is overwhelming evidence of the carcinogenicity of sex hormones in both experimental animals and humans.[17] The pharmaceutical and feed additive industries have attempted to minimize or explain away these findings on the grounds that natural hormones or chemicals based on them cannot possibly be carcinogenic, and that even if they are the risks involved are more than outweighed by the massive benefits. There is no question that the balance between the normal production and levels of sex hormones is delicate and sensitive, and that imbalance occurring naturally or following hormone administration to humans and experimental animals is associated with excess risk of cancer. This carcinogenic effect appears to involve some interaction between the steroid sex hormones and other hormones produced by the anterior pituitary gland, particularly prolactin. We will examine separately the animal and human studies:

In Experimental Animals Natural and synthetic estrogens and progestins have been found to induce cancer in animals in experiments dating back thirty years.[18] Estradiol has been extensively tested in several rodent species, in which it produces a wide range of cancers both in reproductive and other organs. These include cancers of the breast, uterus, cervix, vagina, testes, pituitary, and lymph glands in mice; breast and pituitary in rats; uterus, stomach, and spleen in guinea pigs; and kidney in hamsters. Progesterone, the main progestin hormone, induces cancer of the ovary, uterus, and breast in mice, and precancerous ovarian changes in dogs. It also increases the incidence of various tumors in mice, rats, and rabbits that have been pretreated with other carcinogens.

When DES was first synthesized in 1938, it was also found to be carcinogenic, inducing breast cancer in male mice. Subsequent studies showed that DES was approximately ten times more potent as a carcinogen than natural estrogens. Experiments in 1964 showed that daily feeding of mice with 6.25 ppb of DES in their diet, equivalent to a daily dose of about 0.02 μg, produced breast cancers in female mice. Doubling this dose produced similar cancers in castrated male mice.*

In addition to breast cancer, experiments in 1959 and 1962 showed that feeding dogs with DES induced a high incidence of ovarian cancers. Injection of DES caused cancer of the cervix and leukaemia in mice, and kidney cancer in hamsters. Feeding hamsters with DES in late pregnancy resulted in tumors and other abnormalities in the reproductive tract of their female offspring and abnormalities in the testes of the males.[19] Implantation of DES pellets under the skin of rodents, a standard route for administration to poultry and cattle, induces cancers of the testes in mice, breast in rats, kidney in hamsters, and uterus in monkeys.

---

*These doses are in the same order of magnitude as those prescribed for menopausal women, 10 μg/kg.

In Humans   Administration of female sex hormones has been shown to induce cancer of the uterus, cervix, vagina, breast, and ovary in women, and of the breast in men.[20]

Many independent epidemiological studies have established that administration of Premarin increases the risks of cancer of the endometrial lining of the uterus from four to fourteen times.[21] These and other studies also showed that the risk is proportionate to dose and duration of dosage, but was unaffected by the particular type and brand of estrogen prescribed, whether natural, such as Premarin (Ayerst Laboratories), or synthetic, such as Genesis (Organon, Inc.) and Estrace (Mead Johnson Laboratories).[22] There seems little question that the recent dramatic increase in the incidence of uterine cancer is due to the large-scale use of estrogen replacement therapy, which started in the early 1960s and nearly tripled between 1965 and 1975. In some parts of the United States the incidence of uterine cancer has been increasing at a rate of 10 percent per year, an increase that has rarely if at all been paralleled in the whole history of cancer research.[23] The maximum incidence has occurred in women over fifty in high socioeconomic groups, those most likely to be given estrogen replacement therapy.

Premarin has also been recently incriminated as a cause of ovarian cancer, generally a rapidly developing and fatal disease which attacks about 10,000 women each year in the United States.[24] A 1977 NCI study has found that while there has been a gradual decrease in the incidence of ovarian cancer in younger women, this has been balanced by an increase in older women, the ones most likely to be given estrogen replacement therapy. The NCI study also found evidence of a strong relationship between Premarin dosage and the incidence of ovarian cancer. Besides uterine and ovarian cancer, risks of breast cancer seem to be approximately doubled by replacement therapy, this being particularly marked among those women receiving high and prolonged dosage and developing benign breast disease during treatment.[25]

Worldwide use of birth control pills, in spite of conclusive evidence of carcinogenicity of estrogen in experimental animals, constitutes the largest uncontrolled experiment in human carcinogenesis ever undertaken. This reflects the failure of both industry and government to develop any large-scale system designed to detect and report long-term adverse effects, particularly cancer. While many scattered investigations of cancer and the pill have been undertaken, their results have been somewhat ambiguous or negative. The number of women studied generally has been too few, not enough time has yet elapsed for an increased incidence of cancer to become apparent, and little or no attention has been directed to identifying subsets of susceptible women defined in terms of other risk factors (such as benign breast diseases). Nevertheless, suggestive evidence of a relationship between oral contraceptives and excess breast and cervix cancers has appeared periodically. A study involving a total of 34,000 women by New York researchers concluded that pill users had a higher cervical cancer rate than diaphragm users. While there are possible objections to the significance of these findings, including the fact that pill users tend to belong to lower socioeconomic groups who are known to have a higher risk of cervix cancer, than diaphragm users, and that use of the diaphragm could block a possible sexually transmitted cancer virus, the study nevertheless merited publication. When an article based on the study was submitted to the *Journal of the American Medical Association*, which is heavily supported by advertisements from the pharmaceutical industry, the editors insisted that it could be published only if accompanied by a rebuttal statement in the same issue. Faced with these unusual demands, the authors instead published their findings in the *British Medical Journal.*[26]

Another condition associated with pill usage over the last decade is *benign hepatic adenoma*, a proliferative liver tumor the incidence of which is now sharply increasing.[27] These can prove fatal by eroding large blood vessels, with subsequent massive abdominal hemorrhages, and can also progress to frank liver cancers.

In April, 1971, the Massachusetts General Hospital reported seven cases of a rare form of cancer of the cervix and vagina in young women aged fifteen to twenty-two.[28] In most cases, these women had first consulted their doctors because of irregular or heavy periods, and were treated with hormone therapy on the assumption that this was due to irregular ovulation. Only after treatment had proved ineffective were thorough pelvic examinations performed, including direct microscopic inspection of the cervix, using an instrument known as a colposcope. Vaginal cancers were found, in addition to other possibly premalignant lesions of the cervix and vagina called adenosis. One of these seven women died eighteen months later, after unsuccessful surgery. A common thread was found linking the victims. Their mothers had been treated with DES during pregnancy for habitual or threatened miscarriage some two decades ago.[29]

It is variously estimated that between 500,000 and 2 million young women have been exposed to DES *in utero* in the the United States since its first clinical use in 1946, and that between 20,000 and 100,000 pregnancies were treated each year from 1960 to 1970. While the incidence of vaginal cancer so far recorded is still relatively rare, vaginal adenosis occurs in 30 percent to 90 percent, the incidence depending more on how early DES was given in pregnancy rather than on dosage. There is no way of telling how many adenosis cases will in time progress to cancer. All these women will require careful and regular follow-up.

Some women who took DES in the early 1950s did so apparently unwittingly as part of a large-scale clinical trial, the object of which was to investigate the value of DES in the prevention of complications of late pregnancy, including threatened miscarriage. These events took place at the Lying-In Hospital of the University of Chicago, where about 2,000 women were each given about 10 to 12 g

DES, and an equal number received a control placebo.*
The explanation given to these women was summarized in
a 1953 publication by W. J. Dieckmann of the Department
of Obstetrics and Gynecology of the University of Chicago
and the Chicago Lying-In Hospital:

> Each patient was told that previous reports indicated that
> the tablets were of value in preventing some of the com-
> plications of pregnancy and that they would cause no harm
> to her or to the fetus.[30]

Not only were the women treated with a carcinogenic drug—evidence for this was established over two
decades prior to the test—but according to some they
were told that the pills they received were vitamins.† The
initial tests produced somewhat ambiguous results and
were forgotten until the discovery in 1970 and 1971 of vaginal cancers in the daughters of DES-treated women.‡

The vaginal cancer scare brought many of these
DES-treated mothers into contact with each other. One of
the original mothers was Assistant Secretary of State Patsy
Mink, former Congresswoman from Hawaii. Ms. Mink
filed a class action suit against the University of Chicago
and Lilly on behalf of herself and about 1,000 other
mothers in the experiment. In this she has been joined by
the Health Research Group and the Citizen Litigation
Group (both Nader affiliates). A motion by the University of Chicago to dismiss this case was rejected by the
courts in March, 1978. Other such cases which are also

---

*The DES and placebos were supplied by Eli Lilly Company, a leading
DES manufacturer.

†It should be recognized that medical ethics as then practiced did not
require "informed consent" of a patient for experimental treatment.

‡Subsequent studies have also shown that sons of the DES-treated
women have not escaped and have been found to suffer from a wide range of
congenital genito-urinary defects, and a high incidence of infertility and sterility.[31]

pending include the $100 million damage suit and a $1 billion class action for punitive damages filed in March, 1976, by three Long Island mothers against a score of major pharmaceutical companies and five physicians.

Fuel has been recently added to the fire of the University of Chicago–Eli Lilly lawsuit by preliminary data indicating an approximate doubling of the incidence of breast, besides an increase in other hormone-related cancers in the women given DES in the 1950s.[32] These data, based on an August, 1977, progress report to the National Institutes of Health by the University of Chicago, were obtained by the Health Research Group under the Freedom of Information Act. Additionally, these breast cancers occurred in younger women than in untreated controls. While the University of Chicago has challenged the statistical significance of these conclusions, they seem consistent with the results of the 1977 NCI study which found a higher incidence of breast cancer in women treated with estrogen replacement therapy.

DES, used in the past for estrogen replacement therapy, has been incriminated, together with Premarin, as a cause of ovarian cancer. Cancer of the breast in elderly men has developed following treatment with DES and other estrogens for prostate cancer. Similar cancers have developed in young transvestites taking large doses of estrogen to promote female secondary sexual characteristics. While there is little in the way of substantive epidemiological evidence on the carcinogenicity of progestins, recent studies have incriminated progesterone as a cause of ovarian cysts.

Other Toxic Effects of Estrogens

Apart from cancer, various studies from all over the world over the last twenty years have focused suspicion on the pill as a cause of premature heart disease and stroke.[33] The FDA decision to market the first oral contraceptive in

1960 was based on tests with only 132 women for only 38 months. On this basis was begun the first mass prescription in medical history of a nonmedical drug. Early studies suggesting blood clotting (*thrombo-embolic* disease) and other dangers of the pill were countered by authoritative FDA reassurances, such as those by Joseph Sawdusk, FDA's top physician and later vice-president of Parke Davis, that the pill is "safe when given under a doctor's supervision." The FDA was joined in these assurances by the medical journals, the medical establishment, leading physicians such as John Rock and Alan Guttmacher of Planned Parenthood, and the promotional literature of the industry.

In January, 1966, when the long-compliant FDA Commissioner George P. Larrick was replaced by James L. Goddard, an advisory committee warned of possible blood clotting problems due to oral contraceptives. The press, which had for years been silent on the dangers of the pill, belatedly and slowly started covering the growing information on this problem. In May 1968, a study published in the *British Medical Journal* clearly implicated the pill with excess thrombo-embolic disease, in which a blood clot forms within the vein and if dislodged can lead to a fatal stroke.[34] The FDA obtained agreement from the manufacturers to include a warning about blood clotting in the package labeling given to the pharmacists, but without any direct warning to the patient. In August, 1969, the FDA Advisory Committee on Obstetrics and Gynecology confirmed the thrombo-embolic risks of the pill and summarized the data on experimental carcinogenicity of estrogens, but nevertheless concluded that the pill was "safe."[35]

In January, 1970, Senator Gaylord Nelson held widely publicized hearings on the safety of oral contraceptives before his Subcommittee on Monopoly. The hearings summarized the known hazards of the pill and made it clear that users were not being adequately informed of these. It was also emphasized that the pill had not been adequately tested prior to its massive use. Industry, the FDA, and the medical establishment, including family planning and birth control organizations, on the other hand, insisted that the pill was perfectly safe and that users were being told all they needed to know. Nevertheless, after the hearings, about 19 percent of pill users quit.[36] Critics of Nelson claimed 100,000 unwanted pregnancies resulted and dubbed them "Nelson babies," an allegation which has never been substantiated.

These issues came to a climax in a 1977 publication of two British studies in *Lancet,* one conducted by the Royal College of General Practitioners on 46,000 women, and the other on 17,000 women by the Oxford Family Planning Association.[37] Both studies concluded that death from coronary heart disease, hypertension, and stroke were five times more common among pill users than controls, and ten times as frequent among pill users who had been on the pill for over five years. The excess death rate among pill users was also further increased by cigarette smoking. Both studies recommended that all women over thirty-five years should stop taking the pill, that women between thirty and thirty-five should consider changing to different contraceptives, but that women under thirty need not worry. These findings supplemented previous knowledge that estrogen usage increases the risk of thrombo-embolic disease. Pill usage also affects fat metabolism, increasing serum triglycerides and thereby increasing the risk of coronary artery disease, especially in the presence of other risk factors such as smoking or hypertension. Both the pill and estrogen replacement therapy increase the risks of gall bladder disease by two to three times.

Several reports have also suggested a marked association between intrauterine exposure and congenital birth defects of the heart and limbs. The use of hormonal tests for pregnancy has also been incriminated as a cause of congenital defects of the central nervous system.

Recent Occupational Problems

In 1966, the Oil, Chemical, and Atomic Workers Union organized the Dawes Laboratories in Chicago Heights, Illinois, an agricultural products and DES manufacturer.[38] Ventilation was practically nonexistent and the whole interior of the plant, including the cafeteria and toilets, was covered by dust containing as high as 10 percent DES by weight. From 1968 to 1971, many workers complained of sexual impotence and some men developed enlarged breasts, in one case requiring surgical removal.

In their subsequent contract negotiation, in 1971, the union demanded and obtained full medical examinations of all workers, provided by the company, as well as a commitment to improve working conditions. The union also requested an independent evaluation program of the effects of exposure to DES. On this program, eight male employees were admitted in 1973 to the National Institutes of Health Hospital in Bethesda, Maryland, where they were given testosterone therapy to relieve some of the symptoms. Following this evaluation, medical consultants of the union explained to the workers the effects of DES, and the workers renewed their demands for improved working conditions.

The years passed by without the plant being cleaned up. The recommendations for improved industrial hygiene made by Dawes' own insurance company were ignored. Then, in March, 1977, the Oil, Chemical, and Atomic Workers Union again inspected the plant and confirmed that conditions had not materially changed since 1971. This was followed by an OSHA inspection which resulted in a citation for willful negligence and a fine of $46,000, one of the largest ever imposed for a health violation. Dawes will probably never pay the full amount, as the Act permits appeal of the dollar value of fines based upon subsequent cleanup or even a mere show of "good faith." The company has since appealed and the fine was lowered to $21,000. An interesting legal sideline is that

OSHA was obliged to cite the "General Duty Clause" of the Occupational Safety and Health Act as authority for these actions, since there is no occupational standard for DES.[39]

A similar recent incident occurred at an oral contraceptive plant in Puerto Rico. Following complaints of enlarged breasts in male employees and menstrual disorders in females, NIOSH investigated the plant in May, 1976, and found evidence of excessive estrogen exposure. In this case, management instituted the necessary dust control measures and improved work practices, which appear to have resolved the problem.[40]

Regulatory Developments

The large-scale use of female sex hormones as both feed additives and human drugs poses two sets of regulatory problems which, however different, are linked by the common theme of cancer risk.

Feed Additives   It is currently the responsibility of the feed additive and animal drug manufacturers, when submitting an application for approval, to provide "a description of practicable methods" for the specific analysis and routine monitoring of animal drug residues in foods. The FDA has responsibility for approving the registration and use of human drugs and feed additives, besides other animal drugs, and for setting tolerances for permissible residues of animal feed additives and drugs in meat and other dairy products.*

---

*From a regulatory standpoint, there are three kinds of residues: first, *permissible residues* of noncarcinogenic drugs below prescribed tolerance levels; second, illegal residues of noncarcinogenic drugs above tolerance levels, or *excessive residues;* third, illegal residues of any detectable level of carcinogenic drugs, *prohibited residues.* The USDA has authority to prevent the occurrence of illegal, prohibited, and excessive residues by monitoring meat and products from food-producing animals and birds, generally at the time of slaughter, using FDA-approved methods.

Although the carcinogenicity of DES was established in tests as early as 1938,[41] the USDA in 1947 approved the fattening and caponizing of chickens by implanting 15 mg pellets under the skin of the necks. Warning signals of trouble came quickly. Within three years the USDA was sued by mink ranchers whose animals had become sterile after eating the heads and necks of chickens containing DES residues. The USDA still allowed the use of DES in chickens. In 1954 permissible uses of DES were extended to cattle, which could be fed with 5 to 10 mg daily, providing treatment was stopped forty-eight hours prior to slaughter in order to prevent residues occurring in the meat. Highest residue levels are found in liver, and these are about ten times greater than in muscle meat.

Concerned by the mounting evidence on the carcinogenicity of DES, which the FDA seemed to be ignoring, Congressman James Delaney (D-N.Y.) introduced a statement to this effect in the Congressional Record in February, 1957.[42] The FDA immediately denied that DES was a carcinogen. Ensuing congressional concerns with DES were one of the main factors leading to the passage of the 1958 Delaney Amendment to the Federal Food, Drug, and Cosmetic Act which flatly prohibited the introduction to food of additives found to be carcinogenic in either animals or humans. At that time, the amendment made no distinction between chemicals added directly to food as food additives, and those which might enter human food indirectly through the diet of food-producing animals. This amendment, however, did not prevent the continued use of DES, as the FDA argued the technicality that it could not be applied retroactively to DES but could only be used for future applications on carcinogenic food additives.[43]

Using improved analytic techniques, residues were found in poultry in 1959, each carcass containing about 25 μg DES, about a thousand times greater than daily doses found to induce breast cancer in mice. The situation was only resolved with the decision to ban the use of DES in chickens and the willingness of the USDA to buy and remove from the market an estimated $10 million worth of treated poultry. The poultry ruling did not affect the use of DES for cattle and sheep, as residues had not apparently been found in their meat. Alarmed by the poultry ban, the industry lobby introduced the Kefauver-Harris 1962 Drug Amendment to the 1938 Federal Food, Drug, and Cosmetic Act. This is known as the Feed Additive Amendment or the DES Clause, and it specifically exempted DES and other carcinogenic feed additives, such as dinestrol diacetate, from the Delaney requirement. Their use was allowed, provided that the manufacturer made available a "prescribed and approved" monitoring method for the detection of prohibited residues, and that no residues were left when the additive was used according to "label directions that are reasonably certain to be followed in practice." The clear implication here was that any DES subsequently found in meat would be considered the result of bad feeding practices and not due to any inherent danger of DES. In shifting the burden of responsibility from the legislative to the executive branch of government, Congress seemed willing to gamble on the regulatory discretion of the FDA and USDA.[44]

The USDA and FDA rarely checked on compliance. They sampled only a relatively small number of carcasses with biological assay techniques which were impractical, non-specific, and sensitive only to 10 ppb, in spite of the fact that DES was known to produce breast cancer in mice at levels down to 6.5 ppb. The agencies took the additional precaution of keeping results of these samplings confidential. Meanwhile, use of DES was growing. By 1970, 75 percent of all beef produced in the United States, 30 million head per year, were fed with DES. Responsive to the growing DES market and to a request of Eli Lilly Company, the FDA in 1970 doubled permitted dosage levels to 20 mg per day per animal. The FDA, however, did not then take the opportunity to enforce the 1962 DES Clause requiring the manufacturer to provide a sensitive monitoring method for residues.

With the 1971 discovery of vaginal cancer in the daughters of DES-treated women, the USDA–FDA position on DES came under scrutiny and attack. Agency information was discovered proving that DES residues had been found in beef liver as far back as 1966, when 1.1 percent of 1,023 samples tested were positive, and again in 1967 when 2.6 percent of 495 samples were positive.* As typically found, DES residues of 2 ppb are equivalent to about 0.3 μg in a 150 gm serving of liver, an appreciable addition to natural hormonal levels.[45]

In August, 1971, using a newly introduced chromatographic technique sensitive to 2 ppb, the USDA found high DES residues in the livers of twelve cattle and sheep, in one case as high as 37 ppb.[46] These findings, while initially concealed, created a furor, especially since the USDA had previously denied finding any residues at all. Senator William Proxmire (D-Wisc.), introduced legislation to ban DES as a feed additive, and Representative L. Fountain (D-N.C.) held extensive hearings in November, 1971. DES critics pointed out that the additive had already been banned in over twenty foreign countries, that most Europeans would not buy U.S. meat because of its DES content, that any use of DES must obviously lead to residues in meat, and that there was an overwhelming scientific consensus that there was no known way for setting safe levels for carcinogens. The industry, supported by Agriculture Secretary Earl L. Butz and FDA Commissioner Charles C. Edwards, fought against a ban, claiming that this would cost from $300 to $400 million a year, and that DES residues in meat were so small as to be toxicologically insignificant.

In January, 1972, the USDA attempted to answer growing criticism by extending the 48-hour withdrawal period to 7 days, cattlemen being put on their honor to sign a "certificate of compliance" to this effect. The belief of the safety of a seven-day withdrawal seems to have

---

*The number of cattle sampled continued to dwindle and by 1970 was down to 192.

been based on a single FDA experiment with one cow fed one dose of DES.[47] Furthermore, such withdrawal periods are not only unenforceable, but unresponsive to the standard practice of slaughtering and selling just when the market prices are highest.

Following the finding of DES residues in nearly 2 percent of all cattle tested (in spite of the seven-day withdrawal period), the FDA announced its intent to hold further hearings in June, 1972. The meat lobby objected that the hearings were unnecessary, and public interest groups claimed that more than enough was known to ban without hearings. When asked, the American Cancer Society declined to take any position on the matter. By August, the FDA changed its mind and decided to cancel the hearings. The indecision continued until March, 1973, when the Senate Commerce Committee held hearings on the Federal Food Inspection Act of 1973, largely addressing problems of DES and other animal drugs, in which concerns on the deficiencies in Federal monitoring programs for carcinogenic residues in meat and dairy products were vigorously expressed. These concerns were heightened by the discovery that the FDA was also in violation with regard to a wide range of other carcinogenic animal drugs, as it had no practicable test methods for detecting and measuring prohibited residues of seventeen of nineteen drugs then in widespread use.* Such regulatory casualness was all the more serious in view of the burgeoning market in new animal drugs and feed additives, which by 1971 had increased to 1,372, including approximately twenty carcinogenic additives, a gain of nearly 25 percent over 1970 figures.[48]

---

*Dinestrol diacetate, for example, had been incriminated as a cause of vaginal cancer in young women whose mothers were given it in early pregnancy. In August, 1972, the FDA belatedly requested the manufacturer to provide an appropriate test method, as this drug had been illegally registered in the absence of such a method. Although the manufacturer failed to respond, the drug was still in extensive use in chicken and turkey feed at the time of the hearings seven months later.

Still further concerns at the 1973 Commerce Committee hearings were provoked by a report of the National Academy of Sciences which found that there was only clear-cut evidence of efficacy for 18 percent of 706 animal drugs in current use. The highlight of the hearings, however, was the introduction of an internal FDA memorandum from K. R. Johnson, Director of the Division of Veterinary Medicine, in which, on September 27, 1972, he warned the FDA that "unless FDA resolves this drug residue problem, we will soon be in direct confrontation with Congress and the consumer, defending an untenable position. For the FDA to ignore this problem would be disastrous."[49]

The FDA capitulated and following the hearings announced a partial ban on DES as a feed supplement from January, 1973, but still permitting its use in implants, which were later disallowed on April 25, 1973, when the ban became complete. A coalition of the meat and drug industries, including Dawes Laboratories of Chicago, appealed to the U.S. Court of Appeals in December, 1973, claiming that the ban would cost the country $1.8 billion, a figure some 450 percent in excess of the 1971 estimates. The appeal was sustained on the grounds that the manufacturers had not been afforded adequate opportunity for a public hearing. Thus the ban was reversed, and DES was officially returned to the market on January, 1974. How did the industry cope during the nine months total ban on DES? They simply switched to substitute implants of other carcinogenic estrogens which had not been included in the DES ban, such as Synovex (Syntex Pharmaceutical Inc.) and Ralgro and Zeranol (Commercial Solvents Corporation), which were about six times as expensive as DES, although similarly effective.

Caught between the legislative mandate of the 1962 DES Clause and escalating consumer concerns, the FDA then decided to try to move against DES on two fronts, by attempting to ban its use and by attempting to regulate its residues. On January 12, 1976, the FDA proposed a total ban on all remaining feed additive uses of DES, this time allowing ample opportunity for public hearings. The chemical manufacturers, including Dawes and American Home Products, were the leading opponents of the FDA at the hearings which dragged on until January, 1978. (At this writing a decision is imminent.)

In February, 1977, the FDA moved to tighten control of the uses of all carcinogenic feed additives within the framework of the 1962 DES Clause.[50] Their proposals emphasized the long-standing requirement for manufacturers to provide reliable, practical, and sensitive analytic methods for measuring residues, and also required the use of the most sensitive methods to become available at any time in the future. The required withdrawal period prior to slaughter would be that time, under normal conditions of livestock management, which would be necessary to reduce residues to below the lowest level of reliable measurements.

The proposed regulations were promptly challenged in the District of Columbia Federal District Court by the Animal Health Institute, not an animal producers' lobby but an organization with links to the pharmaceutical industry. In January, 1978, the Court ruled in favor of the drug companies, but the FDA appealed and the issue will probably not be resolved for several years.

Human Drugs   In spite of repeated warnings from the scientific literature and from its own advisory committees, the FDA took no regulatory action against oral contraceptives for over a decade after they were first marketed in 1960.[51] On March 4, 1970, the last day of Senator Nelson's hearings on dangers of the pill, Commissioner Charles Edwards testified announcing an explicit proposed statement, "What You Should Know about Birth Control Pills," that the FDA was considering for package warnings. The American Medical Association and the pharmaceutical industry protested strongly and the FDA backed off, revising out most of the warnings and all mention of cancer.

The modified statement provided the basis for package warnings ordered by the FDA in September, 1970.

By December, 1972, after the FDA had announced a ban on DES as a feed supplement, it had become public knowledge that DES was being dispensed by major university health clinics as post-coital contraceptives, in spite of the fact that it had never been approved for such use. The usual DES dosage of 250 mg was approximately a million times greater than a dose of 0.3 μg in a 100 gm serving of liver containing 2 ppb residues and equivalent to the estrogen content in about a two-year supply of oral contraceptives. The FDA has recently withdrawn from the market the 250 mg DES tablets formerly used for this purpose and has not given approval for any manufacturer to market DES as an oral contraceptive. The FDA, however, will approve use of DES in emergency situations, such as rape or incest, if a manufacturer provides patient labeling and special packaging.

By 1976, evidence had accumulated that the sequential pill was not only less effective than the combination pill, but also even more dangerous in terms of clotting disease, besides being incriminated in excess risks of uterine cancer. At the FDA's request, the manufacturer "voluntarily" withdrew sequentials from the market.

With mounting evidence on the carcinogenicity of Premarin and other forms of estrogen replacement therapy, and following the recommendations of its Advisory Committee on Obstetrics and Gynecology in December, 1975, the FDA finally took firm steps to control the burgeoning use of estrogens and replacement therapy. In October, 1976, the FDA ordered the pharmaceutical manufacturers to insert explicit patient package warnings in formulations of natural and synthetic estrogens in addition to DES. Patients had to be informed and warned against uterine cancer and a wide range of other risks, including other cancers, particularly of the breast and liver, and cardiovascular and thrombo-embolic diseases.

The ruling on labeling of estrogens used in replacement therapy was unusual for the FDA, which in the past has only required a mandatory "patient package insert" for oral contraceptives, intrauterine devices, and isoproterenol drugs used by asthmatics. The Pharmaceutical Manufacturers Association, joined by the American College of Obstetricians and Gynecologists and supported by the American Cancer Society, protested that information on drugs should be withheld from patients, and challenged the constitutional authority of the FDA to require such informative labeling. In September, 1977, the Pharmaceutical Manufacturers Association and the American College of Obstetricians and Gynecologists filed suit in the U.S. District Court in Delaware against the FDA proposal, claiming

> that it interferes with the practice of medicine by physicians according to their best professional judgment and by dictating the way in which they may practice their profession. . . . The regulation will discourage patients from accepting estrogen therapy when prescribed by their doctors which will impair the reputation of estrogens and reduce the sale of the drug and others.[52]

The Center for Law and Social Policy and Consumers Union have intervened against the suit on behalf of the FDA. The case is still pending. A successful outcome to the suit could well open up the Pharmaceutical Manufacturers Association and the American College of Obstetricians and Gynecologists, quite apart from individual gynecologists, to malpractice liability actions by women developing uterine cancer, as well as cancer of other sites, from the continued use of estrogen replacement therapy.

The FDA followed up their move to label estrogens used in replacement therapy by a request to Congress in October, 1977, for authority to order patient package inserts when necessary.* Of particular interest is the recent

---

*The FDA estimates that such warnings on adverse drug effects will be required in 50 percent to 75 percent of all prescription drugs.

announcement by FDA that manufacturers of oral contraceptives must supply physicians and patients with revised labeling, by April, 1978, warning of the dangers of heart attack and cardiovascular disease from the combined effects of smoking and contraceptives. The labels also warn that estrogens can cause cancer in certain animals and may, therefore, also cause cancer in humans, although it is stated that studies to date of women taking currently-marketed oral contraceptives have not confirmed this.*

Summary

Worldwide use of the contraceptive pill, dating back to 1960, constitutes the largest uncontrolled experiment in human carcinogenesis ever undertaken. This was only made possible by the importunity of the drug industry; in its massive marketing and heavy promotional campaigns for a poorly tested product and its unwillingness to face substantive questions on risk of cancer and cardiovascular disease that subsequently developed; by the FDA's allowing the marketing of a poorly tested drug and refusing for years to take minimal regulatory action; and by the silence of the press on the growing evidence of dangers of the pill. Not surprisingly, the public accepted assurances of the pill's safety and abandoned other forms of contraception in its favor.

The carcinogenicity of estrogens and other female sex hormones has been repeatedly demonstrated in animal experiments begun as long ago as fifty years. Use of the contraceptive pill is associated with excessive risks of rare liver tumors, and there is also suggestive evidence of increased risk of cervix and breast cancers. Additional and major risks of the pill include heart disease and stroke, these being particularly marked in women who also smoke. The large-scale and common estrogen replacement

---

*One of the unique elements of these new warnings is the information provided on the relative effectiveness and risks of oral contraceptives compared with other forms of contraception.

therapy of menopausal women with Premarin, which is largely restricted to the upper socioeconomic brackets, is not only generally unnecessary but has also resulted in a virtual epidemic of uterine cancer. In spite of this, the Pharmaceutical Manufacturers Association and the American College of Obstetricians and Gynecologists have challenged the legality of the FDA's recent label warning on the grounds that this will reduce the sale of the drug, and that it interferes with the doctor–patient relationship.

Evidence for the carcinogenicity in animals of DES, a synthetic chemical with estrogenic activity, dates back to 1938. Nevertheless, DES has been widely prescribed in attempts to prevent the complications of late pregnancy, although there is no substantive evidence to support the efficacy of such a use. This has resulted in an excess of breast cancer in the women themselves, vaginal cancers and the more common vaginal adenosis in the daughters of these women, and infertility and genito-urinary abnormalities in their sons. In spite of all the evidence on its dangers, DES is also still commonly prescribed as a post-coital contraceptive, in the absence of clear evidence as to its effectiveness, although the FDA is now attempting to regulate this.

DES was introduced as a feed additive in 1947. Extreme regulatory laxness by both the USDA and FDA, coupled with 1962 legislative exemption, at the urging of the industry, of DES from the Delaney Amendment, has resulted in the extensive and increasing use of DES and other carcinogenic estrogens as feed additives. In spite of the requirement for withdrawal periods prior to slaughter, residues of these additives continue to be found in meat products. A powerful coalition of the meat and drug industries has now effectively blocked FDA attempts to regulate the use of these carcinogenic additives in animal feeds.

Chapter Seven

The General Environment: Case Studies

This chapter deals with two sets of case studies: the pesticides aldrin/dieldrin and chlordane/heptachlor, and nitrosamines, a large group of organic chemicals now found throughout the environment, many of which have been shown highly carcinogenic in animal tests. These are chosen to illustrate some basic problems of exposure to chemical carcinogens that are so widespread in the general environment as to be ubiquitous. While these particular pesticides are synthetic, nitrosamines, in contrast, can be produced by interactions between different classes of chemicals which may be common and naturally occurring.

Pesticides

Pesticides are chemicals that are intended to kill pests such as insects (insecticides); mites (miticides); weeds and unwanted vegetation (herbicides); fungi (fungicides); and, rats and other "vermin" (rodenticides).*

Historical Background[1]

We are now entering what is generally recognized as the "third generation" of pesticide use. The first generation of pesticides, which were developed and used until the 1940s, included naturally occurring organic chemicals such as pyrethrum and rotenone, and inorganic compounds, such as copper, zinc, mercury and lead salts, and arsenates. The inorganic pesticides created significant problems of toxicity, carcinogenicity, and environmental contamination (though these effects were generally confined to the area of application). Another problem with first-generation pesticides was that they were relatively expensive and variable in supply. The second generation was based on synthetic organics, the large-scale production of which commenced about 1940 with the advent of DDT and related organochlorine pesticides. The use of other major classes of synthetic organic pesticides which entered production about this time, including organophosphate insecticides and phenoxy herbicides, has substantially increased over the last decade. The third generation of pesticide use is based on an appreciation of fundamental ecological principles and on the maintenance of pests at economically acceptable levels rather than on futile and counter-productive attempts at eradication. Third generation strategies are based on integrated use of biological control, pest-resistant crop varieties, crop rotation, insect predators, insect hormones, viruses, and sterilizing agents, either alone or in combination with minimal application of highly selective, "narrow spectrum" pesticides. Such programs of pest control, known as "integrated pest management," are still in their infancy, due

---

*Fumigants are another class of pesticides used to kill a variety of pests by volatilization in confined spaces such as grain elevators and other food storage facilities.

largely to industrial indifference and scanty federal support, but they have shown great promise in agricultural and urban pest control, including home lawn and garden applications.[2]

In March, 1977, Secretary of Agriculture Bob Bergland announced that the USDA would work to move farmers away from their dependence on chemical pesticides and encourage greater emphasis on integrated pest management. There is, however, no material evidence yet of this intent.

The Toxic Effects of Pesticides

The second generation of pesticides was initially greeted with uncritical enthusiasm, as a triumph of modern synthetic chemistry, heralding a new era of agricultural efficiency. In nature, however, there are no "free lunches," and problems soon began to surface. First, it was noted that insects can acquire resistance to a particular insecticide or class of insecticides, necessitating progressively greater, more costly applications, and resulting in progressively smaller agricultural yields, until the infestation eventually becomes uncontrollable.[3] This is known as the "pesticide treadmill." Second, many pesticides produce "broad spectrum" effects, damaging various forms of insect, animal, and plant life other than the intended target.[4] Third, many classes of pesticides, particularly organochlorines, are highly stable, resist degradation, and accumulate in the food chain at levels often more than a millionfold in excess of those found in the environment. Fourth, many pesticides have been found to induce a wide range of toxic effects in experimental animals, including birth defects, sterility, and cancer, thus posing grave public health hazards, especially in view of their widespread environmental dissemination and persistence. Finally, some of the more stable pesticides become widely dispersed in the environment, air, food, water, and the human body, at locations far distant from their initial application. Pesticides are thus now one of the most important classes of general environmental pollutants, and result in extensive involuntary exposure and contamination of human populations.

Many of these concerns were lucidly and cogently expressed by Rachel Carson in her 1962 classic *Silent Spring*, with particular and illustrative reference to DDT.[5] Reaction from the agrichemical community—including the Manufacturing Chemists Association, chemical industry equipment manufacturers, farm organizations, land grant colleges, industrial organizations such as the Nutrition Foundation,* industry consultants or grant recipients in university departments of nutrition, and state and federal departments of agriculture—was immediate and strident.[6] Carson was attacked as unscientific and hysterical. Typical of the misleading criticisms leveled against Carson were the self-interested statements by William Darby,† then nutritionalist at Vanderbilt School of Medicine:

> Her ignorance or bias on some of the considerations throws doubt on her competence to judge policy. For example, she indicates that it is neither wise nor responsible to use pesticides in the control of insect-born diseases.[7]

Darby, like most of Carson's critics, made a great show of reporting what she had never said. What in fact

---

*The Nutrition Foundation was incorporated in 1941 to support "fundamental research and education in the science of nutrition." Its membership consisted of fifty-four companies in the food and chemical industries, the president of whose companies served on the Foundation's Board of Trustees. The foundation funnelled industry money, as research grants, to nutrition departments of many prestigious universities, whose recipients were among Carson's most vociferous critics. As part of its educational activities, in 1963 the foundation published a "fact kit" attacking *Silent Spring* and defending large-scale use of chemical pesticides.

†Darby is a veteran member of the Food Protection Committee of the National Academy of Sciences, long dominated by industry, and now the director of the Nutrition Foundation. He is also member of the EPA Science Advisory Board and was recently appointed to a special subcommittee to review EPA policies on pesticide tolerances on food in response to continued grave Congressional charges of mismanagement.

Carson had questioned were the overall methods of combatting insect-borne diseases which relied almost exclusively on massive pesticide use. Carson summarized her position as follows:

> It is not my contention that chemical insecticides must never be used. I do contend that we have put poisonous and biologically potent chemicals into the hands of persons largely or wholly ignorant of their potential for harm—. I contend, furthermore, that we have allowed these chemicals to be used with little or no advance investigation of their effect on soil, water, wildlife, and man himself. Future generations are unlikely to condone our lack of prudent concern for the integrity of the natural world that supports all life.[8]

The book, however, made a deep impact on the independent scientific community and on the nation.[9] President Kennedy requested his Science Advisory Committee to create a special Panel on the Use of Pesticides to review the charges against pesticides. Both the Kennedy Committee and another Science Advisory Committee appointed by President Johnson in 1965 reported that the charges were indeed scientifically well founded. They concluded that organochlorine pesticides were dangerous, quite apart from often being ineffective, and that their production should be phased out as soon as possible. The importance of these recommendations has been more recently emphasized by growing information on the carcinogenicity of organochlorine pesticides as a class (Table 7.1).

Of the twenty-five organochlorine pesticides listed, nineteen have been shown to be carcinogenic in animal tests. There are no data available on four of the remaining six pesticides, while data on the other two (endosulfan and tetradifon), which are claimed to be noncarcinogenic, are still incomplete. Industry has repeatedly attempted to dismiss these findings by such tactics as selective interpretation of the data, challenging their human relevance, and asserting that alleged human experience of safe manufac-

Table 7.1 Organochlorine Pesticides: Production, Use, and Carcinogenicity

Class and Name of Pesticide	Manufacturer	1972 Production, Million Pounds	Major Use	Carcinogenicity
Oxygenated compounds				
Chlorobenzilate (Acaraben)	Geigy	1–4	Miticide	+
Dicofol (Kelthane)	Rohm & Haas	1–4	Miticide	No data
Dieldrin	Shell	Under 1	Insecticide	+
Endosulfan	FMC	1–4	Insecticide	–
Endrin	Shell; Velsicol	1–4	Insecticide	+
Kepone (Chlordecone)	Allied	No data	Insecticide	+
Methoxychlor	Multiple	5–14	Insecticide	+
Ovex (Chlorfenson)	Dow	No data	Insecticide	+
Sulfenone	Stauffer	No data	Miticide	No data
Tetradifon (Tedion)	FMC	No data	Miticide	–
Benzenoid non-oxygenated compounds				
Benzene hexachloride (BHC)	Diamond; Hooker	1–4	Insecticide	+
Dichlorobenzene (PDB)	Multiple	50–99	Fumigant	No data
Dichloropropene-propane (DD)	Dow; Shell	15–29	Fumigant	No data
DDT	Multiple	30–49	Insecticide	+
Lindane (Gamma BHC)	Diamond; Hooker	1–4	Insecticide	+

(*continued on following page*)

Table 7.1 (*continued*)

Class and Name of Pesticide	Manufacturer	1972 Production, Million Pounds	Major Use	Carcinogenicity
Pentachloronitrobenzene (Quintozene)	Olin	1–4	Fungicide˙	+
Perthane	Rohm & Hass	No data	Insecticide	+
TDE (DDD)	Allied; Rohm & Haas	Under 1	Insecticide	+
Non-oxygenated, non-benzenoid compounds				
Aldrin	Shell	5–14	Insecticide	+ +
Chlordane	Velsicol	15–29	Insecticide	+ +
Ethylene dichloride (Dichloroethane)	Multiple	5–14	Fumigant	+
Heptachlor	Velsicol	5–14	Insecticide	+ +
Mirex (Dechlorane)	Allied	Under 1	Insecticide	+ +
Strobane	Tenneco	No data	Insecticide	+ +
Toxaphene (Terpene polychlorinate)	Multiple	50–99	Insecticide	+

Source: Epstein, S. S. "The Carcinogenicity of Organochlorine Pesticides," pp. 243–265, in *Origins of Human Cancer*, Book A. ed. by H. H. Hiatt, J. D. Watson, and J. A. Winsten, Cold Spring Harbor Laboratory, 1977.

ture and use has vindicated their products. In fact, there are no published human epidemiological studies on carcinogenicity and other chronic toxic effects for the majority of organochlorine and other pesticides. Recent review of twelve organochlorine pesticides by an expert committee of the World Health Organization International Agency for Research on Cancer concluded that there are no valid human data which can possibly justify the conclusions of safety claimed by industry.[10]

The Pesticide Market

There are approximately 1,400 active ingredients currently used in some 40,000 different pesticide products. A relatively small number of these products dominate the pesticide market, twenty basic ingredients accounting for 75 percent of total sales of agricultural formulations. Table 7.2 shows that about half of all pesticides are used in agriculture, while remaining uses are divided between industry (for purposes such as mothproofing carpets and fabrics and clearing rights-of-way), government (for brush and pest control on public grounds), and the general public (for home lawn and garden purposes).

Synthetic pesticides are one of the top classes of synthetic chemical products in the United States, with current annual sales in the region of $4 billion, about 6

Table 7.2   Estimated Average U.S. Use of Pesticides

Use	Percent of Sales
Agriculture	55
Industry	20
Home, lawn and garden	15
Federal, state, and local government	10

Source: Environmental Protection Agency, Office of Water Programs, "Patterns of Pesticide Use and Reduction in Use Related to Social and Economic Factors," Washington, D.C., 1972.

percent of the 1975 gross sales ($72 billion) of the chemical industry. From 1950 to 1975 overall pesticide production increased by about 15 percent per year, from an estimated 200,000 pounds to 1.4 billion pounds. The increase in production of herbicides and organophosphate insecticides was even greater during the same period. The only class of pesticides whose growth rate has declined are the organochlorines, particularly those belonging to a subclass known as cyclodienes, which include aldrin and dieldrin (A/D), chlordane and heptachlor (C/H), Endosulfan, and Endrin.

Support for the pesticide market comes from a politically and economically extremely powerful consortium of diverse interests.[11] In addition to the major agrichemical industries, this consortium includes pest control operators; aircraft applicators; agribusiness concerns such as banks, utility companies, and farm equipment manufacturers; food processors; key politicians, particularly from the corn and cotton belts; elements in federal agencies, particularly the USDA; elements in state agencies, particularly state departments of agriculture; segments of the media, such as the chemical and farm journals, rural newspapers, and chemical company house organs; professional societies such as those represented in the Council for Agricultural Science and Technology; elements in land grant universities; and consultants in other universities.

At the bottom of this conglomerate of interests are the pesticide salesmen, who are generally ignorant of the efficacy as well as the hazards of their products.*

---

*Their role in the proliferation of pesticides has been questioned by many, including Robert Van den Bosch, the world's leading expert on integrated pest control: "The greatest absurdity in contemporary pest control is the dominant role of the pesticide salesman who simultaneously acts as diagnostician, therapist, nostrum prescriber, and pill peddler. It is difficult to imagine any situation where society entrusts so great a responsibility to such poorly qualified persons. [This characterization also seems generally apt for drug salesmen.] Pesticides rank with the most dangerous and ecologically disruptive materials known to science, yet under the prevailing system these biocides are scattered like dust in the environment by persons often utterly unqualified to prescribe and supervise their use."[12]

Profits and Losses from Pesticide Use

What have been the agricultural returns for the recent massive uses of pesticides in agriculture? In spite of the fact that the total U.S. harvested acreage has remained steady over the past two decades, expenditures on pesticides for agriculture have increased about tenfold, an increase well above the inflationary rate and disproportionately greater than increases in crop value (Table 7.3).

According to estimates by David Pimentel of the Department of Entomology at Cornell University, the harmful recognized effects of pesticides represent a cost to the nation of at least $3 billion annually, including

> hospitalization costs for 6,000 human pesticide poisonings; costs of about 60,000 days of work lost from the pesticide poisoning hospitalizations; additional medical costs for 8,000 human pesticide poisonings treated as outpatients; and costs of about 30,000 days of work lost from humans not ill enough to be hospitalized.[13]*

To these can be added losses from toxicity to domestic animals, livestock, fish, and wildlife; from losses of crop products; from seizure of food containing pesticide residues above tolerance levels, from the approximately 200 people estimated by EPA to die annually from pesticide poisoning; and from an unknown number of deaths due to the carcinogenic and other chronic toxic effects of pesticides. In sum, the total national losses from use of synthetic pesticides are probably in the same order of magnitude as the $8.7 billion estimated by Pimentel as the cost of annual crop losses due to pest attacks.

---

*Most cases of poisoning by accidental carelessness are due to the use of highly hazardous pesticides instead of less hazardous available alternatives. An important example is the widespread use of the highly toxic organophosphate Parathion. By replacing Parathion with Sumithion (a related but much safer insecticide not available for patent reasons in the United States), the Japanese have reduced their accident rate.

Table 7.3 Increasing Costs of Pesticides, 1955 to 1975

	1955	1975
Number of harvested acres	335 million	340 million
Farmers' expenditure for pesticides	$184 million	$1.96 billion
Cost of pesticides per acre	$0.55	$5.76
Cost of pesticides in relation to farm production value	1 percent	4.4 percent

Source: Statistical Research Service, United States Department of Agriculture, 1978.

I mean there is no fooling around, the major issue is cancer.

Herbert L. Perlman, EPA Administrative Law Judge, 1974

Aldrin/Dieldrin

Aldrin and dieldrin (A/D) are two closely related organochlorine pesticides. The former is naturally converted to the latter by an oxidation process both in the field and in the body.

Sales and Uses

Aldrin and dieldrin were first developed in 1947 and, from 1952 to 1977, were manufactured exclusively in the United States by Shell Chemical Company, a subsidiary of Shell Oil. At first they were chiefly used on cotton, but the increasing resistance of the boll weevil to A/D in the late 1950s caused these uses to decline. With growing concern about insect resistance and its toxicity, A/D sales declined from a peak of 22 million pounds in 1966 to about half that amount in 1972. Even then, A/D ranked sixth in sales among all U.S. insecticides, with registration for about 1,300 products handled by some 350 firms. Apart from termite control, which constituted about 15 percent of total sales, the major use of A/D was on corn. In the eight-state corn belt, where over 70 percent of the nation's five to six billion bushels of corn is grown, A/D were used prophylactically on approximately 8 percent of the crop as insurance against possible future infestation by the corn soil insect complex (rootworms, wireworms, and cutworms), rather than for treatment of actual infestations.

Environmental Contamination[1]

Until about 1970, A/D were applied by aerial spray, even in the vicinity of lakes and streams, causing high levels of contamination of air and water. This contamination was found to persist, although at lower levels, even after use was restricted to direct soil application in accordance with recommended agricultural practice. The routes of this contamination by A/D were threefold: volatilization; transport on dust particles; and agricultural runoff of treated soils and dusts into waterways.

Dieldrin was found in 85 percent of air samples monitored by the EPA from 1970 to 1972, with average national values of 2 ng/m^3 (nanograms per cubic meter), resulting in daily human intakes in the order of 0.1 μg (100 ng). Household dust levels in the corn belt averaged about 2 ppm. An additional and generally unrecognized source of household exposure comes from woolens and rugs which have in the past been routinely mothproofed with dieldrin. Dieldrin was found more often in surface waters than any other insecticide, in average levels as high as 0.4 μg per litre.

Aldrin and dieldrin are highly persistent, and more than 50 percent of an original application of dieldrin can be recovered from soil after four years. Contamination of corn and forage grown on A/D-treated soil was the major source and route of residues in meat and dairy products, and ultimately also the major source of human contamination. Average residues of 10 ppb were found in soybeans rotated with corn in the corn belt. EPA monitoring programs from 1972 to 1974 found dieldrin residues in virtually all human body fat samples analyzed, with average levels of about 0.3 ppm and sometimes ranging as high as 15 ppm.[2] Levels in blacks were about twice those in whites. These residues are relatively stable and persistent: an average of 50 percent of initial residue levels are still present at about nine months.* Further, these residues are of the same order of magnitude, and in some cases greater, than levels in rodents which developed cancers after feeding with A/D.

Economic Losses

The profits Shell made by selling A/D have been at the expense of the national economy, which suffered major direct losses from the extensive environmental contamination caused by agricultural uses of A/D.[3] In 1972, about half the catch of chub and trout from Lake Michigan had to be seized by the FDA, because they were found to contain residues over the permissible levels of 0.3 ppm. This came as a surprise to many, because dieldrin levels in Lake Michigan waters were "only" in the ppt range. However, the persistence and fat solubility of A/D allowed them to accumulate and concentrate in the food chain at levels nearly a billion times greater than those of the lake.

In the whole class or organochlorine pesticides, A/D are second only to Endrin in toxicity to lower species. A/D have been responsible for major kills, a single application resulting in the extermination of one million fish of thirty different species in a Florida marsh. Some fish show toxic effects at 2 ppb levels, and oysters are damaged below 1 ppm, a level which killed 100 percent of quail

---

*The measure of this persistence is known as the biological half-life of a pesticide.

chicks exposed. Egg shell thinning and breakage, induced by very small body burdens of dieldrin, has been particularly destructive for predators at the top of the food chain, and it has been estimated that A/D are responsible for about 10 percent of all bald eagle deaths.

Destruction of livestock and poultry due to excessive dieldrin levels has been commonplace since 1969, when the extent of this contamination was first appreciated. In February, 1974, a routine test by USDA inspectors discovered unusually high residues in a batch of chickens being processed by a Mississippi broiler farm. Within days, more lots of contaminated birds were identified from five poultry plants. As the residues in each chicken exceeded the allowable standard, they were ordered destroyed. By the end of March, more than eight million chickens had been gassed and buried, at a cost approaching $10 million. The source of contamination was thought to be low-grade soybean oil containing dieldrin levels as high as 58 ppm and originally intended for industrial use but diverted instead into more profitable use in poultry feed.[4]

On March 26, 1974, a network of Southern senators headed by Senator James O. Eastland (D-Miss.), and supported behind the scenes by the Nixon administration, then anxious for sympathetic Southern votes against the pending impeachment charges, tried to rush through a bill indemnifying the poultry and egg producers and processors for the losses they had suffered. In fact, the major beneficiaries of this bill would have been five large conglomerates, and not the individual family farmers who serve as their share-croppers. Senator William Proxmire (D-Wisc.) managed to put a last-minute hold on the bill, until the measure could be finally debated, when it was overwhelmingly rejected.

Are such economic losses, quite apart from questions of excess cancer risks, an inevitable and necessary penalty for maintaining the corn yield so vital to the national food supply? The answer seems to be no.[5] There are, in fact, real questions as to whether A/D are of any actual agricultural value against the corn soil insect complex, the major use. A 1972 USDA survey of corn crops found that of all acres treated with A/D, 60 percent were for rootworms, 16 percent for wireworms, and 24 percent for cutworms. However, rootworms and wireworms had by then become largely resistant to A/D. More important, rootworms and wireworms can be effectively controlled by other measures including crop rotation with soybeans. While Shell admitted this by labeling its products "Do not use in areas of suspected rootworm resistance," the pesticide salesmen countered this caution by aggressive sales pitches. As far as cutworms are concerned, infestation is relatively rare, occurs only in limited areas, and can then, if necessary, be treated by acceptable alternative pesticides, rather than by routine preventive application of A/D.

Most farmers are dependent on advice from salesmen for principles and details of pesticide use. Farmers also rely on university entomologists and economists, much of whose research is funded by the industry. There seems little doubt that A/D had been oversold by Shell and pesticide salesmen to farmers as an insurance against the entire corn soil insect complex, against most of which it was ineffective. Even for cutworms, recommended application levels seem to have been more than twice that actually needed for effective control.

A wide range of independent experts, including Robert Metcalf (University of Illinois), Robert Van den Bosch (University of California), and Donald Chant (University of Toronto), are agreed on the major ecological disruption caused by A/D and organochlorine pesticides.[6] Many state entomologists are also agreed that A/D were unnecessary in the treatment of the corn soil insect complex. There is also a consensus that crop rotation is not only a more effective but also a cheaper method of control.

Carcinogenicity of A/D

While information on the ineffectiveness of A/D and on its extensive environmental pollution was becoming in-

creasingly appreciated, it was the question of carcinogenicity that finally influenced EPA to commence regulatory proceedings against these insecticides in 1971.
The major issue in the subsequent agency hearings was
the validity of the experimental carcinogenicity data, and
the relevance of such data to human risk.

Animal Tests By the time the proceedings started, A/D
had been tested for carcinogenicity in several feeding
studies in mice and rats by the FDA, Shell, and other
laboratories under contract to Shell. In general, these
studies had either reported negative findings or that A/D
induced allegedly non-neoplastic liver nodules or "benign
liver tumors" in mice (Table 7.4). In spite of these conclusions, however, the Mrak Commission in 1969 had concluded that A/D were carcinogenic on the basis of the
1962 FDA study.[7]

In an effort to explore these studies further, besides
explaining fundamental principles of carcinogenesis to the
court, EPA assembled a small team of independent experts that included Melvin Reuber, then of the University
of Maryland, Umberto Saffiotti of the NCI, Arthur Upton,
then from the State University of New York at Stony
Brook and now Director of the NCI, and Adrian Gross of
the FDA.*

Apart from evaluating the specific findings of the various carcinogenicity studies, the EPA team made substantial contributions in broader areas of carcinogenesis. These
were subsequently summarized and formulated by EPA as
"nine cancer principles," and were of great importance in
the final stages of the regulatory battle to ban A/D.†[8]

---

*The author was a member of this team.

†These cancer principles have broad general applicability. They summarize the overall conclusions of many national and international committees
on environmental carcinogenesis. (See, for example, Appendix II, the 1970
Surgeon General's Report on Environmental Carcinogens.) In the EPA brief
the principles were followed by 29 pages of citations from reports and testimony.

Table 7.4 Summary of Carcinogenicity Tests on Aldrin/Dieldrin in Mice

Authors	Strain	Concentrations (ppm)		Carcinogenicity		Comments
		Aldrin	Dieldrin	Author's conclusion	Conclusion in subsequent independent re-evaluation	
Davis & Fitzhugh, 1962 (FDA)	C$_3$H	10	10	"Benign liver tumors"	Liver cancer	Liver cancer
Davis, 1965 (FDA)	C$_3$H	10	10	"Benign liver tumors"	Liver cancer	1. Liver cancer 2. Study still unpublished
Song & Harville, 1964	Swiss	15	15	Liver "neoplasia" in unspecified groups	None	Unacceptable
MacDonald et al., 1972		...	3–10	"Non-neoplastic" liver lesions	Liver cancer	1. Liver cancer 2. Study still unpublished
Walker et al., 1973 (Tunstall 1)	GF$_1$	...	0.1–20	"Type A and B" liver tumors	Liver cancer	1. Liver cancer with no apparent threshold at 0.1 ppm, and following only 1–2 months treatment at 10 ppm. 2. Multiple site tumors at low doses. 3. Submitted to FDA 1968, but unpublished till 1973.
Thorpe & Walker, 1973 (Tunstall 2)	CF$_1$	...	10	"Type A & B" liver tumors	None	Liver cancer, with high incidence pulmonary metastases

Source: S. S. Epstein, "The Carcinogenicity of Dieldrin, 1," *Science of the Total Environment*, (4)1975: 1–52.

1. A carcinogen is any agent which increases tumor induction in man or animals.

2. Well-established criteria exist for distinguishing between benign and malignant tumors; however, even the induction of benign tumors is sufficient to characterize a chemical as a carcinogen.

3. The majority of human cancers are caused by avoidable exposure to carcinogens.

4. While chemicals can be carcinogenic agents, only a small percentage actually are.

5. Carcinogenesis is characterized by its irreversibility and long latency period following the initial exposure to the carcinogenic agent.

6. There is great variation in individual susceptibility to carcinogens.

7. The concept of a "threshold" exposure level for a carcinogenic agent has no practical significance because there is no valid method for establishing such a level.

8. A carcinogenic agent may be identified through analysis of tumor induction results with laboratory animals exposed to the agent, or on a post hoc basis by properly conducted epidemiological studies.

9. Any substance which produces tumors in animals must be considered a carcinogenic hazard to man if the results were achieved according to the established parameters of a valid carcinogenesis test.

In an effort to resolve some questions on the interpretation of the pathology findings of the various carcinogenicity tests, Reuber reexamined most of the original liver sections, and found that where "benign tumors" or "nonmalignant" nodular liver lesions had been claimed, these, in fact, were often unequivocal cancers.[9] In some instances, confirmation of the malignant nature of these tumors was obtained by other independent pathologists, and by the fact that some of the tumors spread or metastasized to the lungs and were also transplantable. Following Reuber's reevaluation, G. McDonald, a pathologist who had previously reported one of the industry-sponsored studies as negative, reexamined his original sections and was then obliged to admit that Reuber was substantially correct.

The available information, particularly as modified by the EPA reevaluation, clearly established that A/D were carcinogenic in five separate feeding tests involving three different strains of mice and at concentrations as low as 0.1 ppm and following only two months feeding. Simultaneous administration of the carcinogen DDT markedly enhanced the carcinogenicity of A/D in excess of an additive effect. During the proceedings, evidence of carcinogenicity in two additional strains of mice was revealed. While the major cancer site was the liver, cancers were also found in various other organs, including the lung, particularly at relatively low dose levels.[10]

The rat data were less extensive, largely because the tests had generally been conducted at such high A/D concentrations that the animals died relatively early from toxic effects. Nevertheless, two studies, FDA 1964 and Tunstall 1, confirmed the carcinogenicity of A/D in rats, finding a wide range of multiple site tumors, particularly at lower doses. Reevaluation of the histology of one of these studies also confirmed the occurrence of liver cancers in treated rats.[11]

How then could Shell contest the carcinogenicity of A/D, dragging out the proceedings over 1,700 days, the written record of which occupied nearly thirteen feet of shelf space? The answer is simple. The studies which were largely generated or contracted for by Shell were either handled in such a way as to discount, dismiss, or interpret away any findings of carcinogenicity, or alternatively were so inept as to invalidate the claimed conclusions of noncarcinogenicity. These tactics were facilitated by the practice of not publishing the reports but submitting them in confidence to a then uncritical FDA.

At the hearings, Shell further bolstered its claims that A/D were noncarcinogenic by developing, with the aid of an apparently impressive array of academic consultants, a novel approach to carcinogenesis based on an imaginative set of myths which were used in attempts to explain away the results of the animal tests. The Shell case largely rested on the claim that the liver tumors induced in mice were not real cancers, but only "hyperplastic" nodules or, using a newly invented terminology, benign "Type A" tumors. As a fallback position, Shell also argued that the mouse was an unsuitable animal for carcinogenicity tests, although for over a decade it had used negative data in mouse carcinogenicity tests as proof of safety of its products. The basis for this argument was that the mouse liver is "labile," and that all that A/D did was to somehow "augment" the induction of liver tumors, which were really due to an "unknown oncogenic stimulus."[12]

The tumors at sites other than the liver in A/D-treated mice were an obstacle to this set of propositions that had to be explained. What better way to do this than to produce some fresh information discounting them? This is just what Shell did. In the middle of the proceedings, when discussion on extra-hepatic tumors had become critical, Shell suddenly produced some "missing" data sheets going back to the 1967 studies at its Tunstall Laboratories in England purporting to prove that sixty additional test mice had no extra-hepatic tumors, and that statistical analysis of the new and old data combined proved that the incidence of these tumors was insignificant.[13]

The lengths to which Shell's consultants were willing to go is illustrated by the testimony of Paul M. Newberne, Professor of Nutritional Pathology, MIT, who said, "It is my feeling that mice as a species . . . should not be used for safety testing," and agreed with Shell scientists that all the extensive mouse data on carcinogenicity should be ignored.[14]*

---

*Newberne is also an advisor to the NCI bioassay program for carcinogenicity testing, which was and still is largely based on the use of mice.

The rat carcinogenicity data were sharply contested by Shell, particularly Reuber's finding of an excess incidence of liver cancer in treated rats in his reevaluation of the 1964 FDA study. In an effort to discredit this, Shell created an Ad Hoc Committee of Pathologists headed by Stephen Sternberg, a pathologist at the Sloan Kettering Institute, New York, who had written the section on carcinogenesis in the report of a 1972 advisory committee appointed by the National Academy of Sciences claiming that A/D were noncarcinogenic. The ad hoc committee examined slides from twenty-two treated rats (among whom Reuber had found twenty carcinomas) and reported two carcinomas, one borderline carcinoma, and eleven animals with "hyperplastic nodules." This does not seem to constitute a substantive difference of opinion, particularly as it is generally agreed that nodules are premalignant, and are in fact now classified as neoplastic nodules, and particularly as liver carcinomas and nodules are exceptional in rats other than those treated with carcinogens.[15]

Shell and its witnesses adamantly insisted on a progressive escalation of the standards of proof for the carcinogenicity of A/D, which were so extensive and difficult to meet that their compliance would exclude almost every known chemical carcinogen. These standards included:

1. Induction of carcinogenicity must be statistically significant at all dose levels.

2. A uniformly positive dose – response relationship must be found at all doses, even if there is competing toxicity and high mortality at high doses.

3. A causal association between A/D treatment and carcinogenic effects cannot be sustained unless the mechanism of action of the carcinogen can be demonstrated.

4. Conclusions on carcinogenic effects of A/D cannot be accepted until the possibility of unknown "augmenting factors" has been excluded.

5. A carcinogenic effect must be consistent and re-producible in a series of different tests before it can be accepted.

6. The induction of liver tumors in mice is no indica-tion of carcinogenic effects, even if they are unequivocally malignant.

7. Tumor production in mice, even in various differ-ent organs and even when replicated, cannot be accepted as evidence of carcinogenicity.

8. Even the finding of carcinogenic effects in two or more animal species is unacceptable proof in the absence of evidence in humans.[16]*

Human Evidence   The final fallback position of Shell was that the animal tests should be discounted, whatever their findings, because epidemiological studies on workers ex-posed to "high levels" of A/D had conclusively established that there was no excess of cancers. This claim was based on a study, published by K. W. Jager in 1970, of a cohort of 826 full-time male workers, including maintenance crew and operators, employed between 1954 and 1967 at a Shell insecticide plant in Pernis, Holland.[17] Some of them had additional exposures to unrelated pesticides. During the proceedings, the study was updated to 1973 by a Shell witness. There was a high turnover rate at the plant, as the largest number of workers at any one time, 1962, was only 230, and there was also "more or less fre-quent movement of workers between units" in the plant. Of the 826 workers, only 166 had more than four years exposure and fifteen years observation, and there were only 69 workers with more than ten years exposure and fifteen years observation. Finally, no worker had been ex-

---

*This position was unequivocally reiterated more recently by M. J. Sloan, director of the Regulatory Division of Shell Chemical Company, at a discussion of a paper on "The Carcinogenicity of Organochlorine Pesticides," which the author gave at a conference on "The Origins of Human Cancer" at Cold Spring Harbor Laboratories in September, 1976.

posed for more than nineteen years.[18] Although a leading Shell witness admitted that this study "cannot be considered as statistical proof of noncarcinogenicity," other industry witnesses repeatedly cited it as proving that A/D were noncarcinogenic. Sternberg, for example, made the proposition that if A/D were really carcinogenic, then precancerous symptoms should by now have developed in the exposed workers.[19]

The Pernis study was reviewed in detail by leading independent epidemiologists, including Marvin Schneiderman of the NCI, and Herbert Seidman of the American Cancer Society, who unanimously agreed that the study was so flawed and inadequate that it was not possible to draw any conclusion at all from it. The International Agency for Research on Cancer also agreed, stating that the study "does not allow any conclusions on the existence of an excess risk of developing cancer."[20] Not only was it based on too few workers, exposed and observed for too short a period for any significant excess of cancer other than a catastrophic one to be noted, but it was also clear from blood analyses that over 30 percent of the workers never had any substantial exposure to A/D in the workplace. Additionally the study had failed to follow up hundreds of other exposed employees.

Three studies in the general population have developed suggestive evidence of an association between excess human residues of dieldrin and cancer.[21] A 1967 New Zealand study has shown that dieldrin levels in the lungs of patients with lung cancer are significantly higher than in noncancerous controls. A 1968 study in Hawaii found that dieldrin levels were highest in patients with a variety of cancers. Another 1968 study reported higher dieldrin fat levels in patients dying in Florida with various malignant diseases, including leukaemia and Hodgkin's, than in normal controls.

Other scattered cases of association between A/D exposure and malignant disease have been noted. In 1970 a federal court in Missouri (*Burke* v. *Stauffer Chemical Co.*)

ruled that a case of Hodgkin's disease had been caused by prior exposure of a worker to dieldrin.[22] Since then, there have been several other product-liability suits, most of them brought by pesticide operators involved in termite proofing with A/D formulations, which Shell has settled out of court, presumably to avoid the possibility of creating a legal precedent.

The Battle to Ban A/D

The battle to ban A/D has been long and bitter. In this, Shell was aided by powerful friends in Congress, headed by Senator Eastland and Congressman Jamie Whitten (D-Miss.), and in the USDA, which intervened in support of Shell's position. Useful behind-the-scenes support came from staff of the EPA Office of Pesticide Programs, particularly those who had transferred from the Pesticide Regulation Division of the USDA when EPA was created in 1970. Final and enthusiastic support came from Shell's university consultants and the land grant colleges.

The first round of the battle began in May, 1963, when a special panel of President Kennedy's Science Advisory Committee published a review on "Use of Pesticides," which called for reexamination of FDA tolerances for seven pesticides, including A/D. The review concluded that "elimination of the use of persistent toxic pesticides should be the goal."[23] The panel also noted with concern a 1962 FDA study which had shown that liver tumors were induced in mice by feeding them with 10 ppm of A/D. On the basis of this review, the FDA appointed an Advisory Committee which in 1965 recommended that the tolerances for dieldrin in foods should be reduced, and that further carcinogenicity tests be undertaken on A/D, as it found that the existing information was inconclusive. Accordingly, Shell withdrew some of its A/D registrations, including foliar application to corn, and initiated further extensive carcinogenicity studies, known as the Tunstall 1 tests, in its Tunstall Laboratories in England. The results of these tests, transmitted to the FDA in 1968 though not published until 1973, confirmed the carcinogenicity of A/D contrary to the conclusions earlier claimed by Shell.[24] The FDA, however, took no action and did not seem anxious to share the information with anyone, including a blue ribbon HEW advisory committee appointed by Secretary Robert Finch in 1969 to examine the relationship between pesticides and health and to consider whether DDT should be banned (the Mrak Commission). At one meeting of the Carcinogenicity Panel of the Commission, a senior FDA scientist, O. Garth Fitzhugh, jocularly remonstrated with some members of the panel,* "I don't know why you should be so concerned about the carcinogenicity of DDT, you should see what we have on dieldrin." When asked what the FDA "had" on dieldrin, the answer was, "That's confidential."

The Mrak Commission was nevertheless able to conclude, on the basis of the 1962 FDA test in which Fitzhugh had been involved, that A/D were carcinogenic and should be banned.[25] Under pressure from the environmentalists, armed with this fresh support for their position, USDA reluctantly agreed in March, 1970, to cancel "non-essential" uses of A/D, including its application in aquatic environments.

EPA came into existence by order of President Nixon on December 2, 1970. The next day, the Environmental Defense Fund filed a petition to ban all uses of A/D on the grounds of its adverse ecological effects and its carcinogenicity. One month later, EPA Administrator William Ruckelshaus received the decision of the D.C. Circuit Court to ban DDT and to develop policies for cancellation of other toxic pesticides, whenever their use raised "substantial questions of safety." It was against this background of events that the regulatory struggle on A/D began in earnest.

---

*Including the author.

In March, 1971, EPA announced its intent to move to the cancellation of A/D registrations by hearings before an administrative law judge. This action was taken under the authority of the 1947 Federal Insecticide, Fungicide, and Rodenticide Act, which allows the agency to move against pesticides by cancellation or suspension.*

Like all compromises, the cancellation decision did not please anyone. The Environmental Defense Fund promptly appealed, arguing that the cancer risks of A/D posed an "imminent hazard." The industry demanded their rights, under the terms of the 1947 Act, to have the matter referred to an advisory committee appointed by the National Academy of Sciences—National Research Council, which based on the past track record of such committees could have been expected to be sympathetic to the industry position.† The NAS advisory committee released its report in March, 1972, endorsing the continued major uses of A/D.[26] The section of the report dealing with carcinogenicity written by Sternberg, who was later to appear as a principal witness for Shell, is puzzling. Sternberg only discussed the then unpublished Tunstall 1 study, which had concluded that A/D were not carcinogenic, and ignored the published 1962 FDA study, on the basis of which the Mrak Commission had previously concluded that A/D were clearly carcinogenic. Sternberg

---

*Cancellation proceedings are often protracted over several years, while suspension, which is more rigorous and resembles a preliminary injunction in that it bans continued manufacture and distribution during the proceedings, is much more expedited, and can be justified only on the grounds of "imminent hazard." Suspension orders are, however, only temporary bans, pending the final outcome of more definitive cancellation proceedings.

†See also discussion on the National Academy of Sciences Committee on Toxicology 1976 report on "Health Effects of Benzene," the Food Protection Committee 1972 report on Red #2, and reports on a wide range of other topics. It should be noted that membership of many such NAS committees had in the past often reflected dominance by industry representatives or their consultants, who are appointed by NAS staff. Scientific members of the academy have not been commonly involved in these committees. It must, however, be recognized that the NAS itself appreciates these problems and over the last two years or so has instituted various internal reforms which have improved the quality and independence of its reports.

concluded that "if there is a carcinogenic action in dieldrin, it is likely a weak one at a level much like DDT."

In response to a ruling of the appeals court, EPA reaffirmed the cancellation decision in June, 1972, and requested public comment as to whether the agency should proceed to suspension. Shell responded by demanding a public hearing, again its right under the terms of the 1947 Act. Preparation for the trial began. On the government side, the litigation team was headed by Anson Keller and John Kolojeski of the Office of General Counsel. This team started work in virtual isolation, as the Office of Pesticide Programs, where the supposed scientific expertise on pesticides was located, was and still is highly sympathetic to agrichemical interests, quite apart from resenting the Office of General Counsel's apparent policy-making trends and ease of access to the administrator. The Office of Pesticide Programs was actually hostile to the proceedings. While this office was largely staffed by transfers from the FDA and the Pesticide Regulation Division of the USDA, the Office of General Counsel was staffed by young, environment-minded lawyers. The bitter schism which developed, known as the "scientists v. the lawyers," largely reflected the fundamental political ambivalence between environmental activism and traditional pro-industry conservatism, which had existed in the agency since its inception, rather than focusing on specifics of the A/D proceedings.

The failure of the Office of Pesticide Programs to provide scientific assistance in the proceedings opened the door for the Office of General Counsel to go outside the agency for help. This, however, turned out to be not so easy. Most university agricultural economists and entomologists receive research support from the industry and were unwilling to help the government position. The majority of experts on toxicology and carcinogenesis who were approached were either in a similar position or unwilling to take the time to help. The government case had then to rest on the efforts of the small litigation team and a handful of independent outside scientists. These were pitted against the resources of one of the largest and most powerful law firms in Washington, Arnold and Porter, under the direction of William D. Rogers, supported by a profusion of consultants from universities all over the world. In the government case against Shell conducted by EPA, Shell was supported in court by another branch of government, the USDA. The legal fees of Shell amounted to approximately $1 million. These were more than amply repaid by their annual profits of $10 million from continued sales of A/D during the proceedings, which it was to Shell's advantage to protract.

After months of unsuccessful negotiations, the cancellation hearings began on August 7, 1973. News of the Mississippi chicken massacre of February, 1974, interrupted the leisurely pace of the proceedings.[27] This triggered an EPA announcement that it was again considering suspension. It asked Shell to agree to discontinue its intended A/D manufacture for the 1975 crop year, scheduled to begin around September, 1974. Shell refused. EPA then dropped its plans for suspension, presumably out of deference to Congressman Whitten, whose House Appropriations Subcommittee was then reviewing the EPA budget.

The reluctance of EPA to proceed more aggressively on the suspension of A/D was beginning to draw unfavorable comments from the press. On August 2, 1974, the new EPA administrator, Russell Train, announced his decision to suspend on the grounds of "imminent hazards," noting that production and use of A/D had recently increased, that environmental and body burdens of A/D were also increasing, and that further evidence on carcinogenicity had developed. In spite of the acknowledgment of "imminent hazard" in the suspension order, Train allowed the continued sale of existing A/D stocks. It was no secret that EPA had little option but to permit this or be faced with the statutory requirement of indemnifying Shell for unused stocks.

The cancellation record, consisting of about 24,000 pages of transcript and 950 exhibits comprising another

11,000 pages, was then incorporated into the suspension proceedings, which began on September 1, 1974. Because of the urgent nature of the suspension hearings, only fifteen days were allowed for opposing arguments. The final EPA brief was submitted on September 16,[28] and Judge Perlman submitted his decision to the administrator on September 20, recommending suspension.[29] This was subsequently confirmed by the administrator on October 1, 1974.[30]

Of particular importance was the incorporation of the "nine cancer principles" in the final EPA brief as "established principles of carcinogenicity which can be applied to individual substances to determine their human cancer hazard." These principles, which were similar to the "seven cancer principles" used by EPA in the DDT cancellation proceedings, were developed by Kolojeski of the Office of General Counsel, based on the testimony of its "acknowledged cancer experts," Umberto Saffiotti of the NCI in particular. These nine principles, which were backed up by extensive supporting documentation and references and also by refutation of contrary Shell evidence, were implicitly incorporated in both the recommended decision of Judge Perlman and the subsequent decision of the administrator. These principles were also to become the salient point of contention in the subsequent C/H hearings.

The principles aroused the strident opposition of industry. Industry objections were largely channelled through a task force of the Council for Agricultural Science and Technology (CAST), composed of seventeen trade and largely captive scientific associations.* The CAST task force consisted of thirteen scientists, including Newberne, the Shell witness, and Jesse L. Steinfeld, Professor of Medicine at the University of California and previously U.S. surgeon general. The task force reports reaffirmed the industry position that the burden of prov-

---

*In 1976, agribusiness directly contributed 65 percent of CAST's $116,000 budget.

ing the safety of a pesticide was the responsibility of the public, and recommended that rodents were too sensitive for carcinogenicity tests and should be replaced by monkeys.[31] Not only is the latter suggestion economically prohibitive, but given the longer life span of monkeys it would also mean that any carcinogenicity test would take over ten years, rather than the two years required with rodents.

Both sides appealed the administrator's decision, the Environmental Defense Fund on the grounds that the suspension order still allowed use of existing A/D stocks, and Shell and USDA on the grounds that it objected to the basis of the ruling. There was considerable jockeying as to where the appeal should be heard, the Environmental Defense Fund favoring the D.C. Circuit Court, and Shell favoring the more sympathetic climate of the Fifth Circuit in New Orleans. The case was heard in D.C., and the decision of the administrator was affirmed in a unanimous decision of the court. In April, 1975, Shell announced that it would no longer manufacture A/D for use in the United States. A West Coast firm now manufactures aldrin for those relatively small uses exempted in the original cancellation order.

Dieldrin, meanwhile, continues to be sold and used in most countries outside the United States. The EPA decision banning A/D was rejected in Britain on the grounds that "experts not trial judges were competent to judge the issue" of carcinogenicity. The British experts who concluded that dieldrin is not carcinogenic are members of a Pesticide Safety Precaution Scheme committee of the Ministry of Agriculture and Fisheries, which meets behind closed doors. The ministry is closely linked with industrial and agricultural interests.[32]

Summary

Aldrin/dieldrin (A/D) are highly persistent organochlorine insecticides which have been used mainly for the prevention and treatment of corn infestation, in spite of evidence that the complex of insects involved have become largely resistant. Use of these insecticides has resulted in extensive environmental contamination of air, soil, water, fish, wildlife, and meat products, resulting in major economic losses to the agricultural and fishing industries, and also contamination of the human body.

The carcinogenicity of A/D was established in animal tests by the FDA in 1962 and subsequently confirmed in tests by the manufacturer, Shell Chemical Company, in spite of their claims to the contrary. In regulatory proceedings against these insecticides by EPA, beginning in 1971, Shell and an extensive array of its academic consultants attempted to argue away the findings of carcinogenicity in its own and other tests by developing a set of scientific myths, escalating to the assertion that mice are unsuitable animals for carcinogenicity tests. Shell's confidence in these positions did not seem shaken by the fact that they had regularly used negative results in mouse carcinogenicity tests as proof of the safety of a wide range of their other chemical products, and also by the fact that A/D were carcinogenic in rats, besides mice. As a fallback position, Shell argued that even if the animal tests were positive, these should be discounted, as there was no evidence of carcinogenic effects in workers involved in the manufacture of A/D. However, the number of workers exposed was so few and the period of time over which they were observed was so brief that any possibility of detecting even a powerful carcinogenic effect was virtually excluded.

The success of the regulatory proceedings against A/D, resulting in their 1976 ban on the grounds of imminent carcinogenic hazard, was due to the combined efforts of a public interest group and the EPA's Office of General Counsel aided by a small team of independent experts. These were pitted against the massive legal and scientific resources of Shell and the USDA, which supported Shell's position, aided by the politically powerful Southern congressional network and its own Office of Pesticide Programs, which was hostile to the proceedings.

Chlordane/Heptachlor

Chlordane and heptachlor (C/H) are two closely related organochlorine pesticides of the same general cyclodiene subclass as A/D. Both chlordane and heptachlor are transformed in the environment and in the body to persistent and stable epoxide derivatives, oxychlordane and heptachlor epoxide, respectively. Technical formulations of chlordane contain about 7 to 12 percent heptachlor, besides various other related impurities.

Sales and Uses

Chlordane and heptachlor have been sold since the late 1940s and are exclusively manufactured by the Chicago-based Velsicol Chemical Corporation, a subsidiary of Northwest Industries Inc. (Chlordane is manufactured at Marshall, Illinois and heptachlor at Memphis, Tennessee.) Their major agricultural uses have been as corn soil insecticides. They have also been used for treatment of termite infestation and as general insecticides around the home, lawn, and garden. Even prior to their suspension in 1975, the agricultural uses of C/H were on a gradual decline due to increasing insect resistance and the emergence of alternatives, particularly organophosphate and carbamate insecticides, which are more effective and do not pose comparable problems of environmental contamination. This decline was, however, temporarily arrested between 1973 and 1975, when the regulatory proceedings against A/D created demands for alternative corn soil insecticides.

Environmental Contamination[1]

Chlordane and heptachlor and their principal derivatives are highly persistent, mobile, and fat soluble. Like A/D, their use in accordance with recommended agricultural practice has led to widespread environmental dissemination and the pollution of soil, air, and water. This, in turn, has led to accumulation and concentration of C/H in the food chain and resulted in substantial human contamination.

Residues of C/H are found in soil more than ten years following application.[2] Although the highest levels occur in agricultural areas of the corn belt states, residues are also high in urban soils, with average recorded values in the early 1970s of 0.16 ppm resulting from use around the home and garden. C/H are also highly volatile and escape into the air, whether applied to the soil surface or injected into the subsoil.[3] In addition, C/H are transported as dust, particularly in areas where soil erosion is high. Dust levels of chlordane ranged up to 135 ppm in homes of pesticide formulators, and to about 40 ppm in homes of people who have no occupational exposure. Based on EPA monitoring data, the daily respiratory intake of an average adult would be in the order of 0.6 μg chlordane and 0.2 μg heptachlor, levels of the same order of magnitude as those from food.

Residues of C/H are found in surface waters all over the United States. Stream sediments containing chlordane residues as high as 800 ppb have been found in corn belt states. Chlordane residues are also found in fresh and saltwater fish, with levels reaching as high as 24 ppm. Laboratory experiments have shown that even very low levels of C/H cause mortality and reproductive failure in fish. Significant residues of heptachlor epoxide and oxychlordane have been found in eggs of many birds, including fish eaters. Much wildlife has been killed as a result of using C/H to control fire ants.

Diet is probably the most important source of human contamination by C/H.[4] Once applied to soil, these insecticides begin a continuous movement up the food chain. Root crops grown on land treated with C/H as long as ten years ago absorb measurable quantities of these insecticides. FDA market basket surveys in 1973 and 1974 have shown that C/H, and particularly heptachlor epoxide, are found in the majority of dairy products, meat, poultry, and fish; the data on oxychlordane, while more recent and limited, also indicate extensive food contamination. The calculated total daily intake of heptachlor and its epoxide in the diet of a normal adult, excluding other environmental sources, is about 0.7 μg.

Residues of heptachlor epoxide and oxychlordane are found in virtually all body fat samples, each at levels from 0.1 to 0.2 ppm but ranging as high as 10 ppm for the former and 2 ppm for the latter.[5] Levels in the United States are lower than in France and Italy, where agricultural use of C/H is more intense. Residues are also found in umbilical cord blood and in mothers' milk. It is important to note that human fat residues of heptachlor epoxide are roughly the same magnitude as levels in rats following feeding with the lowest level tested and found to be carcinogenic (0.5 ppm).

Nearly all available information on environmental contamination with C/H is related to agricultural use. It is remarkable that there seem to be no published reports on contamination of air, dust, drapes, textiles, food, and the human body following home and garden use, especially following treatment for termite infestation.

Carcinogenicity of C/H

As was the case with A/D, the regulatory battle to ban C/H largely focused on questions of carcinogenicity. C/H have been extensively tested for carcinogenicity in rats and mice in a total of some eleven studies, most of which have never been published.[6] One exception is a 1965 FDA mouse study on the basis of which the Mrak Commission in 1969 concluded that heptachlor and its epoxide were carcinogenic.[7] Apart from this study and more recent ones by the NCI, the results of which first became available in 1975,[8] the main body of information on the basis of which C/H were claimed to be noncarcinogenic and safe was generated under contract to Velsicol by two commercial testing laboratories, the Kettering Laboratories of the University of Cincinnati, Ohio, and the International Research Development Corporation, Mattawan, Michigan. Studies in the latter laboratory were based on feeding C/H and heptachlor epoxide to mice and concluded that these insecticides were noncarcinogenic, although they noted a dose-related incidence of "liver nodules" in treated animals. Similar negative conclusions were reached in the Kettering rat studies.

In view of the uncertain validity of the conclusions of these various carcinogenicity tests, particularly those of the Kettering and the International Research Development Corporation, EPA decided that the liver sections should be reexamined by a team of independent pathologists headed by Melvin Reuber. Reuber undertook an extensive examination of most available liver sections, and these were spot-checked by four other pathologists in the team, who in general confirmed Reuber's findings.[9] Where the International Research Development Corporation and Kettering had reported either normal conditions or nonmalignant nodular liver lesions in C/H-treated mice and rats, Reuber and his team found a high incidence of unequivocal liver cancers. Reuber's results in many cases were statistically analyzed, showing that the incidence of liver cancers induced by C/H were highly significant. An honest difference of opinion, you might say, but for the fact that there were no discrepancies between the diagnoses of the industry laboratories and the EPA team in untreated control animals. Nor were there discrepancies in diagnoses of the positive control animals treated with the known potent carcinogen acetylaminofluorene, as a check on their sensitivity, which resulted in a high incidence of liver cancers. An additional obstacle to the "honest difference of opinion" theory is that two Velsicol consultants who reviewed the liver sections of the International Research Development Corporation concluded that these showed cancers in the C/H-treated animals. They informed Velsicol of this by letter in December, 1972.[10]

C/H were also tested in the NCI bioassay program, the preliminary results becoming available in 1975 and the final published results in 1977. These studies confirmed the carcinogenicity of C/H in mice, although the results in rats were less clear-cut.[11]

Taken together, the results of all these tests, particularly following independent reevaluation of the industry-generated data, clearly proved that C/H and heptachlor epoxide were carcinogenic in mice. These conclusions were subsequently confirmed by a 1977 Pesticide Committee report of the National Academy of Sciences, which agreed that there was unquestionable evidence of carcinogenicity in mice, and that accordingly, C/H represented a carcinogenic hazard to humans.[12] The rat data, while less extensive, again proved the carcinogenicity of heptachlor and its epoxide. While the results of chlordane testing in rats were equivocal, all the positive data on heptachlor and its epoxide are also applicable to technical chlordane, since heptachlor is a major component of technical chlordane.

As was the case in the A/D hearings, the industry minimized the human relevance of the carcinogenicity findings in rodents.* Industry further asserted that great weight should be attached to the human epidemiological

---

*The scientific and emotional demeanor of some industry witnesses was unusual. William J. Butler, an English pathologist, in response to a question as to whether the induction of liver cancer in rats by C/H in the NCI Tests constituted evidence of carcinogenicity, responded, "This would slightly raise my suspicions."[13] Another consultant, John Rust of the University of Chicago Medical School, responding to a question on the occurrence of metastases in the lungs of rodents from liver cancers induced by C/H, expostulated, "I would like to say right now [gesturing towards respondent's counsel] that Judge Perlman ought to throw you bastards out for bringing this to court."[14] Other industry consultants, such as Klaus Stemmer and Frank Cleveland of the Kettering Laboratories, who had undertaken carcinogenicity tests for Velsicol purporting to show that C/H were not carcinogenic, admitted in court that they had no training or expertise in chemical carcinogenesis.[15]

studies which had failed to demonstrate the carcinogenicity of C/H. Three such unpublished studies have been recently conducted on behalf of Velsicol, two on pest control operators, and one on workers involved in the manufacture of C/H.[16]* All these studies suffered from the major defects of inappropriate methodology, too few workers exposed, too brief duration of follow-up, lack of exposure records, and lack of appropriate controls. As a result, it is impossible to make any valid inferences on safety or carcinogenicity.

Over the last twenty years there has been an accumulation of scattered reports of aplastic anaemia and leukaemia, besides other malignant disease, in humans exposed to C/H, under a wide range of conditions. There have also been recent reports of cancer and leukaemia in infants and young children born to mothers exposed to chlordane during pregnancy following house-proofing for termites.[17] Recent product liability suits filed by workers who have developed cancers of various sites against Velsicol and exterminating companies have been settled out of court, presumably to avoid the possibility of a successful legal precedent.

The "Banning" of C/H

On November 18, 1974, EPA announced its intent to cancel all agricultural and domestic uses of C/H, excluding termite control, on the basis of carcinogenicity and widespread environmental contamination.

In the agency's first pretrial brief of April 1, 1975, the

---

*Typical of these studies was one presented by a Velsicol consultant, Brian MacMahon, Professor of Epidemiology at the Harvard School of Public Health, in testimony at the cancellation proceedings (FIFRA Docket 33, EPA, 1977). Based on a preliminary study of about 16,000 males with some occupational exposure to CH during 1967–1976, MacMahon concluded that there was no evidence of increased cancer mortality, while admitting the relatively short duration of follow-up of this study. The small number of workers who had been exposed for more than five years also invalidates the conclusion of noncarcinogenicity.

"nine cancer principles" developed during the A/D suspension hearings, were presented as "the most advanced research findings and policy of both national and international cancer experts and agencies," in support of the proposed cancellation.[18] Velsicol objected on a broad overall basis, particularly challenging principles number two, which deals with the essential similarity of benign and malignant tumors following administration of carcinogens, and number seven, affirming scientific inability to set thresholds or safe levels for carcinogens.[19] Velsicol attempted to have the validity of these principles referred to a committee of the National Academy of Sciences for review. EPA opposed this motion on the grounds that "benign" and malignant tumors have synonymous scientific and regulatory implications in carcinogenicity testing. The appeal was denied by Judge Perlman, as was a subsequent appeal by Velsicol on more narrowly defined grounds. In these exchanges, Velsicol took the position that any burden of uncertainty in the carcinogenicity data should be borne by the agency and the public, not by industry.

On June 27, the EPA litigation team, led by Jeffrey H. Howard, Frank J. Sizemore III, and William E. Reukauf, moved to have some thirty-eight facts officially noted and incorporated in the hearing record. The first seventeen facts were an amplification of the nine cancer principles and were developed with the assistance of Umberto Saffiotti, on whose testimony the original nine principles had been largely developed in the A/D hearings.

On July 29, 1975, Administrator Train issued a further notice of intent, this time to suspend all uses of C/H other than those exempted in the cancellation order. Train cited new confirmatory evidence on carcinogenicity based on reevaluation by the EPA team of independent pathologists of previously claimed negative carcinogenicity tests, and declared an "imminent hazard of carcinogenicity" as the basis for his ruling. In his order, the Administrator discussed the seventeen cancer principles as "the basis for evaluation" of cancer risks, and thus insured their adoption in the suspension proceedings.*

In a move apparently intended to neutralize the seventeen principles, William M. Upholt† wrote to NCI, then under the directorship of Frank Rauscher, asking for their reevaluation. This matter was handled in NCI by Gary Flamm.‡ Flamm referred the matter to the Subcommittee on Environmental Carcinogenesis of the National Cancer Advisory Board chaired by Philippe Shubik, Director of the Eppley Cancer Research Institute, of the University of Nebraska. Shubik, then and still a member of the National Cancer Advisory Board, is a well-known industrial consultant who has recently faced charges including mishandling federal funds and conflict of interest.[20]

The Shubik Committee discussed the seventeen cancer principles at a meeting on November 10, 1975, and in principle was sympathetic to them. The transcript of the meeting also makes it clear that the committee was anxious to avoid reversal or criticism of the principles. Shubik, however, prepared an unsigned "working draft," which had neither been reviewed nor approved by his committee, and released it through Flamm to Judge Perlman.[21] The draft not only gave the impression that the NCI committee had rejected cancer principles, but also perpetuated the alleged distinctions between "benign and

---

*The author was involved in these proceedings as an EPA expert witness.

†Senior Science Advisor to the acting administrator for Water and Hazardous Materials, EPA, previously of the Pesticide Regulation Division of USDA.

‡Then assistant director of the Division of Cancer Cause and Prevention, a geneticist recently recruited to the NCI from FDA and noted for his public speeches on the need to develop tests to "exculpate chemicals from carcinogenicity, rather than to indict them."

malignant tumors."* The draft report was immediately picked up by the trade journals and publicized as a formal NCI rejection of the cancer principles.†[22]

The draft report had its presumably intended impact on Judge Perlman, who had been saturated by argument and counter-argument on questions of the carcinogenicity of C/H. Not unnaturally, Perlman was inclined to give weight to the findings of what appeared to be a top-level NCI report.[23]

As news of this intervention leaked out, Shubik and Flamm sent a telegram to Perlman in late November asking that the draft should "not be misinterpreted or used prior to its completion." Additionally, Flamm has since claimed that they were forced to release the draft under the requirements of the Federal Advisory Committee and Freedom of Information Acts. However, there is no record of any such demand for the document under the terms of these Acts.

On December 12, 1975, Judge Perlman submitted his conclusion to EPA, that he was "hesitatingly unwilling at this time to find that heptachlor and chlordane are conclusive carcinogens in laboratory animals . . . [and that he could] not find an 'imminent hazard'."[24] This decision was rejected on December 24 by Administrator Train, who emphasized that while Judge Perlman did not find the evidence on imminent hazard from use of C/H to be conclusive, it certainly was not the agency's burden to establish risks, but rather the registrant's burden to establish safety, and this Velsicol had clearly failed to do.[25] Velsicol appealed the decision to the D.C. Circuit Court of Appeals, which upheld the EPA suspension ruling on November 10, 1976. The suspension created the authority for a temporary ban, pending the final outcome of the

---

*This and other current positions of Shubik on chemical carcinogenesis are in contrast to the views he previously expressed in a government document in 1970 (See Appendix II).

†The final report of the NCI Subcommittee on Environmental Carcinogenesis, issued in June, 1976, is, however, essentially consistent with the 17 cancer principles.

cancellation proceedings. These began in June, 1976, and opposing briefs were filed in January, 1978.

The three years of administrative litigation ended on March 6, 1978, with the announcement by EPA that a settlement had been reached between the litigants, including the Environmental Defense Fund, to phase out all agricultural uses of C/H over a five-year period ending in September, 1982, to allow agricultural users to shift to alternative crops and pest control technologies.[26] The settlement allows the production of no more than 7.25 million pounds of C/H annually, compared to the 20 million pounds prior to the EPA restrictions. All uses during the phase-out are restricted to certified applicators and commercial seed-treating companies.

The settlement is no victory for public health. It was apparently forced on a reluctant Environmental Defense Fund by the alliance of industry and EPA, whose Office of Pesticide Programs has been clearly adversarial to the objectives of effective pesticide regulation and to the efforts of the public interest movement in this regard.* The settlement allows continued public exposure to excessive amounts of these carcinogenic and widely disseminated pesticides. Additionally, the language of the settlement clearly underestimates the human health hazard posed by the continued use of C/H. The settlement contains no legal finding of fact that C/H are carcinogenic and is thus open to subsequent challenge by industry other than the litigants.† Finally, the settlement in no way limits continued domestic use of C/H for termite control.

---

*A seeming conflict of interest in this settlement is posed by the fact that Charles Warren, husband of the Environmental Defense Fund attorney who negotiated and signed the agreement, Jacqueline Warren, is Director of EPA's Office of Legislation.

†Velsicol's position on this is understood to reflect their intent to limit the scope of future legal actions brought against the company by pest control operators or householders developing cancer following use of C/H for termite control. This position is further strengthened by the language of the settlement, which asserts that the previous suspension decision by the EPA against C/H should not be considered as findings of fact under federal rules of evidence—an assertion of questionable legality.

Criminal Indictment of Velsicol

On April 4, 1977, it was reported that a special grand jury
in the Federal Court of Chicago was investigating Velsicol
on charges that the company had criminally conspired to
conceal information on the carcinogenicity of C/H.
Specifically, Velsicol was charged with withholding the
findings of carcinogenicity arrived at by its own consultants in 1972 on the basis of their review of the liver sections in tests done by the International Research Development Corporation. In announcing the indictment, EPA
general counsel stated:

> Velsicol Chemical Co. may have violated the reporting re-
> quirements of #6(a)(2) of the Federal Pesticidal Statute
> [which states that] "if at any time after the registration of a
> pesticide the registrant has additional factual information
> regarding unreasonable adverse effects on the environ-
> ment of the pesticide, he shall submit such information to
> the Administration."

In December, 1977, the federal grand jury handed
down an eleven-count felony indictment, naming six present or former company executives, all of whom face prison
terms, charging:

> From August 1972 to July 1975 the defendants . . . con-
> spired to defraud the United States and conceal material
> facts from the United States Environmental Protection
> Agency by failing to submit data which tended to show
> that Heptachlor and Chlordane induced tumors in labora-
> tory animals and thus might pose a risk of cancer to hu-
> mans.[27]

Summary

Chlordane and heptachlor (C/H), like aldrin and dieldrin
(A/D), are highly persistent organochlorine insecticides
used on corn, around the home as general lawn and garden insecticides, and also for treatment of domestic ter-

mite infestation. Like A/D, their use in accordance with recommended agricultural practice has resulted in extensive environmental contamination.

The carcinogenicity tests on C/H were made under contract to their manufacturer, Velsicol Chemical Company, by a commercial and a university laboratory, both of which reported negative results. During subsequent EPA proceedings against C/H, samples of the histological sections from these tests were reviewed by an independent team of experts who proved that these insecticides were in fact carcinogenic and had induced a high incidence of liver cancers. The impact of these findings was, however, blunted by the intervention of Phillipe Shubik, chairman of a National Cancer Advisory Board subcommittee, and a well-known industrial consultant who at this writing faces major charges, including conflict of interest; Shubik sent EPA a working draft of his subcommittee's report, which challenged the nature of the carcinogenic effects induced by C/H but which had not been seen or approved by committee members. The subsequent refusal of the administrative law judge to suspend the insecticides was, however, reversed by Administrator Train.

Bowing to congressional and industry pressures, EPA subsequently reorganized its internal policies to exclude the possibility of initiation of further litigation against pesticides by its Office of General Counsel and to place this responsibility, instead, largely in the hands of its Pesticide Regulation Division, which has been hostile to the proceedings against both C/H and A/D. (Since this reorganization, EPA has failed to develop successful regulatory actions against any pesticides, and has developed regulations allowing the provisional registration of pesticides which have not been tested for carcinogenicity and other chronic toxic effects.)

Faced with an EPA now apparently hostile to pesticide regulation, a settlement to phase out major agricultural uses of C/H over the next five years has been developed between Velsicol, EPA, and the Environmental

Defense Fund, which had prompted the original proceedings against C/H. The settlement excludes any legal "finding of fact" as to the carcinogenicity of C/H, and also permits their continued use for termite treatment. Termite treatment results in exposure of pest control operators and also householders to C/H. Case reports on the development of aplastic anaemia, leukaemia, and cancers following such exposures are now accumulating.

In December, 1977, the Federal Court of Chicago indicted senior Velsicol executives for having suppressed information on the carcinogenicity of C/H. This information had been reported to Velsicol in 1972 by their consultants on the basis of a review of the histological findings of their contracted carcinogenicity tests on C/H.

Nitrosamines

Although several classes of agents, including synthetic organic chemicals, metals, fibers, and radiation, have been shown over the past few decades to induce a wide range of human cancers, there are many types of cancers for which no such carcinogenic agents have been identified.

Over the last decade, there has been growing interest in the possibility that nitrosamines and other N-nitroso compounds may be a major class of universal carcinogens responsible for a substantial number of human cancers and cancers in other forms of life, under the widest possible range of conditions and circumstances, including pre-industrial societies.[1]

Nitrosamines are a large group of chemicals, many of which are found in air, food, and water, and most of which are highly carcinogenic to a great range of organs in all animal species tested.[2] A more important reason why nitrosamines qualify as prime candidates for human carcinogens is that they can be simply and rapidly synthesized by a process called nitrosation, both in the environment and in the body, from two types of common and extensively distributed compounds, amines and nitrites or nitrogen oxides.[3] In addition to naturally occurring amines, a wide range of consumer products, drugs, pesticides, and industrial chemicals are also amines, and can thus be nitrosated to form nitrosamines.

Basic Chemistry

Nitrosamines are characterized by a terminal N-nitroso, $N-N=O$, group. They are typically formed by the interaction of amines and nitrites or oxides of nitrogen, which are therefore called *precursors* of nitrosamines.[4]

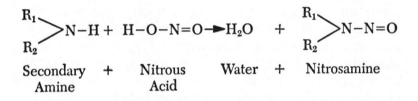

| Secondary Amine | + | Nitrous Acid | Water | + | Nitrosamine |

Chemical analysis and measurement of nitrosamines, particularly at environmental levels in the ppm to ppb range, has until recently been difficult and time-consuming, thus limiting progress in investigating their presence in the environment. These problems have been resolved with the introduction of a highly specific and sensitive instrument, the Thermal Energy Analyzer, developed by the Thermo Electron Cancer Research Center, Waltham, Massachusetts, which is capable of rapid routine analysis of nitrosamines below the ppb level.[5]

Carcinogenicity

Of about 130 different nitrosamines so far tested, 80 percent have been shown to be carcinogenic.[6] Nitrosamines are carcinogenic in more than twenty different animal species tested, and no species has been found to be resistant. Individual nitrosamines produce various types of tumors in many organs of various animal species. Among nitrosamines are some of the most potent known carcinogens: dimethylnitrosamine (DMN), diethylnitrosamine, nitrosopyrrolidine, and dipropylnitrosamine, all of which produce cancers in test animals following administration at the ppm level in food, water, air, or by other routes. The lowest daily level of DMN which has been so far tested in rodents and found to be carcinogenic is 50 μg/kg, which is equivalent to an entire lifetime dose of less than 30 mg.

Formation of Nitrosamines in the Environment[7]

The growing realization that nitrosamines are ubiquitous environmental carcinogens largely reflects the widespread distribution of amines and nitrites or nitrogen oxides. Amines are chemical derivatives of ammonia, and are classified as primary, secondary, tertiary, or quaternary, depending on their increasing degree of chemical substitution. Amines, particularly dimethylamine and diethylamine, are well known constituents of many foods, particularly meat and fish, in which they are found at the 10 ppm range. Many common drugs and pesticides are also amines. Other important sources of amines include nicotine in tobacco smoke, ethanolamines used as emulsifying agents in cosmetics, detergents and pesticides, and air and water pollutants. Finally, amines are a major class of industrial chemicals and are used, for example, as catalysts in the manufacture of plastics, antioxidants in the manufacture of rubber, and fuel additives.

Nitrites are the reduction products of nitrates, the most common form of inorganic nitrogen in the environment. Nitrate/nitrite are present in a wide variety of foods, particularly leafy vegetables, and are also common food additives. Nitrate/nitrite are also normal constituents of drinking water and human saliva. Oxides of nitrogen, often referred to as NO_x, are major air pollutants emitted from all combustion sources, including incinerators and automobiles, and are present at high concentrations in cigarette smoke.

Amines can be nitrosated by nitrite or NO_x to form nitrosamines. These reactions occur in the test tube, air, food, and water—even in the stomach or other organs. A wide range of factors can alter the rates of synthesis of nitrosamines. Rates are increased in acidic conditions, such as those found in the stomach, by bacterial enzymes, and by salts such as thiocyanates, levels of which are particularly high in the saliva of smokers. On the other hand, some chemicals, such as vitamins C and E in high doses, can retard but not block nitrosamine synthesis.

Air

Nitrosamines have been detected by use of the thermal energy analyzer in the air of several American cities, particularly in the vicinity of chemical plants manufacturing or handling amines. In the summer of 1975, levels ranging up to about 0.05 ppb DMN were found in the downtown areas of Belle and Charleston, West Virginia.[8] These were traced to a large Du Pont Chemical complex in Belle, which manufactures a wide range of chemicals and is the largest alkyl amine producer in the United States. Du Pont subsequently reported that they had isolated and plugged the source of the leakage.

DMN levels of about 0.1 ppb have been found in downtown Baltimore, originating two miles away at an FMC Corporation plant which manufactured dimethylhydrazine as a rocket fuel for military purposes. Plant levels were over 300 times higher, ranging up to 36 ppb; levels in an adjacent residential community were about 1 ppb. The rocket fuel production section of the FMC plant was ordered closed in February, 1976.*

It is difficult to translate air levels of DMN into daily human exposures. Making some reasonable assumptions on the average volume and rate of breathing, an atmo-

---

*There is no information available as to where this operation was relocated.

spheric concentration of approximately 1 ppb DMN in air corresponds to a daily intake of about 14 μg or 0.21 μg/kg for an average adult male; this is only about one hundredth of the lowest dose of DMN which has been shown to be carcinogenic in conventional rodent tests. Such intake levels are in excess of DMN concentrations in tobacco smoke and in nitrite-preserved meats.

Among the significant potential sources of amine air pollutants is automobile exhaust. Of approximately seventy registered fuel additives, more than half are amines. These can be nitrosated by NO_X in automobile exhaust or subsequently in the air to form nitrosamines; another common air pollutant, ozone, has been recently shown to catalyze the rate of nitrosation. NO_X are a major class of air pollutants, originating from a wide range of stationary sources, such as municipal incinerators, industrial furnaces and domestic space heating units, besides mobile sources, such as automobiles. Levels of atmospheric NO_X are steadily increasing. According to a recent report of the Council on Environmental Quality, they are the only major pollutants whose concentrations in air have increased since the passage of the Clean Air Act in 1970. Relatively high levels of NO_X, ranging up to 0.4 ppm, are found in the air of large U.S. cities. In a nonindustrial city, mobile and stationary sources contribute about equally to atmospheric levels of NO_X, with the relative proportion from mobile sources increasing during rush hours. In an industrialized city, the contribution of stationary sources is proportionately greater. It may be noted that a current EPA standard regulates automobile emissions of NO_X to levels of 1.5 g/mile, with the goal of reducing emissions to below 0.4 g/mile after 1981. EPA also regulates atmospheric levels of NO_X to an average annual standard of 0.1 ppm, based on short-term acute irritant effects, and without reference to problems of possible long-term effects, including nitrosamine formation. The importance of these problems is further indicated by two recent epidemiological studies, suggesting an association between high atmospheric levels of NO_x and excess cancers of all sites, including breast and lung. Commenting on one of these studies, the National Academy of Sciences concluded:

> The consistent relation postulated by Hickey between cancer death rates and nitrogen dioxide are of enormous potential importance. Hickey reported an association in 38 metropolitan areas for breast, lung and total cancer over a nitrogen dioxide concentration range of 0.08–0.116 mg/m³ (0.04–0.06 ppm), concentrations that are frequently encountered in the ambient air of large cities.[9]

It should be appreciated, however, that such attempted correlations between a single pollution index, NO_x, and several types of cancer may be simplistic, and not necessarily implicate that specific pollutant. Rather, the correlations may reflect an overall increased exposure to a wide range of environmental pollutants. Regardless of possible limitations in these epidemiological studies, recent evidence on environmental synthesis of nitrosamines, and on high levels of atmospheric nitrosamines, lends still further urgency for a long-term NO_x exposure standard reflecting these considerations.

Water

There has been relatively little work on the detection and measurement of nitrosamines in water. High concentrations have been found in a limited number of samples of sea and river water, and effluents from sewage plants treating wastewater from industries using or manufacturing amines or nitrosamines. DMN levels as high as 9 ppb have been detected in effluents from sewage treatment facilities handling wastewater from the FMC plant in Baltimore and the Du Pont plant in Belle, West Virginia. The intake for the drinking water supply of the Du Pont plant was about 500 feet downstream from where it discharged its effluents into the Kanawha River.

Food

Since time immemorial, nitrate has been used to preserve and cure meat. In fact, early European cave paintings show the use of saltpeter for this purpose by the Cro-Magnon man. The typical pink-red color of cured meat is due to the interaction of nitrite, formed by the reduction of nitrate, with myoglobin—a muscle protein related to the blood pigment hemoglobin—to form colored derivatives.

Nitrite has a general anti-bacterial action, besides being particularly effective in inhibiting the outgrowth of spores of *Clostridium botulinum.* For this reason, nitrite is used to avoid the production of the heat-stable toxin responsible for the fatal food poisoning, botulism. Botulism is a very rare disease, mainly occurring under anaerobic conditions in cold cuts and other processed meats.

Over the years, the meat packing and processing industries have found that certain nitrate/nitrite ratios were ideal both for preserving meat and also producing the reddish color which consumers have grown to expect as visual proof of so-called "freshness." As the necessity for preservation has diminished, largely owing to modern refrigeration methods, the "cosmetic" use of nitrite has assumed greater importance to the meat industry. Until recently, USDA and FDA standards have allowed addition of nitrite to meat and fish up to levels of about 200 ppm, regardless of whether its use is preservative or, as is mainly the case, cosmetic.

Nitrosamines have been found in many different meat and fish products, as expected from their content of natural constituent amines and nitrite food additives.[10] The highest concentrations of nitrosamines in food are found in cooked bacon, with DMN levels as high as 10 ppb, and nitrosopyrrolidine levels as high as 50 ppb. Nitrosamine carcinogens have also been found in various other foods such as cheese, salami, hot dogs, nitrite-cured sable fish, salmon, and shad.

Nitrosamine formation in food can largely be avoided by banning the use of nitrite as a food additive, as has been done in Norway, for all purposes except when otherwise required by proven risks of botulism. Even then, minimal levels should be used, and whenever feasible nitrite should be replaced by other effective preservatives, including common salt.

On September 19, 1977, a USDA advisory committee on nitrosamines recommended that the meat industry be given up to three years to find replacements for nitrite in all circumstances where addition of nitrite leads to formation of nitrosamine in meats. However, Carol Tucker Foreman, Assistant Secretary for Food and Consumer Services, USDA, in a statement of October 18, 1977, requested the industry to develop information within six months on the prevention of formation of nitrosamines in cooked bacon, either by finding suitable replacements for nitrite, or by reducing nitrite to levels at which no nitrosamine synthesis can be detected. It must be understood that the USDA proposals are based on prevention of nitrosamine formation in the meat itself, and not in the human stomach, a more difficult and possibly a still more important problem.

As a further move to encourage the sale of nitrite-free meat products, on April 28, 1978, USDA announced plans to propose new rules that would allow use of the name "bacon" on bacon-like meat products that differ from traditional bacon in that they contain little or no nitrite or nitrate. The same new rules will apply to corned beef, frankfurters, ham, and similar products. USDA also announced a proposed ban on nitrite and nitrate in baby, toddler, and junior meat foods. Foreman followed this up by an order on May 15, 1978, reducing levels of nitrite which may be added to meat to 120 ppm, effective June 15, 1978, and to 40 ppm by May, 1979. These requirements would reduce to less than 10 ppb the levels of nitrosamines in cooked bacon.[11]

Foreman has been criticized by the industry for wanting to ban bacon. Her obvious intent, of course, is to ban nitrosamine formation in bacon. How this objective is reached is clearly up to the industry.

Pesticides

Many common pesticides can be nitrosated to form nitrosamines. This happens either if the pesticide is formulated as a basic salt, dimethylamine or ethanolamine, or if the pesticide itself contains amine groups. In either circumstance, the common practice of coating metal containers with nitrite to inhibit rusting further contributes to nitrosation.

Very high concentrations of nitrosamines have been recently found in randomly selected commercial samples of pesticide formulations commonly used around the home and garden, as well as for agricultural purposes. These include Trysben (or Benzac), manufactured by Du Pont as an herbicide designed for use on highways and rights-of-way but also generally available to homeowners, and Treflan, the commercial formulation of Trifluralin, manufactured by Eli Lilly, one of the nation's most commonly used herbicides with an annual market of $230 million, mainly used on cotton, vegetables and soybeans. Trysben was found to be contaminated by DMN in concentrations up to 640 ppm, and Treflan was found to be contaminated by dipropylnitrosamine up to 154 ppm.

At hearings on September 20, 1976, before Congressmen John Moss (D-Calif.) and Andrew Maguire (D-N.J.), the industry admitted to these high nitrosamine levels in their products.[12] Du Pont had already recognized the problem and discontinued the practice of adding nitrite to Trysben containers. Lilly agreed to modify their manufacturing process, thereby reducing nitrosamine levels in Treflan approximately tenfold.

The industry, however, attempted to minimize the public health significance of the contamination of their products.[13] Du Pont insisted that Trysben was not used on food crops nor by homeowners, but only by "professional applicators." In fact, Trysben can be purchased in most hardware stores. Lilly asserted that the "trace levels" of nitrosamines in Treflan posed "no hazard to human health" because they are unstable and rapidly "dissipated and degraded in air" and because "the average farm applicator comes in contact with far less nitrosamines [from Treflan] than from other sources" such as eating bacon and smoking cigarettes. Du Pont gave similar assurances, quoting the views of the Haskell Laboratory of Industrial Toxicology that "there was no imminent hazard." This prompted Congressman Maguire to ask, "Who pays their salary?" The reply was, "Du Pont Corporation."[14]

Farm workers were also not impressed by these assurances. In the spring of 1977, the Migrant Legal Action Program filed suit demanding the banning of Treflan and Trysben on the grounds of imminent hazard to field workers using agricultural sprayers and field cultivators. The suit included statements from several workers, presumably considered by the industry as "professional applicators," complaining that they had been heavily exposed to herbicide spray during application and that they were not warned of possible hazards nor given protective equipment.

In addition to the few pesticides tested and found to contain high concentrations of nitrosamines, EPA admitted at the hearings that similar contamination was probable in as many as 1,000 pesticide products on the market.[15] Exposure to these levels of nitrosamines, by routes including inhalation, ingestion, and skin contact, poses major carcinogenic hazards to occupational groups involved in their manufacture, formulation, and application. Hazards are also posed to the general public using such pesticides around the home and garden. These exposures are avoidable. First, industry should discontinue the practice of formulating pesticides as basic salts, and instead formulate them as acid salts. Second, industry should take precautions to avoid nitrosation of amine-containing pesticides, during both manufacture and application. Third, the use of nitrite rust inhibitors should be abandoned whenever there is any possibility of nitrosation. Fourth, pesticides labeled for use by "professional applicators" should not be made available to unskilled operators or to the general public. Finally, greater control should be developed to prevent hazardous occupational exposure at manufacturing, formulating, and application stages.

Drugs[16]

Many common over-the-counter and prescription drugs contain amine groups which can be nitrosated, particularly under acidic conditions in the stomach, to produce high levels of nitrosamines. Many of these drugs are prescribed or taken voluntarily at high doses for prolonged periods: aminopyrine, an analgesic, chlorpromazine, a tranquillizer extensively used to treat psychoses, and methadone, the heroin "substitute" distributed free to addicts in many cities, all of which yield DMN upon nitrosation; Disulfiram, or Antabuse, used to treat alcoholism, which yields diethylnitrosamine; and phenmetrazine, an amphetamine-type drug prescribed to control obesity, and Tolazamide, an oral hypoglycaemic agent used in the treatment of diabetics, both of which yield nitroso derivatives.

Various recommendations have been made to cope with this difficult problem. These include incorporation of high doses of vitamin C in drug formulations, and the use of encapsulated time-release formulations, from which the active amine-containing ingredient will be released in the small intestine rather than in the stomach. At best, these can only reduce nitrosamine yields, but not prevent nitrosation. The ideal solution would be the development of new classes of drugs containing no amines for use in all except life-threatening or terminal diseases. The ingenuity of the pharmaceutical industry can surely meet this challenge.

Cosmetics

Lotions and shampoos are major classes of cosmetics whose function is in part to moisten and soften skin. Many cosmetics contain ethanolamines as wetting agents, which emulsify the oily ingredients and increase their retention and absorption on the skin. Nitrosation of these amines to form the carcinogenic nitrosodiethanolamine has been recently demonstrated. Nitrosamine levels up to 48 ppm have also been identified in common commercially available cosmetics, including baby lotions (Table 7.5).

Excess risks of cancer, particularly of the lung and bladder, have been suggested by recent epidemiological studies on beauticians, who would be expected to be heavily exposed to a great variety of cosmetics. Whether these are related to exposure to nitrosamines or to other carcinogens in cosmetics, such as amine hair dyes or VC (used until recently as an aerosol propellant) has not been determined. In any case, it is clear that cosmetics should be formulated without ethanolamines, possibly using non-nitrogen-containing glycerol derivatives instead.

Table 7.5   Nitrosodiethanolamine Levels Reported in Common Cosmetics

Product	Concentration, ppb
Max Factor, Ultralucent Whipped Creme Makeup	48,000
Revlon, Moon Drops	3,700
Helena Rubinstein, Silk Fashion	1,200
Clairol, Herbal Essence Shampoo	260
Scholl, Rough Skin Remover	140
Johnson's Baby Lotion	100
Avon, Topaz	100

Source: "N-Nitrosamines Found in Toiletry Products," *Chemical and Engineering News*, March 28, 1977, p. 7.

Tobacco Smoke[17]

Tobacco smoke contains high concentrations of NO_x, at levels from 240 to 1,600 ppm, which are acutely irritating to the lung and which are almost completely absorbed during inhalation. Additionally, NO_x can nitrosate the wide range of amines present in smoke to form nitrosamines. The smoke from a typical American cigarette contains various nitrosamine carcinogens, particularly DMN and N-nitrosonornicotine; .the mainstream smoke from twenty U.S. blended cigarettes contains about 2 μg of the former and 3 μg of the latter. French cigarettes are likely to contain still higher nitrosamine levels because of their greater nitrate content.

A recent study has shown that the concentration of DMN in the sidestream smoke emitted from the glowing tip of a cigarette is much greater than the mainstream smoke directly inhaled by smokers.[18] A nonsmoker at a crowded, smoke-filled bar inhales in one hour approximately the same amount of DMN as that inhaled by the smoker of about twenty-five filtered cigarettes. These facts lend urgent emphasis to the assertion of the rights of nonsmokers to breathe air unpolluted by tobacco smoke, which should be accomplished by the segregation of smokers in restaurants, bars, and other public places.

The Workplace

Countless organic chemists, technicians, and students, in industry and universities, have been involved in the synthesis and use of nitrosamines. Such exposure is a suspected cause of the excess cancer rates, especially pancreatic and lymphatic, found by the NCI in a 1969 survey on organic chemists.

Several nitrosamines have been used extensively as accelerators and antioxidants in the manufacture of various types of rubber. Approximately a million and a half pounds of nitrosodiphenylamine, involving exposure of up to 1,000 workers, are now synthesized each year in the United States. This is used as a retardant in the rubber curing process, involving exposures of an additional 5,000 workers. Preliminary studies on the rubber industry have recently revealed marked excesses of cancer of the stomach, prostate, and lymphatic system. What role nitrosamines play in these excess cancers has not yet been determined. This may well prove difficult, since workers in this industry are also exposed to benzene, a known leukemogen, as well as other carcinogens such as benzo[a]pyrene.

Levels of up to 10,000 ppm (1 percent) nitrosodiethanolamine have been recently reported in commercial cutting oils, used by machine operators in innumerable industries for purposes including cooling, grinding, and lubricating.[19] According to NIOSH estimates, approximately 750,000 workers are exposed to cutting oils. Exposure to nitrosamines from these oils occurs via skin contact and inhalation of mists and vapors. The nitrosamines are formed from nitrite and triethanolamine, which are normal constituents of cutting fluids. NIOSH has recommended the omission of these nitrosamine precursors from cutting fluids and introduction of engineering controls and protective equipment.

The finding in August 1975 of relatively high DMN levels in the air of Belle, West Virginia, in proximity to the Du Pont chemical complex stimulated concerns as to possible hazards from occupational exposure to nitrosamines.[20] In December, 1975, Thermo Electron, working under an EPA contract, sampled the workplace air and found DMN levels comparable to those found outside the plant. Du Pont subsequently challenged these findings. Thermo Electron repeated the tests in February, 1976, but this time found no nitrosamines in the plant except in one unrepresentative location. The mystery was solved when Du Pont workers revealed that the company closed and shipped out all of its amines a few weeks prior to the planned February, 1976, monitoring.

These events led to congressional hearings in New Jersey on May 28, 1976, which were filmed by CBS. Du Pont representatives were invited to testify, but declined to do so on grounds of "short notice." Du Pont management quietly attended the hearings as spectators, however, and were obliged to testify when they were found passing notes to the press offering to "field questions . . . at the noon recess."[21]

An additional issue raised at the hearings was the occurrence of an excess risk of cancer in the Du Pont plant in Belle, particularly cancer of the eye and the kidney, and to a lesser extent the lung.[22] Cancer of the eye is exceptionally rare. The occurrence of five cases in a relatively small group of fifty workers, some of whom had cancers of other sites, is of sentinel importance. Based on Connecticut tumor registry data, this is about forty-four times higher than the incidence of cancer that would be expected in a matched control population. Whether the eye cancers are due to a nitrosamine-like carcinogen such as ethylnitrosourea, which induces similar cancers in experimental animals, has not yet been determined. Du Pont has denied the existence of an excess cancer risk in its workers, but refused to make available to NIOSH the necessary records to substantiate its claims, alleging a need to protect the privacy of its workers. In December, 1977, the courts upheld the rights of NIOSH to these records.

In addition to problems of excess cancer risk in Du Pont employees, it should be noted that Kanawha County, where the Belle Du Pont plant is located, is among the highest in the United States in incidence of lung cancer and leukaemia. The same county also has a high rate of central nervous system birth defects.

The Nitrosamine Balance Sheet

It is difficult to compare the relative amounts of all major possible sources of exposure to nitrosamines. Table 7.6 attempts to give some idea of the relative orders of potential

Table 7.6 .Possible Daily Human Exposure to Nitrosamine Carcinogens

Exposure	Nitrosamines*, μg				
	DMN	NDEA	NPYR	NNN	Other
Cooked bacon, 100 g	1	. . .†	5	. . .	. . .
Tobacco smoke, 20 cigarettes	2	. . .	. . .	3	. . .
Bacon and spinach meal, with synthesis, of nitrosamines in the stomach	7	. . .	. . .	. . .	. . .
Drinking water, New Orleans	. . .	. . .	. . .	. . .	8
Air, Baltimore residential community, 1975	10	. . .	. . .	. . .	. . .
Cosmetics, Max Factor, 10 g	. . .	480	. . .	. . .	. . .
Herbicide spill, Trysben, 1 ml	640	. . .	. . .	. . .	. . .

Source: Based on D. H. Fine et al., "Human Exposure to N-nitroso Compounds in the Environment," pp. 293–307, in *Origins of Human Cancer,* Book A., ed. H. H. Hiatt, J. D. Watson, and J. A. Winsten, Cold Spring Harbor Laboratory, 1977.

*DMN = dimethylnitrosamine; NDEA = nitrosodiethanolamine; NPYR = nitrosopyrrolidine; NNN = nitrosonornicotine.

†No data.

exposures involved. There are many problems involved in such comparisons, including the fact that some exposures occur by eating, others by inhalation, and by skin contact. Perhaps a more important limitation still is the fact that, with one exception, all the exposures listed are based on levels of nitrosamines found in the product itself, rather than on the higher levels that can be expected to be synthesized in the body. In the case of the bacon and spinach meal, the exposure level is based on expected yields of DMN formed by interaction of precursors in the stomach. As can be seen, DMN levels in the stomach are higher than in cooked bacon itself.

The ubiquity of nitrosamines makes it imperative that environmental levels be reduced to the smallest limit possible. Methods for achieving this goal depend almost exclusively on rigorously restricting the further introduction of nitrosamine precursors into the environment, especially under conditions of potential interaction.

Summary

Nitrosamines are a large group of chemicals, most of which are carcinogenic, producing tumors in a wide range of organs of a wide range of test animals. Although there is no direct epidemiological evidence, nitrosamines are considered to be major human carcinogens in both nonindustrialized and industrialized countries, particularly because of their ubiquity in the environment. This is due to the fact that they can be easily and rapidly synthesized by the interaction of common precursors, nitrites or oxides of nitrogen and amines, in a process called nitrosation.

Regulatory control of nitrosamine formation can be achieved by avoidance of the use of amine-containing products, such as pesticides, drugs, detergents, cutting oils and cosmetics, and avoidance of adding nitrite to amine-containing materials, including foods such as bacon, particularly under conditions in which nitrosation can occur.

Cancer in its many forms is undoubtedly a natural disease. It is probably one of nature's many ways of eliminating sexually effete individuals who would otherwise, in nature's view, compete for available food resources without advantage to the species as a whole.

F. J. C. Roe, freelance British consultant,
February, 1978

Chapter Eight

How to Improve Industry Data

The overwhelming bulk of benefit and risk data, on the basis of which most regulatory decisions are based, comes from the industries being regulated. These data are either generated and interpreted by in-house scientists or by commercial laboratories and universities under contract. In-house scientific staff are not immune to pressures from research and development and marketing departments anxious to hurry their product or process into commerce. Industrial contracts with commercial laboratories and universities are usually awarded secretly, without bids having first been solicited on the open market, a practice hardly consistent with the ethos of competitive capitalism. The contractee, anxious about the award of future contracts, is also not immune to unspoken pressures to produce information or interpretations consistent with the perceived interests of the contracting industry. Consultants, generally from prestigious universities or research institutes, provide data with an additional mantle of authority. The industrial interests of these consultants, often unknown to the public and to their own institutions, are either not disclosed to the agencies they advise, or, if disclosed, are usually kept confidential. A similar tendency operates in testimony before law courts and congressional committees.

Faults with Industry Data

Constraints on data, from gross inadequacy, biased interpretation, manipulation, suppression and outright destruction, are commonplace, especially when profitable products or processes are involved.[1] Evidence of such constraints now justifies *a priori* reservations about the validity of data developed by institutions or individuals whose economic interests are affected, especially when the data base has been maintained as confidential at industry's insistence.

Decision-making at all levels of government presupposes the availability of a body of information, on the basis of which the merits of alternate policies can be analyzed. If this data base is constrained or invalid, resulting decisions will also be constrained or invalid. This threatens the very fabric of democratic government.

Constraints in the information base will be illustrated in three general areas relating to its generation, interpretation, and suppression or destruction, with particular reference to problems of occupational and environmental cancer.

Constraints in the Generation of Data

The most common problem with industrially generated data is its poor quality. Complementing this are faults of design and performance consciously or unconsciously built into toxicological and epidemiological studies. These tend to produce results influenced or predetermined by short-term marketing considerations.[2]

Deeply concerned by the inadequacy of data submitted in 1967 to the FDA by industry in support of food additive petitions, Commissioner Herbert Ley complained:

> Almost half of the food additive petitions originally submitted to the Food and Drug Administration have been incomplete or have not adequately supported the regulation requested and, therefore have required subsequent supplementation, amendment, withdrawal or denial.[3]

There is substantive evidence that the situation has not improved over the last decade.

Problems related to improper initial design of animal cancer tests include:

1. Using too few animals

2. Exposures in excess of the maximally tolerated dose, resulting in premature animal deaths before onset of cancer

3. Doses too low for the size of the animal test group, resulting in failure to obtain a statistically significant incidence of tumors

4. Deliberate premature sacrifice of animals for other "studies" during the course of the main test, thus depleting the number of animals remaining alive and at risk for cancer

5. Premature termination of the test before sufficient time has elapsed for the animals to develop tumors.

A second set of performance problems relates to husbandry. These include:

1. Poor housing, diet, and care, resulting in infections, sickness, and premature death

2. Failure to insure that each test and control group receive appropriate prescribed treatments as originally intended

3. Failure to inspect cages regularly so that dead animals become decomposed, resulting in the possibility that tumors may be missed at autopsy

4. Inadequate autopsies

5. Failure to examine appropriate tissues and organs for histological (tissue) study

6. Poor record keeping

7. Alteration, falsification, and even destruction of records.

The following examples illustrate common patterns of experimental deficiencies and misconduct. A 1969 review of seventeen industry-sponsored studies on the carcinogenicity of DDT by consultants to the Carcinogenicity Panel of the Mrak Commission on Pesticides concluded that fourteen of these studies were so inherently defective as to preclude any determination of carcinogenicity.[4]

Having spent $500,000 on the carcinogenicity and toxicological testing of the cosmetic food additive Red #40 by Hazelton Laboratories, which concluded that it was safe, Allied confidently submitted these data to FDA in 1970 and embarked on an ambitious advertising and marketing program. Not only had Hazelton failed to perform the customary mouse carcinogenicity test, but their rat test was of little value, as most animals died early in the test from intercurrent infection, not leaving enough alive to have revealed any but a massive carcinogenic effect.[5]

Carcinogenicity tests in rats of aldrin/dieldrin sponsored by Shell and of chlordane/heptachlor sponsored by Velsicol produced results that were claimed negative by the sponsors. In fact, these results were hardly interpretable because such high and toxic doses of both pesticides were fed the animals that many died early in the experiments, before they could have developed cancer.[6]

Other data submitted by Shell and Velsicol were used to claim that their pesticides were not carcinogenic in mice, and that the liver lesions induced in them were not really cancers, but just nonmalignant nodules. Review by independent experts, however, proved just the contrary.[7] Faced with such major discrepancies and under pressure from Senator Kennedy's Subcommittee on Administrative Practice and Procedures, EPA finally reviewed other industry data on pesticides. Twenty-four pesticides were selected on the basis of their highest permissible residues (tolerances) on common foods. Their extensive toxicological files, which had been previously submitted to EPA by a variety of manufacturers, were then independently reevaluated. In an EPA report of April 9, 1976, it was concluded that with one possible exception these data were so inadequate that it was not possible to conclude whether any of the pesticides were safe or whether there would be any hazard in eating common foods with now legal residues.[8]

These and other grave deficiencies in the EPA data base on pesticides were discussed in a recent Congressional Staff Report:

> EPA almost exclusively rules upon data submitted by the pesticide companies. This data is the informational linchpin in the Agency's regulatory program. Yet in spite of repeated warnings, beginning at least 5 years ago, EPA has failed to take corrective action designed to discover and supplement further data.[9]

More serious than inadequacies of data are the numerous examples of fraud, such as those described in the *Congressional Record* of July 30, 1969.[10] Manipulation of data has been established with such drugs as MER/29, for which officials of Richardson-Merrill Company were criminally convicted; Dornwall, for which Wallace and Tiernan Company were found guilty of submitting false data; and Flexin, about which McNeil Laboratories omitted toxicity data on drug-related liver damage, including eleven deaths, in their submissions to the FDA.

On January 20, 1976, then FDA Commissioner Schmidt testified before Senator Edward Kennedy (D-Mass.) that Hazelton Laboratories, under contract to G. D. Searle Company, reported on nonexistent histological findings in carcinogenicity tests on the drug Aldactone.[11] Hazelton was also charged with falsifying data on the artificial sweetener Aspartame.

A striking example of inept design is the fiasco of nitrilotriacetic acid (NTA).[12] In 1970, Monsanto and Procter and Gamble were poised to launch a new type of detergent onto the market, based on NTA instead of phosphates. This would have resulted in the annual discharge of approximately five billion pounds of the new detergent into the surface waters and ultimately into the drinking waters of the United States. The industries concerned had spent about ten years investigating the toxicological and ecological effects of NTA, concluding that it was noncarcinogenic and that it degraded in water into harmless constituents. In fact, the industries had not done a single test to determine the mechanism of degradation of NTA in water, nor of the possible interaction of such degradation products in water with other water pollutants. The industry had also failed to appreciate that degradation was incomplete over a wide range of operating conditions with the resulting likelihood that drinking water could become contaminated with the detergent. These and other considerations led to the "voluntary" withdrawal of NTA from the market with a loss of some $300 million to the industries concerned.* The detergent was subsequently shown in studies sponsored by the National Cancer Institute and

---

*The major precipitating event to the withdrawal of nitrilotriacetic acid from the market was the report that the author prepared as a consultant to the Senate Committee on Public Works which raised substantial questions on safety of the new detergent, besides challenging the claim that its use would prevent eutrophication in lakes, which was the main basis for its proposed large-scale use as an alternative to phosphate detergents.

the National Institute of Environmental Health Sciences
to produce cancer of the kidney and ureter in mice and
rats.

There are similar examples throughout the field of
safety testing, whether of drugs, pesticides, food additives, industrial chemicals — even motor cars. For instance, in 1972 Ford Motor Company manipulated emission control certification tests on their new fleet of cars.
With approval of the Nixon administration and Department of Justice, the industry managed to ward off a subsequent criminal prosecution and jail sentence by paying
a $7 million fine.[13]

Industry has manipulated economic as well as scientific data. It is now common practice for an industry
"threatened" by an impending regulation or standard designed to protect against occupational cancer, environmental pollution, or some other adverse effect to protest
first that the measure is unnecessary and then that it is so
expensive it will put them out of business. In this they are
supported by economic consultants whose analyses apparently confirm the industry contention. For example, the
economic impact analyses of the anticipated costs of meeting the proposed 1 ppm vinyl chloride standard in the
workplace, undertaken by Foster D. Snell and Arthur D.
Little in the summer of 1974, estimated costs of up to $90
billion and job losses of 2.2 million, supporting the industry claim that the standard would be too expensive and
impractical.[14] These estimates have turned out to be
exaggerated, quite apart from neglecting savings to industry from recovery of VC that would otherwise be lost to
the outside air, and also major costs to society from VC-
induced cancer and other diseases in the workplace and
surrounding communities.

Spearheaded by the Manufacturing Chemists Association and Dow Chemical Company, an essential strategy
in the industry attempt to block toxic substances legislation, which had been languishing in Congress for six years
prior to its passage on October 11, 1976, was the claim

that it would cost too much. In 1975, industry asserted that these costs would be in the range of $2 billion a year. In contrast, EPA and the General Accounting Office estimates ranged from $80 to $200 million, costs which are now seen to be closer to the reality.

Constraints in Interpretation of Data

Explaining away awkward data is part of the now familiar scenario of constraints. Over the years, the industry position on carcinogenicity data has been crystallized into a set of five defensive propositions.

These have been aired on two major occasions:[15] at the 1973 meetings of the Department of Labor Advisory Committee on Occupational Carcinogens, by industries including Dow, Du Pont, Rohm and Haas, and Esso Research, in addition to the Manufacturing Chemists Association and the Synthetic Organic Chemical Manufacturers Association; and at the cancellation/suspension hearings on aldrin/dieldrin, by Shell Chemical Company, and on chlordane/heptachlor, by Velsicol Chemical Company. These five propositions are:

1. *"Tumorigens are less dangerous than carcinogens."* This argument was used at the pesticide hearings to explain away the allegedly "benign liver tumors" induced by DDT, aldrin/dieldrin, and chlordane/heptachlor which were hence claimed by industry to be "tumorigens," not carcinogens. Independent review established that these "tumors" are in fact cancers, which in some cases metastasized to the lungs; it was also shown that they produced cancers in a wide range of sites other than the liver and hence are clearly carcinogens. There is no conceivable basis for drawing any scientific and regulatory distinctions between allegedly "benign tumors" and cancers induced by administration of carcinogens.

2. *"Animal carcinogens are less dangerous than human carcinogens."* In other words, the results of animal

tests must be validated by deliberate and continued human exposure before instituting rigorous controls. This argument was vigorously proposed for occupational carcinogens such as dichlorobenzidine and ethyleneimine, for which there are as yet no human data, and is still pressed, even though the activity of most recently recognized "human" carcinogens, such as diethylstilbestrol and vinyl chloride, was first demonstrated in animal tests.

3. *"Most chemicals are carcinogenic when tested at relatively high concentrations."* This is not consistent with available information. Mice or other animals can be fed with massive doses of most chemicals and they will not develop cancer. For instance, in an NCI contract study by Litton Bionetics from 1963 to 1969, approximately 140 industrial compounds and pesticides, selected because of strong suspicions of carcinogenicity, were tested at maximally tolerated doses in two strains of mice. Less than 10 percent of these chemicals were found to be carcinogenic.[16]

Further, of a total of some 6,000 compounds listed in the NCI's "Survey of Compounds which Have Been Tested for Carcinogenic Activity" only about 1,000 have been reported to be carcinogenic. By current standards only half of those tests are considered valid, and a total of about 500 compounds are now accepted as carcinogenic. The compounds on the NCI list were selected on the basis of known similarity to proven carcinogens.

4. *"Safe levels of exposure to carcinogens can be determined."* It is alleged that no or negligible risks result from exposure to "low levels" of occupational or environmental carcinogens. These low levels are generally determined on the basis of the sensitivity of available monitoring techniques, technical expediency, or other poorly articulated concepts. The American Conference of Governmental Industrial Hygienists has in the past assigned acceptable "threshold limit value" levels for carcinogens such as asbestos, BCME, and nickel carbonyl, but expert national and international scientific committees and

regulatory agencies are agreed that there is no mechanism for setting thresholds or safe levels for any chemical carcinogen.

5. *"Human experience has demonstrated the safety of occupational exposure to 'animal carcinogens' or to 'low' levels of human carcinogens."* These claims are generally based on a lack of positive evidence of excess cancer deaths, or on the basis of undisclosed or partially accessible records covering small working populations at risk, with undefined turnover rates and short periods of follow-up. Clearly, such data do not permit development of valid inferences, and fail to recognize inherent limitations of epidemiological techniques.

Dow and Du Pont were insistent at the 1973 Department of Labor Advisory Committee meetings on occupational carcinogens that their own experience had proved the safety of three widely used "animal carcinogens," ethyleneimine, 1-naphthylamine, and methylene-2-bischloroaniline. After repeated challenge to produce the underlying epidemiological data, the industries finally admitted that they had destroyed the workers' records after ten years exposure as a matter of company policy, thereby making it almost impossible to detect a human carcinogenic effect.[17]

While these assertions cannot withstand elementary scientific scrutiny, they have nonetheless been vigorously and effectively asserted in various public forums and adjudicatory proceedings. They are myths, spawned by pressures on industry scientists and academic consultants to develop and interpret safety data on chemical carcinogenesis consistent with short-term marketing interests, and are calculated to minimize the significance of the effects of human exposure to occupational carcinogens.

Apart from explaining away carcinogenesis, attempts have also been made to explain away other chronic toxic effects, including birth defects (teratogenicity). An example of this is a 1971 Dow publication on the teratogenicity in rats of the herbicide 2,4-D.[18] The summary and text of the publication state that it was tested in pregnant rats and found to be nonteratogenic while tabular data indicates the production of a wide range of congenital defects of the skeleton. However, since some of the affected progeny were shown to be capable of surviving in early infancy, Dow decided that the defects were of no particular consequence and could be dismissed. To bolster this position, Dow redefined the standard term teratology as congenital defects that are fatal or preclude optimal function. If generally applied, this definition would exclude thalidomide-type defects and most congenital heart defects.

Suppression or Destruction of Data

Occasionally data that can't be designed out of existence or interpreted away are suppressed or even destroyed. Known instances of this are legion. The carcinogenicity of the organochlorine pesticide kepone, besides its toxic effects on the reproductive and central nervous systems, were discovered by studies sponsored by the manufacturer, Allied Chemical Co., in the early 1960s.[19] Allied suppressed this information for about a decade, until workers at Life Sciences in Honeywell, Virginia, an Allied spinoff corporation, developed crippling neurological and other diseases from exposure to very high levels of kepone in grossly deficient working conditions.

In December 1972, Velsicol was informed by its own consultants that chlordane/heptachlor were carcinogenic.[20] However, the company suppressed this information, resulting in their criminal indictment by a federal grand jury in December, 1977.[21]

Reserve Mining Company testified in court in the early 1970s that there were no alternate sites which could be used for the daily disposal of 67,000 tons of asbestos-laden taconite tailings into Lake Superior. In fact, the company had previously developed detailed plans for land disposal sites.

The carcinogenicity of vinyl chloride in the liver of rats was discovered in late 1972, but the Manufacturing

Chemists Association suppressed this knowledge for more than eighteen months, until the human evidence could no longer be ignored.[22]

In the course of meetings of the Department of Labor's 1973 Advisory Committee on Occupational Carcinogens, Dow and Du Pont admitted routine destruction of workers' records, including those exposed to occupational carcinogens.[23]

Industrial Biotest Labs, Northbrook, Illinois, a subsidiary of Nalco Chemical Company, faced with federal investigation in April, 1977, for fraud and submission of questionable test data, destroyed files dealing with toxicological and carcinogenicity testing of thousands of federally approved products including drugs, pesticides, food additives, and industrial chemicals.[24] The president of the company, A. J. Frisque, has admitted that he ordered the shredding of laboratory documents immediately prior to the initiation of the investigation, but claimed that this was due to a "misunderstanding."

FDA and EPA investigators have established that Industrial Biotest submitted falsified data on potential carcinogens to the government. It has also been established that at least four unidentified major pesticide manufacturers were aware of this fraud when they submitted the test data in product registration applications.[25]

Industrial Biotest has also been charged by Rep. Thomas Downey (D-N.Y.) with having mismanaged toxicological tests by "shoddy amateurish" laboratory practices on irradiated food in a U.S. Army project dating back to 1953, which has so far cost the taxpayer about $51 million.[26] More recently, Industrial Biotest and Nalco have been sued by former industrial clients, including Syntex Pharmaceutical and Wesley-Jesson, Inc., for alleged breach of contract and misrepresentation of test data.*

---

*In June, 1978, Nalco confirmed reports that it was attempting to sell Industrial Biotest to anyone interested.

Extremely grave questions are being raised about the moral standards or ethical behavior of the business world today.

W. Michael Blumenthal, ex-President Bendix Corp., Treasury Secretary, May 25, 1975

How to Improve Industry Data

What Not to Do

The reaction of industry to recently escalating evidence on the constraints of their data base has been one of angry denial followed by grudging acceptance of the possibility of an occasional unfortunate "slip-up." The present response, from which we can probably expect only "more of the same," is to increase their own toxicological and carcinogenicity testing capabilities. One of the earliest manifestations of this approach was the creation in 1974 of the Chemical Industry Institute of Toxicology, supported by the leading chemical industries. The Institute has recently moved to a new $10 million facility in Raleigh, North Carolina, scheduled for completion by the end of 1978. The institute is headed by Leon Golberg, a long-time industrial consultant dedicated to such standard myths as the "benign" nature of liver tumors induced by carcinogenic pesticides. Golberg, asserting that the institute is oriented toward the "public good," is highly critical of EPA for their "crisis approach" to toxic chemicals and of the NCI because their carcinogenicity testing procedures are "likely to produce false positives."[27] The institute's current research activities are being done by outside consulting laboratories, prominent among whom has been Industrial Biotest Laboratories.

Industry is responding to the recent passage of toxic substances legislation with a massive expansion of its facilities.[28] Du Pont recently enlarged its toxicological capabilities in Newark, Illinois, by about 70 percent. Dow increased its Midland, Michigan, facility by 50 percent, and Monsanto, which until now has contracted out its testing to independent laboratories, is building a new facility in St. Louis. Shell recently announced the creation of a new toxicology laboratory in Westhollow, Houston, to be headed by Donald Stevenson, the leading figure of the Shell toxicology team who attempted to discount the liver cancers induced by mice by aldrin/dieldrin at the 1974 EPA hearings.

There is no apparent basis for assuming that any of these new ventures will be less constrained by their direct linkage to industry than any of their predecessors, or any less a threat to long-term industrial interests.

What to Do

Approaches now being developed by FDA, EPA, and other agencies include formalization of protocols or guidelines, formalized inspection, selective auditing and monitoring, and licensing of testing laboratories, with increased penalties for manipulation or suppression of data.* Congress has recognized this problem by allocating an extra $16.6 million to the FDA in 1977 to insure quality control of the data submitted to the agency in support of the products it regulates. (But contracts still seem to be awarded to laboratories found guilty of such practices.) These approaches, however helpful, do not address the inherent conflict of interest, which remains unchanged. Another useful approach developed by Senator Gaylord Nelson (D-Wisc.) with particular reference to drug testing is based on the concept of "third party testing" by federal laboratories at cost to the industry concerned.

---

*A recent move in the direction of providing guidelines for epidemiologic studies has been made by the Guidelines Committee, Epidemiology Work Group, of the Interagency Regulatory Liaison Group. The committee issued a draft "Documentation Guidelines for Epidemiologic Studies: Cohort Studies," on May 31, 1978. These guidelines, while flexible, recommend minimum criteria for satisfactory epidemiologic studies to be used in investigating environmental and occupational health hazards. These include availability of full supporting documentation and definition of follow-up procedures and methods of statistical analysis, discussion of potential bias, and disclosure of sponsorship and source of funding.

Radical approaches are clearly required to free testing from the crippling constraints of corporate influences. One possible approach is based on the introduction of a neutral "buffer" between those who test and those whose product is being tested. This buffer concept was proposed by the author at congressional hearings about six years ago:

> There is a growing consensus of opinion on the need for legislation to ensure impartial and competent testing of all synthetic chemicals for which human exposure is anticipated. The present system of direct, closed-contract negotiations between manufacturing industries and commercial and other testing laboratories is open to abuse, creates obvious mutual constraints, and is thus contrary to consumer, and long-term industrial interests. One possible remedy would be the introduction of a disinterested advisory group or agency to act as an intermediary between manufacturers and commercial and other testing laboratories. Various legal and other safeguards would have to be properly developed to avoid or minimize potential abuses and conflicts of interest in the operation of this intermediary group. Manufacturers would notify the advisory group or agency when safety evaluation was required for a particular chemical. The advisory group would then solicit contract bids on the open market. Bids would be awarded on the basis of economics, quality of protocols, and technical competence. The progress of testing would be monitored by periodic project site visits, as routine with Federal contracts. At the conclusion of the studies, the advisory group would comment on the quality of the data, make appropriate recommendations, and forward these to the regulatory agency concerned for appropriate action. . . . Additionally, quality checks during testing would ensure the high quality and reliability of data, and minimize the need to repeat studies, and thus also reduce pressure on involved federal agencies to accept unsatisfactory data and *post hoc* situations. This approach would not only minimize constraints due to special client interests, but would also serve to upgrade the quality of testing in commercial and other testing laboratories.[29]

Industry could be protected from the possibility of incompetent work by requiring a contractee to post an indemnifying bond, should tests have to be repeated because they were bungled or for any other reason. Some form of limited liability provisions could also be built into a buffer system. This could insure that industry complying with these requirements would be protected from possible open-ended future testing needs, and also from legal responsibility for future adverse effects not predicted by properly conducted tests.

These proposals seem more consistent with the avowed industrial practice than is the present practice of secret award of unbidded contracts to commercial testing laboratories. It would also free top-level corporate management from the influence of those in the lower corporate structure who are over-responsive to short-term marketing interests at the expense of long-term stability and growth.

Finally, there must be greater appreciation of the enormity and public health consequences of the manipulation or suppression of toxicological, epidemiological, and other data on health, safety, and exposure. Medical malpractice suits are now commonplace; the strong threat of laboratory malpractice suits is clearly needed to police the practice of industrial toxicology and safety assessment. Homicide or assault by toxic chemicals is a serious variant of white-collar crime. The recognition and social stigmatization, including maximum criminal penalties, of those involved in these crimes is long overdue.

Part III

The Politics of Cancer

Chapter Nine

Governmental Policies

Environmental and occupational cancer are now becoming prime topics of national concern. Their underlying political and economic determinants are at last becoming appreciated. The data base of past decision-making is now known to have been massively distorted, or constrained, and responsive to narrowly defined special interests. Accordingly, policy and decision-making are at last moving from closed discussions between the executive branch of government and industry into the open political arena.

Congress

Congress is both initially and ultimately responsible for all agency policies and priorities. Congressional control is exercised in the Senate and in the House through committees serving three basic types of functions. *Legislative committees* hold hearings on a particular bill and report out the bill, which is voted up or down on the floor. If voted up, the bill becomes law and provides overall authority to research and regulatory agencies. The *appropriations committees* decide how much money and staff each agency will receive each year. And both types also have an *oversight function:* they examine the administration of a law by the agency concerned and otherwise monitor its performance to see whether the Congressional intent is being met.

The most concrete generalization that can be made about the government policy on carcinogens is that there is no single such policy yet. Rather, policies and responsibilities are distributed over many diverse agencies and institutes, with widely differing philosophies, priorities, and practices and often with overlapping and poorly defined jurisdictions. While these differences reflect such factors as external pressures, historical background, and personalities, the most substantive determinants are the confused and often inconsistent authorities governing regulatory controls over air, water, food, drugs, cosmetics, industrial chemicals, and the workplace. These authorities have been created piecemeal by Congress over the last few decades and now form a legislative patchwork quilt. Rather than resolving legislative ambiguities and stalemates, such as those allowing the continued use of carcinogenic cattle feed additives, Congress has often abdicated its authority and relegated it to regulatory agencies, using vague, value-laden terms such as "unreasonable risks" or "feasibility." The subsequent actions of the regulatory agencies are then open to challenge in the courts, as is failure to take any action. Congress has thus allowed decision-making to evolve into an uneasy triangular relationship, involving besides itself the executive and the courts.

Federal Agencies

Broadly speaking, there are two types of federal agency: those primarily engaged in research, and those primarily engaged in regulation and enforcement.

Inconsistencies apart, federal priorities in cancer research and prevention have been, and continue to be, very low, reflected in relatively trivial total federal expenditures in environmental health. This conclusion was strongly supported by a 1972 congressional report which contrasted the then $215 *million* total federal effort in environmental health with the $82.5 *billion* value of products regulated in 1970 by one agency alone, the FDA.[1] But even the $215 million figure was misleading, for it included biologic agents such as vaccines. When these are eliminated, the total shrinks to a $96 million effort for chemical and physical pollutants, of which only about $24 million was spent for carcinogenesis research. By 1976, federal expenditures in environmental health and carcinogenesis research had more than doubled, totaling $485.7 million and $76.8 million, respectively; however, they are still minute compared to the value of the products and processes regulated by federal agencies.

The National Cancer Institute

The National Cancer Institute (NCI) is the lead agency for cancer research.

Early History   Created in 1937 under the National Cancer Act, the NCI is the only federal institution with exclusive responsibility in cancer research.[2] Although incorporated into the National Institutes of Health in 1944, the NCI has always been considered by Congress and the public as a semi-autonomous agency. This sense of independence was further consolidated by the 1971 National Cancer Act, which assigned managerial responsibility to the director of the NCI, who reports to the President, through the Office of Management and Budget, bypassing the director of the National Institutes of Health and the HEW Secretary.[3]

When the first annual NCI budget of $400,000 was established in 1937, scientific interests in cancer largely focused on problems of treatment, with little concern for prevention. Congressional and public opinion then re-

Table 9.1 Federal Expenditures in Environmental Health and Carcinogenesis Research

Agency	Total 1976 Research Budgets ($ million)	
	Environmental Health	Carcinogenesis Research*
Department of Health, Education, and Welfare (total)	301.1	70.3
National Cancer Institute	(149.5)	(47.5)
National Institute Environmental Health Sciences	49.1	(8.4)
National Institute Occupational Safety and Health	48.8	(8.4)
National Center for Toxicological Research†	12.9	(6.0)
Other agencies	40.8	
Environmental Protection Agency	51.4	1.0
Department of Energy‡	60.7	5.5
National Science Foundation	4.7	NA
Army	14.1	NA
Department of Labor	16.8	NA
National Aeronautics and Space Administration	1.6	NA
Department of Transportation	18.0	NA
Department of Housing and Urban Development	1.8	NA
Department of Interior	7.1	NA
Department of Defense	8.4	NA
TOTAL	485.7	76.8

Source: NIEHS, Report to the Senate Appropriation Committee on Federal Support for Environmental Health Research, 1977.
*NA (not available) means there is no line item on cancer research in the agency's budget.
†Excludes $4 million from EPA.   ‡Excludes radiation carcinogenesis.

flected this attitude. Although considerable research was being conducted in the United States and elsewhere on chemical carcinogenesis, this was largely viewed as basic science, with little relevance to the prevention of human cancer. This background is important to understanding how NCI priorities have evolved over the subsequent four decades.

Attempts were made to challenge these priorities, particularly by Wilhelm C. Hueper, a German-born physician and distinguished researcher on the carcinogenic effects of radioactive agents and aromatic amine dyes at the Haskell Laboratories of DuPont, who was appointed chief of the Environmental Cancer Section of the NCI in 1948. Hueper's outstanding research on environmental and occupational carcinogenesis was matched by his integrity, obduracy, and the energy of his advocacy. Although he was supported by Rod Heller, then NCI director, Hueper ran afoul of the federal establishment, particularly the Atomic Energy Commission and the FDA, quite apart from drawing the concentrated wrath of the chemical industry.[4] Attempts were made to silence him, to censor his reports and block his research. In 1952, Hueper was refused clearance to testify before Congressman James J. Delaney's (D-N.Y.) Select Committee Investigating the Use of Chemicals in Food and Cosmetics, a move that Hueper countered by testifying as a private citizen. In the same year, he was ordered to discontinue his epidemiologic studies on occupational and community cancer.[5]

To Hueper, harassment came early and recognition late.* Hueper is now widely appreciated as the leading pioneer in the concept of cancer prevention.[6] Among other recent distinctions, Hueper, now in his eighties, was presented with the first Annual Award of the Society for

-----

*Recent interest has been expressed in nominating Hueper for a Nobel prize in physiology and medicine.

Occupational and Environmental Health in March, 1975.*
The concluding remarks of the citation read:

> To Wilhelm C. Hueper, M.D., Head of the Environmen-
> tal Cancer Section, National Cancer Institute, Depart-
> ment of Health, Education and Welfare, in recognition of
> his role in pioneering and fostering the study of occupa-
> tional and environmental cancer and in establishing the
> scientific and public awareness that most human cancers
> are caused by environmental factors and can be pre-
> vented.[7]

Hueper, in fact, had little visible impact on NCI priorities. The annual budget of the NCI in 1948 was $14.5
million, of which Hueper's section received $90,000, a
sum which had not materially increased when he retired
sixteen years later, despite a tenfold increase in the NCI's
total budget.[8]

By the late 1950s, research in the treatment of cancer
had produced some interesting leads, particularly the finding that drugs inhibiting folic acid metabolism could produce remissions in childhood leukaemias and other forms
of malignant disease. The significance of these findings
was exaggerated and hailed as the dawn of a new era when
cancer could be cured by the "magic bullet" of chemotherapy. In fact, the basis for such optimism was slender. The
cancer lobby, headed by the late Sidney Farber, politically
astute director of the Children's Cancer Research Foundation, Boston, and including the American Cancer Society
and Mary Lasker,† a New York philanthropist who had
close contacts with the administrations of successive Pres-

---

*The award was made by the author, then president of the society.

†Mary Lasker is the widow of Albert D. Lasker, the multimillionaire
advertising tycoon, who handled American Tobacco's Lucky Strike account
and who coined what has been called the most successful slogan in American
salesmanship "Reach for a Lucky Instead of a Sweet," aimed at inducing
women to smoke. Mary Lasker, however, has a distinguished record of involvement concerning public health.

idents, exerted a powerful influence on Congress and the public. Both were exhorted and persuaded by hard-sell techniques that the cure for cancer was just around the corner, and only needed more support and funding for the American Cancer Society and the NCI. In the naive search for the "magic bullet," the NCI financed a huge and ill-conceived Cancer Chemotherapy Program for mass-screening of hundreds of chemicals, selected on tenuous pretexts, for anticancer activity in tissue culture and animal tumor systems.

The National Cancer Program   The 1971 National Cancer Act,[9] embodying the Senate Conquest of Cancer Act and the House National Cancer Attack Act, had as its principal objective the launching of the National Cancer Program to cure cancer.[10] The Act reflected a Senate report of the National Panel of Consultants on the Conquest of Cancer, of which Farber was a leading member, which sounded a clarion call to attack and eradicate cancer. In a full-page advertisement entitled MR. NIXON, YOU CAN CURE CANCER in the New York Times of December 9, 1969, paid for by the "Citizens Committee for the Conquest of Cancer," whose leaders included Farber and Lasker, Farber is quoted as follows: "We are so close to a cure for cancer. We lack only the will and the kind of money and comprehensive planning that went into putting a man on the moon . . . Why don't we try to conquer cancer by America's 200th birthday."[11]

The Consultants' Report which was presented to the Senate Committee on Labor and Public Welfare on December 4, 1970, effectively led the Congress into believing that the cure for cancer was imminent, needing only a massively funded national effort.* The report also insisted that NCI had to be removed from NIH and be given autonomy in order to find the cure for cancer.[12]

---

*Only a few members of Congress were not persuaded by the cancer lobby, particularly Sen. Gaylord Nelson and Cong. Paul Rogers who tried to fight the separation of NCI from the NIH.

The 1971 legislation itself is poorly drafted and naive. It reflects the bias of the Consultants' Report and emphasizes immediate possibilities for the cure of cancer without attaching any significance to prevention. The Act also authorizes the establishment of National Cancer Centers "for clinical research, training, and demonstration of advanced diagnostic and treatment methods relating to cancer." The centers were not assigned any responsibility for establishing carcinogenesis or epidemiological programs, nor for any other problem-solving activities relating to cancer prevention.

The National Cancer Advisory Board and Panel The 1971 Act mandates major changes in the NCI by establishing strong links with the President and giving it virtual autonomy, while formally retaining it within the parent National Institutes of Health. This move was consistent with the general policy of the Nixon administration in obtaining direct control over Federal agencies.

The NCI Director is authorized to submit his annual budget for approval to the Office of Management and Budget, thereby bypassing the National Institutes of Health and HEW. In addition to personally appointing the NCI Director, the President also appoints a National Cancer Advisory Panel of three which meets monthly and establishes NCI priorities and policies. Back-up for the panel is provided by a Presidentially appointed advisory board of twenty-three members, five from government and eighteen from the public sector, which meets quarterly. The National Cancer Advisory Board is granted executive function, in contrast to its Advisory Council predecessor, which had only advisory functions.

The chairman of the Cancer Panel was and still is Benno Schmidt, a New York investment banker and a friend of the Nixon administration, with ties to the oil, steel and chemical industries through J. H. Whitney and Co., of which he is managing partner. Schmidt has virtually dictated NCI policies over the last seven years. Membership of the Advisory Board has also included industry representatives, such as Elmer Bobst, Warner Lambert, and Clark Wescoe of the drug industry, but no representatives of labor or the public interest movement. Scientific membership of the board largely reflected expertise in cancer diagnosis and treatment. The National Cancer Advisory Board and Cancer Panel have had close interlocking relationships with the leadership of the American Cancer Society.[13]

Conflicts of Interest on the National Cancer Advisory Board   One long-time member of the board is Philippe Shubik, an experienced carcinogenesis researcher. In November, 1975, as chairman of the Subcommittee on Environmental Carcinogenesis, Shubik played a major role in attacking the "cancer principles," leading to the refusal of the EPA administrative law judge to suspend the registrations of chlordane and heptachlor.[14]

Shubik's influence on the Advisory Board has further weakened the regulation of environmental carcinogens. Apart from attacking the cancer principles, Shubik in November, 1975, argued successfully for abandonment of the system of Memoranda of Alert, by which the NCI warned the community of early findings in its bioassay program (designed for large-scale carcinogenicity tests on chemicals to which humans are likely to be exposed).*

Shubik worked closely with then NCI Director Frank Rauscher and curtailed the bioassay program over the objections of the associate director of the Carcinogenesis Program, Umberto Saffiotti. On some occasions, Shubik attended NCI meetings representing his personal industrial interests. At a 1971 meeting to discuss the carcinogenicity of Procter and Gamble's detergent based on nitrilotriacetic acid, Shubik argued for the continued use

---

*General Foods, to whom Shubik consults, is known to have been particularly incensed by the results of a bioassay program test on trichloroethylene, used to decaffeinate coffee, which was found to be carcinogenic and which resulted in losses to the company of some $20 million.[15]

of the product. When asked by Saffiotti, "Would you for the record identify what capacity you are here under?" Shubik replied, "Procter and Gamble."[16]

Shubik's membership on the board poses problems of conflict of interest with respect to his involvement in NCI policy-making while being a major recipient of NCI research funding.* Shubik consults or has consulted for various companies and organizations, including Royal Crown Cola, Abbott Laboratories, Miles Laboratories, General Foods, Procter and Gamble, Colgate Palmolive, the Flavor and Extract Manufacturers Association and the Calorie Control Council.†[18]

Shubik is also involved in a direct conflict of interest over multimillion-dollar contracts from the NCI to the Eppley Cancer Research Institute, University of Nebraska, Omaha, which he directs.‡ As a member of the National Cancer Advisory Board, Shubik has considerable influence over NCI staff, and normal review mechanisms were waived for his contracts which, apart from being awarded noncompetitively, were instead handled by special *ad hoc* procedures (contracts, unlike grants, are monitored by staff of the agency concerned).[19] In spite of what in July, 1977, Congressman David Obey (D-Wisc.) said were "strongly negative comments by a number of reviewers," Shubik's contracts continued to be renewed.[20] Shubik has been the subject of a Congressional inquiry and a General Accounting Office investigation which

---

*Shubik's potential for conflict of interest is not unique on the NCI Advisory Board. In this, he has been joined by Frank J. Dixon, a consultant for Eli Lilly and Co., and Jonathan E. Rhodes, Chairman of the Board and Director of Penwalt Corp., a chemical manufacturer, quite apart from the industry representatives on the board.[17]

†Shubik is also president of the Toxicology Forum, an industry-sponsored colloquium. The secretary of the Forum is David B. Clayson, Deputy Director of the Eppley Cancer Research Inst. and principal investigator of the NCI contract to the Eppley.

‡In the last 10 years the Eppley has received about $23 million in grants and contracts from NCI.

raised serious questions about poor administrative practices and accounting of $12 million of contract expenditures dating back to 1973, including the use of federal funds to support industrial research.[21] The GAO investigation also questioned the scientific value of this multimillion dollar contract, as evidenced by "NCI's inability to cite more than a few notable accomplishments." According to an article in The Omaha World-Herald,* based on the results of a more recent HEW investigation, the government is demanding refund of $1 million from the University of Nebraska for NCI contract funds which it is claimed that Shubik "used for unauthorized purposes."[22] The Eppley Institute, however, claims that only $85,000 of federal funds are unaccounted for.

Shubik continues to exert considerable influence through various channels, including membership on the National Cancer Advisory Board, which in the absence of his prior resignation will extend until 1982.†

The NCI Budget and Priorities   Over the years, the NCI budget has climbed by leaps and bounds from a 1938 level of $400 *thousand* to a 1958 level of $56 *million*, and to a 1968 level of $183 million. Passage of the National Cancer Act, with its strong emphasis on cure rather than prevention, led to a 1971 budget of $223 million, which by 1978 has quadrupled to almost $1 billion (See Table 9.2). The rapid rate of growth of the NCI budget from 1971 through 1975, however, has now leveled off. For the last four years the NCI budget has accounted for about 30 percent of the total NIH budget.

---

*Prior to this article, all criticisms of Shubik and his conflicts of interest which have appeared in the national press were ignored or toned down in the Omaha World-Herald, the leading Nebraska daily, and in other Nebraskan press in general. This may possibly reflect recognition of the substantial federal research dollars Shubik has brought into the state.

†On March 3, 1978, Shubik was given the 27th Annual Bertner Award by the University of Texas M.D. Anderson Hospital and Tumor Institute for "distinguished contributions to cancer research."

Table 9.2 Growth of NCI Budget from 1971 to 1978 in Comparison with that of NIH

Year	Budgets ($ millions)		NCI Budget As a Percentage of NIH Budget	Percent Increase NCI Budget over Previous Year
	NCI	NIH		
1971	$223	$1,183	18.9	29
1972	379	1,467	25.8	70
1973	492	1,713	28.7	30
1974	527	1,745	30.2	7
1975	692	2,044	33.9	31
1976	762	2,201	34.6	10
1977	815	2,500	32.6	7
1978	872	2,800	31.1	7

Source: National Institutes of Health, 1978.

Under the control of the Cancer Panel and Director Rauscher, the budget of the NCI has been skimpy on prevention. The 1976 budget for each of the NCI's five major divisions (Cancer Research; Resources and Centers; Cancer Biology and Diagnosis; Cancer Treatment; Cancer Control and Rehabilitation; and Cancer Cause and Prevention) is given in Table 9.3.

In testifying before Congress in 1976, Rauscher admitted that only 20 percent of the NCI budget went to environmental carcinogenesis, while agreeing that 85 percent of cancers are environmental in origin. But even this low figure of 20 percent was inflated. To be sure, the budget of the Division of Cancer Cause and Prevention was about 18 percent of the NCI total, but this included programs such as virology, constituting almost half the entire budget of the division, which apart from their intrinsic scientific importance have only limited relevance to environmental carcinogenesis. Thus, the percent of the NCI budget devoted to chemical carcinogenesis, comprised by the programs in Carcinogenesis and Field Stud-

Table 9.3   Analysis of the NCI 1976 Budget

Division	Amounts ($ millions)	Percentage of Total
Cancer Research, Resources and Centers	289.9	42.1
Cancer Biology and Diagnosis	49.8	7.2
Cancer Treatment	110.6	16.1
Cancer Control and Rehabilitation	51.4	7.5
Cancer Cause and Prevention	125.4	18.2
Office of Division Director	(9.6)	(1.4)
Virus Cancer Program	(66.3)	(8.2)
Task Forces Program	(5.6)	(0.8)
Field Studies and Statistics Program	(13.8)	(4.0)
Carcinogenesis Program	(40.1)	(5.8)
Office of NCI Director	38.0	5.5
NIH Management Fund	23.0	3.4
Total	638.2	100.0

Source: National Cancer Institute, 1976.

ies and Statistics, amounted to about 12 percent of the total NCI budget of $638 million, rather than the 20 percent claimed by Rauscher.

What have been the returns for all the billions of dollars spent on cancer treatment? In the last four decades there has been little overall improvement in our ability to treat and cure most cancers. The modest improvement from the 20 percent overall five-year survival rates in the mid-1930s to about 33 percent in the mid-1950s reflects advances in surgery, blood transfusion, and antibiotic treatment, rather than specific advances of cancer treatment. Over the last two decades, there has been no further significant improvement in overall cancer survival rates, nor in survival rates for major cancer sites such as lung, stomach, pancreas, and brain, which are still virtual death sentences, nor for breast, colon-rectum, prostate, cervix, and uterus, whose five-year survival rates continue to range from 45 percent to 75 percent, with little or no change as yet (Table 1.4).[23] These facts in no way diminish the importance of recent striking improvements in treatment and survival of some relatively rare cancers, especially Hodgkin's disease, Wilm's tumor, choriocarcinoma, and some leukaemias.

In 1976, an Environmental Epidemiology Branch with a budget of $2.6 million was created in the Field Studies and Statistics Program. Funding has approximately doubled in 1978, now representing about 20 percent of the overall epidemiology program budget.

Of the 1976 Carcinogenesis Program budget of $40.1 million, only some $11 million, less than 2 percent of the total NCI budget, was spent on the bioassay program, which was initiated in 1968 to undertake large-scale carcinogenicity tests on industrial and consumer product chemicals to which populations are currently exposed. Most testing is done under the management of a prime contractor, Tracor Jitco, Inc., thereby diffusing the responsibility of the NCI. Rauscher neglected this program, and with the approval of the Advisory Board and its Subcommittee on Environmental Carcinogenesis, chaired by Shubik, gave it low priority for manpower and resources, gradually bringing its activities to a near halt. In 1973, about 100 new compounds were being tested each year, but within three years this number had declined to 30. In spite of a major increase in the overall NCI budget during this period, there was no parallel increase in the bioassay budget. In fact, in 1976, a total of only five professional staff were allotted to oversee the contractors, analyze the data and prepare technical reports. Additionally, the bioassay program staff were subjected to bureaucratic roadblocks, including frequent temporary reassignments to other responsibilities. As a result, fewer than a half dozen reports were released in 1976, and a backlog of over 200 bioassays, over half of which had been completed more than twelve months previously, had accumulated.

Criticisms of Rauscher   Criticisms of Rauscher's administration, low NCI priorities on environmental carcinogenesis, and the gross inadequacy of the bioassay program gradually surfaced. These were expressed in a report by the Comptroller General of the United States[24] and by Congressman Obey in House Appropriations hearings in 1976.[25] Rauscher was given additional appropriations and instructed to increase emphasis on environmental carcinogenesis. Specifically, he was told by Congress to create sixty new positions in the Carcinogenesis Program and seventeen new positions in the newly formed Epidemiology Branch in 1977. He was also instructed to make $3 million NCI funds available to NIOSH to support a projected $8 million program on occupational carcinogenesis, an instruction ignored in 1976. The criticisms of Rauscher received further dramatic support on April 14, 1976, with the resignation of Saffiotti from the associate directorship of the Carcinogenesis Program, and his transfer to the Experimental Pathology Branch of the program. In a memorandum subsequent to his letter of resignation, Saffiotti protested against NCI policies in the following terms:

> (1) Lack of manpower to operate a rapidly expanding program of major national importance; (2) Inadequate support for carcinogen bioassay operations and for cancer prevention; (3) Inadequate participation offered to staff scientists in the development of NCI policies in this field; (4) Removal of integral components from the program with resulting fragmentation of program direction; and (5) Administrative action and managerial policies.[26]

Saffiotti's resignation was shortly followed by the resignation of other staff from the Carcinogenesis Program. The program was then further emasculated by being split into two administratively distinct units, the Carcinogenesis Testing Program and the Carcinogenesis Research Program. This move essentially deprived the bioassay activities of needed scientific backup.

It had become clear that Rauscher was not only crippling any possibilities for using the vast resources of the NCI to prevent cancer, but that he failed to understand why he should do so. Criticisms against Rauscher escalated, and he resigned from the NCI on November 1, 1976, to assume his present position as Vice President for Research of the American Cancer Society.* His deputy, Guy R. Newell, became acting director of NCI and continued to perpetuate previous policies of low priorities for environmental carcinogenesis.

In spite of its earlier failure to take a leading role in shaping federal research programs on cancer prevention, NCI in the past few years has made some notable achievements. Its contributions have included: supporting research programs on chemical carcinogenesis; developing criteria for application of animal carcinogenicity data to human experience; funding the International Agency for Research on Cancer in Lyon, France, for the production of an excellent series of monographs summarizing the carcinogenicity and related data on major classes of industrial compounds;† the publication of guidelines on carcinogenesis testing in rodents; and providing advice and guidance to regulatory agencies and congressional committees. Saffiotti has served the latter advisory functions with distinction.

---

*Rauscher attributed his resignation to financial needs. His salary at the American Cancer Society is more than double that he received in government.

†These monographs which have been produced on an ongoing basis since 1971 by the secretariat of the agency, under the direction of Lorenzo Tomatis, supported by *ad hoc* teams of international experts are the best available compendia of comprehensive carcinogenicity data (see Lorenzo Tomatis et al., *Cancer Research* 38 (1978): 877–85).

Recent Developments   Present NCI Director Arthur Upton was appointed in July, 1977, with the backing of the scientific community and with the support of labor and public interest groups. Upton, a scientist with particular expertise in radiation carcinogenesis, expresses deep concerns on problems of environmental cancer, and on the urgency of needs for the NCI to institute more effective programs for the prevention of cancer, which he maintains is, or should be, the primary function of the NCI.

So far, Upton's achievements have included: an in-depth review of the entire range of NCI programs and activities; establishment of a policy that contracts, particularly large ones, are to be largely restricted to supporting applied mission or service, rather than basic research; establishment of an Occupational Cancer Task Force which meets regularly with organized labor; and the provision of critically needed support to regulatory agencies, including endorsement of the proposed OSHA "generic" standards on occupational carcinogens and of EPA's proposal for the regulation of carcinogens and other organic pollutants in drinking water. Upton has also accelerated efforts to wipe out the backlog of bioassay reports (Table 9.4), and is now attempting to increase the quality of the bioassay tests which in the past have been handled through Tracor Jitco, Inc., a prime contractor operating through subcontract laboratories such as Gulf South Research Institute, Galveston, Texas.*

In recent congressional testimony, Upton raised questions on what should be the future role and responsibility of the NCI in the bioassay program:

---

*Deficiencies of these early bioassays include the failure to have an adequate number of matched controls and the failure to make proper initial determination of the maximum tolerated dose (MTD), so that in many bioassays test animals died prematurely from acute toxicity and dosages had to be lowered during the course of the tests. However, it must be borne in mind that NCI did not devote substantial resources to these activities, and that large-scale tests of this type must necessarily go through developmental phases.

Table 9.4 Results of the Bioassay Program as of March, 1978

Compound	Use	Results
Chlordecone (Kepone)	Insecticide	+
Chloroform	Various uses	+
Trichloroethylene	Various industrial uses (solvent)	+
1,1,1-Trichloroethane	Various industrial uses (solvent)	0
Dimethoate	Insecticide	0
Proflavine	Pharmaceutical	+(?)
Nitrilotriacetic acid (NTA)	Detergent	+
Phenformin	Pharmaceutical	0(?)
Chlordane	Insecticide	+
Heptachlor	Insecticide	+
Dichlorvos	Insecticide	0(?)
Trisodium ethlenediamine-tetraacetate trihydrate (EDTA)	Pharmaceutical and food additive	0
Tetrachloroethylene	Various industrial uses (solvent)	+
Lindane	Insecticide	0(?)
Captan	Fungicide	+
Photodieldrin®	Insecticide	0
Dapsone	Pharmaceutical	+
Aldrin/dieldrin	Insecticide	+
Dieldrin	Insecticide	0
Picloram	Insecticide	+(?)
Chloramben	Herbicide	+
Tolbutamide	Pharmaceutical	0
Isophosphamide	Pharmaceutical	+
Chlorpropamide	Pharmaceutical	0
Nitrofen	Insecticide	+
3,3'-Iminobis-1-propanol dimethanesulfonate (ester) hydrochloride (IPD)	Pharmaceutical	+(?)
1,1,2,2-Tetrachlorethane	Various industrial uses (solvent)	+
Dibromochloropropane	Insecticide	+
2-Methyl-1-nitroanthraquinone	Various uses	+

Source: NCI, 1978
*Photochemical conversion product of dieldrin
+ = Carcinogenic effect; 0 = No evidence of carcinogenicity under condition of the experiment; (?) = Equivocal results.

> The role of government will need to change over the next
> decade from one of providing major support for chronic
> toxicity testing to one of primary concern with the devel-
> opment and validation of new test methods and quality
> control of testing conducted by industry.[27]

It should also be asked why the taxpayer, through the
NCI, must pay for the testing of profitable chemicals,
rather than the industries concerned. It is proper that the
burden of financial responsibility for the bioassay program
should, wherever appropriate, be shifted from government to industry. It is also clear, however, that the government will have to maintain a direct supervisory role
over the program.

There have been recent discussions at top levels in
HEW as to whether responsibility for the bioassay program should be transferred from the NCI to the National
Institute of Environmental Health Sciences (NIEHS),
which would administer the program through an interagency advisory committee with pass-through funds from
the NCI. Such a move, apart from relieving the apparent
pressures of limited resources on the Bethesda Campus,
would also relieve NCI from the embarrassment and continuing criticisms which have been directed at its administration of the bioassay program in the past. However, it
is questionable whether the bioassay program should be
physically separated from ongoing basic and applied carcinogenesis research, let alone from problem-solving
research on epidemiology and biostatistics in NCI. While
there is little doubt that NIEHS, currently under the direction of David Rall, would handle the bioassay operation
as well as could be expected, considering its wide range of
other interests and priorities, the move would clearly diffuse the responsibility of the NCI and weaken its authority and role as the lead agency in carcinogenesis and
cancer prevention. Rather than taking over the bioassay
program, a more proper and logical role for NIEHS would

be to act as a central clearinghouse for the coordination of testing of industrial chemicals. On such a basis, NIEHS, with input from other research and regulatory agencies, including the Office of Toxic Substances of EPA, could take a key role in setting priorities and selecting chemicals for testing, the responsibilities for which would be widely shared. NCI would continue to undertake chronic toxicity and carcinogenicity tests; FDA and the National Center for Toxicological Research would be the logical place for teratogenicity testing; mutagenicity testing would logically be undertaken by NIEHS, tests on psychobehavioral function could be undertaken by the National Institute for Child Health and Development and also the National Institute of Occupational Safety and Health; and tests for environmental transport and persistence and monitoring could be the responsibility of EPA. These agencies could undertake some of their testing in-house and contract the remainder to outside institutions, with particular reference to mobilizing the untapped potential national resources of space and talent, such as exist at the Argonne, Los Alamos, and Brookhaven National Laboratories.

Unresolved Dilemmas   Upton faces formidable tasks. The most important of these is to articulate explicitly that the major NCI priorities are to prevent or reduce the incidence of cancer, as opposed to primarily supporting basic science and clinical research on cancer. (This position has yet to receive the public endorsement of Donald Fredrickson, Director of NIH.) Such overall institute priorities must be reflected in allocation of budget and personnel at all division levels. In order to do this effectively, Upton must recognize the nature of the pressure groups and lobbying forces shaping current NCI activities and ensure that their continuing influences do not subvert the implementation of his priorities for the prevention of cancer.

Historically, the NCI has operated as a collection of semi-autonomous fiefdoms, each with its own set of objectives, priorities, loyalties, and outside pressure groups, and often working in conflict with each other in the virtual absence of overall coordination and integration. Outside of government, the basic science and clinical communities regard the NCI as their fiscal and political territory, and believe that the prime responsibility of the NCI is to support and promote their respective interests. The basic science and clinical communities, and their committee representatives on the National Cancer Advisory Panel and Board, generate strong pressures to further influence already sympathetic senior NCI staff to support these narrowly defined professional perspectives.

It must be recognized that the low priority which the NCI has accorded to research on environmental carcinogenesis in the past has been an important factor in limiting possible regulatory initiatives for cancer prevention and control. The absence of adequate information on carcinogenicity testing of suspect carcinogens and on epidemiological investigations on environmental and occupational carcinogens is one of the most common arguments used by industry to oppose regulatory controls.

Future Policies   Upton has already expressed the intent that the NCI should exercise a major role in problem-solving approaches to cancer prevention, over and above preserving excellence in basic and clinical sciences. It is, however, clear, that this intent must be reflected explicitly at all division levels in the NCI by appropriate fiscal and personnel allocations. Just as the primary role of the entire USDA is to encourage the production of food and fiber, so should the primary role of the entire NCI be to reduce the incidence of cancer.

It is likely that the next major reauthorization of the NCI budget will be enacted by May 15, 1981, for fiscal years 1982 and beyond. This review will provide a timely opportunity for critical review of the first decade of the National Cancer Program, and an accounting of its approximately $8 billion expenditures.

It is clear that the hard-sell of the 1970 Senate Panel of Consultants has now been replaced by more somber appreciation of the realities. In Benno Schmidt's 1977 report to the President, he stated, "We are still far away from being able to put either a date or a price tag on the ultimate conquest of cancer."[28] A full accounting of the accomplishments of the National Cancer Program is overdue. This could be undertaken by one or several of the appropriate Congressional committees aided by a special staff established for the review, with additional support from the General Accounting Office. The programs of the NCI should be examined, using a wide range of criteria, in relation to its achievements in cancer prevention, cancer treatment, and basic sciences. Its programs should also be examined in relation to other research agencies and to regulatory agencies.

On a more immediate level, a series of substantive policy changes could be implemented that would improve the responsiveness of the NCI to the need for cancer prevention. For the purpose of illustrating how such changes could be reflected at the operational level in NCI, and without prejudice to consideration of alternatives, the following changes in policies may be considered:

1. *Amendments to the National Cancer Act.* First, consideration should be given to the need to insulate NCI from direct Presidential influence, and to restore it to administrative control of NIH. Second, the dictatorial authority of the Senate Panel of Consultants and the executive role of the National Cancer Advisory Board should be replaced by a more conventional advisory function of a council or committee that would be subject to the public checks and balances of the Federal Advisory Committee Act,[29] including attention to needs for disclosure of

special interests of its members.* Third, senior NCI appointments should be upgraded by recruiting qualified scientists with commitment to problem-solving and cancer prevention, in addition to basic and clinical sciences. Fourth, strong emphasis should be given to the development of high priority programs designed to identify causes of cancer and its prevention. An NCI division with an exclusive commitment to environmental carcinogenesis should be authorized, which should have a clearly defined budget commensurate with its importance.† Finally, legislative provision must be created for the reimbursement of NCI by industry for costs of testing profitable chemicals incurred in the bioassay program.

A useful recent initiative in focusing NCI priorities on problem-solving activities has been provided by Congressman Andrew Maguire (D-N.J.) who has introduced the Cancer Prevention Act of 1978 (H.R. 10190).‡ Maguire's Act is a major contribution to the attempt to focus

---

*As presently constituted, the National Cancer Advisory Board is top heavy with clinicians and basic scientists. There are no problem-oriented epidemiologists or statisticians on the Board or Panel, let alone recognized authorities with activist reputations in environmental and occupational carcinogenesis. There are also critical needs on the Board for professional representation from the Department of Energy. Public members of the Board are appointed as political pay-offs rather than as a reflection of deep commitment to cancer prevention; industry is well represented, unlike labor and public interest groups. Board or Panel membership should exclude those scientists who receive, or whose institutes receive, major NCI contracts.

† In May 1978, Gregory T. O'Conor, a pathologist with expertise in geographical influences on cancer, was appointed director of the Division of Cancer Cause and Prevention of the NCI. Discussions are currently in progress concerning the reorganization of the division into two subdivisions, one primarily concerned with ad hoc basic research on carcinogenesis, and the other with problem solving or applied research. The latter's responsibilities would include the bioassay program, cancer epidemiology, environmental monitoring for chemical carcinogens, and providing resources and guidance to the federal and state agencies involved in regulation of carcinogens.

‡ This is an amendment to the National Cancer Act of 1971, key elements of which became part of the Biomedical Research and Training Act (H.R. 10908), sponsored by Congressman Paul Rogers (D-Fla.).

NCI priorities more clearly. Specifically, the Act directs NCI: to intensify its cancer prevention programs; to submit to Congress an annual report listing all known or suspected carcinogens that have been identified in the year, together with estimates of their potential human impact and the efficacy of regulatory controls; to develop demonstration programs designed to protect occupational and other population groups at high cancer risk; and to ensure that cancer centers develop emphasis on cancer prevention rather than cancer cure. The Act also requires that at least four members of the National Cancer Advisory Board be recognized authorities in environmental and occupational carcinogenesis.

2. *Comprehensive cancer centers.* Continued funding of the nineteen centers should be made contingent on their developing strong programs in cancer prevention, with particular emphasis on carcinogenesis and epidemiology, in addition to their present, almost exclusive, emphasis on treatment. Centers should be required to establish tumor registries, with particular interest in identifying environmental and occupational carcinogens. Special emphasis should also be given to the surveillance of occupational populations at high risk of cancer.

3. *The bioassay program.* This should be singled out as a high priority, with adequate budget and personnel. Besides selecting compounds and supervising their testing, with particular emphasis on industrial chemicals, the program should emphasize critical evaluation of the test data and early development of reports, which should also summarize information relevant to problems of human exposure. The bioassay program should be closely related to programs in epidemiology and biostatistics in the NCI, as well as to basic research in carcinogenesis, and should be extended to cover problems of synergistic and other interactions, especially when clues on such interactions are afforded by epidemiology. Consideration should also be given to requiring the contract laboratories, with ap-

propriate supervision, to prepare bioassay reports rather than maintaining this as a direct NCI responsibility. Some system of interim cancer alerts should be restored to give public warning pending publication of the reports.

Careful thinking and planning are needed for the conduct of future bioassay tests. These should be designed as chronic toxicity tests, in which the discovery of carcinogenicity is a major but not exclusive end. Tests should more clearly recognize other important manifestations of chronic toxicity (including toxic effects on the central nervous and reproductive systems, liver, and kidney) by observation and functional studies during the test and histological studies following its conclusion. Technicians can be taught to elicit a wide range of neurobehavioral effects in animals during routine handling. Chromosome and some reproductive studies can be made in animals without prejudicing the two-year bioassay test. There are a wide range of such possibilities for improving the quality and quantity of information that can be derived from the standard two-year bioassay test, leads from which can be followed up by more specialized procedures.[30]

4. *Tobacco research programs.* The major emphasis should be placed on meeting the needs for aggressive epidemiological and other research on smoking and cancer and to develop explicit antismoking educational campaigns. NCI programs on smoking and cancer must be commensurate with the role of tobacco as a major cause of cancer. Future programs must be segregated from the dominant influence of industry (exercised in the past through the NCI Tobacco Working Group) and protected from past patterns of conflict of interest in its award of research support. There must also be increased emphasis on problem-oriented research, including development of improved test methods, analytic and monitoring procedures for environmental and occupational carcinogens, and carcinogenesis research at the cellular level.

5. *Environmental cancer research programs.* NCI should, with the highest possible priority, develop active,

large-scale internal programs on environmental and occupational carcinogenesis research and also fund such research by outside scientists, to whom all appropriate internal resources of NCI should be made available. These activities should encompass experimental carcinogenesis, epidemiology, surveillance of high risk groups, and analytic and monitoring techniques for chemical carcinogens. Basic scientists should be encouraged to develop interest in these problem-solving activities. NCI should also fund the training of scientific investigators in these various fields.

6. *Conflicts of interest in NCI staff.* A vexing scientific conflict of interest has emerged over the past few years among certain branch chiefs and division heads with regard to the award of research contracts in the millions of dollars range to commercial laboratories, particularly in virology and immunology programs. This practice had its genesis in the early days of the National Cancer Program, when the NCI's newly increased budget outstripped the size of its scientific staff. These "captive contracts" have allowed some NCI scientists to build up large research empires in outside laboratories, which are closely directed to pursue research goals consistent with the career objectives of the scientists concerned. In some instances, the award of captive contracts appears to have been accompanied by the restriction or curtailment of awarding competitive contracts to outside scientists in universities or research institutes.

This is an abuse of power which also stultifies competitive scientific research. It is important that some form of independent external peer review system be developed to examine the scientific relevance and validity of these captive contracts.

7. *Policy statements by the NCI.* A final internal problem is to ensure that ill-informed statements and publications by NCI staff minimizing the dangers of environmental cancer, on topics ranging from carcinogens in drinking water to saccharin, are presented to the public as

individual opinions and not under the mantle of NCI authority.

8. *Relation of NCI and regulatory agencies.* NCI should preserve its primary function as a research agency, with emphasis on problem-solving, and should not become directly involved in regulatory details. NCI should, however, develop special formalized large-scale resources for providing guidance and counsel to regulatory agencies on all scientific matters relating to chemical carcinogens in the general environment and workplace.*

Other Research Agencies

The National Institute for Occupational Safety and Health (NIOSH) has exclusive responsibility for research into all aspects of occupational health and safety, including carcinogenesis. This research provides a critical basis for the development of regulatory standards by OSHA.

A major activity of NIOSH is its conduct of epidemiological surveys and health hazard evaluations for industries where major problems of occupational health and safety are suspected. NIOSH is responsible for funding outside research activities, administers a program for establishing Educational Resource Centers at major universities throughout the country, and has developed educational and training programs for industrial hygienists and other professionals. NIOSH periodically issues Current Intelligence Bulletins to alert the occupational health and safety communities to emerging critical problems, and it publishes an annual Registry of Toxic Effects in Chemical Substances, which in 1976 listed 25,000 different chemicals. Included in this is a list of about 2,000 suspect carcinogens.

The major objective of the various research functions

---

*These have already been developed at an informal level between Upton at NCI, Rall at NIEHS, Kennedy at FDA, Bingham at OSHA, and Costle at EPA.

of NIOSH is the development of criteria documents recommending new or revised standards to OSHA. These documents review and summarize the toxicological, epidemiological, industrial hygiene, and control technology information on specific chemical and physical agents and industrial processes. The documents make recommendations on regulatory standards, work practices, and medical surveillance. Nearly eighty have so far been transmitted to OSHA,[31] of which five have brought about new standards. Even before promulgation as regulatory standards, criteria documents are distributed and used widely by industry and labor as a basis for control practices.

NIOSH carries out a number of programs in occupational carcinogenesis. The budget for the carcinogenesis programs has increased from $1.8 million in 1975 to $6.9 million in 1976, reaching $10.7 million in 1977, including $3 million in "pass-through" funds from the NCI.[32] Carcinogenesis funding thus represents approximately 20 percent of NIOSH's total budget of almost $50 million. The occupational carcinogen program includes laboratory studies, field surveillance, and industry-wide epidemiological studies. The surveillance studies, which focus on groups at high risk of developing cancer, have been particularly important. The groups to be studied are identified on the basis of industrial practices, epidemiological data, and information from labor and other sources. Industries recently surveyed by NIOSH include printing, milling and mining, coal gasification, plywood, pulp and paper, steel, metal smelting, and pesticide formulation. NIOSH has also undertaken epidemiological investigations on industries using various carcinogens, including benzene, trichloroethylene, VC, vinylidene chloride, chloroprene, styrene-butadiene, epichlorhydrin, polychlorinated biphenyls, and asbestos-containing talcs.[33]

An important undertaking of NIOSH has been the National Occupational Hazard Survey from 1972 to 1974,[34] covering nearly 5,000 plants and close to one million workers, the results of which were later summarized in a document entitled, "The Right to Know."[35] The survey spelled out the extent and potential costs of exposure of workers to carcinogens:

> One in every four American workers (approximately 21 million) currently may be exposed on either a full or part-time basis to OSHA-regulated hazardous substances. Upwards of 40 to 50 million persons or 23 percent of the general population in the United States may have had exposure to one or more of OSHA-regulated carcinogens or hazardous substances during their working lifetime.
>
> The annual costs to society of monitoring workers with either full or part-time exposures to all OSHA-regulated hazardous substances including carcinogens could range between $675 million and $2 billion.[36]

Besides monitoring, it was estimated that lifelong surveillance costs for just those few carcinogens currently regulated is in the region of $8.5 billion. Such cost estimates ignore possible additional employer liability resulting from discovery of compensable impairment during examination, entitlement under various federal and state programs, recovery for damages under third-party legal action brought by workers, and even greater costs from past exposures to carcinogens not regulated by OSHA.

"The Right to Know" also confirms the fact that a substantial number of workers in industry are exposed to chemicals the identification of which the industry has refused to disclose; over 70 percent of all exposures were found to arise from trade name products of undisclosed composition. According to the document, "A major stumbling block to identifying exposed workers is the failure of chemical re-packagers and primary producers to show the chemical composition of their product."[37] Beyond knowing who has been exposed to what, "There is currently no effective mechanism for locating and notification [of workers]."

Concerns have been growing over the inability to identify workers today who have been exposed to carcinogens in the past. Responding to these concerns and to an amendment to the Internal Revenue Service Code offered by Senator Gaylord Nelson (D-Wisc.), President Carter authorized NIOSH in November, 1977, to obtain from the Internal Revenue Service addresses of workers whom it suspects of having been exposed to carcinogens. Among the first workers targeted for notification are the many who may have been exposed to asbestos, arsenic, benzene, and benzidine.

The previous administration did not give NIOSH high priority. President Ford's request for the 1976 NIOSH budget was $32 million, the same amount as appropriated by Congress in the previous year. His Office of Management and Budget eliminated a proposed line item for occupational carcinogenesis, a move that was countered by Congressman David Obey (D-Wisc.) of the House Appropriations Committee, resulting in an increase in total NIOSH appropriations to $48 million. (Obey has played a major role in overseeing carcinogenesis and related programs and priorities in NCI as well as NIOSH.)

One of the major problems of NIOSH, apart from critical shortages of funds, has been and still is its relatively low political visibility and stature. For example, NIOSH reports directly to the Center for Disease Control in Atlanta, the main HEW institute for infectious diseases. As such, the NIOSH director has no direct access to the HEW secretary (in contrast to the Assistant Secretary of Labor for Occupational Safety and Health, Eula Bingham, who reports directly to the Secretary of Labor). In spite of these problems, NIOSH has made significant strides in its research, epidemiological surveys, training programs (including establishment of Educational Resource Centers), and development of criteria documents.

The previous director of NIOSH was John F. Finklea, who resigned in January, 1978. Prior to Finklea's NIOSH tenure, he was in charge of air pollution biomedical research activities at EPA, where he made important contributions. While at NIOSH, Finklea had to struggle against crippling fiscal limitations imposed by unsympathetic Republican administrations, a Department of Labor more responsive to interests of commerce than health and safety, and the low bureaucratic status of NIOSH.

It has been suggested that NIOSH be dismembered, giving its research functions to the National Institute of Environmental Health Sciences and its health hazard surveys and related activities to OSHA. Merging NIOSH functions with OSHA would risk putting "all one's eggs in one basket." These risks could become very real if Bingham's successors in office were drawn from the same traditions of inactivity that characterized earlier OSHA administrators. However, HEW and the leadership of organized labor appear determined to maintain the integrity of NIOSH as the only federal institution devoted exclusively to research on occupational safety and health. Reaffirmation of HEW's commitment to NIOSH, including projections of promising growth patterns, was vigorously expressed in a recent report by a committee headed by Julius Richmond, Assistant Secretary for Health.

The National Institute for Environmental Health Sciences (NIEHS)   This institute was created within the National Institutes of Health one decade ago. It supports basic research on the toxic effects of environmental pollutants and on ways to predict and avoid possible future crises due to such problems. NIEHS has developed useful programs in chronic toxicity and mutagenesis, besides studies on the environmental transport of toxic agents. Of a 1977 budget of $49 million, about 20 percent was spent on studies of the relationship between carcinogenic and mutagenic effects of chemicals and on the development of short-term predictive tests for carcinogens. NIEHS also funds selected studies in occupational carcinogenesis. There are clearly some ambiguities and areas of jurisdictional overlap between the functions of this institute on the one hand and NCI and NIOSH on the other, as also seen by the recent suggestion to shift responsibility for the bioassay program from the NCI to NIEHS.

The director of NIEHS, David Rall, is competent and enthusiastic. He has also been involved in critical issues such as defending the Delaney Amendment from industry attacks, and in backing the proposed FDA ban on saccharin.

The National Center for Toxicological Research (NCTR)
This center, in Pine Bluff, Arkansas, was established in 1971 by President Nixon, is administered by the FDA, and is jointly funded by the FDA and EPA. Its stated objectives are the development of methodologies for chronic toxicity and carcinogenicity testing, studies on exposure to low levels of carcinogens, and extrapolation of carcinogenicity data from animals to humans. The track record of the NCTR illustrates how research functions are subverted by political considerations. From its inception, senior FDA officials made it clear that they intended using the center to develop data for the purpose of challenging the scientific basis of the Delaney Amendment so as to allow the FDA to set tolerances for carcinogens deliberately added to food. At hearings before Congressman Whitten's Subcommittee on Agriculture and Related Agencies of the House Appropriations Committee in April, 1971, then Commissioner Edwards stated in congressional hearings that "the Pine Bluff testing facility will provide FDA with the scientific basis on which the Delaney anticancer clause may be changed," reiterating his view that the agency is "locked into an all or nothing" position because of the Delaney box. "The FDA didn't want to make it more difficult by recommending changes until it has the scientific data to justify a modification."[38] Four years later FDA made it clear that it had not changed its position of fundamental hostility to the Delaney anticancer clause.[39]

The research programs developed by the NCTR were poorly conceived. The most widely touted of these was the "Mega Mouse" experiment, in which hundreds of thousands of mice were to be tested in attempts to find safe levels for profitable chemical carcinogens, such as DDT, that had been or were about to be banned. Not only did this approach suffer from major statistical problems, but there were not enough personnel available to undertake the necessary autopsies. The center suggested instead that they would spot-check animals at the end of a carcinogenicity test, rather than autopsying them all.*

Responding to mounting criticisms and at the request of HEW, NCI Director Rauscher appointed an expert committee under the chairmanship of the distinguished pathologist, Harold L. Stewart to evaluate the center's programs. The committee's unanimous report in August, 1973, concluded:

> The program will not contribute materially to progress toward its stated objective, viz., improved capability for assessing the carcinogenic hazard for man on the basis of data obtained in laboratory animals.[40]

Morris F. Cranmer, then director of the center, reacted hostilely, asserting that the critics were not familiar with his programs and had failed to understand his objectives. Apparently interested in avoiding embarrassment to the FDA, Rauscher rejected his committee's report. Four years later, however, a National Academy of Sciences committee came to essentially the same conclusions.[41] The immediate problem was resolved in January, 1978, when Cranmer was relieved of his post following investigations by the General Accounting Office and the FBI resulting in charges of conflict of interest and major mishandling of federal funds.[42]

---

*In spite of these problems, results of recent large-scale NCTR tests on the potent carcinogen acetylaminofluorene are consistent with the no-threshold concept of carcinogenesis, as evidenced by a linear extrapolation through zero. In other words, they confirm the extreme difficulty, if not impossibility, of setting "safe levels."

***The Energy Research and Development Administration
(ERDA)*** ERDA was created in 1974 by the Energy
Reorganization Act and is now part of the Department of
Energy. Its Biomedical and Environmental Research Program, budgeted at $122 million in 1977, is responsible for
investigating the public health and environmental effects
of developments in energy technology, including nuclear
power and coal gasification. Most of ERDA's health effects
research is on radiation, but $5.5 million is budgeted for
other aspects of environmental carcinogenesis.

The Council on Environmental Quality (CEQ) The first
official act of President Nixon was the signing of the National Environmental Policy Act, dedicated to improving
environmental quality.[43] The Act also established CEQ in
the executive office of the President, where its primary
duty is to give Congress an Environmental Quality Report each year, setting forth the status and conditions of
the nation's environment. Under the successive leadership
of Russell Train and Russell W. Peterson, the council has
played an important role in developing critical analyses of
environmental pollution problems, in emphasizing the urgent need to develop preventive approaches to environmental problems, particularly cancer, and in stressing the
importance of interagency collaboration in meeting these
objectives. Under the chairmanship of Charles Warren,
who was appointed in March, 1977, the council is living
up to the promise of past performance. Warren came from
the California State Assembly, where he built up a sound
record on energy and environmental concerns. The second member of the three-person council is Gus J. Speth,
appointed in April, 1977, an attorney who was one of the
original founders of the Natural Resources Defense Council and who has strong interests in problems of nuclear
power, water pollution, and corporate policy. Ruth C.
Clusen, president of the League of Women Voters, is considered to be the leading candidate for the third position.

Regulatory Agencies

The function of regulatory agencies is to regulate. This entails not only developing standards but enforcing them as well. The former is cosmetic without the latter. The regulatory function of every agency is mandated by statutory legislative authority, and confusion or ambiguity in the mandate will be reflected in agency practice.[44]

As illustrated in the various case studies in chapters 5, 6, and 7, the track record of federal agencies in regulating carcinogens in the workplace, in consumer products, and in the general environment has been unsatisfactory. Of the few regulatory actions that have been undertaken against carcinogens in the past few years, virtually all have been initiated or instigated by public interest or labor groups (Table 9.5). (See Appendix III for a comprehensive list of substances regulated as carcinogens.) It is clear that the fundamental problem with the regulatory agencies has not been a shortage of laws or ambiguities in the laws, but an unwillingness of the agencies to enforce them.

Statutory Authority   There are two major types of statutory authority governing control of toxic agents and environmental and occupational carcinogens: *product legislation* and *media legislation* (Table 9.6). Product legislation governs the manufacture, distribution, and use of particular products, such as pesticides, food additives, cosmetics, and drugs. Media legislation governs quality of environmental "media," such as air, water, and the workplace.

Product legislation arises from recognition of the basic obligation of a manufacturer to provide a product of "merchantable quality" which has no harmful effects on the consumer other than those explicitly stated on the label.[45] Over the years, the government's authority has extended from simple labelling to the entire composition and manufacture of a product. More important, the burden of proof has gradually been shifted to the manufac-

Table 9.5 Standards Promulgated by Regulatory Agencies to Control or Ban Carcinogens

Legislative Authority	Carcinogen	Agency Action	Action Initiated by Public Interest or Labor Groups*
Occupational Safety and Health Act (Section 6, Workplace standards)	Asbestos	OSHA, 1972	AFL-CIO, 1972
	Package of 14 carcinogens	OSHA, 1973	OCAW and HRG, 1973
	Vinyl chloride	OSHA, 1974	AFL-CIO and URW, 1974
	Coke oven emissions	OSHA, 1976	. . . .
	Benzene	OSHA, 1978	URW, 1976
Clean Air Act (Section 112, Hazardous Air Pollutants)	Beryllium	EPA, 1973	. . . .
	Asbestos	EPA, 1973–1976	
. . . .	Vinyl chloride	EPA, 1976	
Federal Water Pollution Control Act (Section 307, Toxic Pollutants Effluent standards)	DDT	EPA, 1977	EDF, NRDC, CBE, etc.
	Endrin	EPA, 1977	
	Aldrin/dieldrin	EPA, 1977	
	Benzidine	EPA, 1977	
	PCB	EPA, 1977	

(continued on following page)

Table 9.5   (continued)

Legislative Authority	Carcinogen	Agency Action	Action Initiated by Public Interest or Labor Groups*
Federal Insecticide, Fungicide, and Rodenticide Act	DDT	EPA, 1972	EDF, 1969
	Cyanamide	EPA, 1972	....
	Aldrin/dieldrin	EPA, 1974	EDF, 1970
	Vinyl chloride (aerosols)	EPA, 1974	HRG, 1974
	Chlordane/heptachlor	EPA, 1975	EDF, 1974
	Kepone	EPA, 1976	....
	Octamethyl-phosphoramide	EPA, 1976	....
	Safrole	EPA, 1977	....
Federal Food, Drug, and Cosmetic Act	Violet #1	FDA, 1973	CSPI
	Vinyl chloride (aerosols)	FDA, 1974	HRG
	Chloroform (cosmetics)	FDA, 1976	HRG
	Red #2	FDA, 1976	HRG
Consumer Product Safety Act	Vinyl chloride (aerosols)	CPSC, 1974	HRG
	Tris	CPSC, 1977	EDF

Source: S. M. Wolfe, "Standards for Carcinogens: Science Affronted by Politics," in Origins of Human Cancer, Book C, eds. H. H. Heath, J. D. Watson, and J. A. Winsten, (Cold Spring Harbor Laboratory, 1977), pp. 1735–48.

*OCAW = Oil, Chemical and Atomic Workers Union; HRG = Health Research Group; URW = United Rubber Workers; EDF = Environmental Defense Fund; CSPI = Center for Science in the Public Interest; NRDC = Natural Resources Defense Council; CBE = Citizens for a Better Environment.

turer, who now must prove the safety of his products
rather than demanding that the government or public
prove it harmful.

Media legislation attempts to regulate the discharge
or emission of toxic and carcinogenic pollutants into the
community and workplace environment, as recognized by
the subsequent identification of those agents. As such,
media legislation is retrospective rather than anticipatory
in nature. It says, "By all means use the carcinogen, but
don't let any of it or too much of it escape into the envi-

Table 9.6   Legislation Conferring Regulatory Authority for the
Control of Environmental Carcinogens

Type of Legislation	Specific Authority	Regulatory Agency*
Product	Federal Insecticide, Fungicide, and Rodenticide Act	EPA
	Federal Food, Drug, and Cosmetic Act	FDA
	Consumer Product Safety Act	CPSC
	Safe Drinking Water Act	EPA
	Toxic Substances Control Act	EPA
Media	Federal Water Pollution Control Act	EPA
	Federal Clean Air Act	EPA
	Occupational Safety and Health Act	OSHA
	Federal Mine Safety and Health Amendment Act	MSHA

Source: Marion F. Suter and Warren R. Muir, "Federal Programs in Cancer
Research" in *Environmental Cancer*, ed. S. S. Epstein (Springfield, Illinois:
C. C. Thomas, 1979).

*EPA = Environmental Protection Agency; FDA = Food and Drug
Administration; CPSC = Consumer Products Safety Commission; OSHA =
Occupational Safety and Health Administration, Department of Labor;
MSHA = Mine Safety and Health Administration, Department of Labor.

ronment." Media legislation is specifically addressed to one particular environmental component, air, water, or the workplace, without consideration of the essential unity of the environment. In contrast, toxic substances legislation, while generally considered to be product rather than media in type, insofar as it relates to specific chemicals, is unique in that it can exercise multimedia control over chemicals in air, food, and water in the general environment, home, and workplace.

There is considerable overlap and inconsistency between the authorities of the various regulatory agencies. As an example, VC has been regulated separately on five different occasions by four different agencies: in 1974 by OSHA as an occupational carcinogen; in 1974 by EPA as a pesticide propellant; in 1974 by the Consumer Product Safety Commission in various household products; in 1975 by FDA in food and drug products; and in 1976 by EPA as a hazardous air pollutant.

While regulatory agencies depend on research institutes, such as NCI or NIOSH, for providing the essential data base and advice on which standards are developed, most regulatory agencies also have backup research and scientific resources of their own.

Burden of Proof   The ability of an agency to regulate carcinogens and other toxic agents effectively is substantially influenced by whether or not the burden of proof has been determined by statute to be its responsibility as opposed to that of the manufacturer, who may be required to provide the regulatory agency with information on safety prior to marketing and to update such information after marketing. Exceptions to such requirements in product-type legislation are chemicals in consumer products, regulated by the Consumer Product Safety Commission, and cosmetics, regulated by the FDA, where the onus is on government.

In media-type legislation, the burden of proving hazard for carcinogens and other pollutants, in community air and water and in the workplace is placed on the government. Toxic substances legislation offers EPA the discretionary authority to shift the burden of proof to the manufacturer. An exception to the general burden of proof rule can be made when an agency is petitioned to regulate, for instance, a particular carcinogenic chemical. Then the burden rests not with government or the manufacturer, but with the petitioner, almost invariably a public interest or labor group.

The Occupational Safety and Health Administration

OSHA was created in 1970 as an agency within the Department of Labor after considerable lobbying by AFL-CIO and other labor organizations to create an Act that would "assure so far as possible every working man and woman in the nation safe and healthful working conditions."

The Occupational Safety and Health Act authorizes OSHA to establish and enforce three types of standards.[46] The first type are the approximately 400 consensus standards, established under Section 6(a) of the Act, previously developed as threshold limit values by industry or quasi-industry organizations, such as the American National Standards Institute. These were largely designed to protect against immediate toxic effects rather than delayed toxic and carcinogenic effects. In 1974, NIOSH and OSHA developed in a collaborative effort a "Standards Completion Process" to supplement and update the original 400 consensus standards (with the exception of carcinogens and certain other selected substances for which NIOSH is preparing individual criteria documents).

The second type are the new standards, or modification of old ones, which are authorized under Section 6(b) of the Act and designed to assure "to the extent feasible that no employee will suffer material impairment of health."

This is the language of compromise which reflects industrial determination of technological and economic feasibility, rather than the goals of health protection. Although NIOSH supplied OSHA with about eighty criteria documents, the agency, burdened by fiscal constraints and intense political pressures under the Nixon and Ford Administrations, has so far passed only five new standards: asbestos in 1972; vinyl chloride in October, 1974; a package of fourteen carcinogens without monitoring requirements in January, 1974; coke oven emissions in 1976; and benzene in January, 1978 (See Table 9.5)

The third type of standards are the Emergency Temporary Standards, authorized under Section 6(c) of the Act, which may be imposed for a maximum of six months on grounds of "imminent hazard." Also embodied here is the ability of OSHA to abate these hazards without feasibility considerations. Emergency standards must be followed by proceedings to establish new standards or they are voided. Six sets of emergency standards, all based on carcinogenicity, have been developed over the last six years: in 1972, a standard for asbestos of 2 million fibers per cubic meter of air; also in 1972, regulation of a group of fourteen carcinogens, the permanent standard of one of which, MOCA, being subsequently successfully challenged on procedural grounds; a standard of 50 ppm for VC in April 1974; a 1 ppm standard for benzene in May, 1977; an emergency standard for dibromochloropropane in September, 1977; and an emergency standard for acrylonitrile in January, 1978.

Under the Nixon and Ford administrations, OSHA was subverted in a number of ways, including an inducement by Assistant Secretary of Labor George Guenther to stall standards-setting procedures in exchange for business support of the 1972 presidential election campaign.

The past record of OSHA has been one of extreme inactivity.[47] Inspections concentrated on such trivia as misplaced ladders and split toilet seats rather than seriously attempting to assess blatant health hazards from such substances as lead and asbestos. Fines averaged around $50 per inspection, and were often suspended on the company's promise of eventual abatement.

Under the leadership of Secretary Ray Marshall, and Assistant Secretary Eula Bingham, appointed to head OSHA in March, 1977, there has been considerable improvement in the activities of the Department of Labor for protecting workers against occupational carcinogens and other toxic agents. The standard-setting process has been speeded up, and new policies on carcinogens and other health hazards have been proposed. Inspectors have been instructed to overlook trivia and instead pursue obvious health hazards. Bingham has launched an aggressive recruitment campaign to secure committed and capable specialists, and is transforming OSHA into an effective agency.

Bingham has assigned top priority to promulgating generic standards for occupational carcinogens, drafted by Anson Keller, now Special Assistant for Regulatory Affairs at OSHA, during the latter part of the tenure of the previous OSHA Director, Morton Corn.[48] These standards lay down procedures for categorical rule-making to be followed once a chemical is shown to be a carcinogen, and are designed to obviate the virtually impossible task of separate rule-making for each individual carcinogen—an effort characterized by Secretary Marshall as "trying to put out a forest fire one tree at a time." While determination of carcinogenicity in these proposals is generic, as in the Delaney Amendment, subsequent rule-making for each carcinogen is, however, individualized and not generic. Public hearings and informal rule-making on the proposals commenced on May 16, 1978.*

Broadly speaking, three categories of carcinogens are recognized in the OSHA proposals. Category I substances are unequivocal carcinogens, as proven by human evi-

---

*The author testified on behalf of OSHA on May 26.

dence or two independent animal tests. Category I classification must be accompanied by the issuance of an
emergency temporary standard. Exposure to Category I
carcinogens would be allowed only at the lowest levels
technically feasible, under controlled conditions with sensitive monitoring procedures, and with due warnings to all
concerned. If safe substitutes are available, then continued use of the carcinogen could be banned completely.
While emphasizing the goal of zero exposure, the OSHA
proposals are flexible and include a wide range of regulatory options.

Category II classification is extended to chemicals
found to be carcinogenic in a single animal test or in
suggestive epidemiological studies. Continued use of
these carcinogens will be allowed in the workplace subject
to standards designed to limit but not prevent exposure.
Category III is for chemicals about which there is suspicion but insufficient evidence of carcinogenicity. These
will not be regulated, but will be listed in government
documents for public information. Preliminary review by
OSHA of the 2,000 chemicals on the NIOSH list of suspect carcinogens indicates that about 261 fall into Category I. These include some exotic laboratory curiosities
which are unlikely ever to be used in industry, and other
various derivatives of the same carcinogen, such as various
nickel salts. It is, however, likely that the number of carcinogens which will require regulation will be in excess of
100. It must be appreciated that workers are being currently exposed to such carcinogens in the absence of substantive regulatory controls. It is also estimated that there
are about 196 carcinogens in Category II, many of which
will require permanent standards, and about 300 chemicals in Category III.

While the proposed OSHA regulations are clearly a
move in the right direction, not only for the protection of
workers, but also the general public, they clearly do not
go far enough. The burden of proof for elucidating the
status of Category II carcinogens appears to fall on government and the worker, and continued exposure is per

mitted during the interim period. Additionally, the proposals contain broad "rebuttal" powers that allow OSHA to decide on a wide range of undefined grounds whether the carcinogenicity data are appropriate and relevant.

Industry has reacted negatively to these proposals, criticizing the scientific basis of the standards and invoking the familiar specter of impossibly high costs. Industry reaction, however, has been far from uniform. Rohm and Haas and Hardwicke Chemical Company have both agreed that the policy is generally "feasible and workable."[49]

In a concerted effort to fight these proposals, the Manufacturing Chemists Association has set up a special task force, the American Industrial Health Council, that represents more than sixty companies and forty trade associations and has raised funds in excess of $1 million. In January 1978, the council produced a misleading document which minimizes the significance and extent of cancer due to industrial chemicals (ignoring the fact that the majority of industries have not been evaluated for carcinogenic hazards), backed by voluminous statements from other industry and its academic consultants, attempting rebuttal of the OSHA position.[50]* The apparent intent is to preclude effective regulation of occupational carcinogens and to play down the public health impact of car-

---

*One of the more sophisticated industry statements (dated February 24, 1978) was presented by Shubik, together with D. Clayson and P. Issenberg of his staff, on behalf of the American Textile Manufacturers Institute. This statement attempted to perpetuate distinctions between benign and malignant tumors induced by chemical carcinogens in animals and to denigrate the significance of the induction of hepatomas and lung adenomas in mice. In support of his contention, Shubik quoted from a draft preamble to the International Agency for Research on Cancer (IARC) series of monographs of October 1977, which preamble had not been approved by the responsible committee of which Shubik was a member. When Arthur Upton, Director of the NCI, testified on behalf of the OSHA proposals in May 1978 (supported by Saffiotti and Schneiderman), he explained that the initial draft from which Shubik quoted had since been repudiated by the IARC and replaced by an authorized preamble which did not recognize distinctions between benign and malignant tumors. Shubik immediately phoned Lorenzo Tomatis, who is in charge of preparing the IARC monographs, demanding that the earlier draft be approved. The request was rejected by IARC.

cinogenic industrial chemicals in the workplace and general environment.

Another important action by OSHA has been the proposal of a labeling standard which would require industry to identify by trade and chemical name, hazardous chemicals to which workers are exposed. A chemical would be considered hazardous that appears on any list such as the NIOSH list of suspect carcinogens. However, identification would not be required for untested chemicals, to which exposure could continue without the workers' knowledge. NIOSH has estimated that 90 percent of the chemicals in trade-name products to which workers are exposed are not identified by the industries concerned. The chemical manufacturers have "fought tooth and nail" to insist that this is the concern of industry and nobody else.[51] There is, in fact, ample basis in the General Duty Clause and other sections of the 1970 Occupational Safety and Health Act to mandate disclosure and to develop appropriate safeguards in those rare instances in which trade secrets may be involved.

Bingham has also developed close working relationships with EPA, FDA, and the Consumer Product Safety Commission with whom, in October, 1977, she set up an interagency agreement to develop consolidated approaches to the regulation of toxic chemicals, including sharing resources and instituting compatible testing and compliance procedures.

In May 1978, Bertram Cottine, former attorney for the Health Research Group and assistant to Eula Bingham for the last year, won Senate confirmation as one of three members of the Occupational Safety and Health Review Commission following prolonged debate and vigorous opposition from national industrial organizations.

Outstanding problems which OSHA still has to resolve include the major difficulties in enforcing the Occupational Safety and Health Act in small businesses, as well as problems of employee-initiated inspections in non-unionized shops. Industry has fought hard to penalize employees who invoke their OSHA rights, docking their pay for time spent accompanying inspectors or firing them outright. An additional problem that OSHA must now contend with is posed by the Supreme Court decision of May 23, 1978, requiring OSHA inspectors to obtain search warrants before making "surprise" inspections in those instances where an employer does not voluntarily agree. However, OSHA will not have to show "probable cause" when it suspects that an employer is guilty of some violation.

The Environmental Protection Agency (EPA) The current administrator, Douglas M. Costle, was appointed on March 11, 1977. Costle, formerly a member of the Congressional Budget Office staff and head of the Connecticut Department of Environmental Protection, also served in 1969 on the Presidential Ash Committee, which had a major role in designing the EPA.

EPA has extensive legislative authority to control carcinogens under six separate statutes. This includes three media-type laws, the Clean Air Act, the Federal Water Pollution Control Act, and the Resource Conservation and Recovery Act, and three product-type laws, the Federal Insecticide, Fungicide, and Rodenticide Act, the Safe Drinking Water Act, and the Toxic Substances Control Act.

1. *The Clean Air Act.* This 1970 Act provides broad authority for establishing primary ambient air quality standards for dispersed pollutants from stationary and mobile sources, performance standards for stationary sources, regulations for fuel additives, and emission standards for hazardous air pollutants. Section 112 of the Act is designed for the strict and uniform regulation of hazardous air pollutants, those which pose risks of serious adverse effects, particularly cancer, at relatively low exposure levels.[52] While EPA has discretionary authority for listing an air pollutant as hazardous, it has shown a strong reluctance to do so, as opposed to achieving controls through

more flexible provisions of the Act. Once a substance is designated as a hazardous pollutant, mandatory rule-making procedures are put into effect within one year. (This is the shortest time required by any pollution legislation, involving preparation of a criteria document and proposing and promulgating a standard.)

Emission standards have been developed for only three carcinogens, beryllium and asbestos in April, 1973, and VC in October, 1976. In addition, EPA proposed a benzene standard in 1977. However, it is questionable how meaningful these standards really are. That for asbestos is only based on visible emissions and the use of work practices, such as wetting down buildings during demolition, and tends to be more honored in the breach than in the performance. The VC standard is supposed to limit emissions from all sources to the limits of best available technology, but excludes the innumerable PVC fabrication plants scattered all over the country. Recognizing these various problems, the Environmental Defense Fund petitioned EPA in June, 1977, for more stringent standard setting, with the goal of zero emissions for carcinogenic hazardous pollutants.

2. *The Federal Water Pollution Control Act.* This 1948 law, amended in 1972 and 1977, is one of the most complex and extensive pieces of environmental legislation ever passed, and perhaps the most difficult to administer.[53] Its philosophy is that all water pollution is undesirable and should be reduced to the extent technology allows, rather than to the extent dictated by health considerations alone. Like the Clean Air Act, the Water Pollution Control Act contains a wide range of provisions: new source standards (Section 306), oil and hazardous substances regulation (Section 311), water quality standards (Section 303), water quality related effluent standards (Section 302), and toxic effluent standards (Section 307).

Toxic effluent standards are aimed primarily at limiting the industrial discharge of toxic pollutants that can induce cancer and other serious effects.* The standard takes into account problems of persistence and pollutant degradability in water. However, there is a built-in contradiction in a standard which must be set, regardless of economic considerations, at a level which provides an "ample margin of safety," knowing full well that there is no known safe level for any carcinogen.

In 1973, EPA listed nine pollutants under Section 307 and, following a consent agreement stemming from extensive litigation with public interest groups and industry, promulgated standards for six carcinogens in 1977: DDT, aldrin, dieldrin, toxaphene, endrin, PCBs, and benzidine. Zero effluent limits were set for DDT and aldrin/dieldrin, which EPA had already banned, while numerical limits were set for effluents of benzidine and PCB. Under the consent agreement, EPA has designated about 140 other toxic pollutants subject to control by "best available technology" in 21 priority industries.

3. *The Resource Conservation and Recovery Act.* This 1976 Act, which amends the Solid Waste Disposal Act, creates a regulatory framework to control hazardous wastes. The proposed regulations containing minimal criteria for determining which solid waste land disposal facilities shall be classified as having no reasonable probability of adverse effects on health or the environment were published by EPA in the Federal Register on February 6, 1978. This Act creates the authority to regulate disposal of wastes contaminated by carcinogenic substances.

4. *Federal Insecticide, Fungicide, and Rodenticide Act.* Passed in 1947, this Act was designed to protect consumers from ineffective products and to warn with appropriate labels against toxic effects, without consideration of

---

*Industrial discharge from point sources are regulated by the National Permit Discharge Elimination System. This system, however, cannot be used to regulate non-point sources of pollution such as agricultural runoff of pesticides and fertilizers and municipal stormwater runoff.

carcinogenic and other chronic toxic or ecological effects. The Pesticide Regulation Division of USDA failed to enforce even these minimal requirements. This contributed to the decision to transfer regulatory authority for pesticides to EPA after its creation in 1970.[54] The thrust of this move was, however, blunted by the simultaneous transfer to EPA of USDA Pesticide Regulation Division personnel. These personnel were regrouped in the EPA Office of Pesticide Programs, where they have perpetuated USDA traditions of excessive protection of agrichemical interests at the expense of other considerations. In this, they have been further aided by the USDA, which has supported industry against EPA in all major proceedings to ban carcinogenic pesticides.

An additional serious problem which has adversely influenced EPA pesticide policies was and is the congressional jurisdiction which the House and Senate agriculture committees continued to exercise after the transfer of regulatory authority for pesticides from USDA to EPA.[55] The agriculture committees have traditionally been preoccupied with narrowly focused agrichemical interests and have failed to grasp the need to regulate pesticides to protect public health and the environment. On occasions when EPA seems about to deal decisively with a pesticide problem, the agriculture committees threaten to cancel its authority over pesticides and to transfer it back to USDA.

An example of the power exercised by the House Agriculture Committee is the 1976 bill H.R. 8841, amending the 1947 Act, which, as passed in a somewhat modified form by Congress, severely restricts the authority of EPA to regulate pesticides. The thrust of H.R. 8841 is to give the Secretary of Agriculture virtual veto power over EPA's suspension and cancellation decisions. EPA is required to notify USDA at least sixty days prior to proposing any pesticide regulations and also to similarly notify the House Committee on Agriculture and the Senate Committee on Agriculture and Forestry. EPA is further required to publish any comments of the USDA in the Federal Register at the same time of publication of final regulations. These seemingly harmless provisions carry the implicit threat of political reprisals if EPA ignores unfavorable comments by USDA on proposed pesticide regulations.

The exclusive jurisdiction of the agriculture committees over pesticide regulation by EPA is further anomalous in view of the fact that about half of all pesticide usage in the United States is for nonagricultural purposes (See Table 7.2). Strong public support is needed to ensure that the House and Senate commerce committees, which represent more broadly based interests, be given a share in the congressional authority over pesticides.

The 1947 Act was substantively amended in 1972, emerging as the Federal Environmental Pesticide Control Act (FEPCA).[56] The amendments express the intent of protecting against "unreasonable adverse effects on man or the environment," and place the burden of producing evidence of safety on the manufacturer. The manufacturer is required to produce evidence of safety and effectiveness when petitioning EPA for registration of products. Pesticides can then be classified for general use or for restricted use by trained applicators only. Registrations are automatically cancelled after five years, unless the manufacturer reapplies with updated information. EPA has the power to suspend manufacture on an emergency interim basis if "imminent hazard" can be proven. Otherwise, banning is by a protracted adjudicatory hearing that can stretch over years, during which the pesticide can be used without hindrance. EPA also has responsibility for setting tolerance levels of pesticide residues on foods, which are then enforced by the FDA.

Over the past eight years, EPA has taken regulatory action against only a handful of pesticides. Some of these were no longer in production at the time of the action, such as octamethylphosphoramide, and some of these actions were initiated at the manufacturer's request, as was the case with safrole (also used as a flavoring agent in root beer). The agency has undertaken successful proceedings

only against aldrin/dieldrin, chlordane/heptachlor, and
VC (used as a propellant in pesticide aerosols). However,
all these latter actions were only initiated under threat of
legal action by public interest groups (Table 9.5).

These limited regulatory actions taken by the EPA
aroused intense opposition from industry, supported by
the congressional agriculture committees. In July, 1975,
EPA announced new regulations for re-registration of
all currently used pesticides and for registration of new
pesticides.[57] This move coincided with an internal
reorganization of pesticide policy in EPA in November,
1974, which effectively wiped out any authority for the
Office of General Counsel and gave almost exclusive authority to the Office of Pesticide Programs. The new regulations defined EPA's understanding of "unreasonable adverse effects on man or the environment" in terms of
chronic toxic, mutagenic or carcinogenic effects. Pesticides producing these effects are subject to a "rebuttable
presumption" of being banned. The manufacturer is given
ninety days to rebut this presumption on grounds that include the risks being outweighed by the benefits, following which EPA is required to take final action within six
months. While in principle this approach may be sound,
the agency's implementation of the new regulations can
only be regarded as public window dressing. So far, EPA
has initiated "rebuttable presumptions" against about
forty-five pesticides, none of which however, has yet been
brought to final action.* In three instances, the pesticides
concerned, endrin, chlorobenzilate, and chloroform (an
"inert" pesticide ingredient) are carcinogenic.

During the 1977–1978 congressional proceedings to
reauthorize EPA's pesticide authority, the Office of Pesticide Programs formulated and advocated a provisional
registration amendment. This amendment allows new
pesticides to be given provisional or temporary registra-

---

*With the exception of voluntary cancellations of kepone and DBCP,
EPA has initiated no cancellation proceedings against any pesticide since November, 1974.

tion and to be marketed prior to the completion of required tests, including tests for carcinogenicity. If the test
results turn out to be adverse, then the pesticide can be
taken off the market. In the meantime, the public has
been exposed and the industry has accumulated large
stores which EPA cannot afford to purchase, and thus
must allow them to continue to be sold.

EPA's record on regulation of pesticide residues in
food is as gravely deficient as its record of pesticide regulation.[58] EPA is responsible for establishing all tolerances
for pesticide residues on the basis of data submitted by
industry as to the nature, level and toxicity of the residue.
Any residue on food is considered unsafe unless a tolerance has been established and the remaining residue is
within the limits of tolerance. Authority is shared with the
FDA, which is responsible for enforcing pesticide tolerances by testing food samples. FDA can remove from interstate products any food containing residues in excess of
established tolerances.

A 1975 report to Congress entitled "Federal Pesticide
Regulation Program: Is It Protecting the Public and the
Environment Adequately from Pesticide Hazards?"
showed that EPA established many tolerances without sufficient test data to determine levels of pesticide residues
on crops and the potential of the pesticide to induce carcinogenic and other toxic effects.[59] Further, EPA registered pesticides for use on food and feed crops without
setting tolerances.

As of May, 1976, EPA had examined about 890 of the
approximately 1,400 active ingredients of over 40,000 pesticide products.[60] Only about 419 ingredients examined
had sufficient backup data to allow any assessment of risk,
and of these, about 238 fell in a high risk category, 80
percent of which were "suspect carcinogens." These suspect carcinogens are incorporated in about one-third of all
pesticide products currently on the market.

In 1976, an EPA consultant reviewed carcinogenicity
test data on twenty-four pesticides with the highest tolerances on common foods. His report concluded that, with

the possible exception of data on one pesticide, all other data which EPA had used to set tolerances were so inadequate and defective that no reasonable conclusions could be drawn from them.[61]

EPA seems to have effectively eliminated oversight of its pesticide policies at the agency level by disbanding the Federal Working Group on Pesticides and the Pesticide Policy Advisory Committee. However, in April, 1977, EPA informed the General Accounting Office that its Science Advisory Board had been asked to study the tolerance-setting program. A subcommittee appointed for this purpose met first in February, 1978, and is expected to issue a report by the end of 1978.*

Meanwhile, EPA has made little serious attempt to rectify the deficiencies in its tolerance setting programs as indicated in a 1978 General Accounting Office report which concluded "that the American public had not been adequately protected from the potential hazards of pesticide use because of inadequate efforts to implement existing Federal laws."[62]

Even taking into account legislative ambiguities and pressures from industry and the congressional agriculture committees, the record of EPA on pesticides has been and continues to be unacceptable. The strictures of an earlier congressional report seem at least as apt now as when they were written:

> . . . pesticide regulation in the United States is fundamentally deficient. Pesticide regulation has failed to include many obvious and prudent steps to better protect public health and the environment. Moreover, the severe inadequacies of pesticide regulation are not attributable in any significant way to deficient legislation. Rather, the principal cause lies with EPA's poor administration of the program, including its failure to recognize and correct serious program deficiencies as they arose.[63]

---

*The author is a member of this subcommittee.

5. *The Safe Drinking Water Act.* While the Federal Water Pollution Control Act is media-type legislation designed to limit the discharge of toxic pollutants into surface and other waters and to control pollutant levels, the Safe Drinking Water Act is a product-type legislation specifically designed to regulate the purity of treated drinking water. As pollutants discharged into surface water are likely to eventually find their way into drinking water unless they are unstable or infinitely diluted, it is unfortunate that there is not a greater consistency in the language and intents of the two laws.

The Safe Drinking Water Act was passed in 1974 in response to pressures by the Environmental Defense Fund and public alarm at the high levels of carcinogens and organic pollutants found in the drinking water of New Orleans. According to the Act, every community water supply serving twenty-five or more people must meet certain minimum standards of purity, thus involving a national total of about 40,000 community water supply systems. "National Interim Primary Drinking Water Regulations" went into effect in 1977, and cover ten chemicals, including the carcinogens arsenic, cadmium, chromium, endrin, lindane, toxaphene, and methoxychlor. Strangely, EPA's current informational pamphlet "Is Your Drinking Water Safe?" claims that "radioactivity is the only contaminant for which standards have been set that has been shown to cause cancer."

Concerns have been expressed about the finding of high levels of the carcinogenic chloroform in drinking water treated by chlorine. Chloroform and other related (trihalomethane) compounds are produced following chlorination of water heavily contaminated with organic pollutants.* The answer is not necessarily to stop chlorination,

---

*Resulting levels of chloroform and trihalomethanes in drinking water in general far exceed concentrations of other synthetic organic pollutants. Chloroform levels are approximately correlated with total organic carbon levels in water.

but to limit discharge of toxic and carcinogenic pollutants into surface waters, which ultimately reach drinking water supply systems, and also to effectively treat drinking water by passage through activated carbon filtration systems prior to its chlorination.

Responding to further pressures from the Environmental Defense Fund, in January, 1978, EPA proposed to regulate four of the main trihalomethanes, of which chloroform is typical, produced from organic pollutants by the chlorination of water, in order to reduce total levels of trihalomethanes to below 100 ppb.[64] EPA also proposed that all cities with more than 75,000 people should be required to design and operate a treatment system which uses granular activated carbon filters in order to reduce levels of synthetic organic pollutants to the maximum extent feasible. Variances can be granted only if it can be demonstrated that such treatment is unnecessary. Estimated household costs for treatment range from $3 to $17 a year.

These proposals are part of a phased implementation program which, over time, will be expanded to cover all public water supplies in the United States. The proposals represent the most significant advances in drinking water treatment since passage of the 1976 Act. They represent the first serious attempt to control contamination of drinking water with synthetic organic contaminants.* It should be recalled that over 200 synthetic organic chemicals, including many carcinogens such as chloroform, carbon tetrachloride, benzene, vinyl chloride, lindane, aldrin, and bischloroethylether, have been identified in drinking water. The organic chemicals so far identified represent only a small fraction of total organic material in drinking water.

---

*Apart from chloroform and other trihalomethanes which are often found in the 100 ppb range, the other organics most commonly found in the low ppb range are pentachlorophenol, dichlorobenzene, and trichloroethylene.

Illinois and some other states, backed by the American Water Works Association, are opposing these regulations on various grounds.[65] These include questioning the significance and public health relevance of the carcinogenicity of chloroform and other organic contaminants in water and asserting that the costs of carbon treatment are exorbitant. The position of the states reflects lack of appreciation of fundamental principles of environmental carcinogenesis and of the fact that failure to regulate creates costs greatly in excess of those of regulation.

6. *Toxic Substances Control Act.* Passage of the Act on October 11, 1976, culminated six years of bitter struggle during which a powerful industry lobby pulled out all stops to defeat this legislation.[66] The resistance was spearheaded by Dow Chemical Company and the Manufacturing Chemists Association, which formed a semi-autonomous standing committee empowered to lobby without checking back to individual industries for approval. This striking change from previous practices indicates the mood of crisis within the industry.

The legislation authorizes the EPA administrator to require information necessary for standard-setting on new chemicals and for chemicals in current use, with the exception of chemicals covered by other legislation.*[67] The legislation, while not authorizing the routine need for information, shifted the burden of proof away from the government and public and placed it firmly on the manufacturer. While the legislation is specifically directed to chemicals, it reflects patterns of use and distribution in the environment, water, air and the workplace, and is thus multimedia as well as product in type. Key provisions of the law are:

---

*As consultant to the Senate Committee on Public Works, the author developed the first draft of a bill, "The Environmental Protection Act of 1971," which formed the basis of subsequent toxic substances legislation.

• Industry must give EPA ninety days notice before marketing a new chemical, including proposing "significant new uses" of existing chemicals. Data must be provided on structure, composition, uses, quantity to be produced, byproducts of manufacture, health or environmental effects, and numbers of workers expected to be exposed. While some guidelines are offered on data that may be required on health effects, no such information is provided in the Act for environmental effects.

• EPA must draw up an inventory of existing chemicals to be exempted from premarketing notification requirements, but not necessarily from later challenges.*

• Each year, an intergovernmental agency group (known as the Committee of Eight) will select no more than fifty potentially hazardous chemicals, particularly chemicals suspected of being carcinogens, and recommend priority for their testing to the administrator.

• Industry must keep records of significant adverse health effects caused by any chemical for thirty years and of environmental damage for five years.

• Chemicals produced in small quantities for research and development will be exempted from premarket notification. So also will be small businesses, i.e., those with fewer than thirty employees at any one time.

• Pesticides, tobacco, drugs, cosmetics, food additives, and nuclear materials are exempt from the law, since they are covered by other regulations.

• The Act allows petitions and suits from citizen and public interest groups who wish to challenge EPA decisions.

The main thrust of the law is that if, based on premarket data, EPA believes a new chemical to be hazardous, within forty-five days the agency must give industry

---

*Import of toxic chemicals is covered by the law, but inadequately so.

notice of intent to ban. EPA can also seek a court injunction restricting or banning chemicals it believes are "im-
minently hazardous," and can also take appropriate action
against chemicals it considers "unreasonable risks."

This legislation is potentially the most important
single preventive public health measure of the century.[68]
For the first time, there is the opportunity of controlling
industrial chemicals and anticipating carcinogenic and
other adverse effects, rather than reacting to their occurrence. However, there is little indication yet as to how
well this potential for control will be exercised.

Congress initially allocated a first-year budget of $10
million for the Office of Toxic Substances in EPA, created
to implement the new legislation, a figure later increased
to the current level of $23 million. The administration has
recently announced that as of October, 1978, the budget
will be increased to nearly $50 million. Even this in-
creased figure is small compared to the $150 million
budget of the first year of the Clean Air Act, and the current budget of $40 million for pesticides.

The costs to industry of toxic substances legislation
were estimated in 1975 by EPA and the General Accounting Office to range from $80 to $200 million. These estimates contrast strikingly with estimates of $2 billion by
the Manufacturing Chemists Association and Foster D.
Snell. The maximal government estimate of $200 million,
based largely on costs of carcinogenicity and chronic toxicity testing, represents about 0.3 percent of the chemical
industry's total 1975 sales of $72 billion and 3.6 percent of
its net profits after taxes of $6.5 billion.

Enforcing toxic substances legislation is probably the
most complex and ambitious task any regulatory agency
has ever had to face. EPA has been slow to respond, and
its toxic chemical program is still embryonic, although it is
now attempting to scale up recruiting efforts for much
needed professional personnel. So far, EPA has failed to
encourage adequate public participation in its planning
and activities.

The administration's concerns with inflation, together with the apparently waning interest of Congress, are now emerging as possible threats to the toxic chemical program. Illustrative of the administration's position are the emphasis by Commerce Secretary Juanita M. Kreps and Robert Strauss, Special Presidential Counsel on Inflation, on the high costs of regulation to industry. Recent estimates by Chase Econometrics concluded that total costs of EPA programs add less than 0.4 percent annually to the consumer price index. However, as Costle recently pointed out, such estimates do not take into account improvements to public health, reduced property damage by air pollutants, increased crop yields, and many other benefits that result from pollution control spending.

Consumer Product Safety Commission   The commission was established in 1972 under terms of the Consumer Products Safety Act, incorporating the Federal Hazardous Substance Act, the Flammable Fabrics Act, and the Poison Prevention Packaging Act. The commission was given responsibility for over 10,000 consumer products, excluding those covered by other jurisdictions, such as tobacco, drugs, pesticides, cosmetics, and food additives. However, the commission cannot require registration of consumer products, and before it can regulate must meet the burden of proving hazard due to "unreasonable risk of injury" which cannot be prevented by labeling or packaging.

The Act is a poorly conceived attempt to fill in legislative "cracks." It is anachronistic in shifting the burden of proof from the manufacturer to the government, which must prove hazard before it can regulate. These statutory limitations aside, the commission has not been an aggressive regulator. Following petition by the Health Research Group in 1974, the commission banned VC as a propellant in household products not covered by other legislation. On April 8, 1977, at the instigation of the Environmental Defense Fund, the commission banned the use of Tris as a fire retardant on children's sleepwear. Both the VC and Tris actions have been overturned on procedural grounds. The commission is still considering a May, 1977, petition by the Health Research Group and the Center for Occupational Hazards to ban benzene in consumer products, and a petition by the Environmental Defense Fund and the Natural Resources Defense Council to ban fireplace logs and other household products containing asbestos. The commission acted on a petition of the Health Research Group to ban asbestos-containing packaging and spackling compounds as of June, 1978. In April, 1978, the commission published a draft of a cancer policy, which in general bears similarities to the OSHA "generic" proposals.

The commission has come under mounting criticism from consumer groups and from some congressmen for its regulatory tardiness. In December, 1977, the General Accounting Office issued a report criticizing the commission for dragging its feet in developing and issuing safety standards, setting priorities, and for keeping inadequate records on product-related injuries.[69] On February 8, 1978, the embattled chairman of the five-member commission, John S. Byington, announced his resignation, effective June 30, charging that he had been a victim of "political harassment by the Carter Administration."* His resignation was applauded by Rep. John E. Moss (D-Cal.) as "a very significant public service" and by Senator Wendell E. Ford (D-Ken.) as "in the best interests of the Agency."[70]

Speculations as to the commission's future have been cut short by the April, 1978, announcement of President Carter of a three-year reauthorization. It seems likely that this will be endorsed by Congress. The administration has also asked Congress to transfer the commission's responsibilities for scientific research to EPA.

---

*Byington was appointed chairman by President Ford in June, 1976.

Food and Drug Administration   The major regulatory authority of the FDA is mandated by the 1938 Federal Food, Drug, and Cosmetic Act, which gives the FDA authority over food additives, cosmetics and drugs, all of which are regulated with distinct and differing philosophies and practices. The Act prohibits the marketing of food that contains a "natural or added substance which may render it injurious to health." The Act permits the addition of toxic substances to food within prescribed tolerance levels, but shifts the burden of proof to the manufacturer to show that the additive is safe under the conditions of proposed use.[71]

The 1938 Act was extended by the 1954 Pesticide Amendments, the 1958 Food Additive Amendments, including the Delaney Amendment, the 1960 Color Additives Amendments, and the 1962 Animal Drug or Feed Additive Amendments. The overall laws resulting from these various amendments are complex and inconsistent, especially with regard to the regulation of carcinogens.[72]

The 1958 Delaney anticancer clause is a straightforward piece of legislation, stating that

> no additive shall be claimed to be safe if it is found to induce cancer when ingested by man or animal, or if it is found after tests which are appropriate for the evaluation of safety of food additives to induce cancer in man or animal.[73]

This law reflected the then and currently prevailing scientific consensus that there is no known method for setting safe levels for human exposure to carcinogens.[74] The FDA is given authority only to determine whether the carcinogenicity tests are appropriate, then after these limits of bureaucratic discretion are reached an automatic set of rule-making procedures are invoked leading to a ban of the carcinogenic additive. The requirement for appropriate test methods can reasonably be used to exclude carcinogenic effects induced in animals from subcutaneous or intravenous injection of food additives. However, it would seem inappropriate on these grounds to try to exclude carcinogenic effects of additives administered to animals by gastric intubation, a standard practice in carcinogenicity tests, rather than in diets. Nevertheless, the FDA concluded in 1975 that such exemption could be valid.

Although invoked on several occasions, the Delaney anticancer clause has only been formally used twice or so for the purpose of banning a carcinogen: in 1967 for Flectol H and in 1969 for MOCA, both used in food packaging adhesives. The FDA has, however, used the broad statutory authority of general safety provisions of food law to ban several other carcinogens, including: the sweetener dulcin in 1950; coumarin, in Tonka Bean Extracts, in 1954; safrole in 1960; oil of calamus in 1968; the sweetener cyclamate in 1969; diethylpyrocarbonate in 1972; the animal drug DES in 1972; mercaptoimidazoline in 1973; Violet #1 in 1973; FD&C Red #2, FD&C Red #4 and carbon black in 1976.

There are many loopholes in the legislative definition of a food additive that exempt a wide range of carcinogens from the requirements of the Delaney Amendment.

1. Pesticide residues: These are not defined as food additives. EPA has authority to set tolerances in food for carcinogenic pesticides.

2. Unavoidable or unintentional contaminants: Like pesticides, these are exempt. Most common examples are PCBs, benzo[a]pyrene and other such polycyclic compounds formed during broiling, and chemicals migrating from food packaging materials. Additionally, FDA does not require carcinogenicity testing of unintentional additives derived from packaging materials, some 10,000 of which have been approved for use, unless they are present in concentrations over 1 ppm, and unless the FDA believes there is valid reason to suspect carcinogenicity.

3. Prior-sanction additives: By a "grandfather clause," additives sanctioned by the FDA prior to September 6, 1958, are exempt.

4. GRAS additives: Additives "generally recognized as safe" by experts prior to January, 1958, are not regarded as additives from the Delaney standpoint.

5. Color additives in use before July, 1960: Under a "grandfather clause" of the 1960 Color Additive Amendments, color additives in prior use can be provisionally listed for a period of two and a half years to allow completion of tests. The FDA is allowed to extend this period "in good faith" if necessary. Using this stratagem, FDA extended the provisional listing of Red #2 fifteen times from 1960 to 1965, before its final ban in January, 1976.

6. Animal drugs without prohibited residues: The 1962 Feed Additive Amendment (or the DES clause) allows administration to cattle of carcinogenic drugs or feed additives, such as DES, provided no residues can be detected in meat or animal food products. This special-interest legislation was exploited to the utmost by successive FDA commissioners to allow continued use of DES even though residues were consistently detected from the late 1960s until its ban in 1973, a ban which was, however, overturned on procedural grounds.

The 1938 Act created a specific exemption for coal-tar dyes, provided they are appropriately labeled. The FDA cannot now ban them, even though their carcinogenicity has been recently proven. However, congressional moves which will probably abolish this exemption are now pending.

FDA also has authority for enforcing tolerances on foods set by EPA for pesticides and toxic chemicals. It accomplishes this by testing samples of food to determine if there are residues exceeding tolerance levels, in which case the food can be banned and penalties on violators can be imposed. However, a 1975 General Accounting Office Report criticized the FDA tolerance program for failing to test food for residues of 179 out of 233 pesticides for which tolerances were set.[75] A subsequent General Accounting Office Report in 1978 demonstrated that the FDA had failed to rectify these serious deficiencies.[76] Of 268 pesticides with a total of 5,872 individuals' tolerances on various foods, only 38 percent can be detected by currently used FDA multi-residue techniques. Also, 940 of these 5,872 tolerances are for pesticides which are either carcinogenic or suspected of being carcinogenic. About 70 percent of these carcinogens or suspect carcinogens cannot be detected by FDA monitoring techniques. FDA Commissioner Kennedy in subsequent testimony on February 24, 1978, recognized various of these deficiencies in FDA's monitoring program. He indicated his intent to institute various reforms, including more effective coordination with USDA and EPA.

Cosmetics are treated differently from food additives under the Federal Food, Drug, and Cosmetic Act. The burden of demonstrating carcinogenic or other hazards is placed on the FDA. Following petitions by the Health Research Group, the FDA banned the use of VC as a propellant in cosmetics in 1974 and of chloroform as an ingredient in cosmetics in 1976, both on grounds of carcinogenicity. While there is no requirement for manufacturers to undertake toxicological testing of cosmetic ingredients prior to marketing, current labeling laws of the FDA require untested products to be clearly labeled as such.[77]

Drug law is as different from food law as is cosmetic law.[78] Unlike food law, which is based on hazard alone, drug law allows consideration of matching benefits. The 1938 Act requires that drugs be "adequately tested to show that they are safe for use under conditions of use prescribed in their labeling." The 1962 Kefauver-Harris Amendments require formal proof of effectiveness and authorizes banning on grounds of "imminent hazard." There are, however, no formal requirements for carcinogenicity testing of drugs before clinical trials are undertaken. Carcinogenic drugs can be used for both medical purposes, such as Flagyl for trichomonas vaginal infections and griseofulvin for athlete's foot and other superficial fungal infections, and for nonmedical purposes, such as oral contraceptives.

The current commissioner, Donald Kennedy, was appointed to the FDA on April 8, 1977. Kennedy, a Stanford University biologist, has already made significant impact on an agency whose past record of protection of consumer interests has been grossly deficient. Under Kennedy's direction, FDA is moving in the direction of greater concern for consumer safety and interests. Kennedy has so far taken sound positions on various issues such as dangers of saccharin and the labeling of alcoholic beverages (with warnings to pregnant women that too much alcohol may cause birth defects). In May 1978 the FDA announced plans to launch a "cyclic review" of food additives by December. This would include a priority list of about 2,300 substances (some 350 direct additives, 620 natural flavors and spices, and 1330 synthetic flavors and spices) that FDA wants tested now or in the near future.

U.S. Department of Agriculture   The regulatory authority of the USDA over carcinogenic and other contaminants in agricultural products and meat is limited.* The Animal and Plant Health Inspection Service conducts programs to protect wholesomeness of meat and poultry products for human consumption. USDA is responsible for preventing the marketing of adulterated raw meat and poultry, including that containing residues in excess of tolerances set by FDA and EPA. As part of this program, USDA samples and monitors meat and poultry, generally at the time of slaughter, for illegal residues. These illegal residues include excessive residues of noncarcinogenic animal drugs, pesticides and environmental contaminants above tolerance levels, and prohibited residues of any detectable level of carcinogenic drugs such as DES. Apart from

---

*This authority is granted by the 1906 Federal Meat Inspection Act, the 1967 Wholesale Meat Act, and the 1968 Poultry Products Inspection Act.

these, tolerances or action levels have been set for residues of pesticides and other carcinogenic environmental contaminants, even though a safe level cannot possibly be scientifically established for them. These include the banned carcinogenic DDT and dieldrin, residues of which persist in meat and poultry as a result of their agricultural uses several years ago.*

According to a recent congressional report, the USDA monitoring program is seriously deficient.[79] There are at least 143 known drugs and pesticides, including 40 carcinogens and 18 teratogens, besides an unknown number of environmental contaminants likely to leave residues in food-producing animals. USDA's monitoring program tests for only 46 drugs and pesticides, and 8 environmental contaminants. Using USDA data, on the basis of which an overall estimated rate of 2 percent violation with illegal residues was claimed by USDA, the General Accounting Office report showed that from 1974 to 1976 the violation rate may have ranged from 2.6 percent in sheep and goats to almost 16 percent in swine. The actual violation rate is probably very much higher, as USDA fails to test for most drugs and pesticides likely to leave residues. Among pesticides and drugs which are not included in USDA monitoring programs are the carcinogenic drug furazolidone, ethylene-bis-dithiocarbamate fungicides, which break down to the carcinogenic ethylene thiourea, chlorophenoxy herbicides such as 2,4-D, 2,4,5-T, and Silvex, which are teratogenic and some of which contain the highly persistent and carcinogenic tetradioxin contaminant.

High violation rates of carcinogenic contaminants in meat and poultry are still further compounded by the fact that most illegal residues are discovered only after the meat and poultry have been marketed. Furthermore,

---

*USDA tests in 1976 showed that 82 percent of about 900 poultry tested for DDT and 52 percent of 1,800 cattle tested for dieldrin had measurable residues.

FDA and EPA fail to follow up on most residue violations and to take appropriate corrective action.

USDA authority for inspection of illegal and potentially harmful residues in raw meat and poultry is shared with FDA and EPA. FDA is responsible under the Federal Food, Drug, and Cosmetic Act of 1938 (as amended) for insuring the safety of drugs given to food-producing animals, setting tolerances for animal drugs or environmental contaminants allowable in food, and preventing the marketing of raw meat and poultry containing residues that exceed established tolerance levels. EPA is responsible for regulating the introduction of pesticides and toxic substances into the environment. Under the Federal Insecticide, Fungicide, and Rodenticide Act of 1947 (as amended), EPA must approve pesticide products for safety and effectiveness before they can be marketed. Additionally, under the Federal Food, Drug, and Cosmetic Act, EPA must establish safe tolerance levels for pesticides likely to leave residues in food. Finally, under the 1976 Toxic Substances Control Act, EPA regulates the introduction of toxic substances into the environment which can contaminate meat and poultry. Both FDA and EPA are responsible for requiring manufacturers to provide suitable, practical, and sensitive test methods for the detection of chemical residues.

USDA also sets tolerances for nitrate and nitrite in meat, though not in fish, which is an FDA responsibility. The authority of the USDA over nitrate and nitrite in meat is due to a legislative quirk by which these two additives were given a prior sanction under the 1907 Meat Inspection Act and were thus exempt from the 1958 Food Additive Amendments.

Assistant Secretary for Food and Consumer Services of the USDA, Carol Tucker Foreman, has taken vigorous steps to ensure that the meat industry reduce nitrite in bacon to levels at which no nitrosamines can be detected. In congressional testimony on February 24, 1978, Foreman endorsed the criticisms of USDA's monitoring program contained in the 1978 General Accounting Office report. Foreman also announced plans of the USDA to attempt to improve its sampling and monitoring programs.[80]

It is clear that USDA procedures for meat inspection and monitoring are considerably out of date and unresponsive to the grave problems of the modern petrochemical era. Additionally, the fragmentation of authority and responsibility for setting tolerances and food inspection between the USDA and the FDA and EPA is an anachronism which leads to regulatory complexity and diffusion of authority.* In a limited effort to resolve this problem, in December, 1977, the Senate Governmental Affairs Committee recommended that the regulatory function of the USDA over chemical contaminants in food be transferred to the FDA.

Secretary of Agriculture Bob Bergland has shown an apparent sensitivity to toxic and environmental problems of pesticide uses. In March, 1977, he expressed the intent of USDA to wean farmers away from dependence on pesticides and to encourage integrated pest management instead. USDA has not yet implemented such intent.

Other Regulatory Agencies

The Federal Trade Commission, through the 1964 Federal Cigarette Labeling and Advertising Act, requires cigarette packages to be labeled with the familiar warning that smoking "is dangerous to your health." The FTC spends about $125,000 annually to measure the tar and nicotine content of commercial domestic cigarettes, requiring the

---

*OMB is beginning to formulate plans for investigation of current national food policies with regard to production, distribution, nutrition, and safety. This project, headed by Charles French, will also examine the authorities of concerned federal agencies, FDA, EPA, and USDA, for overlap and consistency. It is expected that public comments will be solicited in late 1978.

findings to be printed on the packages. Without this modest pressure, the tobacco industry would have no incentive to reduce the tar and nicotine yield of its products. As it is, the industry has cashed in on the low-tar concept with massive media campaigns to win smokers to the lower-tar brands. Industry efforts to move the testing from the FTC to private concerns were thwarted in 1977. Similar attempts will, however, probably be made in the future. Efforts to regulate the tobacco industry now seem futile in view of its strong support by the administration and a powerful network of Southern congressmen. If there are any possible remedies, they seem to rest in the courts.

The current FTC commissioner, Michael Pertschuk, former chief counsel of the Senate Commerce Committee, is a dedicated consumer activist. He has brought in new staff and has overnight transformed the FTC into an agency aggressively dedicated to protect the interests of the consumer.*

Under the 1974 Hazardous Materials Transportation Act, the Department of Transportation has authority to regulate transportation of various categories of materials, such as flammable liquids or explosives, but not specifically carcinogens.

The Bureau of Mines of the Interior Department has authority under the Federal Coal Mine Health and Safety Act of 1969 and the Federal Metal and Nonmetallic Mine Safety Act of 1966 to enforce federal health and safety in mining operations. The bureau has adopted the 1972 OSHA standards for asbestos and the 1973 threshold limit values for other airborne pollutants.

The Federal Mine Safety and Health Amendments Act of 1977 supercedes the 1966 Mine Safety Act. The 1977 Act established a Mine Enforcement Safety Adminis-

---

*In May, 1978, Pertschuk was charged with bias in his regulation of TV advertising for children by the Toy Manufacturers of America, the American Association of Advertising Agencies, the American Advertising Foundation, and the Association of National Advertisers.

tration, separate from OSHA, in the Department of Labor.

New Trends

The last year has witnessed the emergence of significant new trends in federal agencies. An important element is the overall and explicit emphasis of the Carter administration on integrity and openness.* This has also put new teeth into recent laws governing agency conduct. These laws include the 1973 amendments to the 1967 Freedom of Information Act, making it possible for concerned citizens to obtain copies of documents on the basis of which agencies make decisions and regulatory policies,[81] and the 1972 Federal Advisory Committee Act, governing the conduct of these committees, with particular reference to the needs for balanced representation, disclosure of special interests, and public announcement of meetings.[82]† The administration has also introduced new policies designed to limit conflicts of interest and the "revolving door" between industry and federal agencies.[83] Senior agency officials are now forbidden to accept positions in

---

*While there is no evidence that the Carter administration, which came to Washington pledging "open government" and protection for "whistleblowers," has taken measures similar to those used in the Nixon administration, it has mounted a range of internal inquiries, tightened the National Security Council regulations on interviews, opened the prosecution of an espionage case, filed a breach of contract suit against a former CIA employee who wrote an unauthorized book, and required Justice Department lawyers to sign affidavits about their contacts with reporters as a part of leaking inquiries. Attorney General Griffin Bell has taken still stronger positions on news leaks, and his department has conducted most of the investigations on unauthorized disclosures, including a recently closed investigation on the Washington Star, which refused to disclose its sources of information about alleged corruption in the Interstate Commerce Commission.

†It should be recognized, however, that the National Academy of Sciences, a major source of technical advice to Congress and regulatory agencies, has so far successfully resisted legal challenge to require its compliance with the Freedom of Information Act.

those industries they have regulated for one year after resignation from government. A bill approved by the Senate in 1977 mandates an even stricter two-year ban in certain cases.

There is no question that the overall quality of new appointments of agency heads under the Carter administration has been outstanding from the point of view of their past records. While it is too early to make definitive assessments on the basis of necessarily brief track records, it is possible to observe some emerging trends in performance. In general, these trends are favorable. Bingham at OSHA, Foreman at USDA, Claybrook at Transportation, and Pertschuk at the Federal Trade Commission, have all transformed their agencies for the better. As part of their reforms, they have recruited much needed fresh and skilled new personnel into senior positions. Additionally, Upton at NCI, Kennedy at FDA, and Costle at EPA have also made a substantial impact at their agencies by virtue of their integrity and openness.

Problems of overlapping jurisdictions and regulatory inconsistencies are now being recognized.[84] Attempts are being made to correct this and to develop better coordination of efforts at the fact-finding and regulatory levels. Among the more important cooperative moves that have been made are the formation of an Interagency Regulatory Liaison Group (IRLG), involving EPA, OSHA, FDA, and the Consumer Product Safety Commission, and the formation of an EPA Toxic Substances Strategy Committee, an overall coordinating group which reports directly to the President.

The likelihood for success of these new cooperative ventures is increased by the close contacts and understanding that have developed between Bingham, Costle, and Kennedy, which have been reinforced by similar contacts with heads of research agencies, particularly Upton and Rall. An informal system of "yellow alerts" has been developed between these agencies through which mutual concerns and needs are shared. Some of these cooperative moves, particularly the IRLG, may well foreshadow the emergence of more extensive and formalized consolidation, probably within HEW, of the functions of the several different agencies now dealing with various aspects of environmental pollution and public health.

Chapter Ten

Non-governmental Policies

Until recently, industry and labor have been the only major nongovernment influences on Congress and regulatory agencies in all areas of public health and safety, whether relating to the general environment, consumer products, or the workplace. In the last decade a new element has emerged, the public interest movement, which, in spite of trivial material resources compared to those of industry, has begun to transform the climate of decision making. A discussion of the three—industry, labor, and public interest groups—and also of additional influences with respect to environmental and occupational carcinogenesis follows.

Industry

American industry early gained a reputation for innovation and flexibility. These are among the qualities that established international preeminence for the U.S. free enterprise system. Nowhere has this flexibility been better seen than in the major chemical industries, which have learned to deal with shifting supplies of raw materials and shifting demands of the market.

In spite of this, industry has failed to adequately comprehend the magnitude of health and safety problems entailed in the manufacture and handling of hazardous, particularly toxic or carcinogenic, chemicals. Industry has also failed to comprehend the enormous costs to society of the cancer and other diseases resulting from the use of toxic and carcinogenic chemicals. Industry is not alone in this failure of comprehension, which must also be shared by government and the public.

Top management has also failed to be aware of the shortcomings in its own modes of developing health and safety information. As a result, marketing decisions and all-but-irreversible economic commitments are often made on the basis of information that subsequently proves to be defective or based solely on short-term marketing considerations. The conflicts inherent in this tend to limit the interests and incentives of industry to develop equally effective but less hazardous alternative products and processes—hence to stifle needed innovation.

Big industry faces two distinct types of problems in developing control technology. First, there are the difficulties of effectively refitting old plants with add-on devices to allow them to handle toxic chemicals more safely. It is now generally recognized that in many instances this just may not be practical. This does not exclude the possibility of materially decreasing risk by improving work practices. Part of the problem here is the fact that some industries, particularly steel, have in the past failed to plough back profits into renovating old plants.* This problem of old plants with old technology must be dealt with on an industry-by-industry basis. There are no simple so-

---

*The 1976 OSHA hearings on coke oven emissions made it clear that the newer Japanese coke ovens are better designed than their U.S. equivalents.

lutions or general formulae. It is clear, however, that old plants cannot be allowed to function as before at the continued expense of human health. While they are being phased out, at a pace influenced by industrial economics and public health concerns, improved work practices and engineering controls must be instituted on an interim basis.

The second (and relatively easier) set of problems faced by big business are those involved with the design of new plants. This is where industry can be expected to exhibit bold innovation. Health and safety considerations must be designed into plants at the earliest possible stages. The substitution of safer products and processes must be exploited to the fullest to avoid the use of carcinogenic chemicals. If it can be proven that there are no practical alternatives to the use of a carcinogen, then closed systems must be devised and engineered with all possible precision and safeguards, including constant monitoring with highly sensitive instrumentation. Costs of such controls are a useful incentive to the innovative development of safer alternatives.

The problems of small industry are probably the most difficult and complex. Many of these operate marginally and cannot afford to install expensive engineering controls.* Many also employ poorly educated and transient, nonunionized labor. While some improvement in work practices to reduce risks is feasible, there are clearly practical limitations as to what can be done in the small plant. To add to these pressures, large corporations have historically sided with government in efforts to regulate and destroy competition from small business. It is clear that small business must be gradually weaned away from handling hazardous chemicals. It is also clear that they should be encouraged in this direction and in the direction of im-

---

*It must be stressed that most epidemiological investigations that have so far demonstrated carcinogenic hazards in the workplace, have been undertaken in large chemical corporations that have some degree of protective controls, as opposed to small industry.

proved work practices by special treatment, including tax subsidies and interim variances.

Industry, like labor, represents a heterogeneous array of interests and objectives. Such diversity, however, tends to be replaced by a common front of intransigence in response to proposed regulation of toxic and carcinogenic chemicals. A complex of interrelated factors seems involved in this posture. These include the near-automatic rejection of federal controls (without a parallel rejection of tax subsidies and other forms of corporate protectionism); preoccupation with short-term marketing interests (often in conflict with needs for hazard controls) rather than consideration of long-term growth and stability; excessive reliance on narrowly based, self-interested recommendations of in-house marketing and scientific staff and their consultants on problems of health and safety; and a tendency to wait for health and safety problems to arise (which they then deal with defensively) rather than developing anticipatory strategies based on long-term considerations.

Strategies

In support of the status quo, industry has evolved a complex set of strategies to use individually or in concert to meet the needs of any particular circumstance. These are illustrated by the various case studies discussed in this book. The essence of all of them is to minimize the reality of risks due to a particular product or process, to maximize the social benefits, and to exaggerate the costs and difficulty of regulation. The elements of these strategies are sometimes presented frankly as industry positions, but they often come to us from industry spokesmen and academic consultants as "professional" viewpoints, with no hint of who employs the professionals.

Minimizing the Risk   This standard ploy is exemplified by the Quebec Asbestos Mining Association's position. The association has publicly asserted that asbestos disease is a reflection of poor working conditions in the past which have been so improved that there is now little or no risk. Similarly, the Manufacturing Chemists Association and the academic consultants of industry have testified that benzene-induced leukaemias and other toxic effects reflect high exposures in the past and that now, based on the relatively low exposures encountered under modern working conditions, there is no cause for concern. As a further example, Rohm and Haas, as recently as 1974, denied that exposure to BCME has caused any worker deaths following exposure at their plant. Other illustrative positions include the claim, by such organizations as the Nutrition Foundation and the Council on Agricultural Science and Technology, that there is no risk in being exposed to "relatively low levels" of chemicals found to be carcinogenic in humans, and that there are no substantive risks of exposure to chemicals found to be carcinogenic in animals and for which there are as yet no human data.

Diversionary Tactics   These are generally based on insistence on degrees of precision and legal definition that cannot possibly be met in carcinogenesis tests or in epidemiological studies. Such a demand is often coupled with rejection of experimental carcinogenicity test data and alternative proposals for long-term prospective human studies over the next few decades, pending which, it is claimed, regulatory action should be suspended.

On January 11, 1978, the day HEW Secretary Joseph Califano announced a new "war on smoking," Senator Wendell Ford (D-Ken.), on behalf of his tobacco-producing state, told a news conference that Califano should instead direct the earmarked antismoking funds "into well-founded scientific research. The American people can make their own decisions," implying that still more research was needed and that government should do this research but should not set policy based on its results.

A December 13, 1977, meeting of the Toxicology Forum, an industry-sponsored group of toxicologists and geneticists, decided that saccharin should be given top priority for new studies. These new studies, the group concluded, should be directed to identify "impurities" in commercial saccharin, which members apparently had convinced themselves were responsible for the carcinogenic and mutagenic activity of saccharin.

Propagandizing the Public   The media blitz orchestrated by the Calorie Control Council following the FDA's proposal to ban saccharin was unprecedented in regulatory history. The payoff obviously was worthwhile, for the unexpected and tumultuous public response led to a moratorium on its regulation. The council's use of such high-priced public relations firms as Hill and Knowlton reflects the determination of an industry faced with potential control. The council's propaganda is an outgrowth of an evolving media campaign, in which the chemical and oil industries are striving to improve their public images with all the techniques of modern mass advertising.

"Assuming a leadership role" on behalf of the chemical industry, Monsanto Chemical Company has recently launched a major public advertising campaign directed to the importance and safety of synthetic chemicals. Synthetic chemicals, it is claimed, are no different from all other naturally occurring chemicals to which mankind has been exposed for millions of years, and are essentially harmless in the absence of massive exposure or careless misuse. More specifically, the campaign consists of attacks against standard methods of carcinogenicity testing based on accepted uses of maximally tolerated doses, against the Delaney Amendment, and against other regulatory controls of carcinogenic chemicals, all of which are categorized as irrational and emotional. A Monsanto pamphlet called "The Chemical Facts of Life" explains that the purpose of the campaign is "to explore the benefits and risks of chemicals — to find a clear path through the labyrinth of information and misinformation about chemicals which may help or harm health and the environment."[1]

Monsanto is spending about $5 million this year and is planning to spend similar amounts annually over the next five years on spots on national television, newspaper ads, and pamphlets. Some 500,000 pamphlets have been distributed so far, even to high school children. The campaign has been well planned and seems to limit possibilities of asking for equal time under the Fairness Doctrine. Following protest by the Environmental Defense Fund, Monsanto initially agreed to limit somewhat the scope of its campaign. One sixty-second national television spot features a speaker identified as an agricultural chemist drinking from a glass of water and asserting the dependence of the modern farmer on chemicals such as di-hydrogen oxide — water. He then goes on to discuss the herbicide Vegadex,* explaining that while one would never drink this, it benefits crop growth in several ways. The screen flashes images of weeds being killed and healthy crops growing. The speaker allows that "no chemical is totally safe all the time," but maintains that chemicals such as Vegadex are necessary in circumstances of worldwide food shortages, and concludes that without chemicals life would not be possible.

The Monsanto campaign is not a public service. The

---

*Vegadex, or sulfallate, is a chlorinated dithiocarbamate derivative used as a selective pre-emergence herbicide on vegetable crops. It is structurally similar to a number of other pesticides which were shown to be carcinogenic more than nine years ago. In January, 1978, Vegadex was shown to be positive in the Ames test,[2] and in the following March the NCI bioassay program published a report showing that the herbicide is carcinogenic to rats and mice, inducing breast cancers in females of both species, tumors of the stomach in male rats and of the lung in male mice.[3]

Recent production data for Vegadex are unknown, as this is considered proprietary information. However, a 1971 report estimates U.S. production as about 500,000 kg annually. As the NCI report points out, "The potential for exposure to sulfallate is greatest for agricultural workers, but may also be considerable for workers in sulfallate production facilities. Residents of agricultural communities may be exposed to airborne residues following spraying operations. The herbicide is readily taken up by plant roots . . . and the general population may be exposed via ingestion of residues in food crops."

company would do better to stress concerns that the chemicals they plan to produce should be well tested to avoid future problems such as those posed by the toxicity and carcinogenicity of its products, such as Vegadex and nitrilotriacetic acid. Monsanto should also consider the judgment of its executives and consultants, on the basis of whose advice this mass campaign was presumably authorized.

Blaming the Victim Simply stated, the argument is, "Modern industrial working conditions are so safe that if a worker gets hurt or sick it must be his or her fault and not the fault of the industry." The culprit is either the worker's bad habits, such as smoking, or the worker's high genetic susceptibility to effects which any normal person would shrug off. Applications of this perspective have taken many forms. Perhaps its latest variant is the stance of Johns-Manville's Paul Kotin, in shifting attention from what *chemicals* cause cancer to what *people* get cancer. Kotin has helped resurrect the notion of the "hypersusceptible worker," one who, by his own constitutional or genetic makeup, is at higher risk for occupational disease than fellow workers. Starting from the plausible premise that all biological organisms, including humans, vary in their response to external stimuli such as toxic substances or carcinogens, he then advances the following proposition:

> The workplace, no matter how elegantly controlled, cannot assure uniformity of protection to all workers because of susceptibility variation. . . . A safe, acceptable workplace for hypersusceptible workers is as much a cultural concept as it is a scientific one. . . . It is still the responsibility of management to deny the worker the "right" to place himself at increased risk.[4]

Kotin jumps from the variability premise to the assertion of management's "right" to assign sturdier individuals to riskier jobs, overlooking the difficulty, if not impossibility, of making such judgments on scientifically sustained grounds, especially regarding carcinogenesis. However, the viewpoint has superficial appeal, as it rationalizes management's right to make arbitrary work assignments, and leaves open the possibility that management will somehow attempt to predict or decide in advance which workers are cancer-prone.

Another blame-the-victim ploy tries to shift the responsibility for workplace disability from uncontrolled exposure to lifestyle. Thus, industries (other than the tobacco industry, of course) are quick to blame lung cancer on smoking and in so doing try to absolve dusts and chemicals in the workplace from any role in the disease.

There is no question that smoking markedly increases the susceptibility of asbestos workers to lung cancer, but the risk of the nonsmoking asbestos worker is also significantly greater than that of the person who does not work with asbestos. Also, smoking has no relation to other malignant diseases caused by asbestos such as pleural or peritoneal mesotheliomas.

Similarly, alcoholism programs in industry focus almost solely on family and marital problems as a cause of drinking, rather than looking into frustrations on the job as a possible factor. Recent studies on heart disease are focusing on so-called Type-A behavior (characterized by a hard-driving, aggressive, competitive personality), which is considered to predispose to coronary disease. An employer may thus be provided with a rationale for blaming the disease solely on the employee, without considering that the behavior itself may also be influenced by stresses inherent in the work.

An equally insidious blame-the-victim scheme, characteristic of the cosmetic approach of some industry to occupational hazards, involves exaggeration of the known problems of small numbers of people with genetic or enzyme deficiencies. It would be useful to industry to have it proven that those workers who contract occupational illness were genetically defective and thus hypersusceptible. A deficiency in the respiratory enzyme alpha-1-antitrypsin, for example, is claimed to be associated with chronic obstructive lung disease:

> if susceptible subjects can be identified during pre-employment screening and are effectively excluded from hazardous occupations, some cases of chronic bronchitis may be prevented.[5]

However, a 1975 University of Arizona study demonstrated no association between deficiency of the enzyme and symptoms of chronic obstructive pulmonary disease or reduced lung function, and furthermore, found the frequency of this deficiency in the population to be trivial.[6]

Controlling Information The overwhelming majority of decisions made by regulatory agencies is based on information provided by the industries themselves being regulated. In retrospect, it seems strange that this practice has persisted so long, and that in fact it still persists. In every case study documented in this book, the relevant data base is inadequate or constrained by incompetence, biased interpretation, or even manipulation and suppression. There is no basis for believing that such examples are uncommon.

Influencing Policy The methods by which industry influences the legislative and regulatory processes, both in the passage and enforcement of standards, are legion. Even after scientific evidence can be developed which shows that a chemical is carcinogenic, the ensuing regulatory process and development of exposure standards are strongly influenced by industrial lobbyists and trade associations. Throughout the last stages of the writing of toxic substances legislation, lobbyists from the Manufacturing Chemists Association were in daily conference with congressmen and their staffs.[7] Out of that experience emerged a semi-autonomous lobbying group which promises to challenge the environmental legislative and regulatory process for many years to come.

Exhausting the Agencies Once an agency has determined to regulate, or has been obliged to regulate by concerns of labor or public interest groups, a common tactic of industry is to resort to protracted legal action. This is done in the full knowledge that legal proceedings on one particular chemical product or on one standard alone may extend over months or years, during which no regulatory control can usually be imposed. The legal costs incurred by the industry during such proceedings are usually small compared to the continued sales profits. One or two cases such as aldrin/dieldrin can exhaust the legal resources of an agency, which are small compared to the virtually limitless legal and other resources that industry can muster.

Insistence on the case-by-case approach has been a favored industry tactic. Basic questions on carcinogenesis have to be argued over again and again for every separate proceeding (such as for the chlordane/heptachlor case, which revived all the same set of problems settled before in the aldrin/dieldrin hearings). This seems the basis for industry's vigorous opposition to the "cancer principles" and to the generic approach to regulation of carcinogens proposed by OSHA.

In late 1977, the Manufacturing Chemists Association spun off the American Industrial Health Council to "assist" OSHA and other agencies in developing policies on carcinogens.[8] Convinced that "OSHA may be developing the national standard for the identification and regulation of carcinogens" in the environment as well as the workplace, the council will provide technical and economic analysis on behalf of its member industries. Its counterproposal to OSHA's "generic" carcinogens standard would set up two major categories of carcinogens: "human carcinogens" (Category I) and "animal carcinogens" (Category II). Within each category, it would differentiate high, intermediate, and low-potency agents. More tellingly, it would require OSHA to establish apparent no-effect levels for carcinogens, to assess both risks and benefits before setting workplace exposure levels, and to emphasize the use of controls based on personal protective equipment. This is in contrast to OSHA's and labor's policy favoring stricter work practices. The council's proposals would lay the foundation for unending legal challenges to future attempts to regulate any occupational carcinogen.

The position of the American Industrial Health Council rests on claims that there is no evidence of any recent increase in cancer incidence, that most cancer is due to smoking and diet, that the incidence of occupational cancer is low, only in the region of 5 percent,* that the role of industrial chemical carcinogens in occupational cancer is small, and that the costs of regulation as proposed by OSHA are excessive and as high as tens of billions of dollars.† Apart from the inherent distortions in these claims, they ignore the growing evidence of the occurrence of cancer in the general community due to discharge or release of carcinogens from the workplace to the external environment. They also ignore the likelihood of inducing cancer in the children of exposed pregnant workers, besides in the workers themselves. Finally, apart from inherent questions on the validity of economic impact analyses by industry, they ignore the much greater costs to society of failure to regulate industrial chemicals in the workplace, let alone in the general environment.

The industry position on the allegedly heavy costs of regulation in general and occupational carcinogens in particular appears to be gaining the sympathy of the present administration. A Regulatory Analysis Review Group, recently created by President Carter with representation from the Council of Economic Advisors and the Council

---

*In contrast, Schneiderman of the NCI has estimated that up to 30 percent of all cancers in white males are related to exposures to occupational carcinogens.

†These cost estimates were developed by Foster D. Snell Inc., Division of Booz, Allen and Hamilton, whose earlier analyses on costs of meeting the 1974 1 ppm occupational standard for vinyl chloride have also been shown to be grossly exaggerated.

on Wage and Price Stability, is now requiring agencies to justify all proposed regulation that is perceived to be inflationary, even if this is unproven. As yet, OSHA and other regulatory agencies have failed to develop and present a strong case for the opposing position: that the costs of regulation are trivial in relation to the costs of failure to regulate, which are highly inflationary though still largely unrecognized.

The Flight of the Multinationals   In the past, when faced by the prospect of local regulatory controls, industry has moved or has threatened to move to Southern states, which have traditionally been more receptive to industrial interests and less concerned with occupational health and environmental considerations. With the passage of the 1970 Occupational Health and Safety Act, the opportunity for such evasions in the United States became more limited.* U.S. industry with multinational connections then shifted tactics to exporting their hazardous industries abroad. "Runaway" shops were created in lesser developed countries such as Brazil or Taiwan, where there are virtually no regulatory controls and where cheap and unorganized labor is amply available. More surprising, however, is the increasing flight of segments of the chemical industry to runaway shops in eastern Europe, where regulatory controls and opportunities for public protest are minimal compared to the United States.

The growing flight from regulation poses major threats to foreign workers, and to the environmental quality outside the United States, besides reflecting on the corporate ethics of the industries involved. It also poses two sets of threats to the U.S. economy: loss of jobs and unfair advantage in competition with those segments of

---

*However, the chemical industry in New Jersey is threatening to move elsewhere if the state perseveres in attempts at regulation, with particular reference to limiting the discharge of carcinogenic chemicals into the environment of the surrounding community.

industry complying with pollution control regulations in the United States. In some industries, the flight from regulation is already established.[9] In others, it appears imminent. The greatest flight is seen in the asbestos textile industries, which are being increasingly located in Mexican border towns and in Taiwan and South Korea. There are also indications that other asbestos manufacturers, particularly of friction products such as brake linings and disc pads, will follow this course. Other flights involve arsenic-producing copper smelters and the plastics, benzidine dye, and pesticide industries.*

Vigorous legislative initiatives, such as federal chartering of giant multinational corporations, are urgently needed.[10] Federal chartering would impose specific restrictions on giant industries where four or fewer firms account for over 50 percent of sales in some major markets, and would restructure them internally to prevent such corporate abuses as bribery, illegal domestic and foreign political contributions, price-fixing, monopolistic practices, regulatory violations (including manipulation or suppression of data), and the export of hazardous products and processes. The broad objectives of the proposed federal corporate chartering would be to achieve corporate accountability to the U.S. government and people

> to assure more corporate democracy by giving greater voice or authority, for example to shareholders over the decision of managers; to require greater disclosure of the social and financial performance of companies; to deconcentrate industries and restore competition; to assure employees their civil rights and liberties by a bill of rights for employees.[11]

The recent proposal of the Council on Environmental Quality to require industry to file environmental impact

---

*Following legal action by a coalition of environmental groups, the Agency for International Development announced in 1976 that it would no longer sponsor the export of pesticides banned in the U.S.

statements before exporting hazardous products and processes is also an overdue approach to this problem. Patterns of flight need to be carefully monitored by federal groups and other concerned interests, including organized labor and responsible industry.* Assistance should also be requested from international organizations such as the World Health Organization and international labor groups.

An issue related to the flight of the multinational corporations is the common practice of export of products whose use is not permitted in the United States, such as the pesticide leptophos, or products whose use has been banned in the United States, such as the pesticide dieldrin and children's sleeping garments treated with the flame retardant Tris. In January, 1978, Senator Gaylord Nelson (D-Wisc.) called for a ban on export of pesticides whose use is prohibited in the United States, after samples of imported agricultural products show residues of these pesticides. This whole area needs comprehensive legislation to prevent exposure of foreign workers and consumers to products manufactured by the U.S. industry but considered too hazardous for use here.† A critically related issue which demands vigorous international initiatives is the growing promotional campaign of the tobacco industry in the Third World.

Technological Innovation and Regulation

Some segments of industry have repeatedly expressed concerns that the mounting tide of federal regulation over the last two decades is impeding or stifling technological innovation. The Manufacturing Chemists Association and Dow Chemical Company have claimed that requiring chemicals to be tested prior to their introduction into

---

*The information available on hazard export is extremely scanty, though the trend is already well established.

†Banned products being exported include Tris, DDT, cyclamates, and Red #2.

commerce, in accordance with current requirements of toxic substances legislation, is acting as an obstacle to industrial innovation. (These claims have particularly involved the manufacture of pesticides and contraceptive drugs.) Such claims ignore costs to society of the failure to regulate and they do not bear critical scrutiny even on narrowly defined economic grounds. Costs of carcinogenicity and other chronic toxicity testing and costs of toxic substances legislation are small in relation to the profits of the chemical industry.[12] These claims have even been challenged by some leading industry spokesmen as illustrated by the following protest:

> I emphatically take issue with the line of reasoning that escalating regulatory demands have made the cost of research and development prohibitive, thus drying up an incentive to go develop new agricultural chemicals.
>
> In the first place, new regulations imposed since the creating of EPA affording better protection to fish and wildlife were over-due. More important is the changing aspect of the marketplace, particularly in the pesticide area. Growers now have available to them many first-rate products . . . many of these are quite inexpensive. What the chemical people are really telling you is that while research costs continue to rise, to come with still better compounds costing no more money than what's already being sold is a tough proposition . . . ; the companies with weak research organization, a shaky financial position, are dropping out. They would rather have FDA and EPA take the rap rather than acknowledge the overall problem.[13]

A series of federal and expert committees have also recently examined this problem and their general conclusions were summarized as follows:

> . . . The total value of sales (manufacturers' shipments) of the U.S. drug industry has risen consistently.
> . . . The drug industry is highly research-intensive and appears to be becoming even more so.
> . . . The number of new significant chemical entities developed year by year has remained fairly constant.

The value of sales of basic pesticide chemicals has increased consistently each year between 1962 and 1970. . . . Research and development expenditures over the same period rose 33 percent.

This Panel finds that research and development in the chemical industry has been vigorous and growing the decade since the 1962 FDA amendments. Moreover, we conclude that such R&D promises to continue a healthy rate of growth in the immediate future despite increased government regulation, and in part because of regulation.

It is the Panel's view, after examining a variety of economic issues concerning the industries which manufacture chemical products, that the economic health of these industries remains high. Sales of chemical products continue to increase. The value of shipments of chemical items continues to rise with a doubling time of something over ten years.[14]

Labor

A 1970 University of Michigan survey sponsored by the Department of Labor found that American workers rated health and safety a higher priority than increased wages.[15] This helped explode the common belief that workers relegate health issues to a minor role compared with bread-and-butter and job-security issues. In fact, workers have placed a high premium on safe working conditions throughout the hundred-year history of trade unions.

Organized labor's support of child labor laws and its insistence on an eight-hour working day led to considerable industrial strife in the 1870s. The March 25, 1911, fire at the Triangle Shirtwaist Company in New York City drew public attention to the atrocious working conditions of many young girls, and led to the enactment of corrective legislation.[16]

One of the unions that has long been involved in health and safety issues is the United Mine Workers, whose members are employed in the most hazardous industry in America. The record of the union on health and safety is mixed.[17] During the late 1940s and early 1950s, frustrated by its inability to obtain minimal compensation for disabled workers, and urged on by its medical director, Lorin Kerr, the union paid for the establishment and operation of ten hospitals in mining regions of rural Appalachia and recruited its own doctors and staff. By 1962, affected both by mismanagement and severe recession in the industry, the hospitals were sold to the Presbyterian church and the experiment ended. One of the staff physicians, Donald Rasmussen, also led an effort to have black lung recognized as a compensable illness. The union leadership, while initially hostile to the pressure which quickly developed in its ranks around the black lung issue, was ultimately forced to support federal legislation. It took a disaster, however, the 1968 explosion at a Farmington, West Virginia, mine which killed seventy-four miners, to bring about enactment of the 1969 Federal Coal Mine Health and Safety Act.

The modern era of labor concerns over health and safety and occupational carcinogenesis is a striking tribute to a handful of labor leaders who have had to overcome crippling problems. Not only have they had to emancipate themselves from the self-serving authoritarianism of industry physicians and other professionals, and to educate themselves in the relatively recent area of adverse health effects due to chemical exposures, but they have also had to develop rank-and-file support. To do this, they have sought out advice and guidance from a few independent professionals in the academic community. On a limited scale, they have also developed their own expertise and resources, particularly in industrial hygiene. Additionally, they have had to contend with economic blackmail and threats of job loss by industry whenever they advocate or support attempts to regulate unsafe exposures. Not surprisingly, most of the focus of labor concerns on problems of chemical exposures has so far been expressed in Washington, D.C. rather than at the grass-roots level.

Most prominent among these labor leaders is Anthony Mazzocchi, Vice President of the Oil, Chemi-

cal, and Atomic Workers Union (OCAW). One of Mazzocchi's many contributions has been to extend the arena of
concerns on health issues to the rank-and-file of union
membership. The president of the union, Al Grospiron,
has also made important contributions, particularly as
chairman of the Standing Committee on Safety and Occupational Health, AFL-CIO. Another labor leader who has
taken consistently strong positions on needs to regulate
chemical hazards is George Taylor, executive secretary of
the Standing Committee on Safety and Occupational
Health. Taylor has exerted a powerful influence on the
development of a wide range of occupational standards,
particularly through his chairmanship of the Staff Subcommittee of the Standing Committee. Another important
figure is Peter Bommarito, president of the United Rubber Workers, assisted by his industrial hygienist, Louis
Beliczky. Bommarito is chairman of the Executive Committee on Occupational Health and Safety of the Industrial Union Department, AFL-CIO, and has pioneered
the development of joint labor–management contracts to
universities for research on problems of carcinogenesis in
the rubber industry.

The Industrial Union Department of the AFL-CIO,
established after the 1954 AFL-CIO merger (the current
president is the labor veteran Jacob Clayman), plays a critical role in the whole area of occupational health and
safety. The director of the department's Division of Occupational Safety and Health and the Environment is Sheldon Samuels, whose major contribution has been to translate principles of control of environmental pollution into
the workplace. He also monitors the performance of
OSHA, NIOSH, NCI and other agencies. Additionally,
Samuels has developed educational programs for organized labor on occupational hazards.

Major credit for the development of the 1970 Occupational Safety and Health Act belongs to Jack Sheehan,
legislative director of United Steelworkers of America.
Sheehan is an accomplished lobbyist whose influence has
been felt on most recent major occupational standards.

George Perkel, Director of Research of the Amalgamated Clothing and Textile Workers Union, and Larry Ahern, Research Director of the International Chemical Workers Union, have both contributed materially to expressing labor's informed concerns on standards.

The International Association of Heat and Frost Insulators and Asbestos Workers, whose president is Andy Haas, has also been prominent in the struggle to protect workers from exposure to carcinogenic dusts and fibers. The successes that the union has achieved in this regard reflect the important collaboration they have developed with Irving Selikoff.

AFL-CIO is now developing closer collaboration with unions outside the Federation, particularly the International Brotherhood of Teamsters and the United Auto Workers Union. In this they have been materially aided by R. V. Durham, Research Director of the Teamsters, and Dan McLeod and Frank Mirer, Industrial Hygienists of the Auto Workers.

Recent labor concerns on occupational carcinogenesis have been largely spearheaded by OCAW, whose members operate many of the nation's largest refineries and chemical plants. Throughout 1969 and 1970, many of the union's nine district councils, covering much of the United States and all of Canada, sponsored workshops entitled "Hazards in the Industrial Environment." At these conferences, Mazzocchi discussed with union members the basic facts underlying health and safety problems in OCAW plants. For many, it was the first realization that problems arising from workplace chemicals could be recognized and dealt with.

Mazzocchi sought out and developed close personal contacts with a handful of professional scientists who helped him increase awareness in labor, Congress, and elsewhere in the government of the major hazards posed to workers by uncontrolled exposure to toxic and carcinogenic chemicals. Mazzocchi also sponsored the formation in 1971 of the Scientists Committee for Occupational Health, which, jointly with the United Auto Workers and other New Jersey labor groups, taught several courses at the Rutgers University Labor Education Center. Their students were workers who, instead of hearing just about ladders and fire extinguishers, found out about cancer-causing chemicals in their own workplaces, many for the first time.

In 1973, 4,000 OCAW workers went out on a five-month strike against Shell Oil in California and in four other states, demanding that their new contract embody specific measures to protect health and safety on the job. The union made four key demands:

1. Establishment of a joint union–management health and safety committee in every plant.

2. Periodic inspections of plants, by independent consultants jointly approved by labor and management, to determine whether workers are being exposed to hazards.

3. Medical examination of workers, at company expense, when indicated by plant inspections.

4. Availability to the union of all company records on worker's sickness and death.[18]

Impressed by the importance of the strike, a group of about twenty-five leading scientists and educators signed a statement, published by the union as a full-page advertisement in the New York Times on May 3, 1973.* This statement recognized that the strike was unique in labor history and prompted exclusively by concerns for occupational health:

> Workers have long served as unwitting guinea pigs, providing useful toxicological data which helped to protect the public. The effects of most environmental pollutants, such as carbon monoxide, lead, mercury and also of most human carcinogens were first detected in workmen; the in-plant environment is a concentrated toxic microcosm of that outside. Additionally, many toxic agents disperse beyond the plant and pose public hazards.

---

*The author wrote this statement.

The success of the OCAW strike is critical both to labor and the public. This has already been recognized by ten major environmental and public interest groups who have endorsed the Shell strike and boycott. The demand of labor to participate actively in protecting the health and safety of workers is basic and inalienable and cannot be sacrificed to narrow economic interests. It is hoped that Shell will adopt a posture more consistent with the public interest and the intent of the 1970 Occupational Safety and Health Act . . .[19]

Shell, which at first refused to bargain on "management prerogative" issues, was eventually forced to give in. However, the subsequent enforcement of contract terms continues to be an uphill struggle.

A key labor issue which has been strongly championed by OCAW is the guarantee of full economic protection of a worker in the event he or she is removed from a job classification on the basis of medical examination results. This is known as "rate retention" and means that the worker would, upon transfer, retain the same rate of pay allowed by the previous job classification, as well as all pay increases, seniority, and other benefits accruing to the former position. Another critical area pioneered by the union is the use of the Review Commission of OSHA to protect its members in situations where management contests citations by OSHA for violations against health and safety standards.

Over the recent years, management has encouraged hostility between labor and environmentalists by threatening to close plants when there are major attempts to control in-plant pollution. In 1972, responding to demands to improve working conditions, Union Carbide threatened to shut down its Alloy, West Virginia, plant, elected one of America's ten dirtiest factories by *Business Week* magazine. OCAW President A. F. Grospiron refused to knuckle under to "environmental blackmail," and Union Carbide was eventually forced to improve work practices.[20] In an address to the Union convention in 1973, Sierra Club Executive Director Michael McCloskey commented, "Your Union has been preeminent in recognizing that many environmental threats originate in the workplace and affect the workers first and foremost, before they escape into the community-at-large."

Labor has gradually developed working relationships with NIOSH and OSHA. Representatives of labor, as well as management, now participate in various advisory committees of these agencies. In addition to the more long-standing association of labor with Selikoff (particularly by the International Association of Heat and Frost Insulators and Asbestos Workers), and other such associations of labor as those with Thomas F. Mancuso, occupational physician at the University of Pittsburgh, who contributes an excellent monthly health column in the newsletter of the International Union of Electrical, Radio and Machine Workers (see Appendix IV), labor has recently developed contractual arrangements with a few universities to investigate specific occupational health problems. Unions that have been prominent in this regard include OCAW, the United Auto Workers, and the United Rubber, Cork, Linoleum, and Plastic Workers of America. A major recent resource for labor is the Society for Occupational and Environmental Health, whose meetings and conferences have created an opportunity for independent and expert analysis of health-related issues.*

Realizing the critical importance of developing its own internal scientific and technical resources, several unions have created health and safety departments or units, which are at present largely staffed by industrial hygienists.† OCAW and the United Auto Workers have set up Health and Safety Offices which administer nationwide programs for their members, coordinate activities of individual locals (particularly in testing provisions of the Occupational Safety and Health Act), and help

---

*The first president of the society was Irving Selikoff (1972–1974). The author was the second president (1974–1976). The third and current president is Joseph Wagoner (1976–1978). Eula Bingham is now president-elect.

† These include OCAW, United Steelworkers of America, United Rubber, Cork, Linoleum and Plastic Workers of America, and United Auto Workers.

extend the parameters of the collective bargaining agreement. The only union that has had a medical director for any period of time (Lorin Kerr) is the United Mine Workers of America.

AFL-CIO for several years has been considering the creation of a labor institute of occupational health and safety. Recent occupational health crises have lent further urgency to these plans. Labor now realizes that in the final analysis it must rely on its own resources.*

Another major and overdue development has been the growing awareness in labor that there is an inevitable built-in conflict of interest in the present system of direct employment of occupational physicians by industry. Results of physical examinations on individual workers can thus be directly transmitted to management, with ensuing risks of job transfer or loss.

The role of industry epidemiologists, industrial hygienists, and other professionals involved in occupational health and safety demands critical evaluation. These needs are further emphasized by the growing body of information on the existence and extent of constraints on health and safety data, ranging from inadequacy and biased interpretation to manipulation and fraud.

Clearly the salaries of health and safety professionals is the exclusive responsibility of industry as an essential part of the costs of doing business. This should not mean that the loyalty of these professionals must necessarily be directed to their employers. While the salaries of meat inspectors and grain elevator inspectors are in the final

---

*In three recently publicized occupational catastrophes (involving kepone, a carcinogenic pesticide producing neurotoxic and sterilizing effects in workers at Life Sciences Products Corporation in Virginia; leptophos, a pesticide producing neurotoxic effects in workers in a Velsicol Plant in Bayport, Texas; and DBCP [dibromochloropropane], a carcinogenic soil fumigant producing sterility in workers involved in its manufacture at Occidental Chemical Company in California), it was the workers themselves who first recognized the problem, not the plant physicians and not OSHA. It must be clearly recognized that plant health and safety committees are still the exception in the U.S. and that hygiene and occupational health services are still not available or utilized by most U.S. industries.

analysis paid for by the industries concerned, these inspectors are primarily responsible to USDA. Similarly, health professionals in industry must be primarily responsible to the worker—patient, rather than to industry. It should be a felony for an industrial physician to divulge to management the results of a physical examination. Such information is the exclusive property of the concerned principals, the physician and the worker—patient, and must not be shared with management. This is the only way by which a worker can be protected against economic penalties which management may invoke if a worker is found to be suffering adverse effects from conditions at work. Otherwise, the worker will be forced to choose the Russian roulette of exposure to occupational hazards, rather than risk job loss or transfer to a lower-paid job.

Confidential physician—worker relationships would in no way decrease the ability of an occupational physician to disclose to management and to labor the gross and anonymous results of physical examination and biological monitoring of groups of workers in specific job situations in order to allow necessary corrective action to be taken. Labor has begun to realize that the development of further occupational standards is of limited value, possibly even counterproductive, unless workers can be assured of the independence of the professionals whose responsibility is, or should be, the protection of the worker's health. The worker also must be protected against economic penalties by guarantees of equal pay and seniority rights in the event he is moved from a job with a high level of exposure to one with a lower level.

The Public Interest Movement

The public interest movement, as a modern expression of social ethics and as an instrument of political reform, is now about a decade old. Public interest organizations have generally evolved from the initiatives of young activist lawyers and other professionals, and also from expressions of citizen and consumer concerns. In this, they have been supported by a small number of independent scientists and engineers who have helped bridge the gap between technical and societal considerations.

Public interest organizations embrace a wide spectrum of heterogeneous objectives and styles. While the most influential and best-known groups are Washington-based, citizen and consumer groups more "grass roots" in nature are found in most major metropolitan centers. Student public interest research groups are a nationwide effort. They are autonomous, student-run organizations to be found on most campuses and have a record of local activism. Such groups were inspired in large part by Ralph Nader. (See Appendix V for a summary listing of major public interest groups with particular concerns on environmental and occupational cancer.)

The public interest movement expresses the conviction that the "common good" is inadequately represented in decision-making at federal and local levels, where narrow economic and political interests are joined, often at the expense of social equity. The movement also expresses the conviction that the public health and environmental costs of modern technology are poorly perceived and too readily discounted in regulatory decision-making, and that the burden of proof for such "externalized" costs is too readily accepted by government, or inappropriately shifted from the private to the public sector. As recently stated:

> In almost every judicial, legislative or administrative conflict or policy-making process, the law provides either implicitly or explicitly that the burden of proof rests on one of the parties. The criteria are quite simple. The burden of proof rests on the party, that initiates the risk, that profits from the risk, and that has the greatest resources to do something about the risks.[21]

The public interest conviction of the imbalanced and unrepresentative nature of governmental decision-making has been supported by evidence of major conflicts of interest in senior staff of regulatory agencies, by their unwillingness to involve qualified citizen and consumer representatives in decision-making, by restrictions on public access to data on the basis of which important decisions on health and safety are based, and by evidence of major constraints and deficiencies in this hidden data base.

Broadly speaking, public interest groups are either "resource" or "activist" in nature. The resource function is well illustrated by the activities of the Rachel Carson Trust in gathering, organizing, and interpreting information on pesticides and toxic chemicals, and in disseminating this to other concerned groups and the public.* Activist functions include lobbying, attempting to institute regulatory reforms, monitoring agency performance, and filing legal action as a last resort. Each public interest group tends to specialize in a particular area: drugs, food additives, pesticides, air and water pollutants, or occupational health and safety, to name a few. While in the past labor has tended to resent the "intrusion" of public interest groups into the arena of occupational health, particularly because of the alleged conflict between job security and safer working conditions, informal accommodations, such as the supportive relationship between the Health Research Group and OCAW, have recently developed.

Public interest groups have faced difficulties in establishing themselves and making an impact on public perceptions and government policies, already sensitive and responsive to the massive and well-focused and financed industry lobby. The most limiting of these problems have been financial.† Public interest groups largely depend on

---

*The author is president of the Rachel Carson Trust.

† An important recent development is the "Public Participation in Federal Agency Proceedings Act," sponsored by Senators Edward Kennedy (D-Mass.) and Charles Mathias, Jr. (R-Md.), and Congressman Peter Rodino (D-N.J.), now pending before Congress. The bill would allow public interest groups to participate in agency proceedings and also to file suit against agencies for unlawful acts. It would create a special treasury fund of $15 million annually for three years which would be available for these and related purposes. The prospects for the bill's passage seem good.

voluntary contributions from the general public. Other problems stem from the understandable tendency of the groups to move on to other areas of concern after initial resolution of a particular issue, with resulting inadequate follow-up and the possibility of "winning the battle, but losing the war." Public interest groups have also tended to work in relative isolation from each other, for reasons which include their strong sense of independence and preoccupation with their own immediate aims, sometimes to the exclusion of broader objectives. Recognition of these limitations, in addition to the need to develop closer contact between public interest groups and concerned professionals and labor, led to the creation in 1974 of the Commission for the Advancement of Public Interest Organizations.* Current activities of the commission focus on the development of loose, ad hoc coalitions of public interest groups around critical generic concerns, particularly relating to preventable cancer. These activities include supporting New Jersey citizen and labor groups in their efforts to reduce the high incidence of environmental cancer in their state; nominating qualified professionals to serve on the NCI National Cancer Advisory Board and advisory committees of other agencies with prime responsibility in control of environmental carcinogens; supporting the nomination of qualified scientific and legal professionals to senior positions in federal agencies (for example, the present NCI director, Arthur Upton); and holding "round-tables," where heads of agencies are invited periodically to interact with the public interest and labor communities on such critical questions as environmental and occupational cancer.

The past impact of public interest groups on national perspectives and on the legislative and executive branches of government has been profound and disproportionate to the small size and resources of these groups. In no area of

---

*The author chairs this commission, which is an arm of the Monsour Medical Foundation.

public interest activity has this been better exemplified than in that of preventable cancer. As illustrated in the case studies cited in this book, the great majority of all standards on environmental and occupational carcinogens developed over the last decade have been initiated by petitions and lawsuits of public interest groups and labor against the government (see Table 9.5). The past successes of public interest groups in these actions have been all the more remarkable in that they have generally had to fight on two fronts, against both industry and the regulating agency. Groups that have taken a lead role in these actions are the Environmental Defense Fund, Public Citizen's Health Research Group and Litigation group, and the National Resources Defense Council. Important contributory roles have also been played by other groups, including the Sierra Club, Consumers Union, Consumer Federation of America, Center for Science in the Public Interest, Federation of Homemakers, Action on Smoking and Health, Migrant Legal Action Programs, Friends of the Earth, the Rachel Carson Trust, the National Audubon Society, and the National Wildlife Federation.

Recent Trends

Past contacts between public interest groups and regulatory agencies and industry have necessarily been adversarial. Adversarial tactics, whether in committee meetings or the courts and Congress, have been helpful in defining positions on environmental priorities and posing critical environmental and public health problems. Tentative moves are now being made by a few public interest groups to explore the alternative that nonadversarial dialogue with industry may prove to be mutually beneficial in defined circumstances, such as assuring industry of the essential consistency between long-term industrial growth and protection of the environment and public health.

An interesting example of these exchanges is the National Coal Policy Project, the environmental caucus of which is headed by Laurence I. Moss, former president of the Sierra Club.[22] Another is the Business-Environment Project created by the Conservation Foundation in attempts to suggest improved guidelines for toxic substances testing.* A draft document of the Business-Environment Project dated January 16, 1978, entitled "Approaches for the Development of Testing Guidelines Under the Toxic Substances Control Act" reveals an apparent lack of comprehension of the basic toxicological issues involved. The document has been criticized by an industry scientist as "being more concerned with birds and bees than humans." The document places major emphasis on short-term tests as indirect indicators of carcinogenicity. As a final criterion of carcinogenicity, the document recommends the "heritable translocation test," which is a highly specialized procedure that has so far only been applied to fewer than a dozen compounds.

Questions of expertise apart, there are needs to consider whether the public interest movement now has the necessary scientific resources to develop and sustain the type of rapprochement with industry envisioned in these new exchanges. There is a growing likelihood of an increase in these dialogues between industry and the public interest movement, which is encouraged by the possibility of foundation and agency funding. It seems possible that premature moves of this type may blunt the limited impact of the public interest movement, even to the point of possible co-option.

An important development has been the recruitment of some key leaders of the public interest movement to senior positions in federal agencies. These include Joan

---

*This project is co-chaired by Karim Ahmed of the Natural Resources Defense Council and George Dominguez of Ciba-Geigy, and is headed up by Sam Gusman, just retired as Washington representative of Rohm & Haas.

Claybrooke, former director of the Public Citizen Congress Watch, currently Administrator of the National Highway Traffic Safety Administration; Carol Foreman, former executive director of the Consumer Federation of America, currently Assistant Secretary of Agriculture; Harrison Wellford, formerly of the Center for Study of Responsive Law and chief legislative assistant to the late Senator Philip A. Hart (D-Mich.), currently Executive Associate Director for Management and Regulatory Policy, Office of Management and Budget; Gus J. Speth, formerly of the Natural Resources Defense Council, currently a member of the Council on Environmental Quality; David Hawkins, also of the Natural Resources Defense Council, currently Assistant Administrator Air and Waste Management, EPA; Peter Shuck, formerly of Consumers Union, currently Deputy Assistant Secretary of HEW; and Cynthia Wilson, formerly of the National Audubon Society, currently Assistant Secretary of Interior.

It is premature to assess the impact of this "move to government." While it is generally welcomed as a potential infusion of "new and honest young blood," a caution has been raised to the effect that not only have the slender ranks of the public interest movement been seriously depleted, but also that its unique strength lies in keeping a distance from government. Nader has been more explicit in his criticism of consumer advocates who have joined the administration.

> . . . I think they've been too cautious. I think they've been too defensive, and I think to some degree they've even been apologetic about prior careers as consumer advocates. They won't admit it, but their behavior has been such that they're leaning over the other way to compensate for it.[23]

The public interest movement is now at a critical juncture. It has lost some of its best leaders and most in-

formed lobbyists to government. In the absence of new
initiatives, the future financial base of the movement is
precarious. Competition for public funds among the estimated 2,500 public interest organizations is now becoming
keener. Direct mailing lists soliciting support for public
interest groups have become so overgrazed that they are
now of questionable value. Foundation support for public
interest groups has sharply declined, consistent with usual
foundation policies of initiating but not sustaining. This
growing financial crisis has been compounded by the election of a liberal President, who has taken the steam out of
left-wing social protest, which in the past has been an important source of public interest support. There has not
yet been adequate articulation of this shift of the winds of
fortune by public interest groups to the executive branch,
Congress, foundations, or the public at large.

The public interest movement has not yet adequately
shifted focus from emphasis on specific individual issues,
such as a particular carcinogen, pesticide, or feed additive, to broader approaches which will embody a wider set
of generic concerns. More critical still is the absence of a
grass-roots consumer movement which is clearly the only
practical way consumers will be able to exercise effective
political influence to protect their interests.* Industry, on
the other hand, has mobilized on a massive and well-
financed scale to propagandize the government and an
already apathetic or even antipathetic public against the
need for regulatory controls and to assert, on the basis of
tenuous or misleading evidence, that their costs would be
inflationary, while completely ignoring the much higher
costs to society from failure to regulate. Industry has
launched a new range of well organized and financed

---

*The absence of such a grass-roots base, together with strong pressures
from big business on the House of Representatives, were critical factors in the
defeat in February, 1978, of the long-embattled bill to establish a new federal
consumer protection agency.

cooperative initiatives, such as the Business Round Table, corporate Political Action Committees,* and the American Industrial Health Council, which threaten the future effective control and regulation of industry.

The combination of well-focused intensive legislative pressures from a small army of highly paid lobbyists in Washington, national grass-roots support mobilized through Chambers of Commerce all over the country, and lavish advertisements in the press (such as those of the Calorie Control Council in opposition to the proposed FDA saccharin ban), have created major and unparalleled threats to the whole process of democratic decision-making as well as to the public interest movement. It is now more urgent than ever that public interest groups address this crisis of imbalance in national policies. This is the critical message that must be intensively disseminated on a grass-roots level if public interest groups are to survive, let alone maintain their effectiveness.

The possibility of stronger public interest input into federal agencies was created by a memorandum of April 27, 1978, by President Carter, outlining new functions for the White House Office of Consumer Affairs, headed by Esther Peterson. It is proposed that this office should become actively involved in executive policy-making on con-

---

*Political Action Committees, authorized by recent changes in federal election laws, now number about six hundred, while their labor counterparts have leveled off at about 250. Massive expansion of the corporate committees is being organized and stimulated by a consortium that includes the National Chamber of Commerce, the National Association of Manufacturers, the National Federation of Independent Business, and the Center for the Study of Free Enterprise of the University of Southern California's Graduate School of Business. The avowed major objective of these new committees is to reduce government regulation and bureaucratic paper work. However, as pointed out in a recent OMB report, "Paper Work and Red Tape," much of the paper burden has been created by Congress and the courts, and most complaints mask an opposition to a particular federal program. (Also, major needs for paper work are the necessity to protect the public against fraud and to evaluate government programs.) In fact, despite a large number of new programs with reporting requirements, OMB has shown that there has been a 10 percent reduction in the time spent on report filing since January, 1977.

sumer problems. Existing public interest participation programs in federal agencies will be reviewed. Peterson will also be able to evaluate public interest programs in federal agencies — and other actions that impact on the public interest — and to make necessary recommendations how these may be improved.

Additional Influences on Policy-Making

Independent Professionals

Among other groups influencing national policies, a handful of independent professionals of recognized expertise in fields such as toxicology, carcinogenesis, and epidemiology has been particularly important. Over the last decade, these people have been instrumental in providing a critical data base and scientific guidance to leading labor reformers, and to public interest groups and members of Congress concerned about preventable cancer and other environmental and occupational problems. These professionals have also become an important resource to leading press and science writers.

Professional Societies

On the whole, the professional community-at-large and professional organizations and societies have been indifferent, if not hostile, to environmental and occupational problems and needs for controls. The main reason for this is a not unnatural preoccupation with professional concerns, which is often compounded by conservatism, ·ignorance of the problems, or special interest. The role of the American College of Obstetricians and Gynecologists in joining with the Pharmaceutical Manufacturers Association in opposing the FDA's action on labeling of Premarin with a carcinogenicity warning is illustrative. Other examples include the Society of Toxicology, which has served as a professional base for the protection of industrial interests, such as by fighting against the Delaney Amendment. In a similar class, the American Conference of Governmental Industrial Hygienists has generated so-called safe exposure levels or "threshold limit values," exposure levels for a wide range of chemical agents without adequate consideration of long-term effects, particularly cancer.

On the other side of the coin, organizations such as the Medical Committee on Human Rights have exercised a useful role in informing socially conscious clinicians of needs for safe working conditions. From such activities have sprung a series of Committees on Occupational Safety and Health (so-called COSH groups) many of which continue to play an important long-term role in their communities, such as those in Chicago (CACOSH) and Philadelphia (PHILAPOSH). The Environmental Mutagen Society, created in 1969, has performed and continues to perform a useful service by interesting geneticists in practical problems of genetic hazards from toxic chemicals in the general environment and workplace, and in educating the scientific and regulatory communities on such problems. The American Public Health Association is also developing a contributory role in environmental and occupational areas. The American Association for the Advancement of Science has developed programmatic coverage of major environmental and occupational problems and their social implications in its annual meetings, and in 1976 formed a Committee on Scientific Freedom and Responsibility to examine underlying ethical considerations.

The Society for Occupational and Environmental Health, founded in November, 1972, represents an important milestone in the history of professional societies. The society was created to provide a mutual context for dialogue between government, labor, industry, and academia on scientific problems and information underlying regulatory decisions in the workplace and general environment. The uniqueness of the society stems from its broad-spectrum and staunchly independent approach to problems of critical concerns on health and safety, and its promotion of occasions for focusing independent expertise on these concerns. Society meetings and workshops on such topics as occupational exposure to beryllium, lead and arsenic, occupational carcinogenesis, and reproductive hazards in the workplace provide opportunities for unusually frank discussions of scientific and regulatory problems. This is in sharp contrast to conventional practices in the usually self-congratulatory climate of industry and establishment-dominated professional societies dedicated to preserving and defending the status quo. Recognizing these particular qualities, then Senator Walter Mondale stated in an address at the annual society meeting on December 4, 1973,

> You represent—more than anyone else—the best skills and experience necessary to the accomplishment of the national objective declared by the Occupational Safety and Health Act.

Another important independent organization is the Federation of American Scientists, known as "The Voice of Science on Capitol Hill." The federation is a unique lobbying group of 7,000 natural and social scientists and engineers concerned with problems of science and society. It was first organized in 1946 as the Federation of Atomic Scientists, but its current interests are now broader. It has recently taken an active and informed stand on urgent needs for control of environmental cancer. While the federation is a high-caliber professional society, it also functions as an activist public interest organization.

The American Cancer Society

The American Cancer Society is the largest private philanthropic institution in the country and is devoted exclusively to cancer. It was founded in 1913 by a small group of concerned physicians and lay people in order to educate the public in the need for early diagnosis and proper treatment of cancer. The society was incorporated as a nonprofit organization in 1922, and has grown to include 2,800 local units, organized in fifty-eight major state divisions, and with headquarters in New York. Funding of the society, currently budgeted at about $114 million, comes largely from its annual crusade and legacies, rather than from large corporate gifts.

The overall governing group for the American Cancer Society is the 194-member House of Delegates, which in 1977 included one labor representative and one black, but no representative of public interest or citizen organizations.* The 116-member National Board of Directors is recruited from the House of Delegates. The ultimate leadership of the society is in the hands of a select group of thirty-two Life Members, among whom the banking, insurance, advertising, and pharmaceutical industries are well represented, in the absence of representation from labor or public interest groups. These lay representatives share leadership almost equally with clinicians and research scientists.

Since its inception, the society has been preoccupied by problems of cancer diagnosis and treatment, not unnaturally reflecting viewpoints which generally prevailed until relatively recently. While the society made important contributions to the smoking—cancer problem prior to 1964, its subsequent efforts to control smoking have been weak and diffuse. In fact, it has refused to endorse meaningful activist approaches such as those developed by Action on Smoking and Health, and has yet to develop any effective legislative programs.

Research programs, which are the major emphasis of the fund-raising appeals of the society, accounted for about 26 percent of its 1976 budget. Of about $13 million spent on new research projects in 1976, $394,000 was allotted to chemical carcinogenesis, while no new awards

---

*Of the ninety-four lay delegates, eighteen are senior officers or directors of banks, seven are members of investment firms, and thirteen are business or industrial executives.

were made on problems of environmental carcinogenesis. To its credit, however, the society has supported major experimental and epidemiological research on smoking, and on a wide range of occupational problems. These include studies on carcinogenesis and other hazards among printers, in collaboration with the Printing Pressmen's and the International Typographical Union, and studies on asbestos by Selikoff in collaboration with the Papermakers Union.

The educational programs and publications of the American Cancer Society emphasize the importance of early detection of cancer, even for those cancers with known low cure rates. The society has issued the widely publicized Seven Warning Signs of Cancer (see below). Apart from smoking, however, no reference is made to any other causes of cancer, such as Premarin as a major known risk factor for uterine cancer. By emphasizing individual responsibility for early detection, without providing information on environmental or occupational carcinogens other than tobacco, the American Cancer Society has implicitly created an impression that it endorses industry's "blaming the victim" perspective.

The Seven Warning Signs of Cancer

1. Change in bowel or bladder habits.
2. A sore that does not heal.
3. Unusual bleeding or discharge.
4. Thickening or lump, especially in the breast.
5. Indigestion or difficulty in swallowing.
6. Obvious change in a wart or mole.
7. Nagging cough or hoarseness.

The American Cancer Society, particularly through Mary Lasker, the influential honorary chairperson of the National Board of Directors, lobbied hard and effectively for the passage of the 1971 National Cancer Act and for the development of autonomy for the NCI. Passage of the

Act, with massively increased financial appropriations for the NCI but without parallel increases in personnel slots, whether an error of omission or commission, virtually ensured dependence of the NCI on the American Cancer Society for direction of its programs and priorities. Rep. David Obey (D-Wisc.) has charged that the society "wants to keep the Cancer Institute strong in bankroll and weak in staff, so that it can direct its spending without too much interference."

The close links that have developed between the NCI and the society have been cemented by the personal relationships between members of the same lobby that supported both organizations, including the late Sidney Farber, Benno Schmidt (Chairman of the NCI Advisory Panel), and Mary Lasker. These interlocking relationships have also helped create a fiscal pipeline from the NCI to clinicians in leadership roles in the American Cancer Society. Certainly, the interlocking relationships between members of the NCI National Cancer Advisory Panel and Board and the American Cancer Society leadership have been important factors in maintaining high NCI priorities on problems of treatment and low priorities in problems of prevention. When Frank Rauscher recently resigned from the NCI directorship, he moved to his present position of Senior Vice President for Research of the American Cancer Society, an appointment apparently reflecting endorsement by the society of Rauscher's policies at the NCI.

Apart from being uninvolved in cancer prevention, other than to a limited extent tobacco, senior officials have developed for the society a reputation of being indifferent if not actively hostile to regulatory needs for the prevention of exposure to carcinogenic chemicals in the general environment and workplace. In early 1977, the past president of the society, Lee Clark, joined by Frank J. Rauscher, attacked the FDA for its proposed ban on the carcinogenic saccharin. This apparent position of the society has not yet been modified or retracted. Sidney Arje,

Vice President for Professional Education, objects to the FDA proposal for inserting cancer warnings in Premarin packages. The society also objects to FDA requirements for reporting adverse drug reactions in humans receiving experimental anticancer drugs in NCI programs, and has demanded legislation to abolish FDA authority in this area. Over the past decade, the society has refused to endorse critical public health moves such as the Clean Air Act and the proposed FDA ban on DES in cattle feed. Its support of the Toxic Substances Act, probably the most important single piece of legislation of the century designed to prevent exposure to carcinogenic and toxic chemicals, was perfunctory and too late to be effective. The American Cancer Society, together with the American College of Radiologists, still insists on pursuing large-scale mammography screening programs for breast cancer, including its use in younger women, even though the NCI and other experts are now agreed that these are likely to cause more cancers than could possibly be detected.

On March 9, 1978, Rauscher told a Rutgers University audience that New Jersey's high cancer rate may be a result of personal habits rather than industrial pollution.

> People are talking about a cancer hot spot here. They are blaming industry. They are blaming everybody but themselves.[24]

Rauscher further stated that there is clear evidence that New Jerseyans smoke more than the national average, thus accounting for their excess cancer rates. However, in response to a subsequent question by Congressman Andrew Maguire (D-N.J.), Rauscher admitted that he had no evidence to support his claim for higher smoking rates in New Jersey.

The problems with the American Cancer Society seem to reflect clinical bias and conservatism to go with their lack of understanding of environmental causes of cancer.[25] Emerging realization of needs of the society to develop new perspectives and policies with regard to cancer prevention is now being reflected at the divisional level, particularly in Illinois and California, where greater interest in problems of cancer prevention is now being expressed. In November, 1977, the Illinois Division recommended that the National Board create "a clearinghouse on cancer causes and risk factors to provide to the Division and to the public the kind of resource the American Cancer Society has long offered regarding improved methods of treatment." The Illinois Division earmarked a special grant of $500,000 for this purpose, and followed up this initiative by creating a special "Cancer Prevention Committee" in February, 1978.*

Clearly, the American Cancer Society needs more informed leadership about the problems of cancer cause and prevention. The society must develop explicit policies on cancer prevention and these must be articulated by responsible spokesmen. There is an emerging basis for optimism that the society may move in this direction, perhaps prompted by an increasingly critical press. A possible pointer in this regard is the fact that the National Board has recently created the position of Vice President for Cancer Prevention and Early Detection and is now soliciting recommendations for an advisory committee to this new position. However, substantive and rapid reforms are needed if the American Cancer Society is to continue to exercise an appropriate role of national influence.

---

*The author is a member of this committee.

He shall be disenfranchised who in times of faction takes neither side.

Solon, quoted in Plutarch Chronicles,
1st century A.D.

Chapter Eleven

What You Can Do to Prevent Cancer

By now, you will have a grasp of the basic political and scientific problems of cancer cause and prevention. Both are problems, though for different reasons. First, the objective scientific data are often not clear-cut. Second, even when they are, their interpretation is usually distorted by economic and political pressures, which have influenced or shaped regulatory policies. In the final analysis, such policies are based on some kind of risk–benefit equation whose elements are usually concealed or poorly articulated, and whose benefits are not necessarily enjoyed by those who bear the risk.[1] Understanding the risk–benefit equation should help reduce the sense of frustration which often overwhelms lay people when faced with technical discussions on cancer. Understanding should also result in shifting public focus on the cancer problem away from the narrowly scientific to the open political arena, where it clearly belongs.

It is perfectly true that we can make changes in our personal lives and habits that may significantly reduce our chances of getting cancer, but the possibilities here are limited. An asbestos worker with a growing family may well have a true grasp of the dangers he is exposed to, but in all probability he is firmly locked into his particular work situation. Modern industrial society offers most people little opportunity to choose freely where to live, where to work, what air to breathe, what water to drink, what food to eat, and what advertisements to read or see. We must be willing to accept the fundamental reality that a *significant* reduction in exposure to environmental carcinogens will result only from organized political action. The system of checks and balances leading to decision-making must protect the overall interests and welfare of the public. This is the essence of democratic practice. Until very recently, congressional decisions and regulatory policy have too often reflected the overwhelming pressures and influences of industry without significant balance by consumer and labor interests.

Depending on your personal circumstances, you have only two realistic options for effective political action: by working with public interest groups or by working with organized labor. Review all the case studies presented in this book. Try to analyze the relative roles of government, labor, and public interest groups in protecting against industrial abuses and irresponsibility. Virtually every major action designed to protect consumers or workers against cancer has been initiated by public interest groups or labor (See Table 9.5). There is little basis for assuming that this pattern will change in the future. This is where we must focus our energies and efforts if we are to reduce the massive national toll of cancer.

What You Can Do on the Political Level

In order to take meaningful action, become as well informed as possible. Many books, periodicals, and newsletters of various groups dealing with occupational, consumer, and environmental concerns are available.*

Public Interest Groups

Public interest groups have taken a key role in forcing improved regulation of environmental and occupational carcinogens. Some groups function purely in an educational or resource capacity, while others are oriented toward legislative, regulatory, legal, and community action. (See Appendix V). While the larger groups are based in Washington, most large cities now have their own local citizen or consumer groups. They generally specialize in different areas, such as food additives, occupational hazards, drugs, and radiation, but there is usually overlap between these various categories. Get in touch with these groups, find out how you can become actively involved, which of them is most suitable for your particular interests and purposes, and how you can best support them with your time, energy, and money. Finally, one of the best legacies you can leave your children and society is the inclusion in your will of public interest groups dedicated to the prevention of cancer. The future of the public interest movement depends on its developing adequate financial support and a national grass-roots base. Help as much as you can on all these levels.

Organized Labor

Encourage your union to fight to strengthen OSHA. While working for tougher standards, persuade your

---

*The references given in this book should be a useful beginning. Your librarian should be able to help you further. Most universities now have adult or continuing education courses in these areas. This is, or should be, a function of the university extension service or labor education center. Make sure, by checking with others in your labor or public interest group, that your lecturer is both bona fide and well informed.

union to follow the lead of some of the more health-conscious unions, particularly the Oil, Chemical and Atomic Workers (OCAW) and the United Auto Workers, in lobbying for better laws, developing their own professional resources and skills, including hiring full-time industrial hygienists and trustworthy consultants, demanding OSHA inspections, and educating their own members.

The ability of your union to protect you and your fellow workers ultimately depends on your self-education and understanding of health and safety problems, particularly in high-risk industries. Work collectively with your union leadership to produce a work environment free of added cancer risk. If you feel that your union leadership is ignorant or not interested in these problems, then lobby and campaign to vote them out of office and replace them with more responsive leadership.

The OCAW has a double-barrelled strategy of working within and without OSHA. On the one hand, OCAW makes maximum use of both the "general duty" clause of the Occupational Safety and Health Act, guaranteeing a safe and healthful workplace, and the "imminent danger" clause, demanding action when life-threatening situations occur. On the other hand, recognizing that OSHA has had a poor track record for rectifying dangerous health conditions, OCAW has written into many of its contracts specific health and safety language, providing for monitoring of workplace hazards, with results accessible to the union's representatives as well as management, and for receiving health statistics compiled by companies. The union has also won an important settlement from the National Labor Relations Board affirming its right to information on the working environment under the representation clause contained in every collective bargaining agreement. The representation clause establishes the union as the sole collective bargaining agent for the employees on matters of "wages, hours, and working conditions." Never before has this clause been used to extract health and safety data. Winning the settlement is an important victory for all organized workers. Thus, even in the absence of specific health and safety clauses, a labor bargaining unit is able to act aggressively on health and safety.

If you are a member of a union which is not health-conscious, seek assistance from any of a number of professional and public interest organizations devoted to labor education on health and safety, or from the new University Labor Educational Centers, such as Rutgers in New Jersey, Cornell in New York, and the University of Wisconsin in Madison.

One area in which an otherwise apathetic union can make an inroad is through its publications.* Ralph Nader has recently pointed out that most union newspapers or periodicals are little more than photogalleries for their officers.

> The feeble state of the labor press means that 30 million union members are left in the dark about some major issues, never review or discuss them, and cannot really come to grips with many of the problems that beset labor . . .[2]

A number of labor publications, on the other hand, do run regular or occasional columns written by health and safety specialists (See Appendix IV), some of which should be syndicated and run nationwide.

Even the most optimistic estimate of cancer-consciousness among workers must deal with the fact that three out of four workers in this country are not organized and so can have very little to say about their working conditions. While every worker is entitled in principle to

---

*The U.S. labor press is comprised of some 800 publications and reaches some 30 million workers.

OSHA protection, the nonunion individual who complains may be ignored or, at worst, fired.

Other Action

Encourage your local media to cover environment-related events, and to run regular columns on topics ranging from congressional legislation on toxic substances to water pollution, particularly as they impact on cancer. During the early 1970s, great sport was made of Boy Scouts bravely paddling up stinking creeks to trace the source of noxious effluents. But it was efforts such as these, particularly because of the television coverage they received, that caught the public's interest and have to some extent sustained it. Aggressive media action may also be the quickest way to uncover hidden relationships between the industrial interests of legislators and of university scientists. It is also worthwhile asking your newspaper editor or publisher some hard-hitting questions, such as why coverage of violent crimes and road accidents is so complete but coverage of tobacco-related cancer and other diseases is nonexistent or disproportionately low. Also, look for hidden influences of advertising interests on the coverage of environmental issues. Is this why your local newspaper won't run the Nader column?

Find out the position of your local Congressman on key environmental issues. Let him know of your interest and that you expect him to take vigorous action on the prevention of cancer, if he wants your future vote. If you are a professional, such as a doctor, lawyer, chemist, engineer, physicist, or social scientist, you have a wider range of options. These include working actively with public interest groups and organized labor, testifying at Congressional hearings, lobbying at the local or federal levels, supporting responsible regulatory agency officials, criticizing irresponsible or indifferent officials, pressuring voluntary health agencies, such as the American Cancer Society, to develop more aggressive preventive programs.

What You Can Do on the Personal Level

You can reduce your own chances of getting cancer by making changes in three major personal areas:[3] your lifestyle and personal habits; your choice and use of consumer products; and your work. These areas obviously overlap, as your work may be an integral part of your lifestyle. In all these overlapping areas, you have only limited options for making decisions that will affect your exposure to environmental and occupational carcinogens and decrease your risks of getting cancer. The major public interest groups publish useful reports dealing in further detail with these various problems, such as carcinogens in food and water. You are recommended to contact them (See Appendix V).

Depending on your particular circumstances, some of the recommendations offered here may possibly be impractical. But you should at least know what are your available options, even if you are unable or unwilling to exercise them.

In addition to your efforts to prevent cancer in yourself and your family, you should appreciate the importance of early detection and treatment, particularly of the curable and manageable cancers. Finally, you should be aware of possible legal remedies if you do contract cancer and have reason to believe that someone else is responsible.

Lifestyle and Personal Habits

1. *Smoking.* The most effective single action you can take is never to start smoking or, if this advice comes too late, to stop smoking as quickly as possible. Smokers develop lung cancer at about thirty times the rate of nonsmokers, and about one out of ten smokers of a pack or more a day will develop lung cancer. Smoking also increases risks of cancer of the larynx, esophagus, mouth, and bladder. The additional benefits of quitting extend

beyond cancer to chronic lung and heart diseases, the incidence of all of which becomes markedly reduced in the ex-smoker.

While many people can quit "cold turkey," most smokers are so physically and psychologically habituated that they need help. Two well-known organizations (there are others) offer structured help in classes or group therapy, and seem to have good success rates: Smoke-Enders is a private group, that charges a reasonable fee to get smokers to give up the habit in a few weeks; the American Cancer Society also conducts smoke cessation clinics in many cities for a nominal fee.

There can be no argument about the cost-effectiveness of quitting smoking. The current direct medical cost of each lung cancer case is about $10,000, which excludes lost wages and other costs borne by the family of the patient, who rarely survives even a few years. The cost of quitting through a progam such as Smoke-Enders is under $200. At current cigarette prices, a one-pack-a-day smoker would save, on the cost of cigarettes alone, enough money to pay for the program in one year. To get ten heavy smokers to quit, and thereby prevent one case of lung cancer, would cost about $2,000, compared to about $10,000 to treat the one who would get lung cancer.

There is no alternative to quitting. Switching to low-tar cigarettes is no substitute for not smoking. Regardless of how low the tar, if you smoke cigarettes your risk will be greater than if you don't. A major danger in changing brands rather than completely cutting out cigarettes is that some smokers compensate for the low nicotine levels in low-tar cigarettes by smoking or inhaling more. An additional problem is that levels of carbon monoxide are higher in low-tar cigarettes, probably increasing the risk of heart attack.

It has been suggested that a cigarette smoker who cannot quit should instead switch to cigars or pipes, since cigar and pipe smokers have lower lung cancer rates than cigarette smokers. However, while lifetime cigar and pipe smokers inhale little of the bitter, alkaline smoke, former cigarette smokers who switch to cigars tend to inhale nearly as much as when they smoked cigarettes. This is not an effective method of preventing cancer.[4]

If you are a nonsmoker, avoid smoke-filled, poorly ventilated places, particularly crowded bars. Also become more aggressive about your rights to clean air in elevators, restaurants, airplanes, and other public places.* Insist, as far as possible, that your employer provide you with a smoke-free workplace.

2. *Alcohol.* While there is no direct evidence that alcohol is itself a carcinogen, heavy drinking, particularly of hard liquor, increases the risk of developing cancer of the mouth, throat, esophagus, larynx, and liver.[5] These risks, particularly for cancer of the mouth and esophagus, are still further increased by heavy smoking; cancer of these sites is about fifteen times higher in heavy smokers and drinkers than in abstainers.

The type of alcohol consumed also seems to influence the cancer risk. Esophageal cancer is highly correlated with both chronic alcoholism and cirrhosis of the liver in certain regions of France, particularly Brittany and Normandy, where Calvados brandy and applejack are popular. The death rate from cancer of the esophagus in France is highest in the four contiguous brandy-producing areas of Calvados, Manche, Mayenne, and Orne.[6]

The mechanism of these alcohol-related cancers is unknown. It may be due to the nutritional deficiencies which are common in heavy drinkers and which may increase susceptibility to tobacco or other environmental carcinogens. Additionally, alcohol may act as a solvent for tobacco or other environmental carcinogens and may, thereby, increase their access to tissues.

---

*Among many examples of the nonsmoker's decreasing reticence to demand clean air is the use of the antismoker's spray can. Developed by Paul L. Wright, a Denver management consultant who has so far sold 30,000 cans, it drenches offending smokers with a lemon-scented mist.

The influence of chronic alcoholism on cancer is difficult to evaluate, since heavy drinkers tend to die early of other causes, including accidents and diseases related to malnutrition. However, a 1977 study of Veterans Administration hospital patients with cirrhosis of the liver, commonly associated with chronic alcoholism, found a greatly increased risk of the otherwise relatively rare liver cancer. Additionally, patients with cirrhosis developed cancer at other sites at earlier ages than noncirrhotic and nonalcoholic patients did.[7] This would seem to suggest that alcoholism may increase susceptibility to cancer in general, besides also increasing liver cancer.

3. *Food.*   Your dietary choices and habits are clearly important. Some diets may reduce your cancer risk, while others may increase it. This is, however, an area where caution and common sense must be exercised, especially as the facts are incomplete, and the consumer is caught between opposing viewpoints. Industry, on the one hand, dismisses as hysterical any questions on the safety or carcinogenicity of food,[8] while on the other hand public interest groups emphasize the carcinogenic hazards of many food additives and contaminants.[9]

These problems are aggravated by the fact that it is difficult for the concerned consumer to know where to go to obtain reliable information on the hazards of food additives and contaminants.[10] With a few possible exceptions, university departments of nutrition are probably the last place to go. Quite apart from the fact that most such departments have no expertise in toxicology and carcinogenesis, many of them are recipients of major support from the food industry or from industry-sponsored organizations such as the Nutrition Foundation. A joint 1976 report by Congressman Benjamin Rosenthal (D-N.Y.) and the Center for Science in the Public Interest detailed the close ties between academia and the food and chemical industry. While a dozen other universities were mentioned, Harvard's nutrition department was singled out as "riddled with corporate influence."[11] Particular reference was made to the intimate relationships between Harvard's previous department chairman, Fred Stare, and the cereal, sugar, and food industries. Less well known is the case of Jean Mayer, President of Tufts University and previous professor in Harvard's nutrition department. Mayer, a responsible nutritionist who writes a widely read, nationally syndicated column on nutrition, has publicly rebuked Stare for being among those "favorable to the sugar interests" who have distorted nutritional evidence, but has himself advocated the use of textured vegetable protein without mentioning that he is director of the product's manufacturer, Miles Laboratories.[12] (Mayer is also a director of the Food and Nutrition Board, which represents interests of the food industry, and a director of Monsanto, which has recently mounted an aggressive campaign to persuade the public of the essential safety of synthetic chemicals.)

Much has been made of the relationship between modern eating habits—particularly high caloric intake, high consumption of animal fats, cholesterol, dairy products, and meat; and low consumption of grain and fiber— and the twentieth century cancer epidemic.* On the basis of indirect evidence, it has been suggested that a low-fiber, high-fat diet increases the risk of cancer of the colon and possibly of other cancers, including breast, while a high-fiber, low-fat diet protects against these.† As far as dietary fat is concerned, there is no question that a very wide range of environmental carcinogens, particularly pesticides and industrial chemicals, are fat-soluble and are likely to accumulate in the food chain. So the more animal

---

*Bread, the high-fiber staple, has been considered the staff of life since time immemorial. Now, only 5 percent of all grain consumed in the United States is eaten by people; the remainder is fed to cattle in feed lots, producing high fat meat.

†There is a high degree of correlation between mortality from colon cancer and also from coronary disease, and high consumption of animal fats and low consumption of grains and fiber. This, however, by no means constitutes proof of causality.

and dairy product fat you eat, the greater will be your intake of these fat-soluble carcinogens. It is also known from carcinogenicity experiments that high-fat and high-calorie diets increase the incidence of cancers in animals fed known carcinogens, and that low-fat diets seem to protect against cancer. The apparent protective effect of low-fat diets may, however, merely reflect a reduced intake of the carcinogenic contaminants found in animal fats.

Many claims have been made for the protective effect of "dietary fiber", although this term describes a variety of different foods with substantially different properties. The fiber craze in America culminated in two popular recent books, one by David Reuben[13] and the other by Carlton Fredricks,[14] which advocate the consumption of greatly increased quantities of fiber. The underlying theory,[15] popularized by Denis Burkitt, a British surgeon originally known for his research on childhood lymphomas in Africa and now consultant to General Foods, that since fiber increases fecal bulk and thereby decreases "transit time" in the colon, this will reduce the contact times of dietary carcinogens in the intestines.* Fiber has also been claimed to promote growth of favorable intestinal bacterial strains, which are said to produce fewer carcinogens or promoting agents than is the case when the diet is low in fiber.

In spite of the lack of evidence supporting the cancer-preventing effects of low-fat, high-fiber diets, there is certainly no evidence that they are in any way harmful. Cancer risks apart, any diet such as the American Heart Association Prudent Diet is likely to reduce your risk of coronary and other diseases.[16]

The principles of low-fat, high-fiber diets are to emphasize vegetables, beans, grains, and fruits, and decrease intake of dairy products, meat, saturated animal fats, and

---

*Burkitt has recently retracted his theory.

cholesterol. Animal protein should be obtained from fish, veal, and poultry, rather than from high-fat beef, lamb, and pork. If at all possible, buy the meat of range or grass-fed cattle rather than cattle fattened in feed lots. Lean cuts of meat should be selected, trimmed of fat, the remains of which should be drained off during cooking, and baked or stewed, rather than deep-fat fried. Soups and stews should be refrigerated after cooking, and the surface fat layer skimmed off before reheating. Egg consumption should be kept down to one or two a week, and skimmed milk and low-fat cottage and hard cheeses, margarine, and corn or soybean oils should be used in preference to whole milk, high-fat soft cheeses, and butter.

Nutritional deficiencies can cause cancer. The best-known example of this is the Plummer—Vinson Syndrome, characterized by painful difficulty in swallowing, associated with iron-deficiency anaemia and vitamin B deficiency, in which the subsequent incidence of cancer of the esophagus and pharynx is high. The disease, which used to be common in northern Sweden, where winter diets were deficient, has virtually disappeared since flour has been supplemented, in Sweden and elsewhere, with iron and vitamin B.[17]

Food is the most important single source of exposure to a very wide range of synthetic chemicals, either as direct additives or as accidental contaminants such as pesticides and industrial chemicals. Many of these additives are carcinogens, and food containing them or suspected to contain them should be avoided to the greatest possible extent.

Avoid all highly processed "junk" foods, which are rich in additives and poor in nutrients. Hot dogs, potato chips, sugary breakfast cereals, and soda pop contain the greatest concentrations of synthetic additives. Exclude as much as possible known or suspected carcinogenic food additives, such as saccharin and Red #40, and all other synthetic coal tar dyes. Don't buy any foods or beverages containing cosmetic food additives, labeled FD&C (Food,

Drug, and Cosmetic) or U.S. Certified Colors. Another major cosmetic food additive is nitrite, which combines with amines in meat and fish to form the highly carcinogenic nitrosamines. Levels of nitrosamines tend to be particularly high in bacon,* and they are present in lower quantities in sandwich meats, salami and bologna, hot dogs, and smoked meats and fish. All of these should be avoided, especially bacon. While this may sound like drastic advice, it is well founded. Nitrite-free hot dogs and, to a lesser extent, bacon are now becoming available in some supermarkets; these products must be kept refrigerated. Their availability will increase if you firmly make your preferences known to your supermarket manager or grocer.

Avoid all food products containing petroleum-derived protein, either as a flavor enhancer or as a food ingredient. As far as is known, Amoco Foods Company, a subsidiary of Standard Oil of Indiana, is the exclusive U.S. manufacturer of petroleum protein.[18] Marketed under the trade name of Torutein, this is a high-protein yeast culture grown on hydrocarbons distilled from crude oil, which has been manufactured at the rate of about 15 million pounds per year since 1975. Torutein is now being sold to U.S. food processors for use in meat products, baked foods, infant foods, and frozen and other prepared foods, particularly for the institutional food market—hotels, restaurants, and schools. Torutein is found in Prince's macaroni, French's croutons, Health Snacks Limited's breadsticks and cake mixes, La Choy food products, and Gerber baby foods. It is difficult, if not impossible, for the consumer to find out whether a particular product contains Torutein. Under current labeling laws, its presence as a flavor enhancer can be hidden in the catch-all term "natural flavor-

---

*The USDA is now taking vigorous steps to reduce nitrosamine levels in bacon by ordering meat manufacturers to decrease amounts of nitrite that may be added to bacon.

ings." Its presence as a protein booster can be described by the term "torula yeast," without giving any indication as to whether this is natural torula yeast or petroleum-derived.

There are many unresolved questions about the safety of Torutein. The only data submitted by Amoco to FDA are the negative findings of subacute rodent toxicity tests, on the basis of which FDA approved the use of Torutein in March, 1974. There are no data available on the nutritional value of Torutein, its chronic toxicity, reproductive or mutagenic effects, or carcinogenicity. While various foreign governments, including Japan, Great Britain and Italy, have withheld approval of petroleum protein because of such questions on safety, there are no current restrictions in the United States, where its use is burgeoning.

There is a critical and overdue need for the regulation of the use of petroleum protein. In the meantime, to be on the safe side, avoid any food whose label bears any reference to torula yeast. You may express your concerns by writing directly to both the FDA and Amoco Foods Company to demand the immediate curtailment of this market until full toxicological and nutritional testing has been completed and independently evaluated.* Should Torutein be then found acceptable, its presence in food must be acknowledged by clear and explicit labeling.

Avoid organ meats, particularly liver (even though this is high in protein and vitamins and relatively low in calories), pancreas or sweetbreads, and kidney, as these concentrate residues of both accidental carcinogenic con-

---

*The needs for such testing prior to the marketing of petroleum protein were in fact spelled out in detail at a tripartite meeting between the United States, Canada and the United Kingdom at the FDA on December 16, 1974, whose recommendations were spelled out in a working document entitled "Single Cell Protein." The Protein Advisory Group of the United Nations made similar recommendations on February 7, 1972 (PAG Guideline No. 12, "Single Cell Protein").

taminants and carcinogenic feed additives. Avoid any food, oil, or beverage sold or stored in rigid PVC containers. Although banned, these are still on the market. Residues of carcinogenic and other chemicals from the plastic are dissolved in the contents.

4. *Water.*   It is now common knowledge that drinking water in most cities, particularly downstream from chemical industries, contains a great variety of synthetic organic chemicals, of which more than 200 have so far been identified, including many known carcinogens.[19]* Demand from local EPA offices as much specific information as possible on the impurities of your drinking water. Do not accept unsubstantiated assurances of safety from water treatment engineers. Your personal options are limited, however. Boiling water will remove some volatile organics, but will actually concentrate others. Distilling is not particularly effective, since many organic chemicals, such as benzene, form "constant-boiling mixtures" with water and will be carried over with the distillate. Depending on source and purity, bottled water may be an improvement on your tap water, but there is no way of knowing, as bottled water labels give no information at all on levels of organic chemical pollutants.

Your best plan, until the local municipal water treatment plant can be persuaded to install an activated carbon filtration system, is to attach a unit directly to your tap. Commercial units which will remove most organic contaminants from your drinking and cooking water are available at low cost. Choose one which is easily fitted, and which contains silver salts or other germicides impregnated on the carbon to prevent bacterial and algal contamination. Also, be sure to replace the filters every few months.

5. *Drugs.*   A wide range of drugs are known to be carcinogenic, as shown by human experience and animal

---

*The chemicals so far identified account for only a small fraction of total organic contaminants in water.

tests.[20] It is unfortunate, but true, that the most effective drugs used to treat cancer can also cause it (Appendix VI). Considering the long latency period of most cancers, it may well be worthwhile taking the risk of being treated with carcinogenic drugs if you have cancer or some other equally serious disease. A possible example of such worthwhile risks is the case of kidney transplants. The recipient of a kidney transplant, for example, must be treated to suppress the immune response and to prevent rejection of the new kidney, and the drugs used for this purpose increase the risk of developing lymphomas up to thirty-five times. It is not, however, worthwhile taking carcinogenic drugs for relatively trivial conditions, such as Flagyl for trichomonad vaginal infections, griseofulvin for athlete's foot or for scalp infestation with ringworm, and Lindane shampoos for head lice. There are alternative noncarcinogenic treatments for all these conditions. Discuss this with your doctor if he appears to be well informed. If he is not, don't be lulled into false security or intimidated by reassurances such as "Those carcinogenicity data are just based on animal tests," or, "I've been using this drug for over twenty years and have never had any problems." Read the label and insert or stuffer in the packaged medicine bottle, and ask the pharmacist whether he has additional information. Check carefully for any reference to cancer.

If you are a menopausal woman, do not take estrogens unless your symptoms are really crippling, and if you do, take the lowest possible dose for the shortest possible time. Your risk of uterine cancer will be greatly increased by "estrogen replacement therapy" with Premarin. If you are a fertile woman who had unprotected intercourse last night, and you would rather not risk pregnancy, never take DES, as commonly prescribed in campus clinics, which apart from being highly carcinogenic may not be particularly effective. Instead, once you are sure you are pregnant, if you feel you must, have a D&C or an abortion by one of the modern vacuum-aspiration techniques.

After tranquillizers, the most commonly prescribed

drug is "the Pill." Millions of women the world over are taking it for a substantial part of their lives. This is the largest carcinogenicity test in human experience, and the answers are not yet all in. Estrogens are carcinogenic in animals, Premarin induces uterine cancer in menopausal women, and the synthetic DES induces vaginal cancer in adolescent girls whose mothers took it while they were pregnant. Epidemiological studies on users of birth control pills have so far been inconclusive, probably because most women have been taking them for too short a time for possible cancers to show up. The pill has, however, been associated with liver tumors, stroke, and other diseases. So consider other forms of contraception. And make up your own mind about this; your gynecologist or physician is likely to tell you not to worry.

6. *Cosmetics.* Under the authority of the 1938 Federal Food, Drug and Cosmetic Act, the FDA has recently required the ingredients of all cosmetics to be listed on the label. Exemptions are granted to ingredients constituting less than 1 percent of the product, and to the names of specific flavors and fragrances. While the agency does not have the authority to require the industry to test their products for safety, it does require that if a product has not been tested, then the label must read: "Warning: The safety of this product has not been determined." Do not buy any products carrying such a warning, nor products containing known carcinogens, such as 2,4-toluene-diamine or 4-methoxy-m-phenylenediamine, which are used in permanent hair dyes, particularly the darker colored ones. Nor should you allow your hairdresser to use these products on your hair. Apart from carcinogenicity, there is also recent information that these hair dyes also cause birth defects. The FDA still lacks the current statutory authority to ban the carcinogenic hair dyes, which are exempt from the requirements of the Federal Food, Drug, and Cosmetic Act. Recognizing this problem, the General Accounting Office in December, 1977, called for a legislative change to bring hair dyes under food, drug

and cosmetic regulations. This was followed in January, 1978, by the announcement of Congressman John Moss (D-Calif.) that his House subcommittee would hold hearings on whether to abolish the hair dye exemption. The dyes, however, could be regulated by OSHA, as about 400,000 workers, including hairdressers, cosmetologists, and furriers, are potentially exposed to them. Accordingly, on January 13, 1978, NIOSH urged that these dyes be handled as occupational carcinogens and proposed a 50 ppm standard.

On December 12, 1977, the FDA banned further use of six carcinogenic color additives in drugs and cosmetics: Yellow #1, Blue #6, and Reds #10, 11, 12, and 13, the red colors mainly being used in lipsticks and soaps. Unfortunately, the FDA did not require these products to be removed from the market. Existing stocks will continue to be sold for years to come, and there is no practical way you can avoid them.

A small market based on cosmetics containing only natural ingredients and free from synthetic chemicals such as coal tar dyes, is now developing. You are encouraged to explore this to see if it meets your needs. If it doesn't, you may want to consider changing your needs.

7. *X-rays.* X-rays are carcinogenic. The more X-rays you submit to and the greater the dose, the greater is your risk of cancer.[21] Avoid unnecessary X-rays like the plague. Make your doctor or dentist spell out to you in detail the benefits you may get from exposure to X-rays. Are they given for "routine reasons," or for "defensive medical practice" to protect against possible malpractice suits, or because they are paid for by Medicaid and Medicare from which your physician may get a fee, or because critical choice of treatment in serious disease or injury is at stake?

You should raise these questions before you consider submitting to X-rays, even at the risk of offending "professional dignity." If you are convinced that X-rays are essential, only have them done in the office of a physician who is a specialist in radiology or in the radiology department of a hospital. Also, make sure that the technician is certified, not just "office trained," that modern equipment is used, that the smallest dose is given, and that your nonirradiated areas are protected with a lead shield.

Whatever you may be told, refuse routine mammograms to detect early breast cancer, especially if you are premenopausal. The X-rays may actually increase your chances of getting cancer.[22] If you are older, and there are strong reasons to suspect that you may have breast cancer, the risks may be worthwhile. Very few circumstances, if any, should persuade you to have X-rays taken if you are pregnant. The future risks of leukaemia to your unborn child, not to mention birth defects, are just not worth it.

At issue here is not the occasional obvious necessity of X-rays, but their indiscriminate use. According to U.S. Public Health surveys, 129 million Americans were given 210 million medical and general X-ray examinations in 1970. The number of medical X-ray examinations per person has increased steadily from 50 per 100 population in 1964 to 56/100 in 1970, a 12 percent jump.[23] The number of dental X-rays per person increased from 27/100 in 1964 to 36/100 in 1970, a 29 percent jump. Not only is the number of exposures increasing, but the dosage is much larger than necessary. Many doctors and hospitals use old, outdated equipment, which is not properly controlled and has not been given needed annual inspections by a qualified health physicist.

Dentists are also often guilty of overexposing their patients.[24] Some dentists require a full set of sixteen to eighteen films every time a patient comes in for a routine checkup. The additional diagnostic information furnished by such a series, over and above inspection aided by a dental pick, is difficult to imagine. The American Dental Association advises that a full set need not be taken more often than every three to five years; and other authorities extend this to between six and ten years.

More than 20 million Americans consult chiropractors, instead of or in addition to physicians. Some chiropractors base entire treatments on extensive use of full body X-rays. Avoid such treatments and all chiropractors who offer them.

8. _Sex._ [25] Cancer of the cervix seems related to sex. The earlier in life you start intercourse, the more your partners, marriages, and pregnancies, and the poorer your prenatal and postnatal care, the greater are your chances of cervix cancer. Intercourse during and immediately after menstruation is thought to increase risk, possibly accounting for the relative rarity of cervix cancer in orthodox Jewish women, who abstain during and immediately after menstruation. The relatively increased risk of this cancer in non-Jewish women has also been attributed to their sexual partners being uncircumcised. These sexual risk factors are further aggravated by poverty, possibly because of poor nutrition and limited opportunities for personal hygiene. The rate among lower socioeconomic groups, particularly low-income blacks, is double that for middle-class whites, and its incidence among other low-income ethnic groups, such as Mexican-Americans, is higher still. There is some evidence that a venereally transmitted Herpes virus is in some way responsible for this cancer.

Risks of breast cancer are increased in women who menstruated before the age of twelve, who have never had children or who had their first child after the age of thirty, who have never breast fed, who have had a history of benign cysts or breast tumors, and who have a familial predisposition. If you fall into any of these high-risk categories, monthly breast self-examination is imperative.

If you are a Jewish male, your chance of getting cancer of the penis is virtually zero, as this is prevented by circumcision. If you are uncircumcised, make sure to retract your foreskin daily and wash away the secretions with soap and water.

There are also some suggestions, based on epidemiological studies, that promiscuity increases risk for prostate cancer, possibly due to a sexually transmitted virus.

9. _Sunlight._ This makes you feel and look good.

But too much sun or exposure to ultraviolet lamps will age your skin and may give you skin cancer, especially if you have a light skin and blond complexion. You have much less to worry about if you are black. Besides avoiding too much sun, wear a good sunscreen ointment; those containing para-aminobenzoic acid are particularly effective. If you work outdoors, use sunblocking creams such as zinc oxide around your lips and nose.

The incidence of skin cancer and melanomas is greatest in farmers and fishermen, who spend a great deal of time outdoors.* The incidence is also greater in southern latitudes, where sunlight is more intense. While most skin cancers are easily curable, melanomas are not, and account for approximately 9,600 new cases and 4,000 deaths a year in the United States.

10. *Where you live.* This influences your overall risks of cancer, and also the particular type you may get. For some, this advice may well be academic; but, you may nevertheless want to think about this if you are about to move or if you have the luxury of choosing where you live. If you can possibly avoid it, do not live close to a chemical plant, refinery, asbestos plant, or metal mining processing or smelting plant. Also avoid living close to major highways and expressways.

From 1969 to 1971, the NCI conducted an intensive survey of new cancers in nine regions of the country and found wide geographic variations in the incidence of different types.[26] Many of these patterns paralleled those previously found in the twenty-year NCI cancer death rates study in each of the nation's counties. This study led to publication of the "cancer maps," which show that an excess of many cancers are clustered in regions of heavy industrialization and concentration of petrochemical plants. The excess incidence of cancers in the heavily in-

---

*The role of environmental factors other than sunlight is suggested by the striking recent increase in the incidence of melanomas in white males, from 2.6 per 100,000 in 1947 to 6.3 per 100,000 in 1975.

dustrialized counties includes women as well as men, and thus cannot be mainly due to occupational exposures. Rather, it is probably also due to breathing and drinking carcinogens discharged into the air and water or dumped with chemical waste products into land disposal sites by the local petrochemical, metal mining, smelting or asbestos plants. There is chemical monitoring information that confirms this for growing numbers of industrial carcinogens.

Among all states, New Jersey leads in overall cancer mortality and in the variety of mortal cancers as well.[27] Every known major industrial chemical carcinogen is manufactured or otherwise handled in bulk in New Jersey.[28] Salem County, New Jersey, has been singled out as having the highest national death rate from bladder cancer in both men and women, possibly related to the location there of a concentration of chemical industries, including a giant Du Pont organic chemical complex, and the fact that 25 percent of the male population in the county work in the chemical industry. New Jersey is now attempting to control the discharge of carcinogens from industry into the environment of the surrounding community.*

New Jersey is not unique. In New Orleans, there is also an excess of overall cancer mortality, as well as of cancer of the bladder and large bowel. This is probably associated with the heavy concentration of organic carcinogens in the drinking water, these being discharged from countless industries along the banks of the lower

---

*Regulations effective by 1979 will require about half of all industries in New Jersey to install new antipollution devices designed to sharply curtail carcinogenic emissions from industry, though these regulations will initially apply to only eight known carcinogens. Questionnaires are also being sent to 12,000 companies in the state to determine whether they use any of 188 known or suspect carcinogens in their operations. Additionally, New Jersey has established a computer terminal linked to an NCI computer data bank which will enable rapid studies on correlation of cancer mortality rates with geographical, ethnic, and other data. Industry has responded by the usual threats to move elsewhere.

Mississippi. The increased incidence of birth defects, and possibly brain tumors, in certain Ohio counties where VC/PVC plants are located has been associated with the discovery of VC leaking from the plants into the air of the nearby communities.

Hazardous industries are by far the main but not the only danger. Avoid, if possible, living downtown in heavily air-polluted cities and live as far as you can from heavily traveled major expressways and highways. A recent Swiss study, based on a relatively small population sample, claims that there is a strong correlation between cancer incidence and proximity of residence to highways.[29] Quite apart from any possible excess cancer risks, levels of carbon monoxide, lead, and other automobile pollutants are also increased near major highways.

11. *Your home.* Your house or apartment can expose you to hidden carcinogenic hazards. These include asbestos insulation and lining of ventilation and heating ducts, and pesticides used for termite treatment and other purposes. Make sure that the apartment house manager is not allowed to disinfect with pesticides he "is sure are safe."

12. *Race.* You should recognize that race and color are factors that may be associated with excess risks of cancer. However, these excess risks are probably due to environmental factors rather than any intrinsic or genetic susceptibility. This is the only reason why questions of race have anything to do with ways and means by which you can possibly reduce your own cancer risks.

The overall cancer risks of black U.S. males are higher than those of white men and higher than those of blacks anywhere in the world.[30] The incidence of lung cancer in black males is particularly high, despite the fact that substantial underreporting is suspected. This is probably due to heavy cigarette smoking, particularly of unfiltered cigarettes, among blacks. The highest incidence of lung cancer in U.S. black males is in Pittsburgh, Pennsylvania, and probably reflects their extensive employment in the most hazardous jobs in the steel industry.

Both black men and women are experiencing an increase in the incidence of esophageal cancer at a time when this is declining in whites. Cancer of the large bowel has increased sharply in blacks, compared to a slow increase in whites. Black women have more uterine and cervix cancers than whites.

Factors which have been incriminated in the excess incidence of cancer in blacks are varied. These include discriminatory employment of black males in high risk jobs; heavy smoking, particularly of unfiltered cigarettes; the high proportion of blacks in the populations of city centers, where air pollution is greatest and where there is likely to be heavy pesticide use; living in areas near high-risk industries; and heavy consumption of dairy products and animal fats, rather than vegetables and fiber. Various surveys have shown that human fat residues of carcinogenic chlorinated hydrocarbon pesticides such as dieldrin and heptachlor epoxide are substantially higher in blacks than in whites.

Consumer Products

1. *Spray cans.* A wide range of consumer products—including insecticides, hair sprays, disinfectants, deodorants, furniture polishes, and cleaners—are marketed as aerosols. While vinyl chloride is no longer used as a propellant, existing stocks of VC-containing aerosols have not been recalled, nor has there been any clear brand identification of these stocks. Labeling may not necessarily help, for although the presence of propellants is stated their identities are not generally disclosed. The fluorocarbon Freons® are being phased out but are still used as propellants and are known to escape into the upper atmosphere and attack the ozone layer, which filters the sun's ultraviolet rays. This will increase your chance—and everyone else's—of getting skin cancer.

Avoid all aerosols, no matter what their propellant. Every time you use one for any purpose, you will inhale high concentrations of its chemical contents, whatever they happen to be.

2. *Pesticides.* A number of common pesticides used in and around the home and garden are carcinogens. Among the more dangerous are chlordane and heptachlor, which are widely used as common garden insecticides, moth and termite proofing, and other purposes.

In the last decade, there have been major advances in the understanding of biological control of insects using integrated pest management systems. These are equally applicable for home, lawn, and garden infestations and other urban uses as for agriculture.

3. *Tris.* Until recently, children's sleepwear was treated with the flame retardant Tris. Don't buy such sleepwear. Tris is absorbed through the skin, persists in fabric even after repeated laundering, and has been recently shown to be both carcinogenic and mutagenic. Instead, try to use only inherently fire-resistant natural and semi-synthetic textiles.

4. *Cleaning agents and solvents.* Do not use *any* products containing carbon tetrachloride, trichloroethylene, perchloroethylene, or benzene, which are all carcinogenic. Use alternatives based on detergents. Be especially careful to avoid all products containing benzene, particularly paint and varnish removers, adhesives, and cements.

Work

1. *Industry.* Your choice of work can greatly affect your chances of getting cancer. Workers in petrochemical, asbestos, steel, smelting, and some mining industries are recognized "high risk" groups (See Table 5.1). While risks are clearly greatest in these manufacturing industries, they also extend to industries that subsequently fabricate products derived from these carcinogens.

The conditions you will experience in different industries vary from the totally uncontrolled, especially in smaller, nonunionized plants, to the partially controlled. One of the major problems, however, has been the chemical industry as a whole, through its politically powerful trade association, the Manufacturing Chemists Association, refusing to disclose the identity of most chemicals used in trade name products in the workplace on the grounds that these are "trade secrets." The likelihood is that you will not even know the names of many or most of the chemicals you work with. Instead you will find yourself handling and breathing chemical mixtures labeled something like AB-347. If you ask your foreman or plant manager what this is, the answer may be "We don't know, we buy it like this," from such a company as Monsanto or Du Pont, who in turn will not be eager to tell you what is in their product, again claiming trade secrecy. Alternatively, management may know what is in the mix, but will tell you that "it is none of your business."

Unless you are fully and completely prepared to take the consequences, you should not go to work in an uncontrolled, high-risk industry, especially one with a bad track record. If you are already working in one, you may only have very limited options, other than leaving, at the expense of loss of seniority and other rights, and trying to find other, safer work. If you decide to stay, work with your union to make conditions safer.

If you do plan to seek work in one of the high-risk industries, try to choose a large, well-organized plant with reliable and informed union leadership, one in which carcinogens are handled in closed systems and the workplace is monitored with sensitive instrumentation. Also make sure the results of the monitoring are promptly made available to you. Avoid any non-organized industry, particularly one that refuses to give you complete information on the names of the chemicals you will be working with. Do not otherwise accept assurances of safety from the plant manager or even the company physician, who is employed by management and may not consider you his first loyalty. Finally, if you possibly can, try to find out from your union or some other independent source the record of this particular industry in the health and cancer area before you accept employment there. But be forewarned that your chances of getting such information are not good.

2. *Arts and crafts.* Arts and crafts are to some a full-time occupation, and to others a hobby. Whichever is the case, you should know as far as possible the composition of all your materials so that you can handle them with due care, and find substitutes for any which are carcinogenic (Table 11.1).

Some construction materials, such as plasterboard and spackle, contain asbestos. Many paints are based on carcinogenic pigments, including chromium, cadmium, nickel, and arsenic, and may also contain carcinogenic solvents, particularly benzene. Artists, especially, should take meticulous precautions when mixing dry pigments, since the dust generated is easily inhaled. Spray paints may still contain VC as propellants, even though its use for this purpose has been banned. Whether an occasional hobbyist or a serious artist, you should avoid handling carcinogenic materials. If you must handle them, do so either with complete ventilation and personal protection, such as a respirator, or with the process completely enclosed.

3. *Schools.* Schools may contain hidden and unexpected hazards, including the hazard of cancer, and children spend as much time there every day as does any workman in a factory or plant. Parents should check on the location of the school, to make sure that it is not near a chemical, mining, or smelting plant, or too close to busy highways and other sources of chemical emissions. The elementary school in Saugus, California, where VC levels of about 3 ppm were found in classrooms in the summer of 1977, is a good case in point. The construction of the

Table 11.1 Carcinogenic Materials Encountered in the Arts and Crafts

Material	Process	Type of Cancer
Arsenic and alloys	Textile prints, metal alloys	Skin and lung
Beryllium	Vapors in sculpture, dust in ceramics	Lung and liver
Cadmium	Silver soldering, brazing, welding	Lung and prostate
Chromium	Paints, lithographic dyes, mordants, printing	Lung
Nickel, oxides, and carbonyl	Welding, nickel alloys	Lung
Asbestos	Mold-making, foundry welding, soldering, spackling	Lung, pleura, and peritoneum
Wood	Carpentry and cabinet making	Nasal sinus
Arsene	Etching	Lung, skin
Benzene	Solvent for resins, glues and rubber cement	Leukaemia and aplastic anemia
Carbon tetrachloride	General solvent, cleaner	Liver cancer
Trichloroethylene	Solvent for oils, resins, dry cleaning, scouring	Liver cancer
Tetrachloroethylene	Solvent for oils, resins, dry cleaning, scouring	Liver cancer
Formaldehyde	Preserving	Produces BCME, a lung carcinogen in acid solution

Source: Based on B. W. Carnow, "Health Hazards in the Arts and Crafts," University of Illinois, School of Public Health, April 19, 1974.

school building should also be examined to avoid the experience of several schools in Howell Township, New Jersey, in which friable asbestos-sprayed surfaces, such as soundproof ceilings, were found in 1976 to be liberating large quantities of asbestos fibers into the air.

The cafeteria menu may also be of concern. Through your PTA, work for the ban of "junk" or convenience foods. Encourage the sale of nuts and fruit for snacking. The trailblazing example set by the West Virginia Board of Education should be followed on a national basis:

> . . . Effective with the 1976–77 school year, the sale of the following non-nutritional foods or beverages is prohibited during the school day in all public schools of the state: candy, chewing gum, soft drinks, flavored ice bars.[31]

In October, 1977, the USDA, under an amendment to the Child Nutrition Act, regained authority, which it had lost in 1972, to regulate what food items can be sold in vending machines in schools. USDA Secretary Bergland recently indicated his intent to ban "junk" foods in schools.

Laboratory courses should not expose students to harmful chemicals.[32] Wood and metal shops should avoid the use of organic cleaning fluids and solvents containing benzene, carbon tetrachloride, or other carcinogens. Ventilation must be adequate. Chemistry laboratories and stockrooms should be completely cleared of all carcinogenic and other toxic chemicals, such as benzene. Some people question whether organic chemistry should be taught at all at the high school level. If it is, all chemicals used in classroom or laboratory work should be cleared by a knowledgeable independent authority. Finally, the unsupervised use of toxic and carcinogenic pesticides by janitorial staff should be completely stopped.

Early Detection and Treatment

Early detection is no substitute for preventing cancer, but it may result in a cure, or at any rate, increase your survival time. The prognosis of a wide range of cancers, particularly skin, breast, cervix, colon, and larynx, depends on how early they are picked up and treated effectively, in which case there is a good likelihood of a complete "cure." Cancers which are localized to their organ of origin at the time of diagnosis and treatment are more curable than cancers that have spread to regional lymph nodes or beyond (Figure 11.1). Curability is usually expressed in terms of cases surviving without apparent recurrence of disease for over five years past initial treatment.

In view of the importance of early diagnosis, particularly for some of the more curable cancers, you should be on the lookout for any warning signs or symptoms and should check for these regularly. Additionally, you should make arrangements to have the following regular screening tests:

• Pap smears for cervix cancer. Every woman over the age of twenty, especially sexually active ones, should have this test annually. Black women should be especially insistent on this, as their risk is higher than for white women.

• Pelvic examination for uterine cancer. Women over fifty years old should have this done periodically, especially if there is abnormal discharge or bleeding.

• Proctosigmoidoscopy for colon cancer. This unpleasant but lifesaving procedure is recommended routinely for men and women over forty, especially those with a family history of high-risk, precancerous diseases, such as polyposis or ulcerative colitis.

• Self-examination of breasts. Every woman from adolescence on should learn and practice this procedure monthly.

• Laryngoscopy. This is recommended regularly for smokers and drinkers, particularly if there is a history of "laryngitis" or hoarseness.

Screening is even more important if you are already at a particular "high cancer risk," several categories of which are recognized:

Figure 11.1　Five Year Cancer Survival Rates for Selected Sites

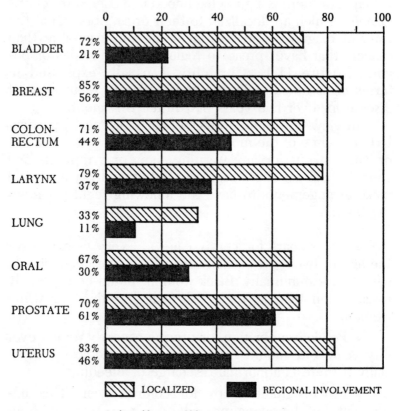

■ LOCALIZED　　　■ REGIONAL INVOLVEMENT

*Adjusted for normal life expectancy.

Source: "1978 Cancer Facts and Figures." American Cancer Society, New York, 1977.

1. *Familial predisposition.*　Certain cancers tend to run in families, for poorly understood reasons.[33] These include cancer of the lung, large bowel, uterus, stomach, and breast, and childhood sarcomas and brain tumors. Your chances of contracting any of these particular cancers seem to be two to four times higher if a close relative has previously developed one of them. The excess risk is re-

stricted to cancers of specific sites; a family history of lung cancer will not predispose to breast cancer.

Familial predisposition to breast cancer is particularly well established. Sisters or daughters of women who developed breast cancer before menopause are known to be about nine times more likely to get breast cancer than the general population. The risk is still further increased if the relative had cancer in both breasts. Risks for postmenopausal breast cancers are much lower.

2. *Genetic predisposition.*   Certain rare cancers or predisposing conditions can be directly inherited. These include multiple polyposis of the colon, which predisposes to colon-rectal cancer, and xeroderma pigmentosum, which predisposes to skin cancer.

3. *History of occupational exposure to carcinogens.* The degree of excess risk will depend on the nature of the carcinogens you work with and the intensity and duration of exposure.

4. *History of treatment with carcinogenic drugs or X-rays.*   As for occupational carcinogens, the excess risks depend on the degree and duration of exposure.

There are certain cancers, however, which are generally death sentences, regardless of how early they are diagnosed. Some of the claims which have been made for improved survival with early diagnosis probably reflect the extra time apparently gained before the cancer would have otherwise been diagnosed. These poorly curable cancers include lung, brain, liver, pancreas, stomach, and some forms of leukaemia. Early treatment may, however, improve chances of survival and increase the quality of remaining life.*

For Hodgkin's disease and some forms of leukaemia, prolonged survival is possible with early diagnosis and

---

*It is important to note that the "cancer surveillance programs" adopted by industry for lung or liver cancer most certainly do not offer prevention, but merely the earlier diagnosis of an inevitable death.

treatment in specialized centers. The importance of going to such a center for these and certain other cancers is critical. It may mean the difference between survival and death, or between prolonged and short survival. Find out what are the best centers in the country, and insist on going there if you possibly can.*

Recognizing the reality that one in four of us will sometime need cancer treatment, and that the costs will not be adequately covered by conventional policies, the ever-responsive insurance industry is now offering cancer policies which you may want to investigate. About 60 percent of these policies are written by the American Family Corporation, at a cost of about $75 a year for individual policies. Profits and a growth rate of 35 percent are expected by this industry in 1978.

Legal Remedies

If you have developed cancer and have reason to believe that this is due to the fault of industry or possibly even government, then there are some legal remedies available to you or your heirs. Your ability to succeed in these, apart from the inherent validity of the case, will depend on your persistence and on the expertise of your attorney. Any successful legal action you take against the industry responsible for your cancer may act as an incentive to prevent further such cancers.

1. *Medical or drug-related suits.* More often than not, drug companies will settle out of court when faced with an obviously legitimate claim for damages in order

---

*There are three major guides to this: accreditation by the American College of Surgeons for cancer treatment; accreditation by the Joint Commission of the American Hospital Association; membership of the Comprehensive Cancer Centers, nineteen NCI-funded national centers for advanced cancer treatment. In addition, there are certain hospitals and centers that specialize in treatment of specific types of cancer and have the best survival rates (See Appendix VII).

not to implicate a particular drug or medicine as a precedent for other suits, which would inevitably follow. As for treatment-related cancer, such as that of the thyroid which developed following irradiation of children for "enlarged thymus glands," a malpractice suit may be difficult to prosecute. Not only has it been a problem to get doctors to testify against each other, but it has also been successfully argued that a given treatment was justified provided it was considered safe and effective at that time, even if it later turned out to be harmful and useless.

2. *Product liability suits.*   If you or any member of your family develops cancer following the use of or exposure to a carcinogenic product, then you have the basis for a product liability suit. The burden to prove your case is less for a food or drug than for other types of products, such as pesticides or paint strippers. In cases involving food and drugs, the courts usually assume that the seller warrants his product as fit and safe for human consumption, and the plaintiff then usually only needs to show that damages were sustained and were caused by the product in question.

For a successful product liability suit, you must prove a "breach of duty of care"; that is, the manufacturer or supplier knew, or it was general knowledge among the industry, that the product was carcinogenic. This duty, when breached, constitutes negligence when the party affected is within the "ambit of risk," and could thus reasonably have been anticipated to be exposed to the product and consequently injured. The product in question must be the proximate or immediate cause of the disease, and the disease itself must be a genuine damage, such as cancer. When all these conditions can be established, grounds then exist for an award for negligence. Some states disqualify the plaintiff if the defense can prove that he somehow contributed to the negligence, while more liberal states, such as New York and Wisconsin, permit partial judgements based upon comparative negligence of both parties.

An alternative, but less well tested, legal approach is based on contract theory. The courts have often recognized that the purchaser of a product expects and receives an implied warranty from the manufacturer that the product is fit for use, or "merchantable." This warranty cannot be waived by mere labeling. The instances where this attack has failed, cigarette suits in particular, have usually involved jury trials, where the purchaser was found to have knowingly assumed a risk. Apart from this, chances of success in product liability suits are increased if the product label contained no indication or warning of its carcinogenicity.

3. *Tobacco cancer.*   Suits against the tobacco industry for lung cancer have so far been unsuccessful. There is, however, some reason for guarded optimism based on as yet untested new legal strategies, which you or your heirs may wish to explore if you have developed lung cancer or other tobacco-induced diseases following smoking. Probably the single most effective measure for the prevention of cancer would be a series of large, successful lawsuits against the industry. This is a potential solution whose time is overdue.

4. *Occupational cancer.*   If you develop cancer after exposure to a known carcinogen, you will be awarded workman's compensation only if you can prove that the exposure was work-related. This, however, is rarely sufficient to cover the total costs of your cancer, quite apart from deprivation of future earnings. It has also the added disadvantage that your acceptance of a settlement absolves the industry of all further liability. An exception is made only if gross negligence can be proven, at best a difficult task for you when pitted against the resources of a giant industry or corporation.

A more practical option, which may sometimes be available, is a third-party suit. You can bring one against the manufacturer supplying a carcinogenic product or process, especially in the absence of appropriate labels and warnings, to the industry in which you worked and contracted your cancer.

The principle of the third-party suit was expanded in 1972 in *Dole* v. *Dow Chemical et al.* (New York Court of Appeals, March 11, 1972) by the heirs of an employee of a small exterminating company who had died of exposure to methyl bromide, a pesticide widely used in fumigation. Unhappy with the trivial workman's compensation award, the heirs sued the third party, Dow Chemical, the manufacturer of the chemical. The grounds of the lawsuit were that the pesticide was not appropriately labeled, and that the worker had thus not been adequately warned of the hazard. Dow, while not explicitly accepting blame, sued the worker's employer for contributing to the negligence by failing to instruct him properly in the chemical's safe use. Dow thus won damages from the company, some of which it then paid the worker's family in its own settlement. The two major precedents set by this case were that liability for negligence could be shared between the defendant and a third party, and that a negligent employer could no longer hide behind workman's compensation to limit his liability for exposing workers to toxic chemicals or other hazards.

The third-party principle was substantially strengthened, especially for carcinogens, when the government, late in 1977, settled a $20 million suit brought by families and former employees of a defunct asbestos plant in Tyler, Texas. The plant, which had been literally dismantled and buried because asbestos levels were so high that it could not be cleaned up, belonged to PPG Industries, which will pay $8 million, and before it, Union Asbestos and Rubber, which will pay $1 million. The government itself will pay the survivors $5 million, admitting that because of a secret agreement with the industry it had failed to warn workers of hazards of asbestos, even after several government inspections over a ten-year period turned up extremely high levels.

Another important option you have is suing your company doctor for medical malpractice if you can show that he failed to warn you of any findings that could have allowed you to limit further exposure or seek early treatment.* Such malpractice suits are likely to increase in the future. It is also likely that their scope will be extended to hold culpable other professionals in the workplace, such as industrial hygienists or chemists, who fail to warn workers of exposure to carcinogenic or other toxic hazards.

5. *Community cancer suits.*   Assume you are a middle-aged or elderly nonsmoking lady living in Salem County, New Jersey, who has developed bladder cancer. It should seem reasonable to take the position that there is a significant probability that your cancer was caused by discharge of aromatic amine carcinogens into your air and water from nearby plants known to be handling these carcinogens. The NCI cancer maps would be helpful in supporting your position, especially if these can be supported by evidence of the leakage of carcinogens from the industry to the outside air. This approach has not yet been tested in the courts, but when it eventually is, it will probably be done on a class action basis for high claims, because the expense is likely to be large and the case difficult to prove. The plaintiffs will also need to establish their case through arguments based on correlation in order to show proximate causes.

Finally, it must be realized that industry itself is not always legally passive. However, the recent failure of industry in the *Galaxy* v. *Capurro* case, besides the climate of current opinion, is likely to dampen any latent initiatives or ambitions in this direction.

---

*Over ten lawsuits, totaling more than $50 million, have been filed against Kent Wise, the former physician of a Johns-Manville plant in Pittsburg, California, on the grounds that he deliberately withheld information from workers on X-ray evidence of asbestos-induced lung disease. Wise in turn is suing Johns-Manville for $100 million, claiming that in his original terms of employment he was "told not to have anything to do with X-rays," which would be read at the Trudeau Institute in Saranac Lake, New York. However, Wise also contends that he had no duty to report the results of the X-rays to the workers concerned but only to Johns-Manville.

The Goal of Public Action

The time has come to summarize the goals of the actions recommended in this book to reduce the national toll of cancer:

1. Cancer must be regarded as an essentially preventable disease.

2. The hidden political and economic factors which have blocked and continue to block attempts to prevent cancer must be recognized.

3. The ineffective past track record of government in cancer prevention must be recognized.

4. The critical roles in cancer prevention that public interest groups and informed labor leadership have exercised must be recognized and their further efforts fully encouraged and supported.

5. Congress must resolve the major inconsistencies in a wide range of legislation on environmental and occupational carcinogens.

6. Substantially higher federal priorities for the prevention of cancer must be developed.

7. Policies of the various federal agencies with responsibilities in cancer prevention must be effectively integrated and coordinated.

8. Top business management must recognize the essential similarities between their long-term interests and goals and those of society. Prevention of occupational cancer and cancer in the community-at-large is of primary importance to both.

9. The American Cancer Society must be influenced to balance its preoccupation with treatment with activist programs designed to prevent cancer.

10. The medical and scientific community must accept a higher degree of responsibility and involvement in

the prevention of cancer by actions on both the professional and political levels.

11. Medical schools and schools of public health
must be persuaded to massively reorient their educational
and training programs from the diagnosis and treatment
of disease and cancer to prevention.

12. Chemicals in consumer products and in the
workplace must be clearly and simply identified and
labeled.

13. Additional new approaches must be developed
for obtaining and for retaining honest and scientifically reliable data on the carcinogenicity and toxicity of new
chemicals, besides of untested or poorly tested chemicals
already in commerce. All such data must be made accessible to public scrutiny. Maximum legal penalties should be
directed against all those responsible, directly and indirectly, for distortion or manipulation of toxicological and
epidemiological data on the basis of which decisions on
human safety and risk are based.

14. Apart from actions on a political level, we all
have limited personal options. To some extent, it may be
possible to reduce our own chances of developing cancer
by making informed changes in lifestyle, use of consumer
products, and work.

The vigorous implementation of policies based on
these goals will reverse the growing epidemic of modern
cancer and restore it to its rightful role of an uncommon
disease.

Epilogue

Over the past few decades, there has been a progressive escalation of available information on the chemical causes of cancer. There has also been a parallel increase in our ability to test for carcinogenic effects of chemicals in animals and also to recognize such effects in humans. Not only is the level of this information in general adequate, but there are also ample laws, in spite of their occasional ambiguities and inconsistencies, to translate such information into regulatory action. The problem is thus not one of inadequate information or inadequate laws.

So then, what is the problem? As the case studies in this book make clear, there has been and continues to be a massive failure to utilize available knowledge and to implement the law. A combination of powerful and well-focused pressures by special industrial interests, together with public inattention and the indifference of the scientific community, has created a major imbalance in decision-making and public policies. In spite of efforts by organized labor and public interest groups, this imbalance has consistently and effectively thwarted, and still continues to thwart, meaningful attempts to prevent the carnage of chemical-cancer, a carnage whose unrecognized costs run each year into the tens of billion dollars.

It is not as if there is any necessary conflict between long-term industrial growth and the prevention of cancer.

469

Many carcinogens are used for purposes that are trivial, or under conditions where they can be replaced by noncarcinogenic substitutes. In those special circumstances where carcinogens perform critically needed and irreplaceable functions, they can be used much more safely, provided industry invests in the appropriate engineering controls.

While much is known about the science of cancer, its prevention depends largely, if not exclusively, on political action. This then is the message of the book.

Appendix I

Chemicals Known to Induce Cancer in Humans

Chemical or industrial process	Humans: Main type of exposure	Humans: Target Organ	Humans: Main route of Exposure*	Animals: Animal	Animals: Target Organ	Animals: Route of Exposure*
1. Aflatoxins	Environmental, occupational	Liver	p.o., inhalation	Rat	Liver, stomach, colon, kidney	p.o.
				Fish, duck, marmoset, tree shrew, monkey	Liver	p.o.
				Rat	Liver, trachea	i.t.
				Mouse, rat	Liver	i.p.
				Mouse	Local	s.c. injection
				Mouse	Lung	i.p.
2. 4-Aminobiphenyl	Occupational	Bladder	Inhalation, skin, p.o.	Mouse, rabbit, dog	Bladder	p.o.
				Newborn mouse	Liver	s.c. injection
				Rat	Mammary gland, intestine	s.c. injection
3. Arsenic compounds	Occupational, medicinal, and environmental	Skin, lung, liver	Inhalation, p.o., skin	Mouse, rat, dog	Inadequate, negative	p.o.
				Mouse	Inadequate, negative	Topical, i.v.
4. Asbestos	Occupational	Lung, pleural cavity, gastrointestinal tract	Inhalation, p.o.	Mouse, rat, hamster, rabbit	Lung, pleura	Inhalation or i.t.
				Rat, hamster	Local	Intrapleural
				Rat	Local	i.p., s.c. injection
				Rat	Various sites	p.o.
5. Auramine (manufacture of)	Occupational	Bladder	Inhalation, skin, p.o.	Mouse, rat	Liver	p.o.
				Rabbit, dog	Negative	p.o.
				Rat	Local, liver, intestine	s.c. injection
6. Benzene	Occupational	Hemopoietic system	Inhalation, skin	Mouse	Inadequate	Topical, s.c. injection
7. Benzidine	Occupational	Bladder	Inhalation, skin, p.o.	Mouse	Liver	s.c. injection
				Rat	Liver	p.o.
					Zymbal gland, liver, colon	s.c. injection
				Hamster	Liver	p.o.
				Dog	Bladder	p.o.

No.	Agent	Exposure	Target organ (man)	Route (man)	Species	Target organ (animal)	Route (animal)
8.	Bischloromethylether	Occupational	Lung	Inhalation	Mouse, rat	Lung, nasal cavity	Inhalation
					Mouse	Skin	Topical
					Rat	Local, lung	s.c. injection
					Rat	Local	s.c. injection
9.	Cadmium-using industries (possibly associated with cadmium oxide)	Occupational	Prostate, lung	Inhalation, p.o.	Rat	Local, testis	s.c. or i.m. injection
10.	Chloramphenicol	Medicinal	Hemopoietic system	p.o., injection		No adequate tests	
11.	Chloromethylether (possibly associated with bischloromethylether)	Occupational	Lung	Inhalation	Mouse	Initiator	Skin
						Lung	Inhalation
					Rat	Local, lung	s.c. injection
						Local	s.c. injection
12.	Chromium (chromate-producing industries)	Occupational	Lung, nasal cavities	Inhalation	Mouse, rat	Local	s.c., i.m. injection
					Rat	Lung	Intrabronchial implantation
13.	Cyclophosphamide	Medicinal	Bladder	p.o., injection	Mouse	Hemopoietic system, lung	i.p., s.c. injection
						Various sites	p.o.
					Rat	Bladder	i.p.
						Mammary gland	i.p.
						Various sites	i.v.
14.	Diethylstilbestrol	Medicinal	Uterus, vagina	p.o.	Mouse	Mammary	p.o.
					Mouse	Mammary, lymphoreticular, testis	s.c. injection, s.c. implantation
						vagina	Local
					Rat	Mammary, hypophysis, bladder	s.c. implantation
					Hamster	Kidney	s.c. injection, s.c. implantation
					Squirrel monkey	Uterine serosa	s.c. implantation

(Continued on page 474)

Chemical	Exposure	Human target organ	Human route	Animal species	Animal result	Animal route
15. Hematite mining (?Radon)	Occupational	Lung	Inhalation	Mouse, hamster, guinea pig	Negative	Inhalation, i.t.
16. Isopropyl oils	Occupational	Nasal cavity, larynx	Inhalation	Rat	Negative; No adequate tests	s.c. injection
17. Melphalan	Medicinal	Hemopoietic system	p.o., injection	Mouse; Rat	Initiator; Lung, lympho-sarcomas; Local	Skin; i.p.; i.p.
18. Mustard gas	Occupational	Lung, larynx	Inhalation	Mouse	Lung; Local, mammary	Inhalation, i.v.; s.c. injection
19. 2-Naphthyl-amine	Occupational	Bladder	Inhalation, skin, p.o.	Hamster, dog, monkey; Mouse; Rat, rabbit	Bladder; Liver, lung; Inadequate	p.o.; s.c. injection; p.o.
20. Nickel (nickel refining)	Occupational	Nasal cavity, lung	Inhalation	Rat; Mouse, rat, hamster; Mouse, rat	Lung; Local; Local	Inhalation; s.c., i.m. injection; i.m. implantation
21. N,N-Bis(2-chloroethyl)-2-naphthyl-amine	Medicinal	Bladder	p.o.	Mouse; Rat	Lung; Local	i.p.; s.c. injection
22. Oxymetholone	Medicinal	Liver	p.o.		No adequate tests	
23. Phenacetin	Medicinal	Kidney	p.o.		No adequate tests	
24. Phenytoin	Medicinal	Lymphoreticular tissues	p.o., injection	Mouse	Lymphoreticular tissues	p.o., i.p.
25. Soot, tars, and oils	Occupational, environmental	Lung, skin (scrotum)	Inhalation, skin	Mouse, rabbit	Skin	Topical
26. Vinyl chloride	Occupational	Liver, brain, lung	Inhalation, skin	Mouse, rat	Lung, liver, blood vessels, mammary, Zymbal gland, kidney	Inhalation

Source: L. Tomatis et al., "Evaluation of the Carcinogenicity of Chemicals: A Review of the Monograph Program of the International Agency for Research on Cancer," *Cancer Research* 38(1978): 877–85.

*p.o. = per os or oral; s.c. = subcutaneous; i.m. = intramuscular; i.t. = intratracheal; i.v. = intravenous.

Appendix II

Evaluation of Environmental Carcinogens*

Report to the Surgeon General, USPHS
April 22, 1970

Ad Hoc Committee on the Evaluation of Low Levels
of Environmental Chemical Carcinogens

Members of the Ad Hoc Committee on the Evaluation of Low Levels of Environmental Chemical Carcinogens

National Cancer Institute
Bethesda, Maryland

---

*This report was introduced as an exhibit and published in full in both the following Senate hearings: "Chemicals and the Future of Man," hearings before the Subcommittee on Executive Reorganization and Government Research of the Committee on Government Operations: United States Senate, April 6 and 7, 1971; and the "Federal Environmental Pesticide Control Act," hearings before the Subcommittee on Agricultural Research and General Legislation of the Committee on Agriculture and Forestry, United States Senate, March 23–26, 1971.

Umberto Saffiotti, Chairman, Associate Scientific Director for Carcinogenesis, Etiology, National Cancer Institute, Building 37, Room 3A21, Bethesda, Maryland.

Hans L. Falk, Associate Director for Laboratory Research, National Institute of Environmental Health Sciences, Research Triangle Park, North Carolina.

Paul Kotin, Director, National Institute of Enviromental Health Sciences, Research Triangle Park, North Carolina.

William Lijinsky, Professor of Biochemistry, The Eppley Institute for Research on Cancer, University of Nebraska College of Medicine, Omaha, Nebraska.

Marvin Schneiderman, Associate Chief, Biometry Branch, National Cancer Institute, Wiscon Building, Room 5C10, Bethesda, Maryland.

Philippe Shubik, Director, The Eppley Institute for Research on Cancer, University of Nebraska, College of Medicine, Omaha, Nebraska.

Sidney Weinhouse, Director, Fels Research Institute, Temple University School of Medicine, Philadelphia, Pennsylvania.

Gerald Wogan, Professor of Food Toxicology, Massachusetts Institute of Technology, 77 Massachusetts Avenue, Cambridge, Massachusetts.

Staff Members: John A. Cooper, Executive Secretary, Richard R. Bates, James A. Peters, Howard R. Rosenberg, Elizabeth K. Weisburger, John H. Weisburger

Introduction

Establishment of this Ad Hoc Committee was requested on October 24, 1969, by the Deputy Assistant Secretary for Health and Scientific Affairs.

The task of the Committee is to review the problems relating to the evaluation of low levels of environmental chemical carcinogens, to consider the scientific bases on which such evaluations can be made, and to advise the Department of HEW on the implications of such evaluations.

The Committee, in addressing itself to the problems of environmental exposures to chemical agents from all sources, has considered the scientific criteria for evaluation of carcinogenic hazards.

Many previous recommendations on the criteria to be used for evaluating environmental chemical carcinogenic hazards have been made for specific sources of exposure or for specific groups of substances (e.g., food additives, pesticides, certain occupational carcinogens). In some cases this approach has led to an uneven assessment of risks from different sources and to an uneven approach to preventive measures.

The task of this Committee covers a broader area and includes an appraisal of the scientific criteria for evaluation of chemical carcinogenesis hazards in the total environment.

I. Recommendations

In full consideration of the past and present states of carcinogenesis investigation this Committee offers the following recommendations:

1.a. Any substance which is shown conclusively to cause tumors in animals should be considered carcinogenic and therefore a potential cancer hazard for man. Exceptions should be considered only where the carcinogenic effect is clearly shown to result from physical, rather than chemical, induction, or where the route of administration is shown to be grossly inappropriate in terms of conceivable human exposure.

b. Data on carcinogenic effects in man are only acceptable when they represent critically evaluated results of adequately conducted epidemiologic studies.

2. No level of exposure to a chemical carcinogen should be considered toxicologically insignificant for man. For carcinogenic agents a "safe level for man" cannot be established by application of our present knowledge. The concept of "socially acceptable risk" represents a more realistic notion.

3. The statement made in 1969 by the Food Protection Committee, National Research Council, that natural or synthetic substances can be considered safe without undergoing biological assay should be recognized as scientifically unacceptable.

4. No chemical substance should be assumed safe for human consumption without proper negative lifetime biological assays of adequate size. The minimum requirements for carcinogenesis bioassays should provide for: adequate numbers of animals of at least two species and both sexes with adequate controls, subjected for their lifetime to the administration of a suitable dose range, including the highest tolerated dose, of the test material by routes of administration that include those by which man is exposed. Adequate documenta-

tion of the test conditions and pathologic standards employed are essential.

5. Evidence of negative results, under the conditions of the test used, should be considered superseded by positive findings in other tests. Evidence of positive results should remain definitive, unless and until new evidence conclusively proves that the prior results were not causally related to the exposure.

6. The implication of potential carcinogenicity should be drawn both from tests resulting in the induction of benign tumors and those resulting in tumors which are more obviously malignant.

7. The principle of a zero tolerance for carcinogenic exposures should be retained in all areas of legislation presently covered by it and should be extended to cover other exposures as well. Only in the cases where contamination of an environmental source by a carcinogen has been proven to be unavoidable should exception be made to the principle of zero tolerance. Exceptions should be made only after the most extraordinary justification, including extensive documentation of chemical and biological analyses and a specific statement of the estimated risk for man, are presented. All efforts should be made to reduce the level of contamination to the minimum. Periodic review of the degree of contamination and the estimated risk should be made mandatory.

8. A basic distinction should be made between intentional and unintentional exposures.

a. No substance developed primarily for uses involving exposure to man should be allowed for widespread human intake without having been properly tested for carcinogenicity and found negative.

b. Any substance developed for use not primarily involving exposure in man but nevertheless resulting in such exposure, if found to be carcinogenic, should be either prevented from entering the environment or, if it already exists in the environment, progressively eliminated.

9. A system should be established for ensuring that bioassay operations providing data upon which regulatory decisions are made be monitored so that their results are obtained in accordance with scientifically acceptable standards.

10. A unified approach to the assessment and prevention of carcinogenesis risks should be developed in the federal legislation; it should deal with all sources of human exposure to carcinogenic hazards.

11. Clear channels should be identified for the regulatory function of different government departments and agencies in the field of

cancer prevention. Establishment of a surveillance and information program would alert all concerned government agencies to the extent and development of information on formation on carcinogenic hazards.

12. An ad hoc committee of experts should be charged with the task of recommending methods for extrapolating dose-response bioassay data to the low response region (1/10000% to 1/10000000%). The low doses corresponding to the responses in this range are the ones which have direct relevance to the human situation.

II. Background

Knowledge of cancer causation by chemicals originates from clinical observations, going back as far as 1775 with Pott's discovery of soot as the causative agent in chimney sweeps' cancer. Several major classes of carcinogenic agents were first discovered by their effects on man. Experimental animal models for the determination of the potential carcinogenic activity of chemicals were only developed in the last 50 years, and most of them have been studied only in the last 20 years.

The effects of carcinogens on tissues appear irreversible. Exposure to small doses of a carcinogen over a period of time results in a summation or potentiation of effects. The fundamental characteristic which distinguishes the carcinogenic effect from other toxic effects is that the tissues affected do not seem to return to their normal condition. This summation of effects in time and the long interval (latent period) which passes after tumor induction before the tumor becomes clinically manifest demonstrate that cancer can develop in man and in animals long after the causative agent has been in contact and disappeared.

It is, therefore, important to realize that incidences of cancer in man today reflect exposure of 15 or more years ago; similarly, any increase of carcinogenic contaminants in man's environment today will reveal its carcinogenic effect some 15 or more years from now. For this reason it is urgent that every effort be made to detect and control sources of carcinogenic contamination of the environment well before damaging effects become evident in man. Similar concepts may apply to the needs for evaluation of other chronic toxicity hazards. Environmental cancer remains one of the major disease problems of modern man.

An agent which is causally related to the occurrence of cancer in man or animals is defined as a carcinogen or oncogen. The number of known carcinogenic agents includes several groups of viruses, various physical factors, and hundreds of chemicals.

Viruses of different types are known to induce cancer in animals; none has yet been proven to evoke cancer in man. If specific viruses are proven to be causally related to cancer induction in man, the frequency of certain human tumors might be reduced in the future by immunization procedures.

Physical factors are known to cause cancers in man and animals. For example, ultraviolet radiation causes skin cancer, and ionizing radiation cancer of various organs (e.g., leukemias, lung cancer, bone sarcomas, skin cancer). Exposure to a "background level" has been widely considered as unavoidable and, in the case of ultraviolet light, even necessary as an integral part of our natural environment. Strong epidemiologic and experimental evidence indicates the existence of a direct dose–response relationship between exposure to radiation and carcinogenic effects. Tolerance levels have been suggested for various forms of radiation and health benefits have been realized from their application. Evaluation of radiation hazards has been approached through measurement of the total cumulative dose of radiation exposure. Some carcinogenic radiation hazards, such as certain occupational exposures (e.g., radiation in uranium mines), are still not effectively controlled.

Chemicals of many classes produce cancer in a large number of organ sites in animals. Cancers in man are known to be caused by several individual chemicals and by materials composed of mixtures of chemicals. Chemical carcinogens have been shown to act by surface contact with skin or mucosae, by inhalation, by ingestion, and occasionally by injection or implantation (medical or accidental). Chemicals may induce cancer at the site of initial contact (e.g., skin cancer from polynuclear hydrocarbons), the site of selective localization (e.g., bone cancer radionuclides), the site of metabolism and detoxification (e.g., liver or kidney cancer from aflatoxin or nitrosamines), or the site of excretion (e.g., urinary bladder cancer from aromatic amines). A complex and often uneven approach to the problem of preventing exposure to chemical carcinogens has developed over the years. It has become increasingly obvious that the hazard from a single chemical carcinogen cannot be evaluated out of context of the total environmental exposure.[1] Estimation of the "cumulative carcinogenic dose" resulting from all possible chemical carcinogens or even from all sources of a single type or class of chemical carcinogens is presently impossible.

Prevention of exposure to known carcinogenic chemicals depends largely on man's ability to control their entry into the environment. Certain chemical carcinogens are natural products (e.g., metabolites of the amino acid tryptophan) or naturally occurring contaminants (e.g., mycotoxins). Others are formed in the processing of natural products. Many, such as polynuclear hydrocarbons (e.g., benzo[a]pyrene), occur almost ubiquitously in our modern industrialized environment. They derive from most sources of organic combustion. A class of very potent carcinogens discovered only in recent years, the N-nitrosamines, include compounds that may be formed in the environment from nitrites and secondary amines. Many other known chemical carcinogens have been introduced as synthetic materials or by-products into man's present environment through a wide range of newly developed industrial processes. Some of these, such as food additives, medicinal products, cosmetics, and certain household products or pesticides, were developed for human use. Several carcinogens derive from products such as tobacco smoke, developed exclusively for human use. In other cases chemical carcinogens not intended primarily for human exposure are introduced into the general environment and eventually come in contact with its inhabitants; many substances (certain polynuclear hydrocarbons, pesticides, metals, dusts, and fumes, etc.) gain widespread environmental distribution, thereby becoming pollutants of the air, soil, water, and food. Prevention of exposure to this broad spectrum of chemical carcinogens must take a variety of forms.

The production of chemicals recognized as carcinogens for uses involving intentional human exposure can be identified and effectively eliminated. Exceptions to this approach should be made for substances that involve a well-defined health benefit (e.g., certain chemotherapeutic drugs). Use of such substances should be accepted on the basis of extraordinary evidence that their health benefit outweighs their risk.

The production of specific carcinogenic chemicals for uses that do not primarily involve an intentional exposure of man, but which result in such environmental contamination that extensive human exposure becomes inevitable, must also be controlled. The most effective prevention of exposure in man is the elimination of carcinogen production, or control of entry into the environment.

A large group of chemical carcinogens (e.g., combustion products, mycotoxins, and other natural products) is widely disseminated in the environment from sources that can only be partly controlled. For these contaminants, as well as for products which have been widely spread in the environment before their carcinogenicity was recognized, the only possible approach to exposure reduction is to monitor their environmental distribution and subsequently minimize their contact with humans

Modifying factors are known to condition the development of neoplasia in man and animals. They can act intrinsically or extrinsically (e.g., hormonal imbalances, metabolic characteristics or abnormalities, caloric intake, dietary factors). Understanding of their specific effects in man, however, is still not adequate to serve as a reliable basis for preventative action.

Interactions among multiple factors have received limited attention to date. There are well-documented instances in animal studies of strong synergistic effects produced by chemicals in combination with radiation, viruses, or other chemicals. The epidemiological patterns of certain human cancers implicate combined effects of multiple agents (e.g., inhalation of radon and radon daughters in uranium mines and cigarette smoking).

The types of cancer in man that are due, directly or indirectly, to extrinsic factors are thought to account for a large percentage of the total cancer incidence.[2] These include tumors of the skin, the respiratory, gastrointestinal and urinary tracts, hormone-dependent organs (such as the breast, thyroid, and uterus), and the hemopoietic system. During the past decade considerable progress has been made in the detection of carcinogenic agents and the analysis of their biological effects. New approaches to the interpretation of quantitative relationships between exposures and carcinogenic effects in man and animals are being developed. It is estimated, therefore, that the majority of human cancers are potentially preventable.[2]

III. Animal Bioassay Results and Evaluation of Risks in Man

In order to evaluate the hazard of a chemical for man, one must extrapolate from the animal evidence. It is essential to recognize that no level of exposure to a carcinogenic substance, however low it may be, can be established to be a "safe level" for man. This concept, put forward in the 1950s, remains true in 1970. The current legislation in the field of food additives, with its "anticancer clause," is based on this principle (Federal Food, Drug and Cosmetic Act, as amended, Sect. 409 (c) (3) (A)).

The reasons for retaining this "anticancer clause" were effectively summarized in 1960 by Secretary of Health, Education and Welfare Arthur S. Flemming in testimony to Congress[3] on the subject of extending the clause to cover the use of food colors, with the following statement.

"The rallying point against the anticancer provision is the catch phrase that it takes away the scientist's right to exercise judgment. The issue thus made is a false one, because the clause allows the exercise of all the judgment that can safely be exercised on the basis of our present knowledge. The clause is grounded on the scientific fact of life that no one, at this time, can tell us how to establish for man a safe tolerance for a cancer-producing agent.

"Until cancer research makes a breakthrough at this point, there simply is no specific basis on which judgment or discretion could be exercised in tolerating a small amount of a known carcinogenic color or food additive.

"As I pointed out in my original testimony, the opposition to inclusion of an anticancer clause arises largely out of a misunderstanding of how this provision works. It allows the Department and its scientific people full discretion and judgment in deciding whether a substance has been shown to produce cancer when added to the diet of test animals. But once this decision is made, the limits of judgment have been reached and there is no reliable basis on which discretion could be exercised in determining a safe threshold dose for the established carcinogen.

"So long as the outstanding experts in the National Cancer Institute and the Food and Drug Administration tell us that they do not know how to establish with any assurance at all a safe dose in man's food for a cancer-producing substance, the principle in the anticancer clause is sound.

"I want to emphasize the statement I made on January 26 that the Food, Drug, and Cosmetic Act, as it now stands, will be enforced to prohibit the addition of cancer-producing substances to food unless a law should be passed directing us to follow another course of action.

"Even though we have this authority in the law, we urge the Congress to join with the executive branch to give added assurance to the consuming public by directing the anticancer clause in the proposed color additives amendment.

"Again, we say, however, that we believe the issue is so important that the elected Representatives of the people should have the opportunity of examining the evidence and determining whether or not the authority should be granted."

The scientific basis on which the government's position was established in 1960 remains valid. The progress of knowledge in carcinogenesis in the last decades has only strengthened the points made in Secretary Flemming's testimony.

IV. Detection of Low Levels of Carcinogens in the Environment

To establish the presence of "low levels of carcinogen in the environment" requires that (1) the presence of the material in question be recognized in the environment and (2) the material be recognized as carcinogenic. To evaluate the impact of a chemical in the human environment, it is useful to prepare an "environmental profile" to reflect the distribution of this material in time and space. Failure to detect the presence of a compound implies only that the compound is present, if at all, in concentrations below the detectable limit of the analytical method used. These "sub-detection levels" cannot be differentiated from "zero." From the distribution profile and additional information on the conditions of uptake in man the approximate level and extent of exposure for population segments can be estimated.

In recognizing a chemical as a carcinogen, the limiting factor is the sensitivity and specificity of the bioassay system used. A bioassay system designed to detect tumor induction only at or above a given level under the conditions of the test (e.g., a 25 percent incidence of a specific tumor type) will fail to reveal carcinogenicity below that level. Compounds whose carcinogenic effects fall below specific bioassay detection limits must not be considered innocuous. Such materials must be characterized as presenting a carcinogenic risk no greater than that defined by this lower limit.

Methodology for the determination of chemical contamination in the environment and of biological activity of carcinogens are discussed in the following sections.

A. Chemical Detection Methods

Methods for detection of low levels of carcinogens in the environment have increased in accuracy and reliability over the past several years. The lower limits of detection for different types of known carcinogenic substances are extremely variable, extending over several orders of magnitude from very sensitive methods (e.g., 1 part per billion of benzo[a]pyrene or aflatoxin) to rather insensitive ones (e.g., for aromatic amines). In principle, analytical methods should be capable of detecting carcinogenic materials at any level or in any condition which has relevance to human exposure. For this reason, increasingly sensitive analytical techniques are needed, and indeed many have been developed over the last 10 years. Much of the improvement in methodology is attributable to the application of gas-liquid chromatographic techniques. Within the next few years sizable additional improvements in the sensitivity of analytical methods are likely to be achieved.

It is important to consider how widely the new analytical methods can be applied for the detection of a given carcinogenic contaminant in different materials. While highly sensitive analytical methods can be devised to detect a chemical in specific materials, these same methods might be powerless in the analysis of the same chemical from other source materials (e.g., dimethylnitrosamine can be detected in the alcoholic beverages at 1 ppb, but in foods only at 10–100 ppb). An uneven evaluation of the sources of environmental contamination may result. Development of widely applicable procedures will provide a more balanced evaluation of environmental contamination.

B. Biological Detection Methods

The carcinogenic activity of materials can only be detected by long-term biological tests. At the present time the chemical structure or physico-chemical properties of a compound do not provide a reliable basis for prediction of freedom from carcinogenic activity. Several structure, activity correlations are valuable indicators of the possible carcinogenicity of a compound, but none can be used to classify the compound as noncarcinogenic. Short-term bioassays that determine the effect of certain chemicals on selected biologic targets have not been reliable for prediction of carcinogenic activity.

The present state of the art requires long-term bioassays in mammalian species for the experimental identification of carcinogenic activity. United States law requires that food additives and various other materials be tested in animals by the intended route of human exposure. Similar tests have not been required for some materials to which humans are exposed by other than the oral route. The expanding production and use of chemicals in household products results in extensive human exposure (via the skin and respiratory tract) to dusts and aerosols; little information is available on the chronic toxicity of these materials by these routes of administration. It would not be wise to wait for the results of these "experiments in man" before instituting animal experimentation.

Bioassays are always performed on a number of animals which is extremely small when compared with the millions of humans exposed to most environmental carcinogens. Such studies can only detect carcinogenic effects resulting in fairly high incidences. For example, an observed outcome of no tumors in a test group of 100 animals, as well as in 100 negative controls, only provides assurance, at the 99 percent probability level, that the true tumor risk is under 4.5 percent. The maximum probable risk is 0.46 percent if groups of 1,000 animals are used. It would require tumor-free results in 450 animals to establish with like probability that the risk is under 1 percent.[4]

The assessment of the carcinogenic activity of a chemical depends on a variety of parameters. These include not only the total number of tumors induced but also their multiplicity, latent period, morphologic type, and degree of malignancy. The induction of tumors diagnosed as benign as a result of treatments has been interpreted by certain groups in the past as not sufficient to demonstrate a "carcinogenic" effect. This is a dangerous position since few, if any, substances are known to have produced only benign tumors and no malignant ones when properly and repeatedly tested. This has been pointed out in the Report of the Subcommittee on Carcinogenesis of the FDA Committee on Protocols for Safety Evaluation.[5]

The important scientific problem of defining the sensitivity of a bioassay system used for testing materials of unknown activity has received insufficient attention. The interpretation of both positive and negative findings is strictly dependent on such definition as well as on the results obtained in negative, vehicle, positive and colony control animals. A bioassay result is meaningful only when accompanied by a statement of the sensitivity and specificity of the bioassay design used. An observed incidence of a given tumor type in a test group has no meaning without adequate information on the appropriate controls. Far too little work has been done using adequate positive controls. Lack of tumor response in a given experimental system cannot be interpreted as negative evidence if positive controls also yield negative results or if no positive controls have been included to show that the experimental system used is appropriate.

A body of knowledge has developed over the years on the response of experimental animals to chemical carcinogens. Several committees of experts in the field of carcinogenesis convened by national and international bodies over the past 15 years have formulated general principles for performance and evaluation of carcinogenesis studies in animals. The recommendations put forth by these committees have shown remarkable unanimity[2, 5-10] and are widely accepted in principle by the scientific community.[11-15] General requirements for testing procedures, which have been outlined by these groups, include specification of criteria for the following:

1. Selection of materials to be tested
2. Chemical and physical characterization of the test materials
3. Selection of appropriate animal species and group size
4. Choice of appropriate routes and levels of administration

In addition, recommendations concerning the lifetime maintenance and pathological examination of experimental animals have been outlined.

Two principles are recognized as fundamental to the evaluation of carcinogenesis bioassays.

1. The minimum requirements for carcinogenesis bioassay should include adequate numbers of animals of at least two species and both sexes with adequate positive and negative controls, subjected for their lifetime to the administration by appropriate routes of a suitable dose range of the test material, including doses considerably higher than those anticipated for human exposure.

2. Any substance which is shown conclusively to produce tumors in animals, when tested under these conditions, should be considered potentially carcinogenic for man.

V. Quantitative Relationships

The major new argument presented today against the "anticancer clause" is that the marked increase in sensitivity of many analytical methods makes it possible to detect low levels of carcinogens in a broader segment of the environment and that, therefore, the immediate enforcement of regulations requiring a zero tolerance becomes more difficult, in some instances impossible.

New and very potent classes of chemical carcinogens, such as aflatoxin and nitrosamines, have been detected in the environment. Striking examples of potentiation in cancer induction have been reported in experimental animal tests and in epidemiologic observations. Bioassays have revealed the carcinogenicity of such widespread environmental chemicals as DDT and cyclamate, to which a large majority of the American population has been exposed.

In contrast to the analytical methods, bioassay methods have remained tools of low sensitivity, capable only of detecting the highest peaks of carcinogenic activity. The factor which limits bioassay sensitivity is usually the small number of test animals used. If the bioassay design has a low probability of detecting carcinogenic effects produced by hazards at levels comparable to those present in environmental samples, then tests at such levels are wastes of time, effort and money. The need to test levels higher than those found in the environment is thus founded. Some substances, on the other hand, are potent carcinogens in animal test systems at levels not currently detectable in the environment. An example is provided by the recent evidence on aflatoxin. Its lowest analytically detectable level is 1 ppb. One hundred percent tumor incidence was produced in rats by a dose as low as 15 ppb. in the diet. Experiments now under way suggest that aflatoxin, when fed to rats at the lowest detectable level (1 ppb), is still carcinogenic.[16] It has already been demonstrated to be carcinogenic at 1 ppb in the trout. These data indicate that aflatoxin may be present in food at undetectable levels and still be capable of producing cancer incidences so high as to be detectable in tests involving relatively small numbers of experimental animals.

It is impossible to establish any absolutely safe level of exposure to a carcinogen for man. The concept of "toxicologically insignificant" levels (as advanced by the Food Protection Committee of the NAS/NRC in 1969), of dubious merit in any life science, has absolutely no validity in the field of carcinogenesis. Society must be willing to accept some finite risk as the price of using any carcinogenic material in whatever quantity. The best that science can do is to estimate the upper probable limit of that risk. For this reason, the concept of "safe level for man," as applied to carcinogenic agents, should be replaced by that of a "socially acceptable level of risk."

While science can provide quantitative information regarding maximum risk levels, the task of ultimately selecting socially acceptable levels of human risk rests with society and its political leaders. The evaluation of the balance of benefits and risks, required for such a decision by society, should not be the result of uninformed guesswork but should be reached on the basis of complete and pertinent data, social as well as scientific. It is necessary, therefore, to define the extent in the processes of interpreting animal response data and subsequently extrapolating them to man. The principle of zero tolerance should be applied in all but the most extraordinary of cases.

VI. Conclusion

Modern society has been extremely fortunate—given the technical limits on detection of carcinogenic effects—that at least some environmental carcinogens have been identified. So-called negative data, obtained in bioassays often incapable of detecting effects below the 10 percent level, are grossly inadequate to give assurance of safety for man. Information on about 2,500 compounds tested for carcinogenic activity up through 1960 has been compiled and published.[17] Most of these materials, however, are of no environmental significance. Data on tests reported since 1960 will be published shortly. It is estimated that data on 3,500 previously unevaluated chemicals will be included in the forthcoming volume. It is seen, then, that about 6,000 chemicals are documented as having undergone carcinogenesis bioassay to date. Many of the referenced tests, however, were inadequate according to presently recommended standards.

If this nation wishes to identify a large segment of existing and potential carcinogenic hazards, it must institute a comprehensive program involving a concert of activities. Scientific and technical plans for the development of methodological standards should be provided by experienced agencies in collaboration with qualified advisors. It is essential that the objectivity of these advisors not be damaged by any conflicting interests.

Resources needed for the extensive bioassay screening of environmental chemicals will be considerable. In addition to the myriad of substances presently in the environment, several thousand new compounds are introduced each year. Up to 20,000 materials should be tested for carcinogenicity as a first screening of the environment. Testing 20,000 compounds by bioassay would cost about $1 billion. This estimate would increase accordingly for the more extensive testing required in less superficial evaluation. Yet even were such funds available today, they could not nearly be spent effectively. Bioassay laboratory and professional resources are just not available in quantities capable of supporting a huge testing program. A great deal of "tooling up" is prerequisite to any such expanded level of effort.

Because the latent period in human carcinogenesis is so long, epidemiologic evidence develops only over periods of 15 to 20 years. Timely decisions to exclude materials from uses involving exposure to man, therefore, must be based solely on adequately conducted animal bioassays. Retrospective human evidence of risk must not be allowed to show itself before controlling action is taken. Chemicals should be subjected to scientific scrutiny rather than given individual "rights"; they must be considered potentially guilty unless and until proven innocent. Valid evidence must come from biological assays; every bioassay report should include a statement of its limits of sensitivity. Experimental design should provide for reproducibility of test results. Since the bioassay plays such a key role in a total carcinogen control scheme, more effort must be devoted to setting standards for both the performance of tests and the interpretation of results. Only given good bioassay data can science possibly provide sound information to those who are charged with making social decisions regarding the acceptability of carcinogenesis risk levels.

An effective program to protect man from the mass of environmental cancer hazards is within reach. No more time should be allowed to pass before the recommendations set forth in this report are applied to reality.

References

[1] Shubik P. Clayson DB. Terracini B: The Quantification of Environmental Carcinogens. UICC Technical Report Series, Volume 4. Geneve, Switzerland, Braillard E., 1970, 33 p.

[2] Report of a WHO Expert Committee: Prevention of cancer. Wld Hlth Org Techn Rep Ser 276:1–53, 1964.

[3] Fleming AS: Statement of Arthur S. Fleming, Secretary, DHEW, *In* Hearings before a Subcommittee on the Committee on Interstate and Foreign Commerce of the House of Representatives Regarding Color Additives; 86th Congress, 2nd Session. Washington DC, US Govt Print Office, 1960, pp. 499–501.

[4] Mantel N. Bryan WR: "Safety" testing of carcinogenic agents. J Nat Cancer Inst 27:455–470, 1961.

[5] FDA Advisory Committee on Protocol for Safety Evaluation: Panel on Carcinogenesis: Report on cancer testing and the safety evaluation of food additives and pesticides. Toxicol Appl Pharmacol: (in press), 1970.

[6] Committee on Causative Factors of Cancer and Committee on Cancer Prevention: Report of symposium on potential cancer hazards from chemical additives and contaminants to foodstuffs. Acta Un Int Cancer 13:179–193, 1957.

[7] Fifth Report of the Joint FAO/WHO Expert Committee on Food Additives: Evaluation of carcinogenic hazards of food additives. Wld Hlth Org Techn Rep Ser 220:1–32, 1961.

[8] Food Protection Committee, Food and Nutrition Board: Problems in the Evaluation of Carcinogenic Hazard from Use of Food Additives. Washington

DC, National Academy of Sciences—National Research Council Publ No 749, 1960, 44p: Cancer Res 21:429–456, 1961.

[9] Berenblum I: Carcinogenicity Testing, UICC Technical Report Series, Volume 2, Geneve, Switzerland, de Bursen G, 1969, 56 p.

[10] Technical Panel on Carcinogenesis: Carcinogenicity of pesticides. *In* Report of the Secretary's Commission on Pesticides and Their Relationship to Environmental Health. Washington DC, US Govt Print Office, 1969, pp 459–506.

[11] Shubik P, Sice J: Chemical carcinogenesis as a chronic toxicity test: A Review, Cancer Res 16:728–742, 1956.

[12] Clayson DB: Chemical Carcinogenesis. Boston, Massachusetts, Little Brown and Company, 1962, 467 p.

[13] Hueper WC, Conway WD: Chemical Carcinogenesis and Cancers. Springfield, Illinois, Thomas CC, 1964, 744 p.

[14] Weisburger, JH, Weisburger EK: Tests for chemical carcinogens. *In* Methods in Cancer Research, Volume I (Busch H, ed.). New York, New York, Academic Press Inc, 1967, pp 307–387.

[15] Arcos JG, Argus MG, Wolf G: Testing procedures. *In* Chemical Induction of Cancer, Volume I (Arcos JG, Argus MG, Wolf G. eds.). New York, New York, Academic Press Inc., 1968, pp 340–463.

[16] Wogan GN: Personal communication.

[17] Hartwell JL: Survey of Compounds Which Have Been Tested for Carcinogenic Activity, 2nd ed., Public Health Serv Publ No 149, Washington DC.

Appendix III

Substances Regulated as Recognized Carcinogens

1. Workplace Standards under §6, Occupational Safety and Health Act

Substance	Date of Final Action
Asbestos	June 7, 1972 (37 Fed. Reg. 11318)
14 Carcinogens 2-Acetylaminofluorene Alpha-naphthylamine 4-Aminodiphenyl Benzidine Beta-naphthylamine Beta-propiolactone Bischloromethylether 3,3'-Dichlorobenzidine 4-Dimethylaminoazobenzene Ethyleneimine Chloromethylmethylether	Jan. 29, 1974 (39 Fed. Reg. 3756)

4,4'-Methylene bis(2-chloroaniline)
   (MOCA)   (deleted)
4-Nitrobiphenyl
N-Nitrosodimethylamine

Vinyl chloride	Oct. 4, 1974 (39 Fed. Reg. 35890)
Coke oven emissions	Oct. 22, 1976 (41 Fed. Reg. 46741)

2. *Hazardous Air Pollutants under* §12, *Clean Air Act*

Substance	*Date of Final Action*
Asbestos	April 6, 1973 (38 Fed. Reg. 8820) May 3, 1974 (39 Fed. Reg. 15396) Oct. 14, 1975 (40 Fed. Reg. 48302)
Vinyl chloride	Oct. 21, 1976 (41 Fed. Reg. 46559)

Source: Marion F. Suter and Warren R. Muir. "Federal Programs in Cancer Research," in S.S. Epstein, ed., *Environmental Cancer* (Springfield, Illinois: C. C. Thomas, in press).

3. *Toxic Pollutants Effluent Standards Under* §307, *Federal Water Pollution Control Act*

Substance	*Date of Final Action*
DDT (and DDE, DDD)	Jan. 12, 1977 (42 Fed. Reg. 2587)

Aldrin/dieldrin	Jan. 12, 1977 (42 Fed. Reg. 2587)
Benzidine	Jan. 12, 1977 (42 Fed. Reg. 2587)
PCBs	Feb. 2, 1977

---

4. *Food, Color, and Cosmetic Products Banned Under Federal Food, Drug, and Cosmetic Act*

Substance	Date of Final Action
Dulcin, P-400	15 Fed. Reg. 321 (1950)
Coumarin	19 Fed. Reg. 1239 (1954)
Safrole, oil of sassafras, dihydrosafrole, iso-safrole	25 Fed. Reg. 12412 (1960)
DES (for use in poultry)	21 CFR 510.120 (1960)
Flectol H (1-2, Dihydro-2,2,4-trimethquinoline, polymerized)	32 Fed. Reg. 5675 (1967)
Oil of calamus	33 Fed. Reg. 6967 (1968)
Cyclamates	34 Fed. Reg. 17063 (1969)
MOCA (4,4′-methylenebis-(2-chloroaniline))	34 Fed. Reg. 19073 (1969)
DEPC (diethylpyrocarbonate)	37 Fed. Reg. 15426 (1972)

Mercaptoimidazoline	38 Fed. Reg. 33072 (1973)
FD&C Violet #1	38 Fed. Reg. 9077 (1973)
Vinyl chloride	39 Fed. Reg. 26842 (1976)
FD&C Red #2	41 Fed. Reg. 5823 (1976)
Chloroform	41 Fed. Reg. 26842 (1976)
FD&C Red #4	41 Fed. Reg. 41852 (1976)
Carbon black	41 Fed. Reg. 41857 (1976)
Acrylonitrile	42 Fed. Reg. 13546 (1977)
Nitrofurans	42 Fed. Reg. 17526, 18611, 18619, 18660 (1977)
Graphite	42 Fed. Reg. 60734 (1977)
D&C Red #10-13	42 Fed. Reg. 62475 (1977)
D&C Yellow #1	42 Fed. Reg. 62482 (1977)

5. *Consumer Products Under Consumer Products Safety Act/Federal Hazardous Substances Act*

Substance	*Date of Final Action*
Vinyl chloride	39 Fed. Reg. 30114 (1974)
Tris	42 Fed. Reg. 18856, 61621, (1977)
Asbestos products	42 Fed. Reg. 63354 (1977)

6. *Pesticides Under Federal Insecticide, Fungicide, and Rodenticide Act*

Substance	*Date of Final Action*
DDT	37 Fed. Reg. 13369 (1972)
Vinyl chloride	39 Fed. Reg. 14753 (1974)
Aldrin/dieldrin	39 Fed. Reg. 37265 (1974)
Heptachlor/chlordane	41 Fed. Reg. 7552 (1976)
Kepone	41 Fed. Reg. 24624 (1976)
Mirex	41 Fed. Reg. 56694 (1976)
DBCP (dibromochloropropane)	42 Fed. Reg. 57543 (1977)

Appendix IV

Labor Publications on Occupational Health*

ACTWU Labor Unity
Amalgamated Clothing and Textile Workers Union (AFL-CIO)
15 Union Square
New York, N.Y. 10003

Aluminum Light
Aluminum Workers International Union (AFL-CIO)
818 Olive St., Suite 338
St. Louis, Mo. 63101

American Flint
Glass Workers Union of North America (AFL-CIO)
1440 S. Byrne Rd.
Toledo, Ohio 73614

Butcher Workman
Amalgamated Meat Cutters and Butcher Workmen of North America
2800 N. Sheridan Road
Chicago, Ill. 60657

---

*All are published monthly unless noted otherwise.

Carpenter
United Brotherhood of Carpenters and Joiners of America
101 Constitution Ave., N.W.
Washington, D.C. 20001

Chemical Worker
International Chemical Workers Union (AFL-CIO)
1655 W. Market St.
Akron, Ohio 44313

Facts and Analysis
Industrial Union Department (AFL-CIO)
815 16th St., N.W.
Washington, D.C. 20006

Glass Workers News
United Glass and Ceramic Workers of North America (AFL-CIO)
556 E. Town St.
Columbus, Ohio 43215

Health and Safety Bulletin (6 issues annually)
International Union of Electrical, Radio and Machine
Workers (AFL-CIO)
AFL-CIO/CLC
1126 16th St., N.W.
Washington, D.C. 20036

International Firefighter
International Association of Firefighters (AFL-CIO)
1750 New York Ave., N.W.
Washington, D.C. 20006

International Teamster
International Brotherhood of Teamsters, Chauffeurs, Warehousemen,
and Helpers of America
25 Louisiana Ave., N.W.
Washington, D.C. 20001

IUE News
International Union of Electrical Radio and Machine Workers
(AFL-CIO)

1126 16th St., N.W.
Washington, D.C. 20036

Labeletter
Union Label and Service Trades Department (AFL-CIO)
815 16th St., N.W.
Washington, D.C. 20006

Lifelines
Oil, Chemical, and Atomic Workers Union (AFL-CIO)
Health and Safety Department
P.O. Box 2812
1636 Champa St.
Denver, Colo. 80201

Light
Utility Workers Union of America
815 16th St., N.W., Suite 605
Washington, D.C. 20006

The Machinist
International Association of Machinists and Aerospace Workers
(AFL-CIO)
1300 Connecticut Ave., N.W.
Washington, D.C. 20036

Metaletter
Metal Trades Department (AFL-CIO)
815 16th St., N.W.
Washington, D.C. 20006

Monitor (8 issues annually)
Labor Occupational Health Program
Institute of Industrial Relations
Center for Labor Research
2521 Channing Way
Berkeley, Calif. 94720

NABET News (bimonthly)
National Association of Broadcast Employees and Technicians
(AFL-CIO)
1601 Connecticut Ave., N.W.
Washington, D.C. 20009

Occupational Health and Safety (6 issues annually)
International Union of Auto, Aerospace, and Agricultural Implement
Workers of America
8000 E. Jefferson Ave.
Detroit, Mich. 48214

Painters and Allied Trades Journal
International Brotherhood of Painters and Allied Trades of U.S. and Canada
(AFL-CIO)
United Unions Building
1750 New York Ave., N.W.
Washington, D.C. 20006

Paper Worker
United Paperworkers International Union (AFL-CIO)
163-03 Horace Harding Expressway
Flushing, N.Y. 11365

Pennsylvania AFL-CIO News
Pennsylvania AFL-CIO
101 Pine St.
Harrisburg, Pa. 17101

Plasterer and Cement Mason
Plasterers' and Cement Masons' International Association of the United
States and Canada (AFL-CIO)
1125 17th St., N.W.
Washington, D.C. 20002

Service Employee
Service Employees International Union (AFL-CIO)
2020 K St., N.W.
Washington, D.C. 20006

Solidarity
International Union of Auto, Aerospace and Agricultural Implement
Workers of America
8000 E. Jefferson Ave.
Detroit, Michigan 48214

Spotlight on Health and Safety (quarterly)
Industrial Union Department (AFL-CIO)

815 16th St., N.W.
Washington, D.C. 20006

Steel Labor
United Steelworkers of America (AFL-CIO)
Five Gateway Center
Pittsburgh, Pa. 15222

UE News (biweekly)
United Electrical, Radio, and Machine Workers of America
11 E. 51st St.
New York, N.Y. 10022

United Rubber Worker
United Rubber, Cork, Linoleum, and Plastic Workers of America
(AFL-CIO)
URWA Building
South High St.
Akron, Ohio 44308

Union Tabloid (10 issues annually)
Graphic Arts International Union (AFL-CIO)
1900 L St., N.W.
Washington, D.C. 20036

United Mine Worker Journal (bimonthly)
United Mine Workers of America
900 15th St., N.W.
Washington, D.C. 20005

Voice of the Cement, Lime, Gypsum, and Allied Workers
United Cement, Lime, Gypsum, and Allied Workers (AFL-CIO)
7830 W. Lawrence Ave.
Chicago, Ill. 60656

Appendix V

Public Interest Groups Concerned with Cancer Prevention

Action on Smoking and Health
A national organization concerned with problems of smoking; also represents the rights of nonsmokers through legal action.
2000 H St., N.W., Washington, D.C. 20006
Tel: 202-659-4310

Center for Science in the Public Interest
Concerned with energy conservation, nuclear energy, nutrition, and toxic chemicals, particularly in food, and the performance of voluntary health agencies. Publishes *Nutrition Action*, reports and books.
1757 S St., N.W., Washington, D.C. 20009
Tel: 202-322-4250

Commission for the Advancement
of Public Interest Organizations
A public interest group supported by the Monsour Medical Foundation. Concerns include increasing contacts between the professional, governmental, and public interest communities, and with creating loose, ad hoc coalitions of public interest and labor groups around

critical issues such as control of environmental and occupational carcinogens.
1875 Connecticut Ave., N.W., Washington, D.C. 20009
Tel: 202-462-0505

Consumer Federation of America
A federation of consumer, cooperative, and labor groups, which lobbies for consumer protection legislation and publishes *Monthly News* and pamphlets.
1012 14th St., N.W., Washington, D.C. 20005
Tel: 202-737-3732

Consumers Union (CU)
The largest consumer group in the country, with a membership of approximately 190,000; primarily devoted to advancing the well-being of the consumer and to testing consumer products for their effectiveness and safety, as well as such concerns as contamination of water with organic pollutants and carcinogens. Publishes *Consumer Reports* (monthly) and a *Consumers Union News Digest* (bimonthly). Regional offices in Washington, D.C., and San Francisco, files suits and petitions on consumers' rights.
265 Washington St., Mount Vernon, N.Y. 10550
Tel: 914-664-6400

Environmental Action
Founded in 1970, when it convened the first "Earth Day" in the U.S. Researches and lobbies on environmental issues, including toxic and carcinogenic substances.
1346 Connecticut Ave., N.W., Washington, D.C. 20036
Tel: 202-833-1845

Environmental Defense Fund
A public interest law firm with an effective track record in the banning of toxic and carcinogenic chemicals, including DDT, aldrin/dieldrin, chlordane/heptachlor, and Tris. Has also played a major role in passage of the Safe Drinking Water Act.
1525 18th St., N.W., Washington, D.C. 20036
Tel: 202-833-1484

Environmental Improvement Associates
A recently formed group dedicated to workers' rights to air unpolluted by tobacco smoke in the workplace.
109 Chestnut St., Salem, N.J. 08079
Tel: 606-935-4200

Federation of American Scientists

A nationwide lobbying group of natural and social scientists and engineers concerned with problems of science and society, including environmental carcinogens.
203 C St., N.E., Washington, D.C. 20002
Tel: 202-546-3300

Federation of American Homemakers

A public interest group representing interests of consumers and housewives with particular interests in problems of food and consumer product safety.
P.O. Box 5571, Arlington, Va. 22205

Health Policy Advisory Center
(HEALTH/PAC)

Concerned with monitoring and interpreting the health system to change-oriented groups of health workers, consumers, professionals, and students. Publishes a bimonthly journal, the *Health/Pac Bulletin*, on important developments in the health system, including occupational and environmental health.
17 Murray St., New York, N.Y. 10007
Tel: 212-287-8890

Health Research Group of
Public Citizens, Inc.

A highly effective medico-legal group with concerns that include the quality of medical care, carcinogenic drugs, food and feed additives, and occupational health and safety. Has published a series of hard-hitting reports and is active in petitions and congressional testimony.
2000 P St., N.W., Washington, D.C. 20036
Tel: 202-872-0320

National Clean Air Coalition

A national coalition of environmental and other groups concerned with air pollution and lobbying for improvements in the Clean Air Act.
620 C St., S.E., Washington, D.C. 20003
Tel: 202-543-0305

National Public Interest Research Group

Provides technical resources to nationwide PIRGs.
1346 Connecticut Ave., N.W., Washington, D.C. 20036
Tel: 202-833-3934

Natural Resources Defense Council

A public interest law firm with a good track record in successful petitions on carcinogenic food contaminants and air and water pollutants.
15 West 44th St., New York, N.Y. 10036
Tel: 212-869-0150

Rachel Carson Trust for
the Living Environment

A resource group devoted to increasing public awareness of hazardous pesticides and other toxic chemicals.
8940 Jones Mill Rd., Washington, D.C. 20015
Tel: 301-652-1877

Sierra Club

Apart from its primary conservation interests, has played an important role in lobbying for toxic substances legislation and monitoring its implementation.
530 Bush St., San Francisco, Calif. 94108
Tel: 415-981-8634

Urban Environment Conference

An organization founded by the late Senator Philip A. Hart which convenes representatives of environmental, labor, and minority groups for training, information exchange, and developing joint positions on environmental issues of common interest.
1302 18th St., N.W., Washington, D.C. 20036
Tel: 202-466-6040

Appendix VI

Human Cancers Following Drug Treatment

Drugs	Related Cancer
Radioisotopes	
Phosphorus (P^{32})	Acute leukaemia
Radium, mesothorium	Osteosarcoma and cancer of nasal sinuses
Thorotrast	Liver angiosarcoma
Immunosuppressive drugs (for renal transplantation)	
Antilymphocyte serum	Reticulum cell sarcoma
Antimetabolites	Soft tissue sarcoma, other cancers (skin, liver)
Cytotoxic drugs	
Chlornaphazine	Bladder cancer
Melphalan, cyclophosphamide	Acute leukaemia

Hormones
  Synthetic estrogens
    Prenatal   Cancer of the vagina and
                                          cervix
    Postnatal   Cancer of the uterus
  Androgenic-anabolic steroids
    (for treatment of aplastic   Liver cancer
    anemia)

Others
  Arsenic   Skin cancer
  Phenacetin-containing drugs   Kidney cancer
  Coal tar ointments   Skin cancer
  Diphenylhydantoin?   Lymphoma
  Chloramphenicol?   Leukaemia
  Amphetamines?   Hodgkin's disease
  Reserpine?   Breast cancer

Source: Based on R. Hoover and J. F. Fraumeni, Jr., "Drugs," ch. 12, in J. F. Fraumeni, Jr., ed., *Persons at High Risk of Cancer,* (New York: Academic Press, 1975).

Appendix VII

Some Specialized Cancer Treatment Centers

Cancer Site	Recommended Center
Lung	Roswell Park Memorial Institute, Buffalo Mayo Clinic, Rochester, Minnesota Johns Hopkins Medical Institution, Baltimore
Breast	M.D. Anderson Hospital, Houston Massachusetts General Hospital, Boston Cleveland Clinic
Uterus	Fred Hutchinson Cancer Center, University of Washington, Seattle
Prostate and genito-urinary	Roswell Park Memorial Institute, Buffalo, New York
Lymphomas and leukaemias	Memorial Sloan-Kettering, New York Stanford University Medical Center, Palo Alto, California

508

Sarcomas	Moffett Hospital, University of California, San Francisco University of Arizona, Tucson Sidney Farber Cancer Center, Boston
Melanoma	Tufts-New England Medical Center, Boston
Thyroid	Rush-Presbyterian-St.Luke's, Chicago
Pancreas	Ohio State University Hospital, Columbus
Brain	Moffett Hospital, University of California, San Francisco

Abbreviations

Agencies

CEQ	Council on Environmental Quality
CPSC	Consumer Product Safety Commission
EPA	Environmental Protection Agency
FDA	Food and Drug Administration
FTC	Federal Trade Commission
HEW	Health, Education and Welfare
NCI	National Cancer Institute
NCTR	National Center for Toxicological Research
NIEHS	National Institute of Environmental Health Sciences
NIH	National Institutes of Health
NIOSH	National Institute for Occupational Safety and Health
OSHA	Occupational Safety and Health Administration (in Department of Labor)
PHS	Public Health Service
USDA	United States Department of Agriculture

Chemicals

A/D	aldrin/dieldrin
AN	acrylonitrile
BCME	bischloromethylether
C/H	chlordane/heptachlor
CMME	chloromethylmethylether

510

DES	diethylstilbestrol
DMN	dimethylnitrosamine
NO_x	nitrogen oxides
PCBs	polychlorinated biphenyls
PVC	polyvinyl chloride
VC	vinyl chloride

Units

kg	kilogram (2.2 pounds)
g	gram (1/1000 kilogram)
mg	milligram (1/1000 gram)
μg	microgram (1/1000 milligram)
ppm	parts per million (1 ppm = one ten-thousandth of one percent)
ppb	parts per billion (1 ppb = one ten-millionth of one percent)
ppt	parts per trillion (1 ppt = one thousandth of a ppb)

References

Chapter 1

The Impact of Cancer

1. Testimony before Subcommittee on Health, House Commerce Committee, March 21, 1977. See also B. J. Culliton, "Fight Over Proposed Saccharin Ban Will Not Be Settled for Months," *Science* 196 (1977): 276–78.
2. S. S. Epstein, "Environmental Determinants of Cancer," *Cancer Research* 34 (1974): 2425–35; "1978 Cancer Facts and Figures" (New York: American Cancer Society, 1977), p. 3.
3. J. L. Young, S. S. Devesa, and S. J. Cutler, "Incidence of Cancer in United States Blacks," *Cancer Res.* 35 (1975): 3523–33.
4. Ibid., p. 3525
5. Epstein, "Environmental Determinants of Cancer"; S. S. Epstein, "Cancer and the Environment," *Bulletin of the Atomic Scientists (of Chicago)* 26 (1977): 22–30.
6. Ibid.
7. D. Greenberg, "Cancer: Now the Bad News," *Washington Post*, January 19, 1975; D. Greenberg, Science and Government Report, Washington, D.C., April 1, 1975; SEER Program, "Cancer Patient Survival," SEER Program Report no. 5 DHEW Publication (NIH) 77–992 (Washington, D.C., 1976). It should be noted that survival data are difficult to collect,

and debates rage concerning their accuracy. See, for example, J. E. Enstrom and D. F. Austin, "Interpreting Cancer Survival Rates," *Science* 195 (1977): 847–51.

8. "Cancer Patient Survival," SEER Program Report.

9. S. S. Devesa, and M. A. Schneiderman, "Increase in the Number of Cancer Deaths in the United States," *American Journal of Epidemiology* 106 (1977): 1–5.

10. M. S. Zdeb, "The Probability of Developing Cancer," *Am. J. Epidemiology* 106 (1977): 6–16.

11. American Industrial Health Council, "AIHC Recommended Alternatives to OSHA's Generic Carcinogen Policy" (Scarsdale, N.Y., January 9, 1978).

12. R. Doll, "Prevention of Cancer: Pointers from Epidemiology" (London: Nuffield Hospital Trust, 1967); J. Higginson, "Present Trends in Cancer Epidemiology," *Proceedings of the Canadian Cancer Conference* 8 (1969): 40–75; J. Higginson, "The Role of Geographical Pathology in Environmental Carcinogenesis," in *Environment and Cancer* (Baltimore: Williams and Wilkins, 1972), pp. 69–89; Epstein, "Environmental Determinants of Cancer"; B. Armstrong and R. Doll, "Environmental Factors and Cancer Incidence and Mortality in Different Countries with Special Reference to Dietary Practices," *International Journal of Cancer* 15 (1975): 617–31.

13. W. Haenszel, ed., *Epidemiological Study of Cancer and Other Chronic Diseases*, National Cancer Institute Monograph 19 (Bethesda, Md., 1966).

14. Doll,"Prevention of Cancer."

15. AIHC, "Alternatives to OSHA's Generic Carcinogen Policy"; E. L. Wynder and G. B. Gori, "Contribution of the Environment to Cancer Incidence," *Journal of the National Cancer Institute* 58 (1977): 825–32.

16. I. J. Selikoff, E. C. Hammond, and J. Churg, "Asbestos Exposure, Smoking and Neoplasia," *Journal of the American Medical Association* 204 (1968): 106–12; R. Saracci, "Asbestos and Lung Cancer: An Analysis of the Epidemiological Evidence on the Asbestos–Smoking Interaction," *Intl. J. Cancer* 20 (1977): 323–31.

17. T. J. Mason and F. W. McKay, "U.S. Cancer Mortality by County, 1950–1969," DHEW Publication (NIH) 74–615 (Washington, D.C., 1973); R. Hoover et al., "Geographic Patterns of Cancer Mortality in the United States," in J. F. Fraumeni, Jr., ed., *Persons at High Risk of Cancer* (New York: Academic Press, 1975), pp. 343–60; W. J. Blot, "The Geography of Cancer," *The Sciences* 17 (1977): 12–15.

18. C. Noller, *Chemistry of Organic Compounds* (Philadelphia: Saunders, 1957), p. 73; *Chemical and Engineering News*, Nov. 7, 1977, p. 16.

19. T. H. Maugh, "Chemicals: How Many Are There?" *Science* 199 (1978): 162.

Part I The Science of Cancer

Chapter 2

Cancer: The Human Experiment

1. A. M. Lilienfeld, *Foundations of Epidemiology* (Oxford University Press, 1976); B. MacMahon and T. F. Pugh, *Epidemiology: Principles and Methods* (Boston: Little, Brown, 1970); J. Mausner and A. K. Bahn, *Epidemiology* (Philadelphia: Saunders, 1973); R. Doll, "The Contribution of Epidemiology to Knowledge of Cancer," *Revue Epidemiologie et Sante Publique* 24 (1976): 107–21.
2. U.S. Department of Health, Education, and Welfare, *Vital Statistics of the United States, 1970*, vol. 2, "Mortality," (Washington, D.C.: Department of Health, Education, and Welfare, Public Health Service, 1974).
3. See, for example, B. Christine, J. T. Flannery, and P. D. Sullivan, "Cancer in Connecticut, 1966–1968" (Hartford: Connecticut State Department of Health, 1971).
4. I. Adler, *Primary Malignant Growths of the Lung and Bronchi, a Pathological and Clinical Study* (London: Longmans, Green and Co., 1912), p. 1.
5. F. H. Muller, "Tabakmissbrauch und Lungencarcinom," *Zeitschrift für Krebsforschung* 49 (1939): 57–84.
6. "Smoking and Health: Report of the Advisory Committee to the Surgeon General of the Public Health Service," (Washington, D.C.: Department of Health, Education, and Welfare, Public Health Service, 1964). The classic "Surgeon General's Report" exhaustively summarizing the evidence that smoking causes cancer and many other health problems.
7. E. C. Hammond, "Smoking in Relation to Death Rates of One Million Men and Women," National Cancer Institute Monograph 19 (Washington, D.C., 1966), pp. 124–204.
8. E. C. Hammond et al., "'Tar' and Nicotine Content of Cigarette Smoke in Relation to Death Rates," *Environmental Research* 12 (1976): 263–74.
9. "The Health Consequences of Smoking—1974," (Washington D.C.: Department of Health, Education, and Welfare, 1974); E. L. Wynder, and S. D. Stellman, "Comparative Epidemiology of Tobacco-Related Cancers," *Cancer Research* 37 (1977): 4608–22; W. Haenszel, ed., *Epidemiological Study of Cancer and Other Chronic Diseases*, National Cancer Institute Monograph 19 (Bethesda, Md., 1966). A hard-to-find technical monograph containing much fundamental data on smoking and cancer. Also contains British-Norwegian migrant studies which form one

of the cornerstones for belief in environmental rather than genetic causes of cancer.

10. D. Hoffmann and E. L. Wynder, "Environmental Respiratory Carcinogenesis," ch. 7 in C. E. Searle, ed., *Chemical Carcinogenesis,* American Chemical Society Monograph 173 (Washington, D.C., 1976); E. L. Wynder, M. Mushinski, and S. D. Stellman, "The Epidemiology of the Less Harmful Cigarette," *Proceedings of the Third World Conference on Smoking and Health,* (1976): 1–13.

11. "Smoking and Health: Report to the Surgeon General," p. 7.

12. See, for example, I. J. Selikoff, "Lung Cancer and Mesothelioma during Prospective Surveillance of 1,249 Asbestos Insulation Workers, 1963–1974," *Annals of the New York Academy of Sciences* 271 (1976): 448–56.

13. A. J. Fox and P. F. Collier, "Low Mortality Rates in Industrial Cohort Studies Due to Selection for Work and Survival in the Industry," *British Journal of Preventive and Social Medicine* 30 (1976): 225–30.

14. S. D. Walter, "Determination of Significant Relative Risks and Optimal Sampling Procedures in Prospective and Retrospective Comparative Studies of Various Sizes," *American Journal of Epidemiology* 105 (1977): 387–97.

15. Testimony of J. Jandl at OSHA hearings on proposed benzene standard, 1977.

16. M. Segi and M. Kurihara, *Cancer Mortality for Selected Sites in 24 Countries,* Tohoku University School of Medicine, Department of Public Health Monograph 2 (Sendai, Japan, 1972).

17. Joint Iran–IARC Study Group, "Esophageal Cancer Studies in the Caspian Littoral of Iran: Results of Population Studies—a Prodrome," *Journal of the National Cancer Institute* 59 (1977): 1127–77.

18. Segi and Kurihara, "Cancer Mortality for Selected Sites," p. 72.

19. D. J. Jussawalla and V. M. Deshpande, "Evaluation of Cancer Risk in Tobacco Chewers and Smokers: An Epidemiological Assessment," *Cancer* 28 (1971): 244–52.

20. T. J. Mason et al., *Atlas of Cancer Mortality for U.S. Counties: 1950–1969* (Washington, D.C.: Department of Health, Education, and Welfare, 1975).

21. T. J. Mason et al., *Atlas of Cancer Mortality among U.S. Non-Whites: 1950–1969* (Washington, D.C.: Department of Health, Education, and Welfare, Public Health Service, 1976).

22. W. J. Blot et al., "Cancer Mortality in U.S. Counties with Petroleum Industries," *Science* 198 (1977): 51–53.

Chapter 3

Cancer: The Animal Experiment

1. S. S. Epstein, "Environmental Determinants of Cancer," *Cancer Research* 34 (1974): 2425–35. Cites detailed references.

2. M. D. Kipling and H. A. Waldron, "Polycyclic Aromatic Hydrocarbons in Mineral Oil, Tar, and Pitch, Excluding Petroleum Pitch," *Preventive Medicine* 5 (1976): 262–78. A semi-historical review.

3. K. Yamagiwa, and K. Ichikawa, "Uber die Kunstliche Erzeugnung von Papillom," *Verhandlungen der Japanischen pathologischen Gesellschaft* 5 (1915): 142–58.

4. J. A. Murray, "Experimental Tar Cancer in Mice," *British Medical Journal* 2 (1921): 795–96.

5. E. L. Kennaway, "On Cancer Producing Tars and Tar-Fractions," *Journal of Industrial Hygiene* 5 (1934): 462–88.

6. See, for example, H. G. M. Fischer et al., "Properties of High-Boiling Petroleum Products: Physical and Chemical Properties as Related to Carcinogenic Activity," *Industrial Hygiene and Occupational Medicine* 33 (1951): 315–24.

7. Kennaway, "Cancer Producing Tars."

8. J. H. Cook, C. L. Hewitt, and I. Hieger, "Coal Tar Constituents and Cancer," *Nature* 130 (1932): 926–27.

9. W. C. Hueper, *Occupational Tumors and Allied Diseases* (Springfield, Ill.: Charles C. Thomas, 1942).

10. W. C. Hueper, F. H. Wiley, and H. D. Wolfe, "Experimental Production of Bladder Tumors in Dogs by Administration of Beta-Naphthylamine," *J. Ind. Hyg.* 20 (1938): 46–84.

11. R. H. Glasser, *The Greatest Battle* (New York: Random House, 1977). A good general account of the cancer process.

12. National Academy of Sciences, National Research Council, Food and Nutrition Board, *Problems in the Evaluation of Carcinogenic Hazards from Food Additives*, Food Protection Committee Publication 749, (Washington, D.C.: National Academy of Sciences, 1960).

13. F. W. Sunderman, Jr., "A Review of the Carcinogenicities of Nickel, Chromium, and Arsenic Compounds in Men and Animals," *Prev. Med.* 5 (1976): 279–94.

14. L. Tomatis, C. Partensky, and R. Montesano, "The Predictive Value of Mouse Liver Tumour Induction in Carcinogenic Testing: A Literature Survey," *International Journal of Cancer* 12 (1973): 1–20; L. Tomatis, "Validity and Limitations of Long-Term Experimentation in Cancer Research," in U. Mohr, D. Schmahl, and L. Tomatis, eds., *Air Pollution and Cancer in Man*, International Agency for Research on Cancer Scientific Publication 16 (Lyon, France, 1977), pp. 299–307.

15. H. F. Kraybill, "The Toxicology and Epidemiology of Mycotoxins," *Tropical and Geographical Medicine* 21 (1969): 1–18.

16. A. W. Horton, D. T. Denman, and R. P. Trosset, "Carcinogenesis of the Skin, 2: The Accelerating Properties of Aliphatic and Related Hydrocarbons," *Cancer Res.* 17 (1957): 758–66.

17. "Guidelines for Carcinogenesis Bioassay in Small Rodents," NCI Carcinogenesis Technical Report Series, 1, February, 1976.

18. M. B. Shimkin, "Species and Strain Selection," in L. Golberg, ed., *Carcinogenesis Testing of Chemicals* (Cleveland, Ohio: CRC Press, 1973), pp. 15–16.
19. NCI, "Carcinogenesis Bioassay in Small Rodents."
20. M. G. Hanna, Jr., P. Nettesheim, and J. R. Gilbert, eds., "Inhalation Carcinogenesis," U.S. Atomic Energy Commission Symposium Series, 18 (1970); Epstein, "Environmental Determinants of Cancer."
21. Epstein, "Environmental Determinants of Cancer."
22. Ibid.
23. D. B. Clayson and R. C. Garner, "Aromatic Amines and Related Chemicals," in C.S. Searle, ed., *Chemical Carcinogenesis* (Washington, D.C.: American Chemical Society, 1976).
24. Epstein, "Environmental Determinants of Cancer."
25. For a comprehensive review see R. Montesano, H. Bartsch, and L. Tomatis, eds *Screening Tests in Chemical Carcinogenesis*, IARC Scientific Publication 12 (Lyon, France, 1976); National Cancer Institute, *In Vitro Carcinogenesis: Guide to the Literature, Recent Advances, and Laboratory Procedures*, Technical Report Series, 44 (Washington, D.C., 1978).
26. B. N. Ames and J. McCann, "Carcinogens are Mutagens: A Simple Test System," in Montesano, *Screening Tests in Chemical Carcinogenesis*, pp. 493–501.
27. S. Odashima, "The Cooperative Development in Japan of Methods for Screening Chemicals for Carcinogenicity," in Montesano, *Screening Tests in Chemical Carcinogenesis*, pp. 61–75.
28. S. J. Rinkus and M. S. Legator, "Mutagenicity Testing Under the Toxic Substances Control Act," *Cancer Res.* (in press).
29. C. A. H. Bigger, J. E. Tomaszewski, and A. Dipple, "Differences between Products of Binding of 7,12-dimethylbenz(a)anthracene to DNA in Mouse Skin and in a Rat Microsomal Liver System," *Biochemical and Biophysical Research Communications* 80 (1978); 229–35.

Part II   The Science and Politics of Cancer

Chapter 5

The Workplace: Case Studies

1. U.S. Department of Labor, Bureau of Labor Statistics, "Occupational Outlook Handbook," 1974–75 ed., bull. 1785, (Washington, D.C.: 1974).
2. National Institute for Occupational Safety and Health, "The Right to Know" (Washington, D.C.: NIOSH, July, 1977.).

3. "Chemical Dangers in the Workplace," Thirty-Fourth Report by the Committee on Government Operations (Washington, D.C., September 27, 1976).
4. "The Medical/Industrial Complex," *Lancet,* 2 (1973): 1380–81.
5. U. Saffiotti and J. K. Wagoner, eds., *Occupational Carcinogenesis,* Annals of the New York Academy of Sciences, vol. 271 (New York, 1976). Proceedings of a conference on occupational carcinogenesis held March 24–27, 1975, at the New York Academy of Sciences. Many papers present up-to-date reviews and data on occupational cancer studies. This is one of the best modern scientific references on occupational carcinogenesis; B. M. Boland, ed., *Cancer and the Worker* (New York: New York Academy of Sciences, 1977), a lay version of *Occupational Carcinogenesis* written specially for workers from the perspective of NIOSH scientists; L. McGinty, "Controlling Cancer in the Workplace," *New Scientist* 76 (1977) 758–61.

Asbestos

1. P. Brodeur, *Expendable Americans* (New York: Viking, 1974). A masterful history of the occupational hazards of asbestos and the politics of their discovery and control.
2. H. Berger and R. E. Oesper, "Asbestos with Plastic and Rubber" (New York: Chemical Rubber Co., 1966).
3. I. J. Selikoff, "Cancer Risks of Asbestos Exposure" in H. H. Hiatt, J. D. Watson, and J. A. Winsten, eds., *Origins of Human Cancer,* vol. 4 (Cold Spring Harbor Laboratory, 1977), pp. 1765–84.
4. *Occupational Exposure to Asbestos: Criteria for a Recommended Standard* (Washington, D.C.: National Institute for Occupational Safety and Health, 1972), ch. 3, p. 4.
5. Ibid., ch. 3.
6. R. Doll, "Mortality from Lung Cancer in Asbestos Workers," *British Journal of Industrial Medicine* 12 (1955): 81–97.
7. I. J. Selikoff and E. C. Hammond, "Multiple Risk Factors in Environmental Cancer," in J. F. Fraumeni, Jr., ed., *Persons at High Risk of Cancer* (New York: Academic Press, 1975).
8. Brodeur, *Expendable Americans,* pt. 3.
9. D. Kotelchuck, "Asbestos Research: Winning the Battle but Losing the War," *Health/PAC Bulletin* 61 (November/December, 1974): 1–32. A good summary of the interconnection between scientists and the asbestos industry.
10. W. J. Nicholson, "Occupational and Environmental Standards for Asbestos and Their Relation to Human Disease," in Hiatt, Watson, and Winsten, eds., *Origins of Human Cancer,* pp. 1785–1796. A concise historical summary of the failure of government to regulate asbestos.
11. Ibid.; *Federal Register,* October 9, 1975, pp. 47652–65.
12. Quoted in Brodeur, *Expendable Americans,* p. 130.

13. J. C. McDonald et al., "Mortality in the Chrysotile Asbestos Mines and Mills of Quebec," *Archives of Environmental Health* 22 (1971): 677–86.
14. H. L. Seidman, American Cancer Society statistician, letter submitted to U.S. Department of Labor at 1972 asbestos hearings.
15. J. C. McDonald to David Kotelchuck, published in *Health/PAC Bull.* 71 (July/August, 1976).
16. National Cancer Institute, "Current Cancer Research on Environmental and Occupational Factors in Human Cancer, and Related Studies on Major Inorganic Carcinogens," Document NCI/ICRDB/SL-76/53 (Washington, D.C., November 4, 1977).
17. J. D. Gillam et al., "Mortality Patterns among Hard Rock Gold Miners Exposed to an Asbestiform Mineral," in U. Saffiotti and J. K. Wagoner, eds., *Occupational Carcinogenesis*, Annals of the New York Academy of Sciences, vol. 271 (New York, 1976), pp. 336–44.
18. P. Kotin and G. R. Chase, "Comments on 'Mortality Patterns Among Hard Rock Gold Miners Exposed to an Asbestiform Mineral' and 'Asbestos Fiber Exposures in a Hard Rock Gold Mine'," Johns-Manville Corp., Health and Safety Department (Denver, Colo., 1976).
19. J. K. Wagoner, et al., "Comments on 'Critique of Mortality Patterns among Hard Rock Gold Miners Exposed to an Asbestiform Mineral' and 'Asbestos Fiber Exposures in a Hard Rock Gold Mine,'" (Washington, D.C.: National Institute of Occupational Safety and Health, 1976).
20. J. F. Finklea to Assistant Secretary for Health, "Evaluation of Data on Health Effects of Asbestos Exposure and Revised Recommended Numerical Environmental Limits," December 15, 1976.
21. P. A. Greene, "OSHA Serves a Corporate Client, Ignoring Asbestos in Vanderbilt Industrial Talc" (Washington, D.C.: Public Citizen Health Research Group, 1976).
22. Ibid., p. 18.
23. Occupational Safety and Health Review Commission, Docket 10757 OSHD 20, 947, June 28, 1976.
24. International Agency for Research on Cancer, *Asbestos*, IARC Monographs on the Evaluation of Carcinogenic Risks of Chemicals to Man, vol. 14 (Lyon, France, 1977). This is the best available summary on the carcinogenicity of asbestos.
25. J. C. Wagner, C. A. Sleggs, and P. Marehand, "Diffuse Pleural Mesothelioma and Asbestos Exposure in the North Western Cape Province," *Brit. J. Ind. Med.* 17 (1960): 260–71.
26. W. Nicholson, Mt. Sinai School of Medicine, New York, quoted in Brodeur, *Expendable Americans*, p. 172.
27. R. Nader and R. Harris, "Don't Drink the Water, Don't Breathe the Air," *Environmental Action*, September 15, 1973; E. W. Lawless, *Technology and Social Shock* (New Brunswick, N.J.: Rutgers University Press, 1977) pp. 288–307.

28. T. Temple, "Protecting Lake Superior," *EPA Journal* 4 (1978): 5–9. Contains a chronological summary of the Reserve Mining case.
29. Selikoff, "Cancer Risks of Asbestos Exposure"; Nicholson, "Occupational and Environmental Standards for Asbestos"; IARC, *Asbestos.*
30. Nicholson, "Occupational and Environmental Standards for Asbestos "; IARC *Asbestos.*
31. D. L. Bayliss et al., "Mortality Patterns among Fibrous Glass Production Workers," in Saffiotti and Wagoner, eds., *Occupational Carcinogenesis*, pp. 324–35.
32. P. Kotin, *New Times*, November 25, 1977.
33. B. Castleman (1733 Riggs Place, N.W., Washington, D.C. 20009), "The Export of Hazardous Factories to Developing Nations," unpublished report, March 7, 1978.

Vinyl Chloride

1. I. J. Selikoff and E. C. Hammond, eds., *Toxicity of Vinyl Chloride–Polyvinyl Chloride*, Annals of the New York Academy of ciences, vol. 246 (New York, 1975). Proceedings of a conference on vinyl chloride with papers by most of the world's VC researchers, and with a detailed bibliography.
2. Environmental Protection Agency, "Scientific and Technical Assessment Report (STAR) on Vinyl Chloride and Polyvinyl Chloride," EPA-600/6-75-004 (Washington, D.C., June, 1975).
3. Ibid.
4. Ibid.; H. R. Simonds, *Handbook of Plastics*, 2nd ed. (Princeton, N.J.: D. Van Nostrand, 1949); E. A. Boettner and B. Weiss, "An Analytic System for Identifying the Volatile Pyrolysis Products of Plastics," *American Industrial Hygiene Association Journal* 28 (1967): 535–40; E. A. Boettner, EPA Report 670/2-73/049, July, 1973.
5. EPA, "Report on Vinyl Chloride and Polyvinyl Chloride."
6. P. L. Viola, "Cancerogenic Effect of Vinyl Chloride" (abstract), *Proceedings, X International Cancer Congress*, Houston, Texas, 1970.
7. C. W. Heath, H. Falk, and J. L. Creech, "Characteristics of Cases of Angiosarcoma of the Liver Among Vinyl Chloride Workers in the U.S." in Selikoff and Hammond, eds., *Toxicity of Vinyl Chloride–Polyvinyl Chloride*, pp. 231–36; D. Byren, and B. Holmberg, "Two Possible Cases of Angiosarcoma of the Liver in a Group of Swedish Vinyl Chloride–Polyvinyl Chloride Workers" in Selikoff and Hammond eds., *Toxicity of Vinyl Chloride*–Polyvinyl Chloride, pp. 249–50.
8. C. Maltoni, and G. Lefemine, "Carcinogenicity Bioassays of Vinyl Chloride: Current Results," Selikoff and Hammond eds., *Toxicity of Vinyl Chloride–Polyvinyl Chloride*, pp. 195–218.

9. C. Maltoni, "Vinyl Chloride Carcinogenicity: An Experimental Model for Carcinogenesis Studies," in H. H. Hiatt, J. D. Watson, and J. A. Winsten, eds., *Origins of Human Cancer*, vol. 4 (Cold Spring Harbor Laboratory, 1977), pp. 119–46.

10. J. T. Edsall, "Report of the AAAS Committee on Scientific Freedom and Responsibility," Science 188 (1975): 687–693; M. Turshen, "Disaster in Plastic," *Health/PAC Bulletin* 71 (July/August, 1976): 1–6.

11. Edsall, "Report of the Committee on Scientific Freedom and Responsibility."

12. B. W. Duck, J. T. Carter, and E. J. Coombes, "Mortality Study of Workers in a Polyvinyl Chloride Production Plant," *Lancet* 2 (1975): 1197.

13. "Exposure to Vinyl Chloride," *Federal Register* 39 (October 4, 1974).

14. S. Rattner, "Did Industry Cry Wolf?: Polyvinyl Chloride Health Rules Can Be Met," *New York Times*, December 28, 1975.

15. E. Mastromatteo et al., "Acute Inhalation Toxicity of Vinyl Chloride to Laboratory Animals," *Am. Ind. Hyg. Assoc. J.* 21 (1960): 395–401; T. R. Torkelson, F. Oyen, and V. K. Rowe, "The Toxicity of Vinyl Chloride as Determined by Repeated Exposure of Laboratory Animals," *Am. Ind. Hyg. Assoc. J.* 22 (1961): 354–361.

16. S. L. Tribukh et al., "Working Conditions and Measures for their Sanitation in the Production and Utilization of Vinyl Chloride Plastics," *Gigiena: Sanitariya* 10 (1949): 38.

17. W. N. Sokol, Y. Aelony, and G. N. Beall, "Meat-Wrapper's Asthma: A New Syndrome?" *Journal of the American Medical Association*, 226 (1973): 639–641.

18. R. J. Waxweiler et al., "Neoplastic Risk Among Workers Exposed to Vinyl Chloride," in Selikoff and Hammond, eds., *Toxicity of Vinyl Chloride–Polyvinyl Chloride*, pp. 40–48.

19. University of Louisville, Health Education Program, Vinyl Chloride Project, "VC Health Notes," vol. 5 (Louisville, Ky., 1977).

20. A. M. Kuzmack and R. E. McGaughy, "Quantitative Risk Assessment for Community Exposure to Vinyl Chloride," (Washington, D.C.: EPA, December 5, 1976).

21. Environmental Protection Agency, Office of Enforcement, "Survey of Vinyl Chloride Levels in the Vicinity of Keysor-Century, Saugus, California," EPA-330/2-77-017 (San Francisco: National Enforcement Investigation Center, Region IX, June, 1977).

22. P. F. Infante, "Oncogenic and Mutagenic Risks in Communities with PVC Production Facilities," in Saffiotti and Wagoner, eds., *Occupational Carcinogenesis*, pp. 49–57.

23. G. P. Theriault and L. Goulet (Department of Social and Preventive Medicine, Laval University, Quebec, Canada), "Birth Defects in a Community Located Near a Vinyl Chloride Plant," unpublished report, 1977.

24. B. W. Gay et al., "Measurements of Vinyl Chloride from Aerosol Sprays," in Selikoff and Hammond, eds., *Toxicity of Vinyl Chloride-Polyvinyl Chloride*, pp. 286–95.
25. R. E. Shapiro (FDA) to K. Bridbord (NIOSH) on "Vinyl Chloride Migration Data," December 18, 1974.
26. "Vinyl Chloride Emission Control," *Chemical Engineering Progress* 71 (1975): 1–62.
27. W. A. Mack, "VCM Reduction and Control," *Chemical Engineering Progress* 71 (1975): 41–44.

Bischloromethylether

1. H. E. Christensen and C. Zenz, "Compounds Associated with Carcinogenesis," in C. Zenz, ed., *Occupational Medicine: Principles & Practical Applications* (Chicago: Yearbook Medical Publishers, 1975), p. 859.
2. W. S. Randall and S. D. Solomon, *Building Six, The Tragedy at Bridesburg* (Boston: Little, Brown, 1977). Expanded from the authors' award-winning *Philadelphia Enquirer* article, "54 Who Died," a well-researched account of the Rohm & Haas Company and how it dealt with the growing evidence that many of its employees were dying of occupationally induced lung cancer.
3. Ibid., pp. 96–103.
4. Ibid., pp. 246–52.
5. Ibid., pp. 57–58.
6. Ibid.
7. Ibid., pp. 79–80.
8. S. Laskin, et al., "The Inhalation Carcinogenicity of Alpha Halo-Ethers, 2: Chronic Inhalation Studies with Chloromethyl Methyl Ether," *Archives of Environmental Health* 30 (1975): 70–72; N. Nelson, "The Chloroethers—Occupational Carcinogens: A Summary of Laboratory and Epidemiology Studies," in U. Saffiotti and J. K. Wagoner, eds., *Occupational Carcinogenesis*, Annals of the New York Academy of Sciences, vol. 271 (New York, 1976), pp. 81–90.
9. W. Weiss and K. R. Boucot, "Respiratory Effects of Chloromethyl Methyl Ether", *Journal of the American Medical Association* 234 (1975): 1139–42.
10. W. G. Figueroa, R. Raszkowski, and W. Weiss, "Lung Cancer in Chloromethyl Methyl Ether Workers," *New England Journal of Medicine* 288 (1973): 1096–97.
11. R. A. Lemen et al., "Cytologic Observations and Cancer Incidence Following Exposure to BCME," in Saffiotti and Wagoner, eds., *Occupational Carcinogenesis*, pp. 71–80.
12. A. M. Thiess, W. Hey, and H. Zeller, "Zur Toxicologie von Dichlorodimethyläther-Verdacht auf Kanzeroge Wirkung auch beim Menschen," *Zentralblatt für Arbeitsmedizin und Arbeitsschultz* 23 (1973): 97–102.

13. L. S. Frankel, K. S. McCallum, and L. Collier, "Formation of Bis-Chloromethyl Ether from Formaldehyde and Hydrogen Chloride," *Environmental Science and Technology* 8 (1974): 356–59.
14. W. C. Bauman, November 30, 1948, cited by M. Kelyman, Safety Manager, Midland Division, Dow Chemical USA, at OSHA hearings on Standards on Occupational Carcinogens, July 9, 1973.
15. H. M. Donaldson, and P. J. Shuler, "Field Survey of Dow Chemical Company Chloromethyl Ether Facilities, Midland, Michigan," (National Institute for Occupational Safety and Health, September 8, 1972).

Benzene

1. U.S. Department of Labor, Occupational Safety and Health Act, "Occupational Exposure to Benzene," *Federal Register* 42 (May 3, 1977): 22516–29. Contains a general review of experimental and human studies on benzene carcinogenesis, with many references to the primary scientific literature.
2. "High Hazards Found," *Chemical Week*, October 12, 1977, p. 19.
3. S. J. Mara and S. S. Lee, "Human Exposures to Atmospheric Benzene," Center for Resource and Environmental Systems Studies Report 30 (Stanford, Calif.: Stanford Research Institute, 1977).
4. Ibid., p. 54.
5. Ibid., pp. 129–52.
6. Ibid., p. 13
7. Ibid., p. 63.
8. Ibid., p. 65.
9. Ibid., p. 38.
10. Ibid., p. 51.
11. Ibid., p. 87
12. R. J. Young et al., "Benzene in Consumer Products," *Science* 199 (1978): 248.
13. M. McCann (Art Hazards Project, Center for Occupational Hazards, New York) to S. J. Byington (Chairman, Consumer Products Safety Commission), June 30, 1977.
14. For a narration of the Galaxy case, including an interview with Capurro, see L. Agran, *The Cancer Connection* (Boston: Houghton Mifflin, 1977).
15. "Doctor Links Galaxy, Cancer," *Washington Post*, December 14, 1977; see also P. V. Capurro and J. E. Eldridge, "Solvent Exposure and Cancer," *Lancet* 1(1978): 942.
16. B. D. Goldstein, "Benzene Health Effects Assessment" (Washington, D.C.: EPA Office of Research and Development, 1977). This EPA report summarizes information on the toxic effects of benzene on animals and humans, including a critical review of epidemiological literature indicting benzene as a leukemogenic agent.
17. M. Aksoy et al., "Acute Leukemia Due to Chronic Exposure to Benzene," *American Journal of Medicine* 52 (1972): 160–66.

18. A. Forni, and L. Moreo, "Cytogenetic Studies in a Case of Benzene Leukemia," *European Journal of Cancer* 3 (1967): 252–55; idem, "Chromosome Studies in a Case of Benzene-Induced Erythroleukemia," *Europ. J. Cancer* 5: (1969) 459–63.
19. K. Freage, J. Reitalu, and M. Berlin, "Chromosome Studies in Workers Exposed to Benzene," unpublished report, University of Lund, Sweden, 1977.
20. M. Aksoy, S. Erdem, and G. Dincol, "Leukemia in Shoe-workers Exposed Chronically to Benzene," *Blood* 44 (1974): 837–41.
21. OSHA, "Occupational Exposure to Benzene"; Goldstein, "Benzene Health Effects Assessment"; E. C. Vigliani, "Leukemia Associated with Benzene Exposure," in U. Saffiotti and J. K. Wagoner, eds., *Occupational Carcinogenesis*, Annals of the New York Academy of Sciences, vol. 271 (New York, 1976), pp. 143–51.
22. J. J. Thorpe, "Epidemiologic Survey of Leukemia in Persons Potentially Exposed to Benzene," *Journal of Occupational Medicine* 16 (1974): 375–82.
23. S. M. Brown, "Leukemia and Potential Benzene Exposure," *J. Occup. Med.* 17 (1976): 5–6.
24. P. F. Infante et al., "Leukemia in Benzene Workers," *Lancet* 2 (1977): 76–78.
25. Goldstein, "Benzene Health Effects Assessment," p. 105.
26. Ibid., p. 124–29.
27. I. M. Tough et al., "Chromosome Studies on Workers Exposed to Atmospheric Benzene," *Europ. J. Cancer* 6 (1970): 49–55.
28. S. Horiguchi, H. Okada, and K. Horiguchi, "Effect of Benzene on the Leucocytic Function of Mice," *Osaka City Medical Journal* 18 (1972): 1–8.
29. American Conference of Governmental Industrial Hygienists, "Threshold Limit Values for Substances in Workroom Air Adopted by ACGIH for 1963," (Cincinnati, Ohio, 1963).
30. Aksoy et al., "Leukemia in Shoe-workers"; Vigliani, "Leukemia Associated with Benzene Exposure."
31. National Institute for Occupational Safety and Health, "Criteria for Recommended Standard: Occupational Exposure to Benzene" (Washington, D.C., 1974), pp. 74–75.
32. National Academy of Sciences, Committee on Toxicology, "Health Effects of Benzene: A Review," (Washington, D.C., June, 1976).
33. National Institute for Occupational Safety and Health, "Occupational Exposure to Benzene: Revised Criteria for a Recommended Standard" (Washington, D.C., August, 1976).
34. Infante et al., "Leukemia in Benzene Workers."
35. Arthur D. Little, Inc., "Economic Impact Statement for Benzene" (March, 1977); see also *Chemical and Engineering News*, August 1, 1977, p. 12.

36. OSHA, "Occupational Exposure to Benzene."
37. Ibid.
38. Reported by Sylvia Krekel in *OCAW Lifelines* (see Appendix IV), July, 1977.
39. D. Hunter, *The Diseases of Occupations*, 4th ed. (Boston: Little, Brown, 1969), pp. 506–21.
40. I. R. Tabershaw, and S. H. Lamm, "Benzene and Leukemia," *Lancet* 2 (1977): 867–68.
41. P. F. Infante et al., reply to Tabershaw and Lamm "Benzene and Leukemia," *Lancet* 2 (1977): 868.
42. R. E. Olson, testimony before OSHA, Docket H-059, Washington, D.C., 1977.
43. Goldstein, "Benzene Health Effects Assessment."
44. Mara and Lee, "Human Exposures to Atmospheric Benzene."
45. R. E. Albert, "Carcinogen Assessment Groups Preliminary Report on Population Risk to Ambient Benzene Exposures" (Washington, D.C.: EPA, 1977).
46. J. D. Kilian and R. L. Daniel, "Cytogenetic Study of Workers Exposed to Benzene in the Texas Division of Dow Chemical USA," and M. C. Benge et al., "Cytogenic Study of 290 Workers Exposed to Benzene," unpublished reports, February 27, 1978; see also R. Scott, "Danger of Low-Level Benzene Reported: Dow Withheld Report on Danger," *Washington Post*, June 11, 1978.
47. W. J. Blot et al., "Cancer Mortality in U.S. Counties with Petroleum Industries," *Science* 198 (1977): 51–53.
48. Health Research Group petition to the Consumer Product Safety Commission, submitted by S. M. Wolfe and P. A. Greene, May 5, 1977.

Chapter 6

Tobacco

1. B. Ramazzini, *De Morbis Artificum Diatriba*, trans. W. C. Wright (New York: Hafner, 1964).
2. Clearinghouse for Smoking and Health, "Adult Use of Tobacco, 1975" (Atlanta, Ga.: U.S. Public Health Service, Center for Disease Control, 1975).
3. U.S. Department of Health, Education, and Welfare, "The Health Consequences of Smoking—1974" (Washington, D.C., 1974), a summary of relevant data and conclusions on smoking and health; see also U.S. Department of Health, Education, and Welfare, "Smoking Digest, Progress Report on a Nation Kicking the Habit" (Washington, D.C., October, 1977).
4. E. L. Wynder, L. S. Covey, and K. Mabuchi, "Lung Cancer in Women: Present and Future Trends," *Journal of the National Cancer Institute* 51

(1973): 391–402; see also E. L. Wynder and S. D. Stellman, "The Comparative Epidemiology of Tobacco-Related Cancers," *Cancer Research* 37 (1977): 4608–22.

5. E. L. Wynder and S. Hecht, ch. 6 in E. L. Wynder and S. Hecht, eds., *Lung Cancer* (Geneva: International Union Against Cancer, 1976). A multiauthor monograph on causes of lung cancer, including sections on epidemiology, pathology of lung cancer, immunological aspects, animal experiments, and chemistry of tobacco smoke.

6. E. C. Hammond et al. "Some Recent Findings Concerning Cigarette Smoking" in H. H. Hiatt, J. D. Watson, and J. A. Winsten, eds., *Origins of Human Cancer*, vol. 4 (Cold Spring Harbor Laboratory, 1977), pp. 101–12; for sources and original literature, see Wynder and Hecht, *Lung Cancer*, ch. 2, and Wynder and Stellman, "Comparative Epidemiology of Tobacco-Related Cancers."

7. E. L. Wynder and K. Mabuchi, "Lung Cancer Among Cigar and Pipe Smokers," *Preventive Medicine* 2 (1972): 529–42.

8. Ibid.

9. Wynder and Stellman, "Comparative Epidemiology of Tobacco-Related Cancers," p. 4615.

10. E. C. Hammond, "Tobacco," in J. F. Fraumeni, Jr., ed., *Persons at High Risk of Cancer* (Bethesda, Md.: National Cancer Institute, 1975), pp. 131–38.

11. Wynder and Stellman "Comparative Epidemiology of Tobacco-Related Cancers," p. 4613.

12. Ibid.

13. E. L. Wynder, M. Mushinski, and S. D. Stellman, "The Epidemiology of the Less Harmful Cigarette," in E. L. Wynder, D. Hoffman, and G. B. Gori, eds., *Smoking and Health*, Proceedings of the Third World Conference on Smoking and Health, 1975, pp. 1–13; E. C. Hammond et al., "'Tar' and Nicotine Content of Cigarette Smoke in Relation to Death Rates," *Environmental Research* 12 (1976): 263–74. The latter contains the latest results of the American Cancer Society's million-person prospective study, showing that smokers switching to low-tar cigarettes had a lower death rate from lung cancer than smokers of high-tar cigarettes.

14. Wynder and Hecht, eds., *Lung Cancer*, ch. 2.

15. S. J. Cutler and J. L. Young, "Demographic Patterns of Cancer Incidence in the United States," in Fraumeni, ed., *Persons at High Risk of Cancer*, pp. 307–42.

16. J. Berkson, "Smoking and Lung Cancer: Some Observations on Two Recent Reports," *American Statistical Association Journal* 53 (1958): 28–38.

17. I. Schmeltz, D. Hoffman, and E. L. Wynder, "The Influence of Tobacco Smoke on Indoor Atmospheres," *Preventive Medicine* 4 (1975): 66–82.

18. W. S. Aronow, "Carbon Monoxide and Cardiovascular Disease," in Wynder, Hoffman, and Gori, eds., *Smoking and Health*, pp. 321–328.

19. J. M. Stellman, *Women's Work, Women's Health* (New York: Pantheon, 1977).
20. E. Eckholm, "The Unnatural History of Tobacco," *Natural History*, May, 1977, pp. 22–32; see also B. R. Luce and S. O. Schweitzer, "Smoking and Alcohol Abuse: A Comparison of their Economic Consequences," *New England Journal of Medicine* 298 (1978): 569–71.
21. G. Gori, "Low-Risk Cigarettes, a Prescription," *Science* 194 (1976) 1243–46.
22. M. Schneiderman, paper given before the American Society for Preventive Oncology, April 9, 1977.
23. *Washington Star*, January 11, 1977, p. 1.
24. *New York Times*, January 13, 1978.
25. Ibid.
26. P. R. J. Burch, *The Biology of Cancer: A New Approach* (London: MTP Press, 1975). Burch is the leading British proponent of the claim that smoking is not the main cause of lung cancer. This book summarizes his arguments, most of which have been rejected by scientists.
27. A. L. Fritschler, *Smoking and Politics: Policymaking and the Federal Bureaucracy* (New York: Appleton-Century-Crofts, 1969).
28. DHEW, "The Health Consequences of Smoking—1974."
29. Quoted in *The New Yorker*, June 27, 1977, p. 23.
30. Quoted in letter from M. Daniel and M. F. Jacobson (Center for Science in the Public Interest) to V. Weingarten (Chairman, National Commission on Smoking and Public Policy), July 15, 1977.
31. Quoted in the *New York Times*, November 30, 1964.
32. Quoted in the *New York Times*, January 27, 1968.
33. Green v. American Tobacco Co. (5 Cir. 1969) 409 F.2d 1166.
34. Shimp v. New Jersey Bell Telephone Co., New Jersey Superior Court, Chancery Division, Para. 21, 421, December 20, 1976.
35. Clearinghouse for Smoking and Health, "Adult Use of Tobacco, 1975."

Red Dyes #2 and #40

1. B. T. Hunter, *Food Additives and Federal Policy: The Mirage of Safety* (New York: Scribner, 1975). A well-documented general account of food additives and governmental failure to regulate them.
2. M. F. Jacobson, "Food Colors" (Washington, D.C.: Center for Science in the Public Interest, 1972). See Appendix V.
3. C. R. Noller *Chemistry of Organic Compounds*, 2nd ed. (Philadelphia: W. B. Saunders, 1957), pp. 672–73.
4. D. B. Clayson, "Occupational Bladder Cancer," *Preventive Medicine* 5 (1976): 228–44.
5. A. J. Johnson and S. Wolfe, "Hazards of Food Colors," Report of Public Citizen, Health Research Group (see Appendix V), to FDA, January 11, 1977.

6. National Academy of Sciences, Food Protection Committee, "Food Colors" (Washington, D.C., 1971).

7. Report of the Comptroller General of the United States to Senator Gaylord Nelson, "Need to Establish the Safety of the Color Additive FD&C Red No. 2," MWD-76-40 (Washington, D.C., 1975); P. M. Boffey, "Death of a Dye," *New York Times Magazine*, February 29, 1976.

8. M. M. Adrianova, "Carcinogenic Properties of the Red Food Dyes Amaranth, Ponceaux SX, and Ponceaux 4R," *Voprosij Pitaniya* 29, no. 5 (1970).

9. Boffey, "Death of a Dye," p. 49.

10. Report of the Comptroller General, "Safety of the Color Additive FD&C Red No. 2."

11. Boffey, "Death of a Dye."

12. G. Moreland, "Warning: Red Dye #40 May Be Hazardous to Your Health," *Nutrition Action*, February, 1977, pp. 4–6; P. M. Boffey, "Color Additives: Is Successor to Red Dye No. 2 Any Safer?" *Science* 191 (1976): 832–34.

13. FDA, "Summary of Toxicological Evaluation of FD&C Red No. 40," Feb. 7, 1972.

14. Quoted in Moreland, "Red Dye #40 May Be Hazardous to Your Health," p. 4.

15. Joint FAO/WHO Expert Committee on Food Additives, 18th Report, 1974.

16. Moreland, "Red Dye #40 May Be Hazardous to Your Health."

17. Ibid.

18. Ibid.

19. M. F. Jacobson and S. S. Epstein, "Statement to FDA's Working Group on Red No. 40 Dye;" December 16, 1976.

20. Interim Report of the FDA Working Group on FD&C Red No. 40, January 19, 1977, p. 4.

21. Quoted in "Red Dye No. 40 Given Initial Clearance As Not Cancer-Causing; More Study is Set," *Wall Street Journal*, April 28, 1978.

Saccharin

1. R. W. Rhein and L. Marion, *The Saccharin Controversy: A Guide for Consumers* (New York: Monarch Press, 1977). A good guide to the history and politics of saccharin in the United States.

2. R. Q. Brewster and W. E. McEwen, *Organic Chemistry*, 3rd ed. (Englewood Cliffs, N.J.: Prentice-Hall, 1961), p. 528.

3. *Chemical Week*, March 23, 1977, p. 13.

4. Calorie Control Council, news release, June 24, 1977.

5. E. Kun and I. Horvath, "The Influence of Oral Saccharin on Blood Sugar," *Proceedings of the Society for Experimental Biology and Medicine* 66 (1947): 175–77; M. M. Thompson and J. Mayer, "Hypo-

glycemic Effects of Saccharin in Experimental Animals," *American Journal of Clinical Nutrition* 7 (1959): 80–85; E. S. Valenstein and M. L. Weber, "Potentiation of Insulin Coma by Saccharin," *Journal of Comparative and Physiological Psychology* 60 (1965): 443–46.

6. R. Friedhoff, J. A. Simon, and A. J. Friedhoff, "Sucrose Solution *vs.* No-Calorie Sweetener *vs.* Water in Weight Gain," *Journal of the American Dietetic Association* 59 (1971): 485–86.

7. M. B. McCann, M. F. Trulson, and S. C. Stulb, "Non-Caloric Sweeteners and Weight Reduction," *J. Am. Diet. Assn.* 32: (1956): 327–330.

8. National Academy of Sciences, Institute of Medicine, Committee on Saccharin, "Sweeteners: Issues and Uncertainties" (Washington, D.C., 1975), p. 165.

9. S. M. Wolfe and A. Johnson, Public Citizens Health Research Group, testimony before Subcommittee on Health, House Commerce Committee Hearings on Saccharin, March 21, 1977.

10. *Congressional Record*, September 14, 1977.

11. M. D. Reuber, "Preliminary Review of the Carcinogenicity Studies on Saccharin," unpublished Report, September 12, 1977. Summarized in Wolfe and Johnson testimony, pp. 1–6.

12. C. Noller, *The Chemistry of Organic Compounds*, 2nd ed. (Philadelphia: W. B. Saunders, 1957), p. 557.

13. C. J. Kokoski (Division of Toxicology, FDA) to R. Ronk (Director, Division of Food and Color Additives), May 3, 1977.

14. Quoted in J. E. Brody, "Scientist Says Animal Cancer Tests Must Consider Number of Causes," *New York Times*, April 6, 1977.

15. "Saccharin and Health Studies: A History of Safety" (Atlanta, Georgia: Calorie Control Council, June, 1977).

16. Ibid., p. 6.

17. R. M. Hicks, J. J. Wakefield, and J. Chowaniec, "Co-Carcinogenic Action of Saccharin in the Chemical Induction of Bladder Cancer," *Nature* 243 (1973): 347–49.

18. R. P. Batzinger, S-Y. L. Ou, and E. Bueding, "Saccharin and Other Sweeteners: Mutagenic Properties," *Science* 198 (1977): 944–46.

19. F. Burbank and J. F. Fraumeni, Jr., "Synthetic Sweetener Consumption and Bladder Cancer Trends in the U.S.," *Nature* 227 (1970): 296–97.

20. E. L. Wynder and R. Goldsmith, "The Epidemiology of Bladder Cancer: A Second Look," *Cancer* 40 (1977): 1246–68; I. I. Kessler, "Non-Nutritive Sweeteners and Human Bladder Cancer: Preliminary Findings," *Journal of Urology* 115 (1976): 143–46.

21. I. I. Kessler, "Cancer Mortality in Diabetics," *Journal of the National Cancer Institute* 44 (1970): 673–86.

22. G. R. Howe, et al., "Artificial Sweeteners and Human Bladder Cancer," *Lancet* 2 (1977): 578–81.

23. General Accounting Office, "Need to Resolve Safety Questions on Saccharin," Publication HRD-76-156, August 16, 1976.

24. Calorie Control Council, "Why is the Verdict Almost in on Saccharin When All the Evidence Isn't?" *New York Times,* May 12, 1977.
25. *New York Times,* April 6, 1977.
26. K. Isselbacher, testimony before the Subcommittee on Health and Environment, House Interstate and Foreign Commerce Committee, March 21–22, 1977.
27. Wolfe and Johnson, testimony before Subcommittee on Health.
28. *Chemical and Engineering News,* March 28, 1977, p. 22.
29. "Cancer Testing Technology and Saccharin" (Washington, D.C.: Office of Technology Assessment, U.S. Congress, June 7, 1977). A detailed analysis of the problem, with a good bibliography.
30. *Congressional Record,* September 14, 1977.

Acrylonitrile

1. "Pepsi Finds Polyester Bottles to Its Taste," *Chemical and Engineering News,* March 7, 1977, p. 5.
2. J. F. Quast et al., "Toxicity of Drinking Water Containing Acrylonitrile (AN) in Rats: Results after 12 Months," unpublished report, Toxicology Research Laboratory, Dow Chemical USA, Midland, Michigan, March 1977.
3. F. J. Murray et al., "Teratologic Evaluation of Acrylonitrile Monomer Given to Rats by Gavage," unpublished report, Dow Chemical USA, November 3, 1976.
4. S. Venitt, C. T. Bushell, and M. A. Osborne, "Mutagenicity of Acrylonitrile in *E. Coli,*" unpublished and undated report submitted to G. Newell, NCI, by Manufacturing Chemists Association (together with other attachments) on April 11, 1977.
5. M. T. O'Berg (Du Pont de Nemours Co.), "Epidemiologic Study of Workers Exposed to Acrylonitrile," unpublished report, May 13, 1977; see also I. Schwartz, "Facing up to Acrylo Problems," *Chemical Week,* June 22, 1977, pp. 38–40.
6. *Chemical Week,* January 25, 1978, p. 14.
7. "Emergency Standard Set for Acrylonitrile," *Chemical and Engineering News,* January 23,1978, p. 4.
8. Ibid.

Chapter 6

Female Sex Hormones

1. G. Pincus, *The Control of Fertility* (New York: Academic Press, 1965), a comprehensive medical text on fertility, drugs, and endocrinology; K. W.

McKerns, *Steroid Hormones and Metabolism,* (New York: Appleton-Century-Crofts, 1969), a monograph on the biochemistry and metabolism of sex hormones.

2. Forrestal, "Estrogen Hurting, Corticoids Healthy," *Chemical Week,* November 23, 1977, p. 23.
3. Ibid.; J. Rock, C. M. Garcia, and G. Pincus, "Synthetic Progestins in the Normal Human Menstrual Cycle," *Recent Progress in Hormone Research* 13 (1957): 323–39; E. W. Lawless, "Oral Contraceptive Safety Hearings," in *Technology and Social Shock* (New Brunswick, N.J.: Rutgers University Press, 1977), pp. 28–45.
4. Lawless, "Oral Contraceptive Safety Hearings," p. 30.
5. Ibid., p. 31.
6. "Estrogen Replacement Therapy: The Dangerous Road to Shangri-la," *Consumer Reports,* November, 1976.
7. P. Weideger, *Menstruation and Menopause,* (New York: Knopf, 1976).
8. E. B. Astwood, "Estrogens and Progestins," ch. 69 in L. S. Goodman and A. Gilman, eds., *The Pharmacological Basis of Therapeutics,* 4th ed. (New York: Macmillan, 1970), p. 1546.
9. J. M. Stellman, *Women's Work, Women's Health* (New York: Pantheon, 1977).
10. P. Christy, "Diseases of the Endocrine System," in P. B. Beeson and W. McDermott, eds., *Cecil-Loeb Textbook of Medicine,* 13th ed., (Philadelphia: Saunders, 1971), p. 1722.
11. R. I. Pfeffer, "Estrogen Use in Post-Menopausal Women," *American Journal of Epidemiology* 105 (1977): 21–29.
12. Astwood, "Estrogens and Progestins," pp. 1546–48.
13. Lawless, "The Diethylstilbestrol Ban," in *Technology and Social Shock,* pp. 70–82.
14. This incident is discussed in N. Wade, "DES: A Case Study in Regulatory Abdication," *Science* 177 (1977): 335–37; see also, J. N. S. White, "The Stilbestrol Conspiracy," *Natural Food and Farming,* March, 1973, pp. 15–19.
15. Discussed and quoted in M. Mintz, "Kennedy Sets Hill Hearings on Continued Use of DES," *Washington Post,* July 14, 1972.
16. Ibid.
17. *Sex Hormones,* International Agency for Research on Cancer monograph on the Evaluation of Carcinogenic Chemicals to Man, vol. 6 (Lyon, France, 1974). A compendium of experimental data on carcinogenicity of male and female sex hormones.
18. Ibid.
19. J. A. McLachlan and R. L. Dixon, "Transplacental Toxicity of Diethylstilbestrol: A Special Problem in Safety Evaluation," ch. 13 in M. A. Mehlman, R. E. Shapiro, and H. Blumenthal, eds., *Advances in Modern Toxicology,* vol. 1, pt. 2, "New Concepts in Safety Evaluation," (Washington, D.C.: Hemisphere Publishing Corp., 1976), pp. 423–448.

20. *Sex Hormones,* IARC monograph.
21. H. K. Ziel and W. D. Finkel, "Increased Risk of Endometrial Carcinoma among Users of Conjugated Estrogens," *New England Journal of Medicine* 293 (1975): 1167–70.
22. "Estrogen Drugs," *Science* 191 (1976): 838–41.
23. R. Hoover et al., "Geographic Patterns of Cancer Mortality," ch. 20 in J. F. Fraumeni, Jr., ed., *Persons at High Risk of Cancer* (New York: Academic Press, 1975), pp. 343–60.
24. R. Hoover, L. A. Gray, and J. F. Fraumeni, Jr., "Stilbestrol and the Risk of Ovarian Cancer," *Lancet* 2 (1977): 533.
25. R. Hoover et al., "Menopausal Estrogens and Breast Cancer," *N. Eng. J. Med.* 295 (1976): 401–5.
26. M. R. Melamed et al., "Prevalence Rates of Uterine Cervical Carcinoma *in situ* for Women Using the Diaphragm or Contraceptive Oral Steroids," *British Medical Journal* 3 (1969): 195.
27. H. A. Edmondson, B. Henderson, and B. Benton, "Liver-Cell Adenomas Associated with Use of Oral Contraceptives," *N. Eng. J. Med.* 294 (1976): 470–72.
28. A. L. Herbst and R. E. Scully, "Adenocarcinoma of the Vagina in Adolescence: A Report of 7 Cases Including 6 Clear-Cell Carcinomas (So-called Mesonephromas)," *Cancer* 25 (1970): 745–57.
29. A. L. Herbst, H. Ulfelder, and D. C. Poskanzer, "Adenocarcinoma of the Vagina: Association of Maternal Stilbestrol Therapy with Tumor Appearance in Young Women," *N. Eng. J. Med.* 284 (1971): 878–81; K. L. Noller, et al., "Clear-Cell Adenocarcinoma of the Cervix After Maternal Treatment with Synthetic Estrogens," *Mayo Clinic Proceedings* 47 (1972): 629–30.
30. W. J. Dieckmann et al., "Does the Administration of Diethylstilbestrol during Pregnancy Have Any Therapeutic Value," *American Journal of Obstetrics and Gynecology* 66 (1953): 1062–81.
31. M. Bibbo, et al., "Follow-up Study of Male and Female Offspring of DES-Exposed Mothers," *Journal of the American College of Obstetrics & Gynecology* 49 (1977): 1–8.
32. S. Wolfe (Public Citizen Health Research Group) to HEW Secretary Joseph Califano, December 12, 1977.
33. "Mortality Associated with the Pill," *Lancet* 2 (1977): 747–48; "Mortality and Oral Contraceptives," *Br. Med. J.* 2 (1977): 918.
34. M. Mintz, *By Prescription Only* (Boston: Houghton-Mifflin, 1967). An early report to laymen on potential hazards of pill usage.
35. W. H. W. Inmann and M. P. Vessey, "Investigation of Deaths from Pulmonary, Coronary, and Cerebral Thrombosis and Embolism in Women of Childbearing Age," *Br. Med. J.* 2 (1968): 193–99; M. Mintz, *The Pill: An Alarming Report* (Boston: Beacon Press, 1970). An update of Mintz' earlier book on the problems of pill usage.
36. Mintz, *The Pill.*

37. Royal College of General Practitioners' Oral Contraception Study, "Mortality Among Oral Contraceptive Users," *Lancet* 2 (1977): 727; M. P. Vessey, K. McPherson, and B. Johnson, "Mortality Among Women Participating in the Oxford Family Planning Association Contraceptive Study," *Lancet* 2 (1977): 731.
38. "OSHA Fines Dawes Labs $34,100," *OCAW Lifelines,* July, 1977.
39. Ibid.
40. U.S. Public Health Service, Center for Disease Control, *Morbidity and Mortality Weekly Report,* April 1, 1977.
41. *Sex Hormones,* IARC monograph.
42. Mintz, "Kennedy Sets Hearings on DES."
43. Wade, "DES: A Case Study in Regulatory Abdication"; White, "The Stilbestrol Conspiracy"; B. Doerschuk, "The DES Controversy: Beyond the Tip of the Iceberg," *Nutrition Action,* April, 1976; see also H. Wellford, *Sowing the Wind* (New York: Grossman Publishers, 1972).
44. Ibid.
45. Wade, "DES: A Case Study in Regulatory Abdication"; White, "The Stilbestrol Conspiracy."
46. Doerschuk, "The DES Controversy"; Wellford, *Sowing the Wind.*
47. Wade, "DES: A Case Study in Regulatory Abdication," pp. 336–37.
48. S. S. Epstein, "Federal Food Inspection Act of 1973," testimony before the Senate Commerce Committee, Hearings of Toxic Substances Control Act of 1973, U.S. Senate, March 21, 1973.
49. Ibid., quotation, p. 261.
50. "Food Producing Animals: Criteria and Procedures for Evaluating Assay for Carcinogenic Residues," *Federal Register,* February 22, 1977, pp. 10412–37.
51. Lawless, "Oral Contraceptive Safety Hearings."
52. Pharmaceutical Manufacturers Association et al. v. Food and Drug Administration et al., Civil No. 77-291, U.S. District Court for the District of Delaware, 1977.

Chapter 7
The General Environment: Case Studies

Pesticides

1. U.S. Department of Health, Education, and Welfare, *Report of the Secretary's Commission on Pesticides and Their Relationship to Environmental Health,* (Washington, D.C.: December, 1969), ch. 1; J. E. Blodgett, "Pesticides: Regulation of an Evolving Technology," in S. S. Epstein and R. Grundy, eds., *Consumer Health and Product Hazards: Cosmetics and Drugs, Pesticides, Food Additives,* Legislation of Product Safety, vol. 2 (Cambridge, Mass.: MIT Press, 1974), pp. 198–287.
2. W. Olkowski et al., "Ecosystem Management: A Framework for Urban Pest Control," *Bioscience* 26 (1976): 384–89; H. Olkowski and W. Ol-

kowski, "How to Control Garden Pests without Killing Almost Everything Else," (Washington, D.C.: Rachel Carson Trust for the Living Environment, 1976); M. F. Jacobson, "Agriculture's New Hero: IPM," *Nutrition Action*, January, 1978, pp. 3–12; "Farmers and the Environment," *EPA Journal* March, 1978; R. van den Bosch, *The Pesticide Conspiracy* (New York: Doubleday, 1978).

3. Van den Bosch, *Pesticide Conspiracy;* H. Wellford, *Sowing the Wind* (New York: Grossman Publishers, 1972), ch. 9.
4. Van den Bosch, *Pesticide Conspiracy.*
5. R. Carson, *Silent Spring* (Boston: Houghton-Mifflin, 1962).
6. F. Graham, *Since Silent Spring* (Boston: Houghton-Mifflin 1970).
7. Ibid., p. 57.
8. R. Carson, *Silent Spring,* p. 12.
9. Blodgett, "Pesticides: Regulation of an Evolving Technology."
10. International Agency for Research on Cancer, "Some Organochlorine Pesticides," IARC Monographs on the Evaluation of Carcinogenic Risk of Chemicals to Man, vol. 5 (Lyon, France, 1974).
11. Van den Bosch, *Pesticide Conspiracy;* Wellford, *Sowing the Wind;* L. Tallian, *Politics and Pesticides* (Los Angeles: People's Lobby Press, 1975).
12. Van den Bosch, *Pesticide Conspiracy.*
13. D. Pimentel, "Ecological Effects of Pesticides on Non-Target Species" (Washington, D.C.: Office of Science and Technology, June, 1971); see also E. H. Smith and D. Pimentel, *Pest Control Strategies,* (New York: Academic Press, 1978); and D. Pimentel et al., "Environmental and Social Costs of Pesticide Use," draft report to the EPA Pesticide Policy Committee, May 16, 1978.

Aldrin/Dieldrin

1. C. F. Wurster, "Aldrin and Dieldrin," *Environment* 13 (1971): 33–45; U.S. Environmental Protection Agency, Office of the General Counsel, Attorneys for Respondent, "Respondent's Brief, Proposed Findings and Conclusion on Suspension," in re Shell Chemical Company et al., Consolidated Aldrin/Dieldrin Hearing, FIFRA Dockets 145 et al., Washington, D.C., September 16, 1974. The latter is a good and concise account of environmental contamination, carcinogenicity and other hazards, and lack of efficacy of aldrin/dieldrin.
2. EPA, "Respondent's Brief," pp. 146–64.
3. Wurster, "Aldrin and Dieldrin."
4. B. D. Ayers, "Killing of Contaminated Chickens Begins in Mississippi," *New York Times*, March 14, 1974; V.K. McElheny, "Animal Feed Oils Tainted by Insecticide Recalled," *New York Times*, April 19, 1974.
5. EPA, "Respondents Brief," pp. 188–215.
6. EPA, "Respondent's Brief."

7. U.S. Department of Health, Education, and Welfare, "Reports of the Secretary's Commission on Pesticides and Their Relationship to Environmental Health" (Washington, D.C., December, 1969), p. 470.

8. EPA, "Respondnt's Brief," pp. 28–56; see also L. Gibney. "EPA Broadens Approach to Pesticide Decisions," *Chemical and Engineering News,* November 3, 1975, p. 15.

9. S. S. Epstein, "The Carcinogenicity of Dieldrin," *Science of the Total Environment* 4 (1975): 1–52, 205–217; see also National Cancer Institute, "Bioassays of Aldrin and Dieldrin for Possible Carcinogenicity," Technical Report Series, 21 (1978); and idem, "Bioassay of Dieldrin for Possible Carcinogenicity," Technical Report Series, 22 (1978).

10. Ibid.

11. Ibid.

12. EPA, "Respondent's Brief," pp. 127–45; Epstein, "The Carcinogenicity of Dieldrin."

13. EPA, "Respondent's Brief," pp. 75–78.

14. Ibid., p. 131. See also EPA Suspension Hearings, 1974, testimony of P. Newberne, Shell Ex. S-9, p. 20.

15. Ibid., p. 95–98.

16. Ibid., p. 140

17. K. W. Jager, *Aldrin, Dieldrin, Endrin, and Telodrin* (Amsterdam: Elsevier, 1970).

18. Epstein, "The Carcinogenicity of Dieldrin," pp. 15–16.

19. EPA, "Respondent's Brief," p. 113.

20. Epstein, "The Carcinogenicity of Dieldrin," pp. 15–16; EPA, "Respondent's Brief," pp. 109–13.

21. EPA, "Respondent's Brief," p. 109.

22. Ibid.

23. President's Science Advisory Committee, "Use of Pesticides" (Washington, D.C., April 15, 1963).

24. Epstein, "The Carcinogenicity of Dieldrin"; NCI, "Bioassays of Aldrin and Dieldrin"; idem, "Bioassay of Dieldrin."

25. U.S. Department of Health, Education, and Welfare, "Report of the Secretary's Commission on Pesticides."

26. National Academy of Sciences, National Research Council, "Advisory Committee Report on Aldrin/Dieldrin" (Washington, D.C., March, 1972).

27. Ayers, "Killing of Contaminated Chickens Begins"; McElheny, "Animal Feed Oils Recalled."

28. EPA, "Respondent's Brief."

29. H. L. Perlman, (Chief Administrative Law Judge), "Recommended Decision, Aldrin/Dieldrin Suspension Hearings," FIFRA Dockets 145 et al., September 20, 1974.

30. "Opinion of the Administrator, EPA, on the Suspension of Aldrin-Dieldrin," FIFRA Dockets 145 et al., October 1, 1974.

31. Council for Agricultural Science and Technology (CAST), "The Environmental Protection Agency's Nine 'Principles' of Carcinogenicity," CAST Report 4, (Ames, Iowa: Iowa State University, Department of Agronomy, 1976); see also "Comments on Health Risk and Economic Impact Assessments of Suspected Carcinogens: Interim Procedures and Guidelines," CAST Report 73, December 30, 1977.
32. B. Gillespie, D. Eva, and R. Johnston, "A Tale of Two Pesticides," *New Scientist* 77 (1978): 350–52.

Chlordane/Heptachlor

1. U.S. Environmental Protection Agency, Office of the General Counsel, Attorneys for Respondent, "Respondent's Final Brief," in re Velsicol Chemical Corporation et al., Chlordane and Heptachlor, FIFRA Docket 384, Washington, D.C., December 8, 1975. A good and concise account of environmental contamination, carcinogenicity and other hazards of chlordane/heptachlor.
2. Ibid., pp. 77–85.
3. Ibid., pp. 135–39.
4. Ibid., pp. 115–33.
5. Ibid., pp. 140–56.
6. S. S. Epstein, "The Carcinogenicity of Heptachlor and Chlordane," *Science of the Total Environment* 6 (1976): 103–54.
7. U.S. Department of Health, Education, and Welfare, Report of the Secretary's Commission on Pesticides and Their Relationship to Environmental Health (Washington, D.C., December, 1969), p. 470.
8. National Cancer Institute, "Bioassay of Chlordane for Possible Carcinogenicity," Technical Report Series, 8 (Washington, D.C., 1977); idem, "Bioassay of Heptachlor for Possible Carcinogenicity," Technical Report Series, 9 (Washington, D.C., 1977).
9. Epstein, "Carcinogenicity of Heptachlor and Chlordane."
10. Ibid., pp. 116–17.
11. NCI, "Bioassay of Chlordane"; idem, "Bioassay of Heptachlor."
12. National Academy of Sciences, National Research Council, Advisory Center on Toxicology, Pesticide Information Review and Evaluation Committee, "An Evaluation of the Carcinogenicity of Chlordane and Heptachlor" (Washington, D.C., October, 1977).
13. EPA, "Respondent's Final Brief," p. 221.
14. Ibid., p. 222.
15. Ibid., pp. 230–40.
16. Ibid., p. .82–92.
17. P. F. Infante and S. S. Epstein, "Blood Dyscrasias and Childhood Tumors and Exposures to Chlorinated Hydrocarbon Pesticides," in *Proceedings of the June 17–19, 1976, Conference on Women and the Work-*

place (Washington, D.C.: Society for Occupational and Environmental Health, 1977), pp. 51–74.

18. U.S. Environmental Protection Agency Office of the General Counsel, Attorney for Respondent, "Respondent's First Pretrial Brief," in re Velsicol Chemical Corporation et al., Consolidated Heptachlor/Chlordane Hearings, FIFRA Dockets 336 et al., April 1, 1975.

19. Velsicol's first prehearing brief, FIFRA Dockets 336 et al., May 1, 1975.

20. D. Zinman, B. Wyrick and D. Hevesi, "Scientist's Role is Questioned," *Newsday*, January 18, 1977; see also, "Rep. Obey Questions Contract on Cancer," *Washington Post*, June 12, 1977.

21. EPA, Respondent's Final Brief, pp. 331–41.

22. "NCI Carcinogenesis Draft Sparks Backlash," *Blue Sheet* 19, no. 4, January 28, 1976.

23. H. L. Perlman, (Chief Administrative Law Judge), "Recommended Decision," in re Velsicol Chemical Corporation et al., FIFRA Docket 384, December 12, 1975.

24. Ibid.

25. "Decision of the Administrator, EPA, on the Suspension of Heptachlor-Chlordane," in re Velsicol Chemical Corporation et al., FIFRA Docket 384, December 24, 1975.

26. *Federal Register*, March 24, 1978, pp. 12372–75.

27. N. Sheppard, Jr., "Maker of Pesticides Indicted on Charges of Hiding Test Data," *New York Times*, December 13, 1977.

Nitrosamines

1. W. Lijinsky and S. S. Epstein, "Nitrosamines as Environmental Carcinogens," *Nature* 225 (1970): 21–23.

2. P. N. Magee, R. Montesano, and R. Preussmann, "N-Nitroso Compounds and Related Carcinogens," in C. E. Searle, ed., *Chemical Carcinogens* (Washington, D. C.: American Chemical Society, 1976), pp. 491–625; Lijinsky and Epstein, "Nitrosamines as Environmental Carcinogens."

3. J. Sander, "Formation of Carcinogenic Nitroso Compounds under Biological Conditions," in *Environment and Cancer* (Baltimore, Md.: Williams and Wilkins, 1972), pp. 109–117.

4. Magee, Montesano, and Preussmann, "N-Nitroso Compounds and Related Carcinogens"; Sander, "Formation of Carcinogenic Nitroso Compounds"; S. S. Mirvish, "Formation of N-Nitroso Compounds: Chemistry, Kinetics and *in vivo* Occurrence," *Toxicology and Applied Pharmacology* 31 (1975): 325–51.

5. D. H. Fine et al., "N-Nitroso Compounds: Detection in Ambient Air," *Science* 192 (1976): 1328–30.

6. Magee, Montesano, and Preussmann, "N-Nitroso Compounds and Related Carcinogens."

7. International Agency for Research on Cancer, "Environmental N-Nitroso Compounds, Analysis and Formation," IARC Scientific Publication 14 (Lyon, France, 1976), an excellent collection of a wide range of multi-authored chapters; D. H. Fine et al., "Human Exposure to N-Nitroso Compounds in the Environment," in H. H. Hiatt, J. D. Watson, and J. A. Winsten eds., *Origins of Human Cancer* (Cold Spring Harbor Laboratory, 1977), pp. 293–307.
8. Fine et al., "N-Nitroso Compounds: Detection in Ambient Air."
9. National Academy of Sciences, "Air Quality and Automobile Emission Control," vol. 2, (Washington, D.C., 1974) pp. 282–83.
10. IARC, "N-Nitroso Compounds, Analysis and Formation."
11. S. S. King, "Nitrate Reduction Ordered in Bacon," *New York Times*, May 16, 1978.
12. U.S. House of Representatives, Committee on Interstate and Foreign Commerce, Hearings before the Subcommittee on Overnight and Investigations, May 28 and September 20, 1976.
13. Ibid., pp. 302–21.
14. Ibid., p. 218.
15. Ibid., p. 281.
16. IARC, "N-Nitroso Compounds, Analysis and Formation."
17. Ibid.
18. "N-Nitrosamines Found in Sidestream Smoke," *Chemical and Engineering News*, June 13, 1977, p. 18.
19. Hearings before the Subcommittee on Oversight and Investigation, p. 248–73.
20. Ibid.
21. Ibid., p. 71.
22. J. K. Wagoner et al. to Director, NIOSH, "NIOSH Investigation of Cancer Hazard at E.I. Du Pont de Nemour & Company, Belle Plant," February 2, 1977.

Chapter 8
How to Improve Industry Data

1. S. S. Epstein, "Cancer and the Environment," *Bulletin of the Atomic Scientists (of Chicago)* 26 (1977): 22–30.
2. Ibid.
3. *Federal Register*, August 8, 1967.
4. U.S. Department of Health, Education, and Welfare, Report of the Secretary's Commission on Pesticides and Their Relationship to Environmental Health, Washington, D.C., December, 1969.
5. P. Boffey, "Color Additives: Is Successor to Red Dye No. 2 Any Safer?" *Science* 191 (1976): 832–34; see also G. Moreland, "Warning: Red Dye

#40 May Be Hazardous to Your Health," *Nutrition Action*, February 4, 1977.

6. S. S. Epstein, "The Carcinogenicity of Dieldrin," *Science of the Total Environment* 4 (1975): 1–52, 205–17; S. S. Epstein, "The Carcinogenicity of Heptachlor and Chlordane," *Science of the Total Environment* 6 (1976): 103–54; see also idem, "The Carcinogenicity of Organochlorine Pesticides," in H. H. Hiatt, J. D. Watson, and J. A. Winsten eds., *Origins of Human Cancer* (Cold Spring Harbor Laboratory, 1977), pp. 243–45.

7. Ibid.

8. M. D. Reuber, "Review of Toxicity Test Results Submitted in Support of Pesticide Tolerance Petitions," *Science of the Total Environment* 9 (1977): 135–48.

9. Staff Report to the Subcommittee on Administrative Practice and Procedures of the Committee on the Judiciary, U.S. Senate, "The Environmental Protection Agency and the Regulation of Pesticides," December, 1976.

10. S. S. Epstein, "The Delaney Amendment and on Mechanisms for Reducing Constraints in the Regulatory Process in General, and as Applied to Food Additives in Particular," Hearings before the Select Committee on Nutrition and Human Needs, U.S. Senate, September 20, 1972.

11. A. M. Schmidt, Statement before the Subcommittee on Health of the Committee on Labor and Public Welfare, and the Subcommittee on Administrative Practice and Procedures of the Committee on the Judiciary, U.S. Senate, January 20, 1976.

12. S. S. Epstein, "Toxicological and Environmental Implications on the Use of Nitrilotriacetic Acid as a Detergent Builder," Staff Report to the Committee on Public Works, U.S. Senate, December, 1970; see also, S. S. Epstein, *International Journal Environmental Studies* 2 (1972): 291–300; 3 (1972): 13–21.

13. S. S. Epstein, "The Public Interest Overview," *Environmental Health Perspectives*, 10 (1975): 173.

14. Epstein, "Cancer and the Environment."

15. Ibid.

16. J. R. M. Innes et al., "Bioassay of Pesticides and Industrial Chemicals for Tumorigenicity in Mice: A Preliminary Note," *Journal of the National Cancer Institute* 43 (1969): 1101–14.

17. U.S. Department of Labor, transcript, Occupational Safety and Health Advisory Committee, Proceedings Standards, Advisory Committee on Occupational Carcinogens, August, 1973.

18. B. A. Schwetz, G. L. Sparschu, and P. J. Gehring, "The Effect of 2,4-D and Esters of 2,4-D on Rat Embryonal, Foetal, and Neonatal Growth and Development," *Food Cosmetics Toxicology* 9 (1971): 801–17.

19. S. S. Epstein, "Kepone: Hazard Evaluation," *Science of the Total Environment* 9 (1978): 1–62.

20. Epstein, "Carcinogenicity of Heptachlor and Chlordane"; idem, "Carcinogenicity of Organochlorine Pesticides."
21. "Hiding Danger of Pesticides," *New York Times*, December 18, 1977.
22. J. T. Edsall, "Report of the AAAS Committee on Scientific Freedom and Responsibility," *Science* 188 (1975): 687–93.
23. See note 17 above.
24. "Lab Officials Admit Shredding Test Data," *Washington Post*, September 20, 1977; "Testing Lab Errors Hinder Army Food Project," *Chemical and Engineering News*, November 14, 1977; B. Richards, "Probers Say Pesticide Makers Knew of Faulty Lab Test Data," *Washington Post*, March 9, 1978.
25. Ibid.
26. Ibid.
27. "Filling in Toxicology Gaps," *Chemical Week*, November 17, 1976, pp. 36–37.
28. W. Reddig, "Industry's Preemptive Strike Against Cancer," *Fortune*, February 13, 1978.
29. S. S. Epstein, "The Delaney Amendment and on Mechanism for Reducing Constraints in the Regulatory Process, in General, and as Applied to Food Additives, in Particular," testimony before the Select Committee on Nutrition and Human Needs, U.S. Senate, September 20, 1972.

Part III   The Politics of Cancer

Chapter 9
Governmental Policies

1. Office of Science and Technology, Council on Environmental Quality Ad Hoc Committee, "Report on Environmental Health Research," (Washington, D.C., June, 1972).
2. S. P. Strickland, *Politics, Science, and Dread Disease: A Short History of United States Medical Research Policy.* (Cambridge, Mass.: Harvard University Press, 1972). A historical analysis of the background and development of the National Cancer Institute and national policies on cancer research prior to 1971.
3. Public Law 92-218, 85 Stat. 778 (42 U.S.C. 218 *et seq.*), December 23, 1971.
4. L. Agran, *The Cancer Connection and What We Can Do about It* (Boston: Houghton-Mifflin 1977), pp. 171–186.
5. Ibid.
6. Examples of Hueper's 350 scientific publications on cancer include: *Occupational Tumors and Allied Diseases* (Springfield, Ill.: Charles C. Thomas, 1942); *Occupational and Environmental Cancers of the Respira-*

tory System (New York: Springer Verlag, 1966); *Occupational and Environmental Cancers of the Urinary System,* (New Haven, Conn.: Yale University Press, 1969); "Medicolegal Considerations of Occupational and Nonoccupational Environmental Cancer," in C. J. Frankel and R. M. Patterson, eds., *Lawyers' Medical Cyclopedia,* vol. 5B, rev., (Indianapolis, Ind.: Allen Smith Company, 1972), pp. 293–568.

7. S. S. Epstein, "Presentation of the First Annual Award of the Society for Occupational and Environmental Health to Wilhelm C. Hueper," in U. Saffiotti and J. K. Wagoner, eds., *Occupational Carcinogenesis,* Annals of the New York Academy of Science, 271, (New York, 1976).

8. Agran, *The Cancer Connection,* pp. 171–186.

9. Strickland, *Politics, Science, and Dread Disease.*

10. R. A. Rettig, *Cancer Crusade: The Story of the National Cancer Act of 1971* (Princeton, N.J.: Princeton University Press, 1977). A blow-by-blow legislative history of the Act, describing the influences of the various pressure groups.

11. Rettig, *Cancer Crusade,* p. 79.

12. U.S. Senate, Report of the National Panel of Consultants on the Conquest of Cancer, S. Doc. 92-9, 92nd Cong. 1st Sess., 1971.

13. Rettig, *Cancer Crusade,* pp. 18–41.

14. H. L. Perlman (Chief Administrative Law Judge), "Recommended Decision," in re Velsicol Chemical Corporation et al., FIFRA Docket 384, December 12, 1975.

15. D. Zinman, B. Wyrick, and D. Hevesi, "Scientist's Role is Questioned," *Newsday,* January 18, 1977.

16. Ibid.

17. Ibid.

18. Ibid.; see also K. Gage and S. S. Epstein, "The Federal Advisory Committee System," *Environmental Law Reporter* 7 (1977): 50001–12.

19. Zinman, Wyrick, and Hevesi, "Scientist's Role is Questioned."

20. "Rep. Obey Questions Contract on Cancer," *Washington Post,* June 12, 1977.

21. Report of the Comptroller General of the United States, "Need to Improve Administration of a Carcinogen Testing and Carcinogenesis Research Contract" (HRD-78-44), Washington, D.C., February 10, 1978.

22. L. Parrott, "Regent: HEW Wants Eppley to Repay," *Omaha World-Herald,* April 23, 1978; see also J. Shapiro, "Dr. Shubik and Eppley Institute: From Hope to Embarrassment," Sun newspapers of Omaha, special report, June 15, 1978.

23. D. Greenberg, "Cancer: Now the Bad News," *Washington Post,* January 19, 1975; Greenberg, D., Science and Government Report, April 1, 1975; "Cancer Patient Survival," Surveillance, Epidemiology and End Results (SEER) Program, Report no. 5, Publication (NIH) 77-992 (Washington, D.C., 1976).

24. Report to the Congress by the Comptroller General of the United States, "Federal Efforts to Protect the Public From Cancer-Causing Chemicals Are Not Very Effective" (MWD-76-59), Washington, D.C., 1976.
25. U.S. House of Representatives, Cong. D. Obey, Hearings before the Subcommittee of the Committee on Appropriations, 94th Cong., National Cancer Institute, February 25, 1976, pp. 64–208.
26. U. Saffiotti to Director, NCI, April 23, 1976; see also, *Cancer Letter* 2 (1976): 5–8; N. Wade, "Cancer Institute: Expert Charges Neglect of Carcinogenesis Studies," *Science* 192 (1976): 529–31.
27. A. Upton, "On Cancer Cause and Prevention Activities of NCI," testimony before the Subcommittee on Oversight and Investigation, House Committee on Interstate and Foreign Commerce, January 23, 1978.
28. Rettig, *Cancer Crusade*, p. 320.
29. Gage and Epstein, "Federal Advisory Committee System."
30. S. S. Epstein, "A Catch-all Toxicological Screen," *Experientia* 25 (1969): 617–18.
31. National Institute of Occupational Safety and Health, Division of Criteria Documentation and Standards Development, "Summary of NIOSH Recommendations for Occupational Health Standards" (Washington, D.C., June, 1977).
32. "Occupational Carcinogenesis Program," DHEW (NIOSH) Publication 77–111, (Washington, D.C., September 30, 1976); see also Hearings before a Subcommittee of the Committee on Appropriations, House of Representatives, pt. 3, 1977, pp. 162–163.
33. *Chemical and Engineering News*, December 16, 1976.
34. U.S. Department of Health, Education, and Welfare, Center for Disease Control, National Institute for Occupational Safety and Health, *National Occupational Hazard Survey*, vol. 1, "Survey Manual," DHEW (NIOSH) Publication 74-127 (Rockville, Md., 1971); vol. 2, "Data Editing and Data Base Development," 77-213 (Cincinnati, Ohio, 1977); vol. 3, "Survey Analysis and Supplemental Tables," 78–114 (Cincinnati, Ohio, 1977).
35. U.S. Department of Health, Education, and Welfare, Center of Disease Control, National Institute for Occupational Safety and Health, "The Right to Know: Practical Problems and Policy Issues Arising from Exposures to Hazardous Chemical and Physical Agents in the Workplace" (Washington, D.C., July, 1977); see also, "Chemical Dangers in the Workplace," Thirty-Fourth Report of the Committee on Government Operations, House of Representatives, September 27, 1976.
36. NIOSH, "The Right to Know," p. 3.
37. Ibid., p. 33.
38. U.S. House of Representatives, C. Edwards testimony, Hearings before a Subcommittee on Agriculture and Related Agencies, House Appropriations Committee, April, 1971; see also *Food Chemical News*, April 26, 1971.

39. U.S. House of Representatives, FDA testimony Hearings before a Subcommittee on Agriculture and Related Agencies, House Appropriations Committee, pt. 5, 1975, pp. 141–42.

40. H. L. Stewart, "Report of the Director's *ad hoc* Committee on Testing for Environmental Chemical Carcinogens" (Washington, D.C.: NCI, August, 1973).

41. National Academy of Sciences, National Research Council, "The National Center for Toxicological Research: The Evaluation of its Program" (Washington, D.C., 1977).

42. "NCTR Conflict of Interest Allegation Referred to Justice Department," *Food Chemical News*, April 24, 1978, pp. 3–6.

43. Environmental Quality Improvement Act of 1970, Public Law 91–190, January 1, 1970.

44. E. Dolgin, *Federal Environmental Law*, (St. Paul, Minn.: West Publishing, 1974); M. L. Karstadt, "Protecting the Public Health from Hazardous Substances: Federal Regulation of Environmental Contaminants," *Environmental Law Reporter* 5 (1975): 50165–78. A useful summary of scientific problems underlying regulation.

45. S. S. Epstein and R. Grundy, eds., *Consumer Health and Product Hazards*, vol. 1, "Chemicals, Electronic Products, Radiation"; vol. 2, "Cosmetics and Drugs, Pesticides, Food Additives," Legislation of Product Safety (Cambridge, Mass.: MIT Press, 1974).

46. Public Law 91-596, 91st Congress S. 2193, December 29, 1970; see also, Occupational Safety and Health Act of 1970 (Oversight and Proposed Amendments), Hearings before the Select Subcommittee on Labor, Committee on Education and Labor, House of Representatives, 92nd Cong., 1972, and 93rd Cong., 1974.

47. N. Ashford, *Crisis in the Workplace*, (Cambridge, Mass.: MIT Press, 1976).

48. U.S Department of Labor, Occupational Safety and Health Administration, "Identification, Classification and Regulation of Toxic Substances Posing a Potential Carcinogenic Risk," *Federal Regulation*, pt. 6, October 4, 1977.

49. L. Ember, "OSHA on the Move," *Environmental Science and Technology* 11 (1977): 1142–47.

50. American Industrial Health Council, "AIHC Recommended Alternatives to OSHA's Generic Carcinogen Policy" (Scarsdale, N.Y., January 9, 1978).

51. "Chemical Dangers in the Workplace," p. 8.

52. U.S. Congress, *Clean Air gamendments of 1970*, Conference Report No. 91–1783, 81st Cong. 2nd Sess., 1970, *U.S. Congressional and Administration News*, (1970): 5378–79, 1970; see also W. H. Rodgers, *Handbook on Environmental Law*, (St. Paul, Minn: West Publishing Co., 1977).

53. U.S. Senate Committee on Public Workers, Federal Water Pollution Control Act Amendments of 1971, S. Rep. No. 1414, 92nd Cong. 1st Sess., 1971; See also Rodgers, *Handbook on Environmental Law*, p. 482.

54. J. E. Blodgett, "Pesticides: Regulation of an Evolving Technology," in Epstein and Grundy, eds., *Consumer Health and Product Hazards: Cosmetics and Drugs, Pesticides, Food Additives*, vol. 2, pp. 198–287; H. Wellford, *Sowing the Wind* (New York: Grossman, 1972), pp. 310–53.
55. Blodgett, "Pesticides: Regulation of an Evolving Technology."
56. Ibid.: Federal Environmental Pesticide Control Act, Public Law No. 92–516, 1972.
57. *Federal Regulation* 40 (1975): 28241; see also "Pesticide Decision Making," report to the EPA from the Committee on Pesticide Decision Making, National Research Council, National Academy of Sciences (Washington, D.C. 1978).
58. Report to the Congress by the Comptroller General of the United States, "Federal Pesticide Registration Program: Is It Protecting the Public and the Environment Adequately from Pesticide Hazards?" (Washington, D.C., 1975); U.S. Senate, Committee on the Judiciary, Subcommittee on Administrative Practice and Procedure, "The Environmental Protection Agency and the Regulation of Pesticides" (Washington, D.C., December, 1976).
59. Comptroller General, "Federal Pesticide Regulation Program."
60. Ibid.
61. M. D. Reuber, "Review of Toxicity Test Results Submitted in Support of Pesticide Tolerance Petitions," *Science of the Total Environment* 9 (1977): 135–48.
62. H. Eschwege (U.S. General Accounting Office), testimony before the Subcommittee on Oversight and Investigations, House Committee on Interstate and Foreign Commerce, February 14, 1978.
63. Subcommittee on Administrative Practice and Procedure, "The Environmental Protection Agency and the Regulation of Pesticides," p. 4.
64. U.S. Environmental Protection Agency, Office of Water Supply Criteria and Standards Division, "Statement of Basis and Purpose for an Amendment to the National Interim Primary Drinking Water Regulations on Trihalomethanes" (Washington, D.C., January, 1978); U.S. Environmental Protection Agency, "Interim Primary Drinking Water Regulations: Control of Organic Chemical Contaminants in Drinking Water," *Federal Regulation* pt. 2, February 9, 1978.
65. "AWWA Protests EPA Regulations," *Willing Water*, March, 1978, pp. 12–13; see also "State EPA Questions New Drinking Water Rules," *Illinois EPA News*, March 15, 1978.
66. Toxic Substances Control Act, Public Law 94–469, 90 Stat. 2003 (15 U.S.C. 2601–2629), October 11, 1976.
67. U.S. Environmental Protection Agency, "Toxic Substances Control: Inventory Reporting Requirements," *Fed. Reg.*, pt. 6, December 23, 1977.
68. M. L. Miller, ed., "Toxic Substances Control," II. Proceedings of the Second Annual Toxic Substances Control Conference, December 8–9, 1977 (Washington, D.C.: Government Institute, Inc., January, 1978).
69. A. E. Rawse, "The Consumer Agency Bill: Time for a Recall?"

Washington Post, February 5, 1978.

70. J. Thomas, "Chairman of Consumer Panel Quits, Charging Political Harassment," *New York Times,* February 9, 1978.

71. J. Turner, "Principles of Food Additive Regulation," in Epstein and Grundy, eds., *Consumer Health and Product Hazards,* vol. 2, pp. 289–321.

72. Ibid.

73. Public Law 85–929, September 6, 1958.

74. S. S. Epstein, "The Delaney Amendment," in "Delaney Clause Controversy," *Preventive Medicine* 2 (1973): 140–49; see also "Cancer Prevention and the Delaney Clause," Public Citizens Health Research Group monograph (Washington, D.C.: 1973), revised 1977.

75. Comptroller General, "Federal Pesticide Registration Program," pp. 38–48.

76. Eschwege, testimony before the Subcommittee on Oversight and Investigations; G. J. Ahart, "Testimony on Federal Efforts to Regulate Toxic Residues in Raw Meat and Poultry," before the Subcommittee on Oversight and Investigations, House Committee on Interstate and Foreign Commerce, February 16, 1978.

77. W. Sinclair, "More than 100 Suspect Cosmetic Ingredients Unregulated, GAO Study Finds," *Washington Post,* February 3, 1978; M. Russell and T. R. Reid, "FDA Chief Asks Hill for More Power to Regulate Cosmetics," *Washington Post,* February 4, 1978.

78. R. G. Marks, "Pharmaceuticals," in Epstein and Grundy, eds., *Consumer Health and Product Hazard,* vol. 2, pp. 143–195.

79. Eschwege, testimony before the Subcommittee on Oversight and Investigations; Ahart, "Efforts to Regulate Toxic Residues."

80. S. S. King, "Nitrate Reduction Ordered in Bacon," *New York Times,* May 16, 1978.

81. Freedom of Information Act, Hearings before a Subcommittee of the Committee on Government Operation, House of Representatives, 93rd Cong., May, 1973; see also S. J. Archibald, "Working: The Revised F.O.I. Law and How to Use It," *Columbia Journalism Review,* July/August, 1977.

82. Gage and Epstein, "Federal Advisory Committee System."

83. P. Hausman, "As the Revolving Door Turns," *Nutrition Action,* August, 1976, pp. 3–12.

84. D. Kirsten, "The New War on Cancer: Carter Team Seeks Causes Not Cures," *National Journal* 9 (1977): 1220–25; see also, Ember, "OSHA on the Move."

Chapter 10

Nongovernmental Policies

1. Monsanto Co., "The Chemical Facts of Life" (St. Louis, Mo., n.d.), p. 1.

2. F. de Lorenzo, et al., "Mutagenicity of Diallate, Sulfallate, and Triallate and Relationship between Structure and Mutagenic Effects of Carbamates Used Widely in Agriculture," *Cancer Research* 38 (1978): 13–15.

3. National Cancer Institute, "Bioassay of Sulfallate for Possible Carcinogenicity," DHEW Publication (NIH) 78–1370 (Washington, D.C., March 24, 1978).

4. P. Kotin, Address to the American Occupational Medicine Association, Denver, Colo., October, 1977.

5. C. Mittman et al., "Prediction and Potential Prevention of Industrial Bronchitis," *American Journal of Medicine* 57 (1974): 192–99.

6. J. O. Morse et al., "A Community Study of the Relation of Alpha-Antitrypsin Levels to Obstructive Lung Diseases," *New England Journal of Medicine* 292 (1975): 278–81.

7. See, for example, "How They Shaped the Toxic Substances Law," *Chemical Week*, April 27, 1977, p. 52.

8. American Industrial Health Council, "AIHC Recommended Alternatives to OSHA's Generic Carcinogen Proposal" (Scarsdale, N.Y.,January 9, 1978).

9. B. Castleman, (1738 Riggs Place, N.W., Washington, DC 20009), "The Export of Hazardous Factories to Developing Nations," unpublished report, March 3, 1978.

10. R. Nader, M. Green, and J. Seligman, "Constitutionalizing the Corporation: The Case for the Federal Chartering of Grant Corporations" (Washington, D.C.: Corporate Accountability Research Group, 1976).

11. "Federal Chartering of Giant Corporations," Commission for the Advancement of Public Interest Organizations, *Proceedings of a Conference held on 16 June 1976, Washington, D.C.*, p. iii.

12. J. E. Blodgett, "Pesticides: Regulation of an Evolving Technology," in S. S. Epstein and R. Grundy, eds., *Consumer Health and Product Hazards: Cosmetics and Drugs, Pesticide , Food Additives*, vol. 2, Legislation of Product Safety (Cambridge, Mass.: MIT Press, 1974), pp. 198–287.

13. G. L. Sutherland, "Agriculture Is Our Best Bargaining Tool," *Farm Chemicals* 135 (1972): 44.

14. President's Panel on Science, (Washington, D.C.: The White House, 1973).

15. University of Michigan, Survey Research Center, "Survey of Working Conditions: Final Report on Univariate and Bivariate Tables" (Ann Arbor, Mich., November, 1970).

16. L. Stein, *The Triangle Fire* (Philadelphia: Lippincott, 1962).

17. B. Hume, *Death and the Mines* (New York: Grossman, 1971).

18. B. Weisberg, *Our Lives are at Stake* (San Francisco: United Front Press, 1973).

19. *New York Times*, May 2, 1973.

20. J. M. Stellman and S. M. Daum, *Work Is Dangerous to Your Health* (New York: Pantheon, 1973), p. 22.

21. R. Nader, "Professional Responsibility Revisited," in *Proceedings of the Conference on Science Technology and the Public Interest*, October 8, 1973. Brookings Institutions, Washington, D.C. (Jeannette, Pa: Monsour Medical Foundation, 1977).
22. L. I. Moss, "Pulling Together," *EPA Journal* 4 (1978): 11–37.
23. Quoted in L. E. Demkovich, "Ralph Nader Takes on Congress as Well as Big Business," *National Journal* 10 (1978): 390.
24. G. Lanson, "Industry Doubted as Cancer Cause," [New Jersey] *Record*, March 9, 1978.
25. D. S. Greenberg and J. E. Randal, "Waging the Wrong War on Cancer," *Washington Post*, May 1, 1977; R. Rosenbaum, "Cancer, Inc.," *New Times*, November 25, 1977, p. 29.

Chapter 11

What You Can Do to Prevent Cancer

1. S. S. Epstein, "Information Requirements for Determining the Benefit–Risk Spectrum," in *Perspectives on Benefit–Risk Decision Making*, (Washington, D.C.: National Academy of Engineering, Committee on Public Engineering Policy, 1972), pp. 50–55; see also "Uses and Limits of Benefit–Cost Analysis," in *Decision Making for Regulating Chemicals in the Environment* (Washington, D.C.: National Academy of Sciences, 1975).
2. R. Nader, "Sorry State of the Labor Press," *The Progressive*, October 1977, pp. 29–31.
3. J. F. Fraumeni, Jr., ed., *Persons at High Risk of Cancer: An Approach to Cancer Etiology and Control* (New York: Academic Press, 1975). An excellent collection of multi-authored chapters, each with a full set of references, dealing with a wide range of factors including environmental (occupational, tobacco, alcohol, radiation, drugs) and geographic; also deals with recognition of individuals and groups at high cancer risk.
4. J. A. Turner, R. W. Sillett, and N. W. McNicol, "Effect of Cigar Smoking on Carboxyhemoglobin and Plasma Nicotine Concentrations in Primary Pipe and Cigar Smokers and Ex-Cigarette Smokers," *British Medical Journal* 2 (1977): 1387–89.
5. K. J. Rothman, "Alcohol," in Fraumeni, *Persons at High Risk of Cancer*, pp. 139–150; see also E. L. Wynder and S. D. Stellman, "Comparative Epidemiology of Tobacco-Related Cancers," *Cancer Research* 37 (1977): 4608–22.
6. A. J. Tuyns, "Cancer of the Esophagus: Further Evidence of the Relation to Drinking Habits in France," *International Journal of Cancer* 5 (1970): 152–56.

7. A. Z. Keller, "Alcohol, Tobacco, and Age Factors in the Relative Frequency of Cancer among Males with and without Liver Cirrhosis," *American Journal of Epidemiology* 106 (1977): 194–202.

8. E. M. Whelan and F. J. Stare, *Panic in the Pantry: Facts and Fallacies* (New York: Atheneum, 1975); see also Iowa State University Council for Agricultural Science and Technology (CAST) publications and reports such as "Comments on Health Risks and Economic Impact Assessments of Suspected Carcinogens: Interim Procedures and Guidelines," CAST Report 73 (Ames, Iowa, December 30, 1977). Examples of literatire presenting the industry position that food additives and contaminants pose no dangers to health.

9. See, for example, *Nutrition Action*, an excellent monthly publication of the Center for Science in the Public Interest dealing with problems of nutrition, food additives, and contaminants; M. F. Jacobson, *Eaters Digest* (New York: Doubleday and Co., 1972); see also "Chemical Cuisine," a poster on food additives produced by the Center for Science in the Public Interest, 1978.

10. Good sources include: J. S. Turner, *The Chemical Feast* (New York: Grossman, 1970); J. Verett and J. Carper, *Eating May Be Dangerous to Your Health* (New York: Simon and Schuster, 1974); B. T. Hunter, *Food Additives and Federal Policy: The Mirage of Safety* (New York: Charles Scribner & Sons, 1975); M. Burros, *Pure and Simple: Delicious Recipes for Additive-Free Cooking* (New York: William Morrow, 1978).

11. Congressman B. Rosenthal and M. F. Jacobson, "Study Finds Nutritior Professors 'Feeding at the Company Trough'," press release, August 1 1976; see also J. Mintz, "Boston's Agri-Biz Academics: Go Ahead an Eat It," *Real Paper* (Cambridge, Mass.), December 4, 1976.

12. J. Hess, "The Man Who Loves Additives," *Saturday Review* September 2, 1978.

13. D. Reuben, *The Save-Your-Life Diet* (New York: Ballantine, 1975).

14. C. Fredericks, *High Fiber Way to Total Health* (New York: Pocket Books, 1976); see also C. Fredericks, *Breast Cancer: A Nutritional Approach* (New York: Grosset & Dunlap, 1977).

15. R. D. Smith, "Checking Out the Fiber Fad," *The Sciences*, March/April, 1976, pp. 25–29.

16. American Heart Association, *The Prudent Diet* (New York: McKay, 1973).

17. E. L. Wynder et al., "Environmental Factors in Cancer of the Upper Alimentary Tract: A Swedish Study with Special Reference to Plummer-Vinson's (Paterson-Kelly) Syndrome," *Cancer* 10 (1957): 470–87.

18. M. Harris, "Eating Oil: From the Kitchens of Amoco Comes Petroleum Protein, the New 'Natural' Food," *Mother Jones*, August, 1977, pp. 19–33.

19. R. Harris and E. M. Brecher, "Is the Water Safe to Drink," *Consumer*

Reports 39 (June-August, 1974): 436–43, 538–42, 623–27 (subtitled, respectively, "The Problem," "How to Make It Safer," and "What You Can Do").

20. R. Hoover, and J. F. Fraumeni, Jr., "Drugs," in Fraumeni, ed., *Persons at High Risk of Cancer*, pp. 185–200.

21. S. Jablon, "Radiation," in Fraumeni, ed., *Persons at High Risk of Cancer*, pp. 151–65; see also P. Laws, *Medical and Dental X-Rays: A Consumer's Guide to Avoiding Unnecessary Radiation Exposure* (Washington, D.C.; Public/Citizens Health Research Group, 1974); I. Illich, *Medical Nemesis* (New York: Pantheon Books, 1976); L. R. Tancredi and J. A. Barondess, "The Problem of Defensive Medicine," *Science* 200 (1978): 879–82.

22. J. C. Bailar III, "Screening for Early Breast Cancer: Pros and Cons," *Cancer* 39 (1977): 2783–95.

23. *New York Times*, January 30, 1976.

24. *New York Times*, January 28, 1976.

25. B. E. Henderson, V. R. Gerkins, and M. C. Pike, "Sexual Factors in Pregnancy," in Fraumeni, ed., *Persons at High Risk of Cancer*, pp. 267–84.

26. S. J. Cutler and J. L. Young, Jr., "Demographic Patterns of Cancer Incidence in the United States," in Fraumeni, ed., *Persons at High Risk of Cancer*, pp. 307–42.

27. T. J. Mason and F. W. McKay, "U.S. Cancer Mortality by County: 1950–69," DHEW Publication (NIH) 74–615 (Washington, D.C.: U.S. Government Printing Office, 1973).

28. R. P. Ouellette and J. A. King, *Chemical Week Pesticides Register*, (New York: McGraw-Hill, 1977).

29. M. Blumer, W. Blumer, and W. Reich, "Polycyclic Aromatic Hydrocarbons in Soils of a Mountain Valley: Correlation with Highway Traffic and Cancer Incidence," *Environmental Science and Technology* 11 (1977): 1082–84.

30. J. L. Young, S. S. Devesa, and S. J. Cutler, "Incidence of Cancer in United States Blacks," *Cancer Res.* 35 (1975): 3523–36.

31. B. Doerschuk, "West Virginia Schools Ban Junk Foods," *Nutrition Action*, April, 1976, pp. 10–12.

32. B. S. Trenk, "Health Hazards in the Science Classroom," *American Lung Association Bulletin*, May, 1977, pp. 2–9.

33. D. P. Murphy and H. Abbey, *Cancer in Families* (Cambridge, Mass. Harvard University Press, 1959).

Index

Abbey, H., 550
Abbott Laboratories, 325
Abortion, 445
Acetylaminofluorene, 273
Acne, 216
Acrilan, 211
Acroosteolysis, 107
Acrylic fiber, 210
Acrylonitrile (AN), 207–12, 356
Action on Smoking and Health, 168, 174, 416, 424, 497
Activist function of public interest groups, 414
ACTWU Labor Unity, 501
"Acute Inhalation Toxicity of Vinyl Chloride," 522
"Acute Leukemia Due to Chronic Exposure to Benzene," 524
A/D. *See* Aldrin/dieldrin
Adenocarcinoma, 44, 158, 160
"Adenocarcinoma of the Vagina," 533
"Adenocarcinoma of the Vagina in Adolescence," 533
Adenoma, benign hepatic, 221–22
Adenosis, 222
Adler, I., 515
Adrianova, M. M., 529

"Adult Use of Tobacco, 1975," 526
Advances in Modern Toxicology, 532
Advertising, 389–91; and smoking, 151, 165, 168–70, 171, 173
"Advisory Committee Report on Aldrin/Dieldrin," 530
Aelony, Y., 522
Aerosols, 110–11, 293, 379, 453, 456
Aflatoxins, 24, 59, 61, 472, 488
AFL-CIO, 139, 355, 406–7, 411, 501–5
Age groups: cancer incidence by, 9, 17
Agency for International Development, 401n
Agran, L., 524, 541
Agribusiness Accountability Project, 218
Agriculture. *See* Animal feed additives; Pesticides; USDA
"Agriculture Is Our Best Bargaining Tool," 547
"Agriculture's New Hero: IPM," 535
Ahart, G. J., 546
Ahern, Larry, 407
Ahmed, Karim, 417n
"AIHC Recommended Alternatives to OSHA's Generic Carcinogen Policy," 514, 544, 547
Aircraft applicators, 247

551